THE AMERICAN POLITICAL PROCESS

The American Political Process

Sixth Edition

ALAN GRANT
Senior Lecturer in Politics at Oxford Brookes University

Ashgate

Aldershot • Brookfield USA • Singapore • Sydney

Published by
Ashgate Publishing Company
Gower House
Croft Road
Aldershot
Hants GU11 3HR
England

Ashgate Publishing Company
Old Post Road
Brookfield
Vermont 05036
USA

First published 1979 by Heinemann Educational Books
Second edition 1982
Reprinted 1985 by Gower Publishing Company Limited
Third edition 1986 by Gower Publishing Company Limited
Fourth edition 1991 by Dartmouth Publishing Company Limited
Fifth edition 1994 by Dartmouth Publishing Company Limited
Reprinted 1996
Sixth edition 1997 by Ashgate Publishing Company

British Library Cataloguing in Publication Data
Grant, Alan
    The American political process. — 6th ed.
    1. United States — Politics and
    government — 1945–
    I. Title
    320.973   JK261

Library of Congress Cataloging-in-Publication Data
Grant Alan
    The American political process/Alan Grant. — 6th ed.
        p.   cm.
    Includes bibliographical references and index.
    1. United States — Politics and government.   I. Title
JK274.G68   1994
320.473 — dc20   93–47239
                                                                CIP

ISBN 1 84014 037 2 (HB)
        1 84014 042 9 (PB)

Typeset by Manton Typesetters, 5–7 Eastfield Road, Louth, Lincolnshire.
Printed in Great Britain at the University Press, Cambridge.

Contents

1

The Framework of American Politics

There have been many attempts to find a suitable definition of politics, but most people seem to agree that it is an activity that is related to the governing of a society. David Easton believes that politics is the 'activity of trying to influence the direction of social life and public policy',[1] and he emphasizes that politics is not merely a struggle for power, but that it is related to the goals and direction of a society. The United States is usually described as a 'liberal democracy' and in such societies, where freedom of expression and association are encouraged, there is a more open and active display of political activity than in the closed autocratic systems within which governments do not allow groups to canvass support for alternative policies. As a pluralist society, America has thousands of different factions who wish to promote their own interests and objectives, and the study of American politics can therefore be seen as an examination of the continuous process of groups competing to influence the formal institutions of government in order that official policies reflect their preferences and goals.

The People of the United States

Any consideration of American politics should start with the people of the United States who as individuals and groups effect and are affected by the policies of government. Today there are over 263 million Americans, making the United States one of the world's largest nations in population terms. In 1800 there were only 5 million people but in almost two centuries since then a vast expansion has taken place

[1]D. Easton, *The Political System. An Enquiry into the State of Political Science* (Knopf 1953).

TABLE 1.1

Population Growth in the United States 1790–2000

1790	3,929,214
1810	7,239,881
1830	12,860,692
1850	23,191,876
1870	38,558,371
1900	75,994,575
1920	105,710,620
1940	131,669,275
1960	179,323,175
1980	226,542,199
1990	248,718,301
1995	263,034,000
2000	274,634,000 (projection)

Note: Projection for 2000 is Census Bureau middle-range estimate.

Source: J. MacGregor Burns, J. W. Peltason and T. E. Cronin, *Government by the People*, 13th Edition (Prentice-Hall 1987), p. 12 and *Statistical Abstract of the United States 1996*.

with the population more than trebling in the twentieth century alone (see Table 1.1).

Immigration was the major factor in explaining the tremendous growth in the American population. The United States is, in the words of John F. Kennedy 'a nation of immigrants' since, with the exception of the American Indians, the people of America are the descendants of immigrants. The settlers who arrived on the *Mayflower* in 1620 were religious fugitives from Europe, and the early colonists had both a Protestant background and tradition of individualism and resistance to authority. The 'WASPs' (White Anglo-Saxon Protestants) are still the dominant group in American society today in terms of holding positions of power and responsibility, even though they are now a minority numerically. America's heterogeneity and diversity of ethnic groups arose from the 'open-door' policy of immigration in the nineteenth century. From 1815 to 1914 there were over 30 million newcomers to the country; in the first part of the century they sailed mainly from Britain, Ireland and Germany but, by 1900, over a third were arriving from Southern and Eastern Europe.

TABLE 1.2

Immigrants to the United States 1790–1994

(In thousands)	1820–1978	1961–70	1971–80	1981–90	1991–94
Total	48,664	3,321.7	4,493.3	7,338.1	4,509.8
Europe	36,203	1,123.4	801.3	705.6	599.8
Asia	2,855	427.8	1,633.8	2,817.4	1,366.1
Americas	9,051	1,716.4	1,929.4	3,580.9	2,405.2
Africa	131	29.0	91.5	192.3	117.7
All others	427	25.3	37.3	41.9	21.0

Source: *Statistical Abstract of the United States 1996*, p.11

Fears and hostility among the established population were aroused as masses of people, many poverty stricken and speaking strange tongues, arrived at ports on the Eastern seaboard, and after the First World War restrictions on entry were introduced. In the 1920s quotas were fixed for each nationality, but as the system favoured Northern Europeans critics charged that it was based on racial prejudice. In 1965 a new system was adopted and, as amended in 1976 and 1980, an annual limit was established. Preference was given to family members of US residents. The main impact was to reduce the flow from Northern Europe and to markedly increase the numbers from Asia (see Table 1.2).

The main motivation to come to America for the majority of immigrants was, and still is, a desire to seek a better life and standard of living than they could find in their own countries. Stories began to spread about the opportunities in America and were particularly attractive to those living in rigidly stratified European societies, where there was little hope of personal improvement. Some people fled from the autocratic governments in Eastern Europe to find political or religious freedom in America, while the development of cheaper steam transport made the journey a practical, if still dangerous, proposition.

Immigrants tended to settle in almost self-contained communities within the Eastern cities and they retained their own languages, dress and customs. Gradually over a couple of generations these groups became thoroughly assimilated into American society, while at the same time developing their own political leaders and remaining aware and proud of their ethnic origins. Although at various times there was tension and even violence, in broader perspective it is remarkable that so many millions of people were able to come from so many diverse backgrounds without more social and political instability. America has often been called for this reason 'the melting pot society' although in recent times it has become fashionable to see the country as a mosaic with minority groups retaining their own identities and cultures while being part of the nation as a whole.

The Refugee Act of 1980 established procedures for the admission of refugees from such countries as Cuba, Vietnam and Haiti, while in 1990 Congress passed a major new immigration law which increased the total number of visas available, permitted more European entrants and gave priority to people with particular skills. As a result, the number of legal immigrants has risen in recent years, with an average of about 1 million a year being admitted over the last decade. This has led some experts to believe that America is experiencing its second great wave of legal immigration, while at the same time seeing a large flow of illegal immigrants into the country.

There are approximately 4 million illegal aliens residing in the United States with approximately 300,000 more arriving each year, mostly across the long land border with Mexico. Legislation passed in 1986 and 1996 has attempted to deal with this problem by increasing border patrols, speeding up detention and deportation procedures and improving methods of identifying illegal immigrants in the workplace. Many observers believe that such measures are doomed to failure unless accompanied by a national database and the requirement that employers verify the legal status of every job applicant—moves that have been resisted by both business and civil liberties lobbies. Many Americans have increasingly shown their resentment at the mounting costs to the taxpayer of illegal immigration. California spends an estimated $2 billion per year educating the children of such people and, in 1995, voters passed a proposition denying even the most basic public services to illegal aliens—an action that was immediately challenged as illegal in the courts.

During the 1990s there has also been a vigorous debate as to whether there should be a substantial tightening of restrictions on legal immigration as well. Some politicians and business leaders continue to argue that immigration helps fuel economic growth and fills jobs ranging from unskilled agricultural work to computer engineer positions which too few Americans are willing, or able, to do. Some also believe that America has an historic mission and duty to be open to people seeking opportunities denied to them at home. However, there has been increasing criticism about the impact of immigration on the availability of jobs and the wage levels available to American citizens, and concern has also been expressed that many of the new wave of entrants are not being effectively assimilated into society and that this will have worrying implications for the future stability of the nation. This has led to attacks on the development of multiculturalism and bilingualism, with a growing movement in recent years demanding that English be named as the country's official language.

One section of American society that has not been integrated so easily has been the black community which constitutes about 12.6% of the total population. It is not surprising that the legacy of slavery, and the subsequent attempts to prevent blacks from participating in the political system, led to apathy and alienation. In the 1980s black Americans increasingly played an important role and the number of black elected officials rose rapidly. In 1993 there were 7,984 compared with 6,056 after the 1984 elections, 4,963 in 1980 and only 1,479 in 1970.[2]

TABLE 1.3

Black Members in Congress

	Senate	House
80th (1947–49)	0	2
85th (1957–59)	0	4
90th (1967–69)	1	5
95th (1977–79)	1	16
100th (1987–89)	0	22
101st (1989–91)	0	24
102nd (1991–93)	0	25
103rd (1993–95)	1	38
104th (1995–97)	1	38
105th (1997–99)	1	37

Note: Does not include non-voting delegate from District of Columbia.

Source: *Congressional Quarterly Guide to Congress*, 4th Edition, 1991, p. 703, updated to include 103rd–105th Congresses.

[2]*Statistical Abstract of the United States 1996*, p. 284.

The biggest rises have been in the South where until the 1960s segregation of the races was openly practised. This change was symbolized by the election in November 1989 of Douglas Wilder, a descendant of slaves, to be Virginia's Governor, the first elected black Governor in American history. The 103rd Congress, elected in 1992, included 38 black members in the House of Representatives, while Carol Moseley Braun became the first black US Senator since 1978 as well as becoming the first black woman to serve in the upper chamber (see Table 1.3). The most dramatic increase has been among black mayors who now number over 300 compared with 86 in 1972. In recent times many major cities, including Washington DC, Philadelphia, Los Angeles, Detroit, Atlanta and Baltimore, have had black mayors. The election of New York's first black mayor, David Dinkins, in 1989, after defeating three-term incumbent Ed Koch in the Democratic primary, was also seen as a landmark, while the election of black mayors in Seattle and New Haven was notable in that they are cities with relatively small black populations. Since the Voting Rights Act of 1965 which led to federal supervision of elections in areas which had used discriminatory methods to deter them from registering to vote, millions of blacks have been added to the electoral rolls and this was further stimulated by the Presidential primary campaigns in both 1984 and 1988 of the Reverend Jesse Jackson who inspired many blacks to take part in politics for the first time. In the 1996 Presidential election there was both a notable increase in the turnout of black voters and a decline in overall participation.

This increase in political power has been accompanied by the growth of a substantial black middle class which has been helped by anti-discrimination legislation and affirmative action programmes that have led to improved access to higher education and professional and managerial jobs. The contrast between the success of these black Americans, most of whom are among the quarter of black families living in the suburbs, and the problems of an increasing 'underclass' based in decaying city centres and afflicted with drug addiction, violence, widespread illegitimacy and the threat of AIDS is a stark one. The problems of America's inner cities were once again highlighted by the riot in Los Angeles in the summer of 1992, following the acquittal of white policemen on a charge of assaulting Rodney King.

America's fastest growing minority group is the Hispanic population (mainly Mexican-Americans, Cubans, Puerto Ricans and Dominicans).

Twenty-seven million Hispanics live in the United States as compared with 33 million blacks. By the year 2000 it is projected that Hispanic Americans will total 31 million or 11.3% of all US residents. The Voting Rights Act has also been important for Hispanics because it bans literacy tests and requires certain states and localities to provide assistance in voting in languages other than English. In 1994 5,459 Hispanics held public office, while the 105th Congress had 19 Hispanic members.[3] Leaders of the Hispanic communities saw increasing voter registration and participation among their people as their major political task in the next decade.

Blacks and Hispanics have registered substantial gains in membership of the House of Representatives, thanks in large measure to judicial interpretations of the Voting Rights Act that have led to 13 states redrawing their Congressional district maps specifically to provide minority groups with the maximum opportunity of electing members

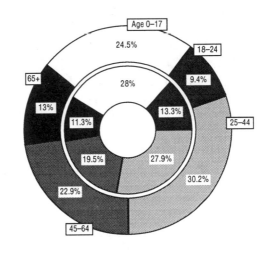

Inner circle: 1980
Total pop. 228 million

Outer circle: 2000
Total pop. 274 million
(projected)

FIGURE 1.1

US Population by Age 1980 and 2000

[3]*Statistical Abstract of the United States 1996*, p. 279.

of their own ethnic background to Congress. However, in a number of cases, the US Supreme Court found that the priority given to race in the drawing of electoral boundaries was unconstitutional and ordered that new districts be created (see Chapter 4).

There was also a growing backlash in the 1990s among white males against affirmative action programmes that are seen to discriminate in favour of racial and ethnic minorities as well as women. Resentment against measures that provide for quotas with reserved places for these groups in higher education or in employment led to challenges in the courts and to voters in California passing a measure in 1996 that would end such practices in state government and public education. President Clinton was aware of this public mood and ordered a review of federal government affirmative action programmes. Although he made some modifications, the President announced that the overall goals of the policy remained sound and that the structure would remain.

The median age of Americans in 1995 was 34.3 years and, as a result of a declining birth rate in the 1960s and increasing life expectancy,

TABLE 1.4

Profile of the Population 1995

262.7 million total
134.4 million females
128.3 million males
218.1 million whites
33.1 million blacks
27.0 million Hispanics
187.1 million residents of urban areas
61.7 million residents of rural areas
19.6 million under 5s
33.5 million over 65s
15.0 million in college or university
116.7 million married
43.9 million single
17.6 million divorced
13.4 million widowed
99.0 million total households
25.0 million single person households

Source: *Statistical Abstract of the United States 1996*, compiled from various pages.

this will continue to go up. An ageing population has brought into focus the issues of the future of social security (retirement pensions) and the Medicare programme which provides for the health care costs of the elderly. The political influence of senior citizens and in particular the American Association of Retired Persons, the largest pressure group in the country, has grown substantially in recent times.

A Mobile Society

The United States has always been a mobile society, geographically and socially. These two aspects of mobility have been closely connected as settlers have moved within America primarily in search of a better standard of living and future for themselves and their families. In 1992–93 16% of Americans moved house, with 3% settling in a new state. Mobility was greatest in the West (20%) and the South (18%) and least in the North-East (11%) and Mid-West (16%).[4]

In regional terms, the main trend has been the move to the West. The pioneers who with rugged determination developed the country westwards are part of American legend, but their hard-won paths to the Mid-West and the Western coast have been followed, albeit more comfortably, by thousands and millions searching for the promised land of opportunity. The Western United States (the states of California, Oregon, Washington, Arizona particularly) grew at a rate of 500% in population in the first half of the twentieth century, compared with a 67% increase in New England. The 'Sunbelt' states of the South and West accounted for over 90% of the total population growth of 12 million between 1980 and 1985. Figure 1.2 shows that the ten fastest growing states between 1990 and 1995 were all in the West and South, while Table 1.5 illustrates the changing regional balance within the population since 1960.

Political power has shifted with the population, to the more conservative areas of the South and West and away from the cities of the North-East, long the bastions of New Deal liberalism. The reapportionment of the House of Representatives seats to take account of the demographic changes revealed in the 1980 Census led to a loss of nine seats in the North-East and eight in the Mid-West while there were gains of eight in the South and nine in the West (with Florida obtaining four and Texas

[4]*Statistical Abstract of the United States 1996*, p. 32.

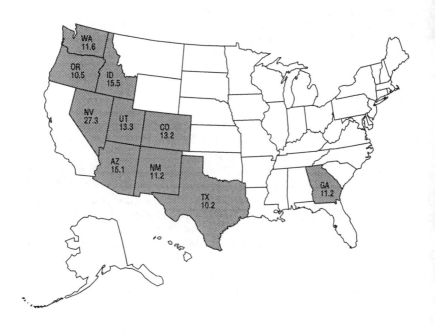

Source: Charts prepared by US Bureau of the Census; *Statistical Abstract of the United States*, p. 7.

FIGURE 1.2

The Ten Fastest Growing States: Percentage Population Change 1990–95

three extra seats). Similar effects resulted from the redistribution of
seats following the 1990 Census; for example, California's population
had grown to over 30 millions and increased its representation from 45
to 52 members, approximately 12% of the total seats in the House of
Representatives.

Another important trend in population mobility was the movement
of blacks from the Southern states to the Northern cities in search of
jobs and racial equality. In the 1970s, however, this trend slowed down

TABLE 1.5

US Population by Region 1960–95

| | 1960 | | 1980 | | 1995 | | Pop. per sq. mile 1995 |
	Millions	%	Millions	%	Millions	%	
US	179.3	100	226.5	100	262.8	100	74.3
North-East	44.7	24.9	49.1	21.7	51.5	19.6	317.2
Mid-West	51.6	28.8	58.9	26.0	61.8	23.5	82.2
South	55.0	30.7	75.4	33.3	91.9	35.0	105.5
West	28.1	15.6	43.2	19.1	57.6	21.9	32.9

Source: Compiled from the *Statistical Abstract of the United States 1996*, pp. 29 and 31.

and was even reversed as industrialization and reform of racial laws took place in the South.

The most marked change in population structure has been the movement from rural to urban areas and, more recently, from city centres to suburban developments. In 1900 the population of America was approximately 60% rural and 40% urban (people living in towns of over 2,500). By 1990 there had been a complete transformation with three-quarters of the population living in urban areas and only one-quarter in the country. In that year 187 million people lived in urban areas and 61.7 million in rural communities.

The movement of middle class white people to the suburbs has left the cities increasingly unbalanced socially and they are now often inhabited by the poor, the elderly and ethnic minority groups; the political and economic problems have multiplied as services have declined, property tax revenues have slumped and businesses, and with them employment, have moved out to the suburbs.[5] By the 1980s only 25% of white Americans lived in central city areas and 48% resided in the suburbs; on the other hand 58% of blacks had their homes in metropolitan centres and only 23% lived in the suburbs.

Social mobility has been helped to a large extent in the past by the continually expanding economy and wealth of the country. With the development of service industries there are more white collar than

[5]See Chapter 8, 'The Problems of Modern Federalism'.

manual jobs and many people have been able to move up the social ladder to a higher income bracket and the attributes of a middle class lifestyle. With the recession in the early 1990s many Americans began to feel increasingly economically insecure and more people worried whether 'the American Dream' of improving living standards and upward mobility would be available to their children in the future. More families relied upon two wage packets to make ends meet, and changes in the economy reduced the number of secure and well-paid blue-collar jobs. Such factors contributed to the defeat of George Bush in the 1992 Presidential election and the rise of populist politicians such as Ross Perot and Pat Buchanan who blamed US free trade policies and accused American business of exporting jobs to countries with lower labour costs. On the other hand, the American economy continued to create jobs, with 10 million more becoming available between 1992 and 1996. The unemployment rate, at 5.3% in July 1996, was less than half the average for the European Union. There was also evidence that opportunities still existed for most people in the lowest income groups to move up the social and economic scale over time.[6]

Class consciousness has not been as prevalent as in Europe and although there have been greater economic inequalities than in most European countries, many visitors to America, going back to the Frenchman Alexis De Tocqueville writing in the 1830s, have noted the markedly more egalitarian nature of social relationships. This was partly a result of the absence of feudalism with its established hierarchies and aristocracy, hereditary landed wealth and titles. The nation was fortunate to start with a clean slate and the history of fierce class divisions with the need to struggle for universal suffrage and basic political and economic rights for the working classes have not been so much a part of the American heritage. The possibility of social mobility and sustained economic growth was enhanced in America by two major factors. The size of the United States territory has grown considerably since the early days of the Republic. In 1800 the United States covered 888,811 square miles and 16 states and this had grown to 3,615,211 square miles and 50 states by 1970. At the same time America was fortunate in possessing enormous reserves of raw materials and its coal, iron ore and oil have been the bases of America's development as a 'Super-Power' militarily and industrially.

[6]Anatole Kaletsky, 'Clinton, Jobs and Keynes', *The Times*, 9 July 1996; Irwin Stelzer, 'Myth of America's Crushed Workers', *Sunday Times*, 12 January 1997.

The American economic system is usually described as 'capitalist', and the United States Constitution was drawn up partly to protect private property rights and provide the right governmental framework for an expanding economy based on private ownership of capital and land. However, America certainly cannot be said to have a *laissez-faire* economy; even in the nineteenth century the federal government carried out policies designed to build up the economy and in the 1880s and 1890s considerable regulatory legislation was passed. American government has favoured regulation of business and commerce by specialist agencies and boards while leaving the means of production in private hands, rather than the direct nationalization of industries experienced in Europe. Federal government intervention in the economy increased markedly in the 1930s. Large-scale unemployment and the slump in economic production led President Franklin D. Roosevelt to instigate a series of measures known collectively as the 'New Deal' in order to mitigate the worst effects of the Depression. In the period after the Roosevelt era (1933–45) Washington became closely concerned with managing the economy and a Republican President, Richard Nixon, even introduced a series of wage and price controls in the early 1970s. A reaction against widespread federal government intervention took place in the 1980s under the Presidency of Ronald Reagan, but regulation by agencies concerned with, among other things, environmental protection, consumer safety and civil rights is widespread, and the federal government continues to spend large amounts of public money on subsidies to particular industries.

The federal government has not only increased in size and scope but the balance of its spending has also altered substantially in the last 30 years. Figure 1.3 shows that, despite the rapid build-up of America's armed forces in the 1980s, defence spending accounted for only one-fifth of the budget in 1992 compared with almost half in 1962. The major reason for this change is the huge increase in spending, both in absolute and proportional terms, on 'entitlement' programmes such as social security (pensions), health care and welfare payments to individuals.

There can be little doubt that the market economy has allowed a rapid development of America's vast natural resources and produced the wealth that gives most of its citizens a high standard of living in comparison with the rest of the world. Capitalism is not without its critics, of course, but there is little real support for socialism or nationalization, and the most that critics of the American system usually demand is that government more strictly regulate business activity so that profits are limited in

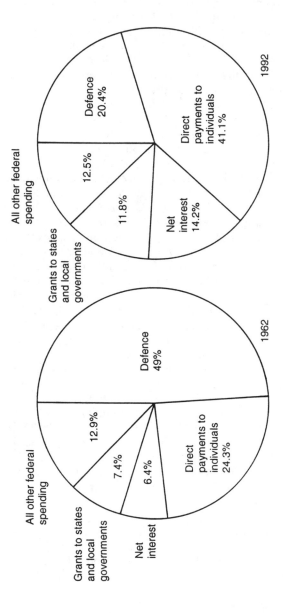

Note: Grants to states and local governments include federal payments to states for social programmes such as Medicaid.

Source: *Congressional Quarterly Guide to Congress*, 4th edition, 1991, p. 146.

FIGURE 1.3

The Federal Budget in 1962 and 1992

the interests of the community as a whole. The oil crisis of 1973–74 and the increasing US dependence on imported oil damaged the self-confidence of Americans in the ability of their economy to expand continually. Public awareness of the dangers of environmental pollution and the need for conservation of natural resources also acted as a check on economic and industrial development in the 1970s.

By the 1980s it had become increasingly clear that the economic dominance enjoyed by the United States in the immediate post-war period was at an end. America has become far more interdependent with the rest of the world while the dollar fluctuated wildly and the US share of world trade declined. The productivity of American industry deteriorated in relation to most other industrial nations. The Reagan years saw increasing prosperity as a result of strong economic growth with low inflation and increasing numbers of jobs, but also a spiralling federal budget deficit and a trade deficit such that the United States for the first time became a net debtor country. The federal budget deficit cast a shadow over the American economy and arguments about how to deal with the problem and related issues of taxation and spending dominated American political debate in the early 1990s.[7] Figure 1.3 demonstrates that the net cost of servicing that debt accounted for 14.2% of total federal expenditure in the 1992 fiscal year while Figure 1.4 shows how the budget deficit grew in recent decades.

Improved economic growth in the mid-1990s allowed President Clinton to benefit in the 1996 Presidential election from a reduction in the deficit from $290 billion when he took office to $116 billion, the lowest annual figure since 1981. However, the trend was projected to turn upwards again in the later years of the decade unless action was taken. The debate between Clinton and the Republican controlled Congress on how to balance the budget created a major conflict between the two branches in the winter of 1995–96 and led to renewed demands for a Constitutional Amendment requiring the government to balance its expenditure with its revenues (see below).

The Historical Framework: From Independence to Philadelphia

> We hold these Truths to be self-evident, that all Men are created equal, that they are endowed by their Creator with certain unalienable Rights, that

[7]Tim Hames, 'The Budget Process and Deficit Politics', in *Contemporary American Politics*, Alan Grant (ed.), (Dartmouth 1995).

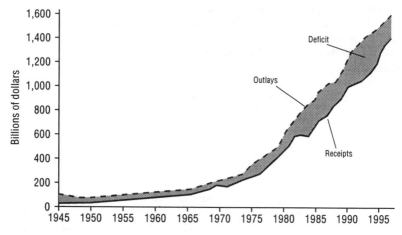

Source: *Statistical Abstract of the United States*, p. 329.

FIGURE 1.4

The Growth of the Federal Deficit 1945–96

among these are Life, Liberty and Pursuit of Happiness. That to secure these Rights, Governments are instituted among Men, deriving their just Powers from the Consent of the Governed that whenever any Form of Government becomes destructive of these Ends, it is the Right of the People to alter or to abolish it, and to constitute new Government ...

In these famous words the Declaration of Independence, drafted by Thomas Jefferson, sets out the basic arguments that justified the act of rebellion by the thirteen American colonies in breaking away from allegiance to the British Crown in July 1776. The settlers had a growing list of grievances including imprisonment of people without trial, cutting off their trade and quartering soldiers in their homes. But the decision by the British that the colonies should pay part of the cost of protecting them militarily, but without representation in the Westminster Parliament, acted as a catalyst in uniting them in opposition to George III. The Declaration of Independence explained to the world why the revolution had taken place.

It is important to remember that this statement was a revolutionary one because, at a time when most nations had hereditary monarchs who ruled on a 'divine right' basis, it was declaring that the only real and legitimate basis of government is the consent of the governed. The argument, and indeed the language, of the Declaration owed a great deal to the British political writer, John Locke. His theory of 'natural rights' and the idea of a social contract between government and the people had wide support among the liberal and educated classes in America.

By 1781 a plan for a confederation had been ratified by the thirteen states which, although only a weak association with little central authority, did show that fighting and winning the war against Britain had succeeded in integrating the colonists into a viable political community. The Articles provided for a Congress in which each state would have one representative, but there would be no separate executive or judicial bodies. The Congress would have jurisdiction over foreign policy and defence, territorial disputes between the states, coinage, weights and measures, the Post Office and relations with the Indians, but the states would retain their independence and sovereignty over all other matters.

Within a few years it became clear that the Articles did not provide a sufficiently strong national authority or central leadership for the future development of America. The Congress had been unable to prevent commercial rivalries between the states and the imposition of tariffs, and there was very little development of a national identity. What is more, the Congress could not raise taxes itself but had to rely on contributions from the state legislatures to meet its expenditure.

By 1786 disillusionment with the Articles was rife and it was decided to hold a constitutional convention where proposals to reform the system could be considered. Most of the delegates who attended the Philadelphia Convention in May 1787 were young, fairly wealthy landowners, lawyers and businessmen and were committed to the notion of a stronger union. These men, who have been subsequently known as the 'Founding Fathers', went beyond their strict terms of reference and proceeded to write a completely new constitution.

Throughout the long summer of 1787 these men tackled three main problems. Firstly, how to strengthen national identity through a more effective central government and, at the same time, recognize the diverse interests of the states. Secondly, they also had to remember that they should not, in creating this new central authority, allow individual rights to be threatened by too strong a government. Lastly, they had to establish a republican and representative system of

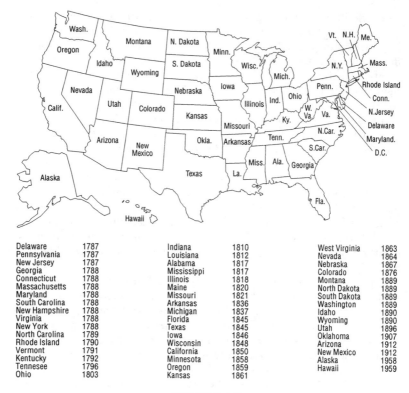

Delaware	1787	Indiana	1810	West Virginia	1863
Pennsylvania	1787	Louisiana	1812	Nevada	1864
New Jersey	1787	Alabama	1817	Nebraska	1867
Georgia	1788	Mississippi	1817	Colorado	1876
Connecticut	1788	Illinois	1818	Montana	1889
Massachusetts	1788	Maine	1820	North Dakota	1889
Maryland	1788	Missouri	1821	South Dakota	1889
South Carolina	1788	Arkansas	1836	Washington	1889
New Hampshire	1788	Michigan	1837	Idaho	1890
Virginia	1788	Florida	1845	Wyoming	1890
New York	1788	Texas	1845	Utah	1896
North Carolina	1789	Iowa	1846	Oklahoma	1907
Rhode Island	1790	Wisconsin	1848	Arizona	1912
Vermont	1791	California	1850	New Mexico	1912
Kentucky	1792	Minnesota	1858	Alaska	1958
Tennesee	1796	Oregon	1859	Hawaii	1959
Ohio	1803	Kansas	1861		

FIGURE 1.5

The States and Dates of Admittance to the Union

government that would be acceptable to the peoples of the 13 states. The answer that the Philadelphia Convention arrived at has been called 'the Great Compromise'. A practical accommodation was achieved between those wanting a strong national government and those seeking to defend the powers of the state authorities, and the conflicting interests of the large and small states. A federal system was therefore created so that national and state governments would each have their own responsibilities (see Chapter 8). At the same time a bicameral national legislature would be established; one chamber would be elected directly by the people with the number of representatives apportioned on the basis of population, while in the upper chamber each state would have two indirectly elected members regardless of size and thus the interest of the smaller states would be protected. Other compromises in the package-deal included a more flexible amendment process, the promise of an early inclusion of a bill of rights to safeguard the freedom of individuals and the powers of the states and a system of electing a single-person executive which avoided both the selection by Congress and direct popular election by the public. Eventually all 13 states ratified the document in special conventions with Rhode Island, which had boycotted the Philadelphia meeting, giving its support in May 1790. It is worth reading the full text of the Constitution, contained in Appendix I, to see how the Founding Fathers set out the powers, responsibilities and constraints on the institutions they created.

Amendments to the Constitution

It was agreed at Philadelphia that proposals for amendments were to be made by either a two-thirds vote of both houses of Congress or by a national convention called by Congress at the requests of two-thirds of the state legislatures. An amendment could not be effective until ratified, either by the legislatures or special conventions in three-quarters of the states. The President does not play a formal role in the process and he has no power to sign or veto a proposal passed by Congress. He can, of course, try to use his influence with the legislature and the public in advocating or opposing particular measures. There have been over 5,000 suggested amendments to the Constitution introduced in Congress since 1787, but less than 40 have been submitted to the states and only twenty-seven have actually been ratified. This testifies to the fact that the framers introduced a system which could only be successful if an overwhelming number of people were behind the change. No amendments have ever been proposed by the convention method although by 1985 32 states (two short of the number necessary) had petitioned Congress for such a convention to write a new amendment backed by President Reagan requiring the federal government to maintain a balanced budget and restrict public spending to the levels of revenues raised. There are no rules for a Constitutional Convention and opponents of the move feared that such an assembly might propose much wider changes in the Constitution.

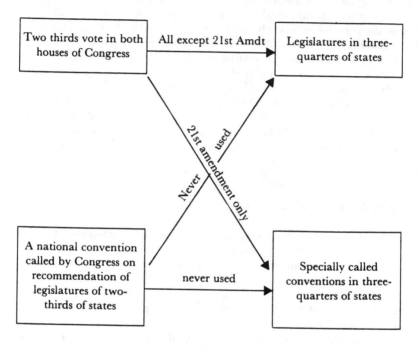

PROPOSALS BY   **RATIFICATION BY**

| Two thirds vote in both houses of Congress | All except 21st Amdt | Legislatures in three-quarters of states |

| A national convention called by Congress on recommendation of legislatures of two-thirds of states | never used | Specially called conventions in three-quarters of states |

FIGURE 1.6

Amending the Constitution

Of the successful twenty-seven amendments all but the Twenty-First, repealing prohibition, were ratified by state legislatures rather than by state conventions.

Some amendments have added to the Constitution and others have revised the provisions of the original constitutional document. It should be remembered that ten of the 27 amendments were ratified by December 1791, as the 'Bill of Rights' which was promised in order to ensure the ratification by some states of the new Constitution.

1 The Bill of Rights—The First Ten Amendments

The first eight amendments set out restrictions on the federal government, specifically limiting its authority over the individual citizen. Many of the restrictions repeat similar limitations already in state constitutions, and they were designed to prevent the growth of a tyrannical dictatorship. The First Amendment sets out guarantees of freedom of speech, assembly and press, as well as the rights of petitioning the government and the free exercise of one's religion. The Second Amendment proclaims the right of the people to keep and bear arms, 'a well-regulated militia being necessary to the security of a free state'. This has been a controversial provision as supporters of gun control and those groups opposed to legislation restricting the ownership of fire-arms have disagreed fiercely over how it should be interpreted. There is also protection against the government quartering soldiers in private homes and against unreasonable searches and seizures of people, their homes, or papers (Third and Fourth Amendments). The next four amendments are concerned with the rights of accused persons, and include the right not to testify against oneself, the right to trial by jury for major crimes and the provision that no-one shall be deprived of 'life, liberty and property without due process of law'. There is the right to a speedy and public trial and the banning of excessive fines or bail, and 'cruel and unusual punishments'. These basic rights are, of course, fundamental to a free society and they retain their importance to this day, although the wording of the amendments has to be interpreted by the courts to fit in with present-day conditions.

The Tenth Amendment was important to the states accepting the new Constitution as it provides that, apart from the enumerated powers of federal government and those specifically denied to the states, all other government powers are retained by, or reserved to, the states or the people. It was supposed to guarantee the states that, although they had given up some powers in comparison with the Articles of Confederation, they were still major participants in the new federal system.

2 Amendments to Extend Voting Rights

The states still retain today the right to determine exactly who is eligible to vote in elections within their boundaries, but they must not infringe any of the various constitutional amendments which have, since 1787, broadened the electorate. The Fifteenth Amendment, passed after the Civil War, laid down that no one should be denied the right to vote on the grounds of race or colour or previous condition of servitude. This was not effective for decades, and in 1964 the Twenty-Fourth Amendment prohibited the payment of poll taxes as a qualification, as this had been used in the Southern states to prevent blacks from voting.

In 1920, the Nineteenth Amendment ensured that women could not be denied voting rights on the grounds of their sex, and the Twenty-Sixth Amendment (1971) guaranteed all citizens over the age of eighteen years the right to vote. This amendment holds the record for speed of adoption, being proposed in April 1971, and ratified by three-quarters of the states by July 1971.

Citizens living in Washington DC, the federal capital, were allowed to participate in the electoral process for President and Vice-President by the Twenty-Third Amendment (1961) and in 1978 Congress passed a proposal to give the District full representation in Congress, but it died in August 1985 with only sixteen states having ratified it.[8]

3 Amendments to Advance Individual Rights

As we have seen, the Constitution guarantees other rights of the individual as well as voting. In the original document there was no restriction on slavery, as the Southern states would certainly not have ratified the Constitution if this had been included. This great moral question, avoided at Philadelphia, was eventually put to the test in the bloody Civil War of 1861–65 and, as a result of the Northern victory, the Thirteenth Amendment abolished slavery in the United States. The Fourteenth Amendment was a very important and major alteration in the Constitution, because it extended the limitations on the federal government, mentioned in previous amendments, to the states as well. It says that states must not abridge 'the privileges or immunities of citizens of the United States', 'deprive any person of life, liberty or property without due process of law' nor deny to any person the 'equal protection of the laws'. The last restriction was later to allow federal

---

[8]The District of Columbia, along with Guam, the Virgin Islands and American Samoa, have delegates to Congress; Puerto Rico's Resident Commissioner has similar status. The delegates may vote in committees but not in the full House.

intervention in states' affairs, like education, when it was felt that the states were not providing equal opportunities for all citizens.

4 Amendments to Alter Government

As the nation developed, so did the need to change some of the institutions and their powers, as set out in the original Constitution. Some amendments were passed to make the system more democratic as the country became more mature; others were necessary as a result of experience which showed the need for improvements and modifications but none has changed the basic structure of government established at the Philadelphia Convention.

The Twelfth Amendment (1804) was necessary after the deadlocked Presidential election of 1800 and provided that, in future, the Electoral College vote separately for the offices of President and Vice-President. The Sixteenth Amendment (1913) allowed the federal government to raise revenue by a graduated individual income tax, thus vastly expanding the amounts of money it could raise and spend. In the same year, the Seventeenth Amendment changed the nature of the Senate by making it a directly-elected chamber.

In 1951, after President Franklin D. Roosevelt had been elected four times to the Presidency, the Twenty-Second Amendment was passed, restricting any individual to two four-year terms in the White House. This was due to fears that a President elected too often to the office would become over-powerful but in August 1986 President Reagan argued for the repeal of the Amendment. Reagan said he did not want to serve a third term himself (he was 78 years old on leaving office in January 1989) but he felt that a restriction to two terms was 'a violation of the people's democratic rights'.

The Twenty-Fifth Amendment (1967) lays down the procedure for filling the post of Vice-President if it becomes vacant between elections. The President makes a nomination which must receive majority approval in both Houses of Congress. This procedure was used by President Nixon to replace Spiro Agnew with Gerald Ford as Vice-President in 1973; in the next year Ford himself as President was able to appoint Nelson Rockefeller.

The amendment also sets out the circumstances when a Vice-President may take over the leadership from the President in the event of the Chief Executive becoming mentally or physically ill or disabled. In July 1985 President Reagan became the first President to invoke this provision by transferring his powers temporarily for an eight hour period to Vice-President Bush when undergoing surgery. The amendment was passed after the heart attack suffered in office by President Eisenhower and the assassination of President Kennedy.

5 Recent Proposals

In 1992 a new amendment was added to the Constitution which delays the implementation of an increase in Congressional salaries until after an election has been held. What made this development unique was that the proposal had originally been submitted by James Madison in 1789. Only six states had ratified it by 1792, a seventh ratified in 1873, an eighth in 1978 and 32 more by May 1992. Interest in the proposal had been revived by the public outcry against a recent large increase in Congressional pay (see Chapter 2). Despite initial scepticism as to whether an amendment that had taken over two hundred years to complete the ratification process was valid and represented 'a contemporaneous consensus', as required by the Supreme Court, Congress somewhat reluctantly accepted it.[9]

In recent years a number of other proposals for amendments have been initiated but none of them has been able to obtain the necessary support for incorporation as part of the constitution. A proposal known as the Equal Rights Amendment (ERA) which would require that equality of rights under the law should not be denied by the federal or state governments on the grounds of sex was first passed by Congress in 1972 but died in June 1982, three states short of the necessary 38 for ratification. An identical proposal fell six votes short in the House of Representatives in November 1983.

As we have seen, a call by state legislatures for a balanced budget amendment fell short of the 34 required for Congress to call a Constitutional Convention. In Congress itself, supporters of a balanced budget amendment fell short of the necessary majorities on several occasions during the 1990s. However, public concern about the federal budget deficit did keep the proposal alive and, once the Republicans gained control of both houses of Congress after the 1994 mid-term elections its prospects of success improved markedly. The party's 'Contract with America' for House elections contained a proposed amendment that would require a balanced annual budget from the year 2002, permit-

---

[9]*Congressional Quarterly Weekly Report*, 9 May 1992, p. 1230, and 16 May 1992, p. 1323.

ting a deficit only in times of war, if there was a threat to national security or if there were to be a three-fifths majority in both chambers. In January 1995 the House passed the proposal by 300–132, 12 more votes than required, and with all but two Republicans supporting it. However, in March 1995 the Senate failed to muster the necessary two-thirds majority by the slimmest of margins when one Republican Senator, Mark Hatfield of Oregon, refused to support his party colleagues, along with 33 Democrats. With the Republicans' majority in the Senate increased by two seats following the 1996 elections, supporters were optimistic that the proposal would pass in the 105th Congress, but in March 1997 it failed again by one vote in the Senate. Concerns that social security payments might be cut in future to bring the budget into balance influenced some wavering Democratic Senators to vote against the amendment.

Concern about Congressional spending bills being loaded with 'pork-barrel' projects favouring particular districts and other unnecessary expenditure led to calls for the President to be given a line-item veto, allowing him to strike out specific parts of appropriation bills rather than accept all or nothing of the legislation. This proposal, which would have given the President similar powers to those enjoyed by many state governors, was also opposed in Congress by those who argued that it would shift power from the legislature to the executive branch, would have little impact on the deficit problem and would merely substitute Presidential spending preferences for those of the Congress. The Republican 'Contract with America' included a commitment to introduce a line-item veto, but it was decided to avoid the problems associated with proposing and ratifying a Constitutional Amendment on the issue by passing legislation that would provide the President with 'enhanced rescission' authority. This means that he has the power to rescind any spending item contained in appropriations bills or in Congressional reports unless both houses pass a 'disapproval bill' that would overturn his decision. The President could veto such a measure. After strong opposition in the Senate was overcome, President Clinton signed the bill into law in April 1996 and the powers came into effect in January 1997. Opponents immediately challenged the constitutionality of the statute in the courts. They argued that it gave the President, acting alone, the authority to cancel or repeal a federal law, that in so doing, he would be acting in a legislative capacity—a power not given him by Constitution—and that an amendment to the Constitution was necessary in order to make such a change.

Discontent with Congress in the wake of scandals, increased salaries for its members and a seeming inability to deal adequately with the nation's problems has led to an upsurge in popular support for legislative term limits. Proponents of term limits argued that such a radical measure was necessary to remove the power of incumbency which, they maintained, distorted the electoral process. In the 1990s voters in over 20 states passed referendum proposals to restrict the number of terms that legislators could serve in Washington; these were similar to the Twenty-Second Amendment which limits the President to two four-year terms.[10] Many areas had already introduced such restrictions for their state politicians and local government officials. However, in May 1995 the Supreme Court ruled that states did not have the power to set term limits for federal legislators, arguing that to do so would add to qualifications for office established in Article I, Sections 2 and 3—namely age, citizenship and residency. Supporters of term limits therefore perceived their only way forward to be the passage of a Constitutional Amendment. Despite being included in the 'Contract with America' the House of Representatives failed by 61 votes to support passage by the necessary two-thirds majority in March 1995, the only Contract item not to succeed in the chamber. Opposition from many senior Republican members led to an unusual number of defections from the party line, as legislators claimed the measure would deprive Congress of experience and expertise and the voters of democratic choice of candidates. Supporters of the movement were also divided as to whether House members should be able to serve for six or 12 years, while agreeing that Senators should be limited to two six-year terms. The Senate failed to come to a vote on the issue after a debate in April 1996. At the beginning of the 105th Congress a new attempt to pass the proposal fell 69 votes short in the House and gained ten votes less than in 1995.

In two separate 5–4 decisions in June 1989 and June 1990 the Supreme Court declared state and federal legislation outlawing the burning or desecration of the US flag unconstitutional despite its symbolic importance to Americans. Justice William Brennan, writing for the majority, said:

---

[10]Alan Grant, 'Legislative Careerism and the Term Limitation Movement', in *Contemporary American Politics*, Alan Grant (ed.) (Dartmouth 1995); Alan Grant, 'The Term Limitation Movement in the United States', *Parliamentary Affairs*, July 1995, pp. 515–29.

If there is a bedrock principle underlying the First Amendment, it is that the government may not prohibit the expression of an idea simply because society finds the idea itself offensive or disagreeable.

President Bush argued that a Constitutional Amendment was required to give special protection to the flag but such a proposal failed to achieve the necessary two-thirds majority in the House of Representatives in June 1990. In 1995 the House passed an amendment prohibiting desecration of the flag by 312–120 but, despite confident predictions of success by its supporters, a similar proposal failed by three votes, 63–36 in the Senate.

The Separation of Powers

The Founding Fathers were concerned not only with creating an American national government structure that would satisfy the states and the people, but also with avoiding the dangers of an over-powerful government. They felt that the experience of absolute monarchies in Europe showed that centralized control inevitably meant a concentration of power and the creation of a tyranny. The distribution of power between the federal and state governments would prevent excessive centralization but how could an autocracy be avoided within the national government itself? They were determined to prevent any one individual or group securing control over all the powers of government—making the laws, executing or administering them, and settling disputes or adjudicating the law. The Framers turned to the principle enunciated by the French writer, Montesquieu, who felt that if the three processes were divided so that they were each the responsibility of a separate group of people, then a concentration of power could be avoided.

It would be unwise to build a system of government on the basis that office-holders would always be good and honest public servants, but if his plan was followed each institution would act as a check on the other. What is more, the President, Senate and House of Representatives would be elected by different constituencies for terms of different length and at different times.

The separation of powers system means therefore that no-one can be a member of more than one branch of the federal government at any one time; in contrast the British Parliamentary system, for example, requires that the executive, the Prime Minister and Cabinet, *must* be members of the legislature. Negativity is the chief characteristic of the separation of powers doctrine as it is concerned with producing limitations and constraints on government rather than looking at the positive use to be made of such authority.

Checks and Balances

Having separated the three main branches of government, the Framers proceeded to allow a certain amount of participation in, and checking of, each branch by the other two. This was because it was clear that a system of government would be unworkable and inflexible without some connecting links between those people making the laws, those enforcing them and the law adjudicators. In effect, the Founding Fathers created 'separated institutions sharing powers'. Since the Constitution was written, other institutions have developed which may bridge the gaps between the formal branches and help the system to operate. Two examples are political parties and Congressional committees. The President and Congressmen are members of political parties and the ties between members of the same party in the two branches have often helped the passage of legislation by the development of common objectives. Congressional committees, which are not mentioned in the Constitution, are able to question executive branch officers, such as Cabinet Secretaries, about the administration's policies, even though the separation of powers doctrine prevents the President or any of his subordinates being members of Congress.

There are many of these 'checks and balances', mostly written into the Constitution itself, although some important ones have grown up as matters of convention later. Some significant examples include:

1 Congressional Checks on the President

(a) Many Presidential appointments have to be confirmed by a majority of the Senate.
(b) The President's budget and appropriations for the executive departments have to be approved by Congress.
(c) All legislation the President wishes to see enacted has to pass the Congress.
(d) Congress has inserted in legislation the provision that executive

action may be reviewed and approved by the legislature. The 'Congressional veto' included in some 200 laws over the past 50 years was declared unconstitutional by the Supreme Court in June 1983. (See page 113 for details.)

(e) The President's officials have to explain and defend their policies before Congressional committees. (In an exceptional case President Ford himself appeared before a House Judiciary sub-committee to answer questions about his pardon of former President Nixon.)

(f) Congress can impeach the President for 'high crimes and misdemeanors' (or force his resignation by the threat of impeachment, as occurred in the case of President Nixon in August 1974).

(g) The Senate has the power to ratify foreign treaties made by the President, with a two-thirds majority.

(h) Congress can override a Presidential veto on legislation by a two-thirds majority in both houses.

2 Judicial Checks on the President

(a) The Supreme Court can rule that the President has acted unconstitutionally or beyond his powers. (For example, the Supreme Court decided that President Nixon acted unconstitutionally in 'impounding' funds appropriated by Congress for particular legislation; President Nixon had refused to spend the money on these purposes.)

(b) The Supreme Court and federal judiciary can decide against the executive branch in court cases. (For example, the Supreme Court upheld the right of the *New York Times* to publish the Pentagon Papers taken by Daniel Ellsburg from the Defence Department, despite the opposition of the Attorney-General and the President.[11])

3 Presidential Checks on Congress

(a) The President has the power to recommend to Congress measures he feels to be necessary; therefore, he can propose important legislation.

(b) As a recognized head of one of the major parties, he has influence throughout the legislative process.

(c) The President can veto bills which have passed the Congress but which he feels are unnecessary or undesirable.

[11]*New York Times Company v. United States* (1971).

(d) The President has the power of the 'pocket veto'; this means that he can refuse to give assent to legislation he receives after the adjournment of the legislative session and, there being no legislature to consider overriding the veto, the bill dies.

(e) The President has the right to convene extraordinary sessions of Congress so that it will consider matters he believes to be important. These are special meetings outside the normal Congressional sessions.

4 Presidential Checks on the Judiciary

The President makes nominations for the appointment of all federal judges including the Supreme Court. If sufficient vacancies become available during his term, the President may be able to 'reshape' the Supreme Court politically.

5 Congressional Checks on the Judiciary

(a) The Senate has to approve all federal judicial appointments by a majority vote. The Senate Judiciary Committee particularly scrutinizes appointees to the Supreme Court.

(b) Congress has the power to determine the size of the Supreme Court, and the number of inferior courts.

(c) Congress can impeach a judge and remove him from office for misbehaviour.

6 Judicial Checks on Congress

(a) The Supreme Court can decide that an Act passed by Congress is 'unconstitutional' and thus null and void.

(b) The judiciary can interpret the meaning of Acts of Congress, and influence how they are carried out.

Whereas partisan connection may help to bridge the separation of powers when the President and Congress are controlled by representatives of the same party, divided party control of the two branches, which has been a feature of American politics in recent decades, may actually serve to reinforce the formal checks and balances in the constitutional system. For much of the post-war period Republican Presidents have been elected while the Democratic Party enjoyed majorities in one or, more often, both houses of Congress. In the period since 1995 a Democratic President has faced Republican control of both chambers on Capitol Hill and there is strong survey evidence to suggest that, in the 1996 elections, many voters consciously acted to try to secure such a result. By so doing they hoped to achieve a check on partisan extremism and, in effect, voted for a form of coalition government with moderate conservative policies. (See Chapter 3 for a discussion on divided government and Chapters 6 and 7 on split-ticket voting.)

Political Culture

To understand the working of any political system it is important to gain an appreciation of a nation's political culture—that is, the citizens' collection of beliefs and attitudes towards government and their feelings about their own place within the system. The political culture of the United States has a number of distinctive features which have evolved as a result of its particular historical development. The term 'American exceptionalism' has been coined to emphasize the peculiar and unique characteristics of the nation's culture and society that set it apart from other liberal democracies. The introductory survey in this chapter has pointed out the importance of the belief in the freedom of the individual and the suspicion and distrust of government control. Together these may be said to have given rise to an anti-authority political culture that has underpinned such movements as those opposing gun control and expressing hostility to taxation on the basis that it will be used wastefully by inefficient government bureaucracy. A sense of optimism and confidence in the nation's future has been accompanied by a belief that individuals can succeed in America by their own efforts. A lack of deference and a relatively high degree of social equality have been associated with social and geographical mobility. A strong belief in equality of opportunity has co-existed with a substantial degree of economic inequality and lack of support for a socialist movement. A firm commitment to democracy and representative government has been counterbalanced by restraints on majoritarianism and a powerful appointed judiciary that can override the decisions of the elected branches. Finally, the esteem in which the Constitution and the rule of law are held has led to a society in which recourse to the courts to settle disputes and protect rights is commonplace.

Some Further Reading

Philip John Davis and Frederic A. Waldstein (eds), *Political Issues in America Today: the 1990s Revisited* (Manchester University Press 1996)

A. De Tocqueville, *Democracy in America* (Vintage 1965)

Michael Foley, *American Political Ideas* (Manchester University Press 1991)

Alan Grant, *Contemporary American Politics* (Dartmouth 1995)

M. J. Heale, *The Making of American Politics* (Longman 1978)

Richard Hofstadter, *The American Political Tradition* (Cape 1967)

Anthony King (ed), *The New American Political System, Second Version* (AEI Press 1990)

William M. Lunch, *The Nationalization of American Politics* (University of California 1987)

G. Peele, C. Bailey and B. Cain (eds), *Developments in American Politics 2* (Macmillan 1994)

M. J. C. Vile, *Constitutionalism and the Separation of Powers* (Oxford University Press 1967)

2

Making the Laws:
The American Congress

The Role of the Legislature

No other legislative assembly in the world probably fits the description of a 'law-making body' better than the United States Congress. In most democratic countries effective initiation of policies and laws has been taken over by the executive branch, and the legislature has generally become a body that reacts to and passes proposals put forward by the government. Nelson Polsby has described such bodies as 'arena legislatures' where parliaments become principally the forums for debate and approval of executive-inspired legislation. The US Congress, on the other hand, he calls a 'transformative legislature' enjoying an independent capacity, frequently exercised, to mould and transform proposals into law.[1] The Congress was given the function of law-making in the Constitution and, because of the separation of powers principle, it has to a large extent retained its powers over the initiation and passage of laws. Even in the United States, the President has played an increasing role in recommending and proposing legislation, but he still has to rely on friendly Congressmen to introduce his bills into Congress, and he is by no means certain of securing their passage. The legislature is seen as being constantly in a checking and balancing relationship with the President; there will always be friction and tension and occasionally direct conflict between the rival policies and interests of each branch. The Congress has, therefore, been called the most powerful legislature

[1]Nelson Polsby, 'Legislatures', in *Handbook of Political Science*, Vol. 5, Fred Greenstein and Nelson Polsby (eds) (Addison-Wesley 1975).

in the world; every year sees the introduction of thousands of proposals, but only a small minority ever became law by surviving the obstacle
race of the legislative process. In the 102nd Congress, for example,
12,016 bills and resolutions were introduced, many overlapping and
on similar topics, but only 590 became public laws in the two-year
period.[2]

What should the functions of a legislature be, and how far does the
Congress successfully carry out these roles? It would appear that, apart
from initiating and scrutinizing legislation, there are a number of
other things a responsible and representative legislative body should
be doing. Firstly, it should be acting as a check on the executive branch
of government. This means that it should not only investigate carefully
the President's requests for legislative action, but also should rigor-
ously question and examine the administrative activities of government departments—what is known as its oversight function. It should
keep a careful watch over the executive's requests for public money for
the running of the departments. Congress has traditionally been the
'controller of the purse-strings' and the legislature's job is not only to
approve taxation measures, but also to be vigilant against extravagance with the taxpayers' money. Lastly, as a representative body elected
by the people, it should reflect the interests and aspirations of American society as a whole, while individual Congressmen should also be
concerned with articulating the views of their own local constituencies.

Most Americans would accept that these are the major roles that they
expect the Congress to perform, but there have been great differences
of opinion as to how successfully they have been carried out. The American Congress has been the centre of great controversy and criticism,
particularly in the last 30 or 40 years. Its supporters remind us that,
despite the great increase in twentieth-century executive power, the
Congress has remained a powerful body and that, more than any other
assembly in the world, it has retained its central role in the legislative
process. It is argued that it has managed to curtail executive power and
maintain the balance in the constitutional system. Following the Vietnam War and the Watergate crisis of the 1970s Congress reasserted its
authority and reformed its procedures so that it became increasingly
independent, acting as an effective check on the President, whether
Republican or Democrat. Ironically, as Allen Schick has pointed out,
Congressional independence has not been rewarded with acclaim; when

---

[2]*Congressional Quarterly Almanac* 1992, p. 5.

it has acted as a check on the executive Congress has been castigated as an interloper, meddling or interfering and making life difficult for the President.[3] Proponents of Congress feel that it has a greater financial control over the executive branch than any other legislature in the world, and they believe that it has been sensitive to the climate of opinion in the country; given the demands of a heterogeneous society, the American Congress has been prepared to pass reform legislation, when it was convinced the public was behind such changes. It is a generally representative assembly that broadly reflects the wishes and views of the people. When Congress is divided on an issue and fails to act it is usually because the public it represents is also divided. Congress has focused on the important national issues of the day, while also allowing opportunities for members to raise matters of significance in their own local areas. Legislators have also increasingly provided a first-class service to their constituents, keeping in touch with the people they represent and helping them with a wide range of problems.

However, critics of the Congress have claimed that it has too often willingly given up its powers to the executive branch, especially in foreign affairs, and this, for example, led to America's disastrous involvement in the Vietnam War. They have argued that Congress has been prevented by its out-dated procedures from properly scrutinizing legislation or the administrative activities of government departments, and that it has lost almost all control over government spending. Perhaps most serious is the claim that Congress simply has not been responsive to the needs of the majority of the American people, and that it does not pass measures quickly enough when they are required. Procedures in the Congress do give advantage to those people who wish to block legislation, and consequently it may take many years to pass a reform which many regard as urgent. Critics point to the Medi-care legislation of 1965, which provided federally supported health care for the elderly, as a major example; it took over twenty years of effort and frustration for the reformers for this proposal to obtain the necessary backing in Congress. It is often argued, therefore, that Congress is too vulnerable to the pressures of rich interest groups and to the obstruction by minorities in the legislature. Congressmen have also been accused of being too timid in dealing with issues for fear of alienating constituents or of stimulating opposition which would mean

---

[3]Allen Schick, 'Politics Through Law: Congressional Limitations on Executive Discretion', in *Both Ends of the Avenue*, Anthony King (ed.) (American Enterprise Institute 1983), pp. 180–81.

that they would face a rigorous challenge in the next election. Parochial interests have often taken priority over the national interest and, even when the federal budget deficit was escalating, members would routinely support expensive 'pork-barrel' projects in their own districts or states, regardless of the impact on public expenditure. However, budget constraints in recent times did lead to a decline in the amount of substantive legislation dealing with the real problems the nation faces and an increase in what were known as commemorative acts. These provide special recognition of individuals, places, things or events and led to the designation, for example, of Tap Dance Day, Drinking Water Week and National Asparagus Month. In the 99th Congress no less than 46% of all public laws passed were of this type.[4]

Claims of corruption and scandal have also frequently rocked Congress and there have been a number of well-publicized cases in recent years. Five Senators were accused of improperly intervening with the federal authorities on behalf of Charles Keating, the chairman of a savings and loan institution in financial trouble. Keating had provided campaign contributions to the members and in 1991 the Senate Ethics Committee criticized all five for poor judgement in the matter, while accusing Senator Alan Cranston of California of improper conduct. In 1993 another Senator, David Durenberger of Minnesota, was indicted with the felony of charging the taxpayer several thousands of dollars for staying in a house in Minneapolis that he secretly owned. Meanwhile, Senator Alfonse D'Amato of New York was accused of improperly pressurizing officials in the Department of Housing and Urban Development to finance projects that benefited his relatives and campaign contributors.

In the House of Representatives there were the dramatic resignations of House Speaker Jim Wright and Democratic Majority Whip Tony Coelho, in June 1989. Wright finally stood down after the House Ethics Committee investigation of his affairs revealed that illegal gifts had been received by Wright from a Texas businessman and that he had received unusually high royalties for a book of his speeches in order to evade Congressional limits on payments for speaking engagements. Coelho's problems centred around a Justice Department investigation into his investments and their relationship with insider trading. Although the two cases were unrelated they highlighted the question of ethical standards of legislators and led to demands for changes in

[4]Roger Davidson, *The Postreform Congress* (St Martin's Press 1992), pp. 18–19.

the rules whereby Congressmen could supplement their salaries ($89,500 in 1989) by honoraria of up to 30% of the salary for House members and 40% for Senators. In 1987 members of Congress collected $10 million for making speeches and attending meetings or seminars, mostly organized by interest groups. In November 1989 the House of Representatives voted to ban members from taking any such honoraria after 1991 in return for a substantial pay increase to $125,000. The Senate at first would only reduce the ceiling on speaking fees in return for an increase in salaries, but in July 1991 it agreed to adopt a similar proposal to the House. By 1995 Congressional salaries had been raised to $133,600, as a result of indexing for inflation.

In 1991 it was revealed that 325 current and former members of the House of Representatives had abused the privilege of having their own bank on Capitol Hill by routinely floating bad cheques and maintaining overdrafts without incurring any interest charges, a story that damaged many incumbents who were seeking re-election in 1992. In 1993 the powerful Chairman of the House Ways and Means Committee, Dan Rostenkowski of Illinois, came under investigation for embezzlement of funds at the House post office; he was found guilty on corruption and embezzlement charges, among which was the conversion of thousands of dollars' worth of stamps into cash for his personal use.

There is little doubt that increased media attention on Congress in recent years and the more open and adversarial nature of Congress has contributed to these exposures. As Christopher Bailey has pointed out, although there have been accusations of misconduct in the past, what is new is the extent to which the most recent allegations have served to focus concern on the performance of Congress. Bailey suggests that the escalating costs of campaigning have been a factor, and a number of allegations of unethical behaviour have involved campaign contributions. He also highlights the distinction between helping a constituent and exerting improper political influence on behalf of an individual. In the increasingly rancorous and partisan atmosphere in Congress, discussion about substantive issues has often taken second place to debate over ethics.[5] Not surprisingly, the overall impact of these cases damaged the reputation of Congress as an institution in the eyes of the public. It is interesting and somewhat paradoxical that,

---

[5]Christopher J. Bailey, 'Ethics as politics; Congress in the 1990s', in *Political Issues in America: the 1990s*, Philip John Davies and Fredric A. Waldstein (eds) (Manchester University Press 1991), p. 146.

although the public have a generally negative view of Congress as a whole, individual legislators are often popular and almost all of those seeking re-election are victorious.

In the 1994 mid-term elections the Republican Party's sweeping successes gave it control of both houses of Congress for the first time in 40 years. The Republicans argued that Democratic dominance of the legislature over such a long period had led to inefficiency and even corruption, as well as procedures that stifled open and democratic debate. The House Republicans' manifesto, the 'Contract with America', promised to make reforms in the way Congress did its business, as well as pledging radical changes in public policy. The preamble stated that the document was 'a detailed agenda for national renewal, a written commitment with no fine print'. The reforms, the Republicans argued, were necessary 'to restore the bonds of trust between the people and their elected representatives'.

Polls taken during 1995 did indicate a rise in public approval for Congress as an effective legislature, with the House succeeding in passing all but one of the main Contract bills but the budget crisis of 1995–96, which led to a partial shutdown of the federal government with departments running out of funds, changed the public mood dramatically. The majority blamed the Speaker, Newt Gingrich, and the Republicans for intransigence and believed the party's proposals to balance the budget were too extreme. President Clinton won the public relations battle with his Congressional opponents by portraying himself as the defender of vital public services, particularly for the elderly and disadvantaged.

The attempt to show that the Republicans had swept away unethical practices in Congress was also undermined by allegations that Gingrich himself had been guilty of misconduct. After a long investigation which cast a shadow over the Speaker for most of the 104th Congress, the House Committee on Standards of Official Conduct (usually known as the Ethics Committee) eventually found that Gingrich had secured tax-exempt charitable donations to finance a college course he taught, knowing that its objectives were partisan and intended to aid the Republican cause. This offence was compounded by the fact that he provided misleading evidence to the committee. As a result, Gingrich was reprimanded and fined, and there was speculation as to whether he would be re-elected as Speaker at the beginning of the 105th Congress. In January 1997 Gingrich was re-elected by 216–205 votes; he failed, however, to secure an overall majority of the 435 members and four Republicans refused to support him.

The impact of the changes made by the Republicans in the 104th Congress will be examined later in this chapter; they affected not only the way the legislature works but also the distribution of power within Congress.

The Membership of Congress

What sort of people become members of Congress? It is clear that Congress is not, and never has been, a true cross-section of the American people.

In terms of age, the members are generally older than the average age of the American population because of the constitutional restrictions (Senators have to be at least 30 and House members at least 25), and because one can usually only obtain election after some considerable experience in politics or business. In January 1997 the average age of members of Congress was 52.7 (House 51.6; Senate 57.5). In the 1970s the trend had been towards younger legislators but this has been reversed since the 1984 elections. There has been a substantial increase in the number of women in Congress in recent years. The 1996 elections resulted in a record number of 51 female members in the House compared with 29 in 1990. There were also nine women in the Senate as against only two at the beginning of the decade. In the 105th Congress there were 38 blacks, 19 Hispanics and 5 Asians. Black members now constitute 9% of the total and the Congressional Black Caucus, all but one of whom are Democrats, are an influential voting block in the House. There was a preponderance of Protestants with 243 members from the five main denominations, Methodist, Episcopal, Presbyterian, Baptist and Lutheran, and 44 non-denominational Protestants. There were also 151 Catholics (a proportional over-representation), 35 Jews and 15 Mormons.

The most obvious factor, as far as occupational backgrounds are concerned, has been the traditional predominance of the legal profession in Congress. In 1993 239 out of 535 members of Congress were lawyers. Law has traditionally been the main professional avenue to a political career because practice is financially rewarding, is compatible with holding public office, and because a legal background is regarded as advantageous to someone making the laws. However, in the 105th

Congress the total number of lawyers declined to 225 and, in the House, the 172 lawyers were outnumbered, for the first time since records were kept, by the 181 members who gave business or banking as their occupation. This change reflects the changing composition of the House under Republican control. In addition, 33 Senators fell into this category. The other main occupational group are public service (126), educators (87), farmers (30), realtors/estate agents (28) and journalists (21).[6] There is a notable lack of people with manual working-class or trade union backgrounds even among the liberal members. Many Congressmen, particularly in the Senate, are very wealthy and more than a quarter are millionaires, some of them many times over.

Historically Congress drew its membership disproportionately from those with rural and small town backgrounds, contributing, some critics claimed, to a rather parochial perspective. Members tended to have served in state or local government in their own areas and, according to William M. Lunch, were often 'emissaries' from state and local party organizations receiving the party nomination as a reward for years of loyal service. In the 'New Washington' members are 'self starters' who have not relied upon the party organization but have won the nomination through primary elections in which they were responsible for their campaigns. As a result when they are first elected to Congress they are typically much younger, they are more ideological in their outlooks and more concerned about influencing public policy. They are likely to be more cosmopolitan, better educated, well travelled and they do not use the district as an exclusive frame of reference. Today the national legislature, says Lunch, is 'dominated by political insurgents and independent entrepreneurs', making the working and style of Congress very different from that in 'Old Washington'.[7]

It is clear that in the late 1970s both the House and the Senate became more aggressively independent of both the White House and their own leaders. The large turnover of personnel during the 1970s which led to one-third of the 95th Congress having served three years or less gave rise to a younger, more rebellious membership whose voting behaviour was more unpredictable. Most of the changes up to 1978 were the result of senior Congressmen retiring rather than defeats at the polls but in 1980 the big swing to the Republicans gave them 12 new seats in the Senate and a 53–47 majority, while the

[6]*Congressional Quarterly Weekly Report*, 4 January 1997, pp. 27–30.
[7]William M. Lunch, *The Nationalization of American Politics* (University of California Press 1987), pp. 14, 102 and 114.

Democrats lost 30 seats in the House. The 97th Congress thus became the first since 1931–33 to have the two chambers controlled by different parties and this continued until the 1986 elections when the Democrats again obtained a majority in the Senate. By 1988 the concern was no longer the high turnover of members and instability in Congress but rather whether competition for the House of Representatives was becoming obsolete.[8] In the House elections of 1988 an incredible 97.5% of those seeking re-election succeeded; only six out of 408 were defeated and three of these had well publicized ethics problems. In 1954 when the Democrats began their long-running control of the House nearly 100 members had close races and were elected with no more than 55% of the vote. In 1988 only 38 members were elected with 55% or less and 88% won with over 60% of the vote and thus can be described as having 'safe seats'. What is more, nearly one-fifth of the House—81 members—had no major party opposition at all in the November elections. In the 1990 mid-term elections 95% of House incumbents were re-elected despite what appeared to be widespread voter discontent with politicians. However, it is worth noting that in Vermont an incumbent Republican member was defeated by Bernie Sanders who became the first independent socialist member of House in 40 years. As we have seen, public disillusionment with Congress increased in the early 1990s in the wake of scandals and deadlocked government. One consequence of this has been the substantial rise in the number of legislators who have voluntarily retired from office and an increase in the turnover of membership, even without term limits. Over the period 1946–90 an average of 32 House members stood down. However, in 1992 a record number of 65 House members, as well as eight Senators, decided not to seek re-election. A similar pattern of voluntary retirements took place in 1994 and 1996. Some members calculated that the voters would probably reject them but many others expressed a frustration with Congress or Washington politics as a whole. Therefore, although elections continue to see a very high re-election rate for incumbents, there are more open races where existing members are not running and, consequently, a large number of freshmen are elected to every new Congress. For example, in the November 1996 elections, 358 House incumbents were returned and only 21 were defeated, while in the Senate 19 incumbents were

[8]'Is Competition in Elections Becoming Obsolete?', *Congressional Quarterly Weekly Report*, 6 May 1989, p. 1060.

re-elected and only one failed in his attempt. There were 74 freshmen in the House compared with 110 in 1992 and 86 in 1994. The Senate has also seen a substantial turnover of members with a record 13 incumbents retiring in 1996 and 15 freshmen being elected to the 105th Congress. A symptom of the public's frustration with Congress and the careerism of politicians, who could in most cases expect to be re-elected time and again, was the move in a number of states to introduce term limits for legislators (see Chapter 1).

Until the 1960s Congressional House elections were closely tied to the ebb and flow of Presidential elections. Voters supported the party ticket at elections and a popular Presidential candidate could help elect dozens of new members of his party into Congress on his coat-tails. The electoral relationship between Presidents and Congressmen has now been uncoupled. Voters are prepared to 'split their tickets' when voting and the Presidential candidate has 'threadbare coat-tails'. As Austin Ranney has pointed out:

> In short, a President running for re-election these days leads his party's ticket only in the sense that he is its best known candidate, not in the sense that the electoral fate of his party's Congressional candidates depends heavily on how well or how badly he does.[9]

In 1988 the weakness of the relationship between Presidential and Congressional elections was clearly demonstrated by the fact that more than half of all House Democrats elected won in districts that were carried by George Bush. Put another way, in 31% of Congressional districts—and in roughly half the Southern districts—voters elected a Democrat to the House while supporting Bush for President. In 13 districts voters elected a Republican to the House while supporting Democratic candidate Michael Dukakis for the Presidency.[10]

The powers of incumbency are formidable today and the variety of resources open to members but not to challengers has played a major role in the decline in competition. Pressure groups have increasingly contributed to the campaign funds of incumbent legislators, regardless of which party they represent, if they are thought to have supported the groups' interests while in office. In 1994 72% of PAC contributions went to incumbents. Challengers find it far more difficult to raise

[9]Austin Ranney, 'The President and his Party', in *Both Ends of the Avenue*, A. King (ed) (American Enterprise Institute 1983), p. 140.
[10]'Key to Survival for Democrats Lies in Split-Ticket Voting', *Congressional Quarterly Weekly Report*, 8 July 1989, p. 1710.

funds and the spiralling costs of elections create a severe disadvantage. Sometimes Congressmen have collected such a formidable warchest of financial contributions unspent from the last election that strong and credible challengers are deterred and the incumbent faces only a weak candidate or is unopposed. Congressmen have better name recognition in their districts, can claim experience of Washington politics and may have an important position through seniority on a committee of importance to their constituents. They have large staffs both in the capital and in their districts who can help provide a constituency service for the voters. Another important advantage is the 'franking privilege'. This entitles House members to send free of charge six mass mailings a year to their constituents, as well as unlimited amounts of individually addressed first-class mail. Members use this opportunity to send newsletters to the electors and to publicize their activities in Washington on behalf of their constituency. The cost of such franked mail was approximately $114 million in 1990. Unsolicited mass mailings from Congressional offices was one of the areas President Bush proposed placing restrictions on in a speech in June 1989 about election law (see Chapter 5 for details).

Another factor in the equation is the fact that the state legislatures are responsible for drawing the boundaries for Congressional districts. A certain degree of gerrymandering under the guise of creating districts with equal numbers of electors as required by the *Baker* v *Carr* (1962) decision[11] has taken place with the parties using their majorities at state level to design the balance of constituencies in their favour and in effect reducing the number of competitive seats. This does not alter the fact that legislators of both parties increasingly emphasize their independence at election time and often play down their partisan connection.

While the advantages of incumbency apply equally to Senators (with even bigger office and staff budgets for those representing the larger states and more expensive campaigns involved) there are fewer safe seats in the Senate. Because the elections are statewide party competition is likely to be more intense over more heterogeneous areas that include both Democratic and Republican strongholds. In 1980 over half the Senators elected in that year won with less than 55% of the vote, and only 55.2% of incumbents seeking re-election were returned. However, in other years incumbents have performed much better, for

[11]See Chapter 4, p. 184 for discussion on *Baker* v *Carr*.

example 93.3% in 1982 and 75% in 1986. As Senate races often tend to be close there is a greater possibility of change of party control, as happened in 1980, 1986 and 1994.

A Bicameral Legislature: The Senate and the House of Representatives

The Constitution established the bicameral legislature as one of the compromises necessary to secure the agreement of the thirteen states. It was essential that, if the House of Representatives was to have its membership apportioned according to the size of a state's population, this should be balanced by having a second chamber, the Senate, which would represent all the states equally with two members each. This would protect the interests of the smaller states, and today the 26 smaller states with a majority in the Senate have only 17% of the American population. The other aspect of the compromise was that the small Senate, with only 26 members when it was created, would act as a conservative check on a radical House, because it was to be indirectly elected by the state legislatures. This role has, of course, been modified considerably by the 1913 Constitutional Amendment that converted the Senate into a directly elected chamber with each member being chosen in statewide popular elections.

The House of Representatives and the Senate are given equal powers over legislation because bills can be introduced in either house, and both houses must give their consent to a bill in exactly the same form before it is passed to the President. Each house is expected to participate in a declaration of war (really a formal power only, as war was never officially declared against North Vietnam) and both have to approve the nomination of the Vice-President if the Twenty-Fifth Amendment is used to fill the vacant post. However, each house was also given certain special constitutional functions which are its own particular powers. All taxation and financial measures must start their procedure in the House of Representatives (traditionally the lower or people's house) and the House also has the power to draw up the Articles of Impeachment against the President. The Senate, on the other hand, has the important power of approving most Presidential appointments, such as Cabinet Secretaries, federal judges and Ambassadors, and trying the impeachment of the President. It also has the power of ratifying foreign treaties which, although used to effect in the rejection of the Treaty of Versailles in 1919, has not been so important in the twentieth century with the President's ability to make executive agreements with foreign heads of government, rather than formal treaties. However, the need for Senate ratification of the Panama Canal Treaties in 1978, changing the rights of control of the canal in a previous treaty, and more recently in May 1988 the Senate's approval of the INF treaty negotiated by Presidents Reagan and Gorbachev eliminating intermediate range nuclear missiles, once again highlighted this power. The need for funding to carry out foreign policy, and thus the approval of both chambers, has in practice meant that the House is a significant partner in the making of foreign policy. Although the House of Representatives has had a longer history in representing the people, the Senate is known as the 'Upper House', and in practice has greater prestige and status.

The Senate

Why should a chamber that is in some ways so clearly undemocratic, with two members for each state regardless of size, and procedures that allow small minorities to block the will of the majority, be so powerful a part of modern legislature? The Senate has, in the Constitution, stricter rules for qualification than the House; a Senator has to be at least 30 years old and must have been an American citizen for at least nine years, while entry to the House requires only that the individual is at least 25 years old and has been a citizen for seven years. This has led the Senate to have an average age several years higher than the House, and in this respect it is the senior of the two chambers.

Senators are also able to claim to speak for the whole state, and therefore they have more important and larger constituencies than Congressmen, who, except for those from the smaller states with only one member, represent only one district within a state. This role gives the Senator more political influence back home in his constituency, and the tradition of 'Senatorial courtesy' means that he will be consulted on executive appointments to his state if he is of the same party as the President. In effect this means that the Senator can usually recommend to the President the name of somebody he would like to see fill, for example, a vacant post in the federal judiciary.

Senators are elected every six years and this means they have more time to establish themselves within the Senate and make their marks as legislators, and spend less time than members of the House in fighting re-election campaigns. The Senate, moreover, has increasingly provided the recruitment ground for more potential leaders and Presidential candidates of the two parties than the House of Representatives, the most recent being Robert Dole, the Senate Majority Leader and the Republican Presidential candidate in 1996. Presidential candidates, in recent years, have invariably been either Senators or Governors of states, but only a few, such as Richard Gephardt (Democrat) and Jack Kemp (Republican) in 1988, have been drawn from the House. However, despite the number of Senators who have tried to win the Presidency successes have been elusive. The last sitting Senator to win the Presidency was John F. Kennedy in 1960.

Because there are fewer Senators (100 as opposed to 435 in the House), the Senate is seen as a more exclusive chamber; each member is likely to be better known and to obtain more news coverage, and is able to acquire more power at an earlier stage. The difference in size goes a long way to explaining the differences in the procedures and operations of the two chambers. There are fewer people to fill almost the same number of important positions, and therefore there is a more even distribution of power than in the House. Almost every Senator, except the freshman, is able to obtain some position which will give him some particular importance; there are jobs as committee chairmen, sub-committee chairmen, party leaders and whips, and on party policy and campaign committees, that all have to be filled. Senate rules have always conferred greater power on individual members than in the House. Any Senator can generally offer any number of amendments to legislation, even if they are not germane or relevant to the bill before the chamber. Passing reforms to Senate procedures requires a two-thirds majority and, without consensus, proposals have little chance of being implemented. The benefits of the existing rules to individual Senators outweigh the collective costs to the chamber in terms of institutional effectiveness.

Nelson Polsby's assessment, written more than three decades ago, remains true today:

> It is worthwhile to remember that there are only one hundred US Senators. Each one enjoys high status, great visibility, a large staff and substantial powers in his own right.[12]

---

[12]Nelson Polsby, *Congress and the Presidency* (Prentice-Hall 1964), p. 36.

The larger number of committee assignments which Senators, with their more diverse constituencies, take on allows them to become more generalist than their House colleagues and to have influence on a wider number of issues. This also means considerably greater pressures on their time. Perhaps the most convincing evidence that the Senate is a more prestigious chamber than the House comes from the actions of politicians themselves. Members of the House often seek a seat in the Senate (40 Senators in the 104th Congress previously served in the House) and see this as an avenue of advancement and promotion, whereas no Senator in modern times has given up his Senate seat to run for election to the House of Representatives.

What is distinctive about the workings of the Senate? The Senate has often been described as an 'exclusive club' with its small membership, its ornate chamber and longstanding traditions. Donald R. Matthews wrote in the 1970s about the norms or 'folkways' of Senate behaviour which led to Senators becoming socialized so that they were proud of the institution and showed respect and courtesy to each other.[13] Members were expected to serve an 'apprenticeship' by carrying out the least glamorous tasks when they first entered the chamber and to be 'work horses' rather than 'show horses'. While there was always the occasional maverick who did not follow the norms, a Senator earned respect and eventually influence by observing the folkways, being prepared to compromise and bargain on issues and by deferring to the desires of committees and their leaders in return for deference to his own committee's recommendations, a tradition known as 'reciprocity'. Over the last two decades the significance of these rules of behaviour has been much eroded. This has partly been as a result of aspiring Presidential hopefuls in the Senate speaking out on a range of subjects beyond those of the committees on which they sit. New Senators were far more prepared to make speeches which would gain them television exposure and national recognition. The Senate debates have become more partisan and the traditional civilities often ignored. In many respects the Senate has become more like the House, and in June 1986 the Senate followed the House in allowing television cameras into the chamber.

One of the Senate's traditional roles has been to protect minority interests, and the most extreme form of minority action blocking the will of the majority is the use of the 'filibuster'.[14] The Senate's rules are

---

[13]Donald R. Matthews, *US Senators and their World* (Vintage 1973).
[14]The term 'filibuster' comes from the Spanish *filibustero*, meaning 'pirate'.

less formal and rigid than those of the House, and there is the tradition of extended or continuous debate in which Senators can speak for as long as they like on the floor of the chamber and can only be interrupted with their consent. There are no set limits on debates and it is difficult, if a minority is prepared to talk a bill out, to secure agreement on a cloture motion to end the debate and take a vote on the bill.[15] The filibuster device has often been attacked as undemocratic but its supporters claim it is an essential mechanism for protecting minority rights in a diverse society. It has been argued that, without such a method of defeating threats to the vital interests of minorities, states or regions, the Union's existence would be threatened. However, it is not just minorities but individuals who can effectively hold up the proceedings of the Senate. The record for the filibuster is held by Senator Strom Thurmond of South Carolina, who spoke for 24 hours and 18 minutes against the Civil Rights Act 1957; the longest group filibuster was by Southern Democrats against the Civil Rights Act 1964 and lasted 83 days!

Filibusters have been used more frequently and as a partisan tool; in the 1950s they averaged only one a year but this increased to 16.7 per Congress in the early 1980s and 26.7 between 1987 and 1992. The threat of filibuster can also become an effective veto power, especially if used when time is tight before a recess or at the end of a session. It may also be used to extract major concessions from the promoters of a bill. The political reality in the Senate is that 60 votes are needed rather than a simple majority of 51 for leaders to be sure that they will be able to pass legislation. As a result of such threats the Senate majority often has to make accommodations with the minority or factions within it. Therefore, despite increasing partisanship in the Senate, bipartisan coalitions are still more common than in the House.

When considering the House Republicans' 'Contract with America' bills, the Senate in many cases amended, diluted or blocked altogether some of the proposals, despite the party having a 53–47 majority in the upper chamber. Observers pointed out that the Senate was acting in exactly the way that the Founding Fathers had intended when they created a bicameral legislature. As James Thurber noted, in a comment echoing the words of George Washington:

---

[15]Three-fifths of the entire Senate (60 if no vacancies) have to vote for a cloture motion for it to be successful. Until 1975 the rule was two-thirds present and voting; from 1917 to 1975 only 24 out of 104 attempts to obtain a cloture were successful.

The Senate absorbs the populist feelings of the House of Representatives in the same way that you pour hot coffee out of the cup into the saucer to cool. It's deliberative. It's slow. It's politically more moderate.[16]

The House of Representatives

The House of Representatives has traditionally been organized in a more hierarchical way than the Senate, so that there is more clearly an elite who have worked their way to the top. This is partially the result of having fewer positions of leadership in proportion to the number of members, and in the early 1970s it caused considerable frustration among the junior and middle-ranking members of the House, who felt they could make little impact on decision making until they had been in Congress a very long time. The centralization of House leadership was modified by reforms made in the committee system in 1975 (see below).

Congressmen in the House tend to become more specialized in particular fields than Senators as they have fewer standing committee assignments. House members are also likely to be more anonymous in Washington as they go about their work; they attract less public attention and even back in their own constituencies there will be many members of the electorate who will not even know their names. The televising of House debates has focused interest on House members and events in the chamber in a way that was very rare in the past.

The House has to have more rigid rules of procedure in order that an assembly of its size can deal with the legislative work. In contrast to the Senate, there are strict time limits on the length of debate and there are limitations on speeches, so that in some cases Congressmen may only speak for one minute each. Cloture requires only a simple majority, and therefore votes are taken and business dealt with quickly.

One of the most unusual aspects of the 104th Congress was the way in which the House of Representatives became the focus of public and media interest. Based on its 'Contract' manifesto, the Republican majority was able to set the political agenda for the nation in a way that only a newly elected President normally has the opportunity of doing. Indeed, the attention given to the swearing in of the Speaker and the new Congress in January 1995 was reminiscent of a Presidential inauguration. For the first year of the 104th Congress, President Clinton

[16]*Congressional Quarterly Weekly Report*, 1 September 1995, p. 913.

TABLE 2.1

The House and the Senate

The House	The Senate
Larger (435)	Smaller (100)
Short period of office (2 years)	Long period of office (6 years)
Elected by smaller constituencies	Elected by whole state
Special authority over tax bills and impeachment	Presidential appointments and trying impeachments. Ratifying foreign treaties
More formal	Less formal
Rules more rigid	Rules more flexible
Power less evenly distributed	Power more evenly distributed
Less prestige	More prestige
Members less publicly known	Members more widely known
Younger average age	Older average age
Easier qualifications (25 years and 7 years a citizen)	Stricter qualifications (30 years and 9 years a citizen)
Acts more quickly	Acts more slowly
Longer apprenticeship period	Shorter apprenticeship period

Source: Modified from Lewis A. Froman Jr, *The Congressional Process* (Little, Brown 1967), p. 7.

and the Senate were principally concerned with reacting and responding to House initiatives. During their long years as the minority in the House, the Republicans had complained bitterly that the Democrats had imposed rules that prevented open debate and stopped them from introducing or voting on amendments to bills. By the 103rd Congress the Democrats had developed a repertoire of methods to expedite floor debate by limiting amendments that could be proposed, and 70% of the rules governing debate were restrictive in this way. While ideological polarization had intensified conflict, this resentment had contributed to the increasingly partisan and adversarial atmosphere in the House where there was little cooperation between the two sides. In a marathon session on the first day of the 104th Congress the House voted for sweeping changes in its rules and procedures, including those intended to allow more open debate (see below).

The advantage of the larger states in the House of Representatives can be seen by the fact that often a state delegation can work together and manage to secure places for themselves in strategic positions on the most important standing committees. California, for example, has 52 House members, while Wyoming has only one and cannot secure that sort of broad-based committee representation. However, the effectiveness of a state delegation will depend on its leadership and whether its members perceive common interests. Despite its size, California's delegation has been divided on regional and ideological grounds and has not been able to maximize its potential influence.[17] Recently caucuses of legislators representing regions or ethnic groups crossing state boundaries have become increasingly important. Taking House and Senate representation together, some states clearly have more political impact than others and this does not depend necessarily on size. A state's power in Congress is determined by the number of important committee and sub-committee chairmanships and elected leadership positions its members hold.

One of the most notable developments since 1994 has been the dominance of members from the Southern states in positions of power in both chambers. In the House, Speaker Newt Gingrich came from Georgia while Majority Leader Richard Armey and Majority Whip Tom DeLay were both from Texas. A Texan also chaired the Ways and Means Committee and a Louisiana member was Chairman of the Appropriations Committee. In the Senate Southerners held all the key Republican Party positions, following the retirement of Robert Dole and his replacement by Trent Lott of Mississippi as Majority Leader.

Congressional Committees and their Chairmen

Most of the important legislative work of Congress has traditionally been done by standing specialist committees that look at bills in their field and decide whether the full chamber should consider them. The committees, more often than not, decide the fate of a proposal, and therefore the composition of the membership is very important. The committees also investigate the work of the government departments and can call executive officials to appear before them; they often hold public hearings where witnesses will provide evidence and answer

[17]*National Journal*, 9 January 1993, 'Taming the Bear', pp. 66–70.

questions, and pressure groups and other interested bodies, as well as executive departments and agencies, usually send representatives to these meetings. The committee members merely question witnesses at these hearings and do not discuss the issues among themselves until a later occasion. Since 1973 committee meetings, including the markup sessions when bills are put together line by line, have generally been held in public. As Norman Ornstein has pointed out, these reforms dramatically changed the nature of committee business because members' actions and votes could be viewed by the press, their constituents and pressure groups.[18] Consequently the influence of chairmen has been eroded and the ability of legislators to bargain over details has been reduced. William Lunch comments that:

> The committee sessions that are now open are at the heart of the legislative process, and although subjecting them to public scrutiny has made available more public information, it has reduced the capacity of legislators to vote against the immediate interests of their constituents. As a result, the old system in which committee members 'made effective trade-offs and had effective discussions which produced effective legislation' has been rendered unworkable.[19]

Apart from the standing committees of the House and Senate, there are also a number of joint standing committees on which members from both chambers are represented, and special or select committees that investigate a particular problem over a shorter period. Examples of the most publicized select committees include the Senate committee chaired by Senator Sam Ervin on the Watergate events, which had daily television coverage, the Senate Committee on Intelligence which investigated the work of the Central Intelligence Agency (CIA), and the hearings on the Iran-Contra affair in 1988.

House committees are usually considerably larger than the corresponding Senate committees, and each one has the membership divided in proportion to the party strengths in the full house. Committee assignments are made by party committees in each chamber and then ratified by meetings of the full caucus. When deciding who shall represent the party on each committee, the leaders take into account the convention of seniority (that is, in this case, the length of service in the chamber), as

---

[18]Norman Ornstein, 'The Open Congress meets the President', in *Both Ends of the Avenue*, A. King (ed.) (American Enterprise Institute 1983), p. 196.

[19]William M. Lunch, *The Nationalization of American Politics* (University of California 1987), p. 124.

TABLE 2.2

Committees in the Senate and House, 105th Congress (1997–8)

Senate Committees

Committee	Chairman	State
Agriculture, Nutrition & Forestry	Richard Lugar	Indiana
Appropriations	Ted Stevens	Alaska
Armed Services	Strom Thurmond	South Carolina
Banking, Housing & Urban Affairs	Alfonse D'Amato	New York
Budget	Pete Domenici	New Mexico
Commerce, Science & Transportation	John McCain	Arizona
Energy & Natural Resources	Frank Murkowski	Alaska
Environment & Public Works	John Chafee	Rhode Island
Finance	William Roth	Delaware
Foreign Relations	Jesse Helms	North Carolina
Governmental Affairs	Fred Thompson	Tennessee
Indian Affairs	Ben Nighthorse Campbell	Colorado
Judiciary	Orrin Hatch	Utah
Labor & Human Resources	James Jeffords	Vermont
Rules	John Warner	Virginia
Select Ethics	Robert Smith	New Hampshire
Select Intelligence	Robert Shelby	Alabama
Small Business	Christopher Bond	Missouri
Special Aging	Charles Grassley	Iowa
Veterans' Affairs	Arlen Specter	Pennsylvania

All Senate Chairmen are Republicans

House Committees

Committee	Chairman	State
Agriculture	Bob Smith	Oregon
Appropriations	Robert Livingston	Louisiana
Banking	Jim Leach	Iowa
Budget	John Kasich	Ohio

TABLE 2.2 continued

Commerce	Thomas Bliley	Virginia
Education & the Workforce	Bill Goodling	Pennsylvania
Government Reform & Oversight	Dan Burton	Indiana
House Oversight	Bill Thomas	California
International Relations	Benjamin Gilman	New York
Judiciary	Henry Hyde	Illinois
National Security	Floyd Spence	South Carolina
Resources	Don Young	Alaska
Rules	Gerald Solomon	New York
Science	F. James Sensenbrenner	Wisconsin
Select Intelligence	Peter Goss	Florida
Small Business	James Talent	Montana
Standards of Official Conduct	James Hansen	Utah
Transportation & Infrastructure	Bud Shuster	Pennsylvania
Veterans' Affairs	Bob Stump	Arizona
Ways & Means	Bill Archer	Texas

All House Chairmen are Republicans

well as the personal choices and constituency interests of members. They also wish to secure geographical balance and they realize that committee assignments are the main way in which they, as the elected party leaders, can influence the sort of decisions committees will make. Since the mid-1970s junior members have been less prepared, particularly in the House, meekly to accept whatever they were assigned, regardless of relevance to their constituency or personal interests.

Inevitably some committees are more popular with members than others, and some are regarded as having higher status. In both houses, committees dealing with taxation and government spending are highly prestigious. The House Ways and Means Committee and the Senate Finance Committee between them shape all taxation measures; their support is invaluable to a President contemplating tax changes or reforms. The Appropriations Committees allocate funds for government departments and for new and existing programmes. In the

Senate, the Foreign Relations Committee has traditionally been an influential body because of the Senate's special powers in foreign policy. In the House, the Rules Committee, which specifies the conditions under which bills are debated and amended, has a vital controlling voice over legislation, and therefore assignment to this small 16-member body is considered a valuable prize.

The committees of the Senate and the House were long recognized as the control centres of legislation, and therefore the committee chairmen have traditionally been leaders in their own right. The sum of their powers once led Woodrow Wilson to describe American government as being 'government by the chairmen of standing committees'. Until the 1970s, the chairmen could exercise almost dictatorial powers over the running of their committees. The chairman could arrange the dates of meetings, decide the agendas, and control the resources and staff for the committee and its sub-committees. He was able to 'pigeonhole' bills to prevent legislation which he did not like from being discussed by his committee and he also wrote the report on bills which were sent to the full house. He could speak on the floor of the chamber on legislation from his committee, and he would be a leading member on any conference committee set up by both houses to hammer out a compromise version, if this was necessary. He could also appoint members of sub-committees and decide on the jurisdiction of these bodies.

These powers could be used responsibly but they were occasionally abused by autocratic chairmen. There were examples of chairmen calling meetings at very short notice, or when most members were away from Washington, in order to steam-roller a proposal through. Chairmen also sometimes rewarded their friends and penalized their opponents when assigning sub-committee appointments or funds for sub-committee work. Younger members, particularly in the House of Representatives, were often angry at their own impotence, but dared not challenge or antagonize the powerful chairmen. However, by the mid-1970s the pent-up frustration led to fundamental changes in the way the committee system operated. House committee chairmen were subdued by new procedural restrictions and forced to share power with their junior colleagues.

The most important development was the vast increase in the number of sub-committees and the expansion in their influence which decentralized much of the power of the full committees. Until the early 1970s, sub-committees (with the exception of those in the Appropriations Committees) did not play a dominant role in committees or in managing bills on the floor. However, between 1971 and 1975, the authority of committee chairmen was curbed in the House and that of sub-committee leaders strengthened. By the end of 1975, sub-committees were behaving more independently and their chairmen were playing a more active role on the floor of the House and sub-committee members were protected by a 'Bill of Rights' adopted by the House Democratic caucus.

Some observers believe that these reforms had led to a shift from committee to sub-committee government, and there were fears that the decentralization of power in the House had gone too far, creating further fragmentation and problems of leadership and coordination. As a result the number of sub-committees was reduced and their juris-dictions rationalized. In the House the 151 sub-committees in 1975 were cut to around 120 and the Senate, which had 140 such bodies operating in 1975, reduced the total to 87 in the 102nd Congress. Ironically, the trend to decentralization occurred at a time when House Democrats were trying to increase the powers of the Speaker, the Democratic Steering and Policy Committee, and the Democratic cau-cus in order to coordinate party policy on legislation and make them-selves a more coherent body.

Selection of committee chairmen was traditionally a result of the 'seniority system'. This meant that the member of the majority party who had given the longest unbroken service to the committee auto-matically became the chairman with all the powers of that office. The justification for this system was that it prevented disputes about the chairmanship and rewarded experience of the committee's work. On the other hand, the seniority system did not take into account the individual expertise of members, the ability to have a good working relationship with other members, or loyalty to the party's general objectives and programme. The system rewarded those who stayed alive and could get re-elected. Consequently it was criticized for two main reasons. Firstly, it resulted in most of the chairmen being much older than the average member, and some commentators dubbed it 'the senility system'. Secondly, the seniority system inevitably helped those members who were from one-party areas where, in practice, they faced little real competition at elections. This resulted, in the 1960s, in the Southern Democrats having control over not only a disproportion-ate number of chairmanships, but also most of the important and prestigious committees. The problem for the majority of liberal Demo-crats was that these Congressmen, although obtaining their positions by being Democrats, were out of sympathy with the party majority on important policies and usually cast their votes with the conservative Republicans. Therefore they used their positions to thwart the liberal legislation which was promoted and supported by the majority of their own party.

Reform of the seniority system was made a major objective of the liberal 'Democratic Study Group' as well as pressure groups like 'Common Cause', and eventually the House Democrats decided, in 1973, to elect the chairmen by a party caucus (a meeting of all party members in the House) at the beginning of each session. The elections resulted in that year in the same people becoming chairmen who held the posts anyway through seniority. However, in 1975 the election of 75 new House Democrats, mostly young and liberal, led to a revolt that shook the seniority system to its foundations. The chairmen of each committee were subjected to the ordeal of interview by freshmen Democrats and the caucus voted 'Yes' or 'No' on each position, after the Democratic Steering and Policy Committee had given its recommendations. In the cases of three chairmen the caucus voted to replace them with other senior members of the committees. The effect of these elections was to remove three Southern Democrats in their seventies and eighties, men who had often been autocratic and unrepresentative chairmen, and to promote younger and more liberal Democrats. It also increased the powers of the Democratic caucus, and made the House more responsive to Northern liberal and urban opinion. In 1990 the Democratic Caucus voted to replace two elderly chairmen, Glenn Anderson (Public Works) and Frank Annunzio (House Administration), while others beat off challenges to their positions. Two years later the Caucus removed 82-year-old Jamie Whitten, the Chairman of the powerful Appropriations Committee; Whitten had suffered a stroke but refused to stand down voluntarily and was replaced by William Natcher of Kentucky, the next in line (and 83 years old!). The Senate Democrats agreed in 1975 that they would select committee chairmen by secret ballot whenever one-fifth of the caucus requested it.

The expansion of sub-committees' responsibilities, the procedural constraints, and the crumbling of the seniority system combined to erode considerably the power and influence of the committee chairmen in Congress. What is more, the increasing role of party leaders and the stringent budget constraints of the 1990s limited the discretion of committees to pursue policies of their own choosing. The initiative for policy change shifted to party and budget leaders and away from committee and sub-committee chairmen who were accustomed to promoting and developing legislation.[20]

The Elected Party Leaders

Traditionally, committee chairmen provided policy leadership in their own specialized areas, and party leaders were principally responsible for organizational matters such as scheduling bills, building coalitions and maintaining party harmony. The Constitution does mention the Speaker of the House specifically and he did have large personal authority, including the right to appoint members to committees. However, the allegedly 'dictatorial' methods of Speakers Reed and Cannon led to a revolt in 1910 and the stripping of the Speaker of many of his powers, including the chairmanship of the Rules Committee. The House reforms of the 1970s, while decentralizing power away from the committee chairmen, also sought to strengthen the power of the Speaker and the party leadership. For example, the prerogative to nominate the majority party members on the Rules Committee gave him power over scheduling of legislation, while the right to refer bills to more than one committee (multiple referral) led the Speaker to become more involved in policy matters, as he often found it necessary to negotiate agreements between committee chairmen. In the post-reform Congress many of the most important bills are considered by more than one committee and the development of very large omnibus bills, covering many subjects and several thousand pages, has helped to increase the role of party leaders. The introduction of summits between the White House and Congressional representatives in order to break deadlocks over the federal budget gave party leaders more authority to try to reach agreement on behalf of their colleagues (although they still have to persuade legislators to go along with whatever is negotiated). On occasions party leaders have also established a special task force of members to consider a particular issue and have effectively bypassed the official committee structure.

Heightened partisanship, which was stimulated by divided party control of the executive and legislative branches and between the two houses (1981–87) has increased members' expectations, particularly on the Democratic side, that their leaders would take a more proactive

---

[20]Steven C. Smith, 'The Senate in the Post-reform Era', in Roger Davidson, op. cit., p. 187.

role in the legislative process and in relations with the President. As the ideological heterogeneity of the Democratic Party declined in the 1980s, and members elected from the South became more aligned with the rest of the Congressional party, so did the fears that the exercise of strong leadership would pose a threat to individual policy or re-election goals. Democrats increasingly looked to their party leaders to speak effectively on their behalf in the media, to counter the impact of Republican Presidents.[21]

The main party leaders in the House of Representatives are:

1 The Speaker. The Speaker is formally elected at the beginning of each session, but the parties vote in blocs, and therefore the majority party is sure of having its nominee selected. In practice, therefore, he is chosen by the majority party caucus, and often the same person is selected without opposition until he decides to retire.[22] The Speaker is fulfilling two basic roles in the 'Congressional game': he is at the same time 'referee' (or chairman of the House) and 'captain' of one of the teams (the party leader). As chairman, he presides over business, interprets the rules, and puts questions to the vote as well as assigning bills to the specialist committees. As party leader he is one of the major spokesmen for the party's policies, and influences the assignment of members to committees through his chairing of the party Steering Committee. He will only rarely take an active part in debate, although he can vote on every issue. The Speaker is usually able to combine satisfactorily these two potentially conflicting roles, and the element of discretion he has over procedural matters provides him with a possibly decisive influence over legislation. The Speaker is also constitutionally next in line for succession to the Presidency after the Vice-President.

Thomas 'Tip' O'Neill was Speaker from 1977 to 1987. His strong personality made him an influential leader on Capitol Hill and the Carter administration's failure to establish good relations with the Democratic House Leader weakened the President's position with Congress. However, O'Neill was criticized during 1981 for his inability to

---

[21]Barbara Sinclair, 'House Majority Party Leadership in an Era Of Legislative Constraint', in Roger Davidson, op. cit., p. 93. See also Daniel J. Palazzolo, 'From Decentralization to Centralization: Members' Changing Expectations for House Leaders', in the same volume, pp. 112–26.

[22]However, challenges occasionally happen. In 1970, a move by liberal Democrats to defeat Speaker John McCormack's re-nomination was defeated, although he subsequently decided to retire. In 1997 there was some internal opposition among Republican members to the renomination of Newt Gingrich because of charges of ethical violations. As we have seen, in the House vote, strong leadership pressure restricted the number of eventual dissidents to four.

hold the Democratic majority together in votes against President Reagan's tax and budget cuts. There had been some discontent with O'Neill's leadership but no formal challenges from among Democrats. His successor was Jim Wright of Texas who exploited the powers of his office and introduced an aggressive and highly partisan style of leadership. After only two and a half years leading the Democratic opposition to the Republican administration's policies Wright was forced to resign after an Ethics Committee investigation into his financial affairs (see above). He was replaced by Thomas Foley (Washington), a well-respected if somewhat less colourful figure in the House, who moved up from the position of Majority Floor Leader. The Speaker invariably has held this position before taking over the top post. Foley was the most prominent of the House Democrats defeated in the 1994 mid-term elections, following which Newt Gingrich became the first Republican Speaker in 40 years. Gingrich's role is discussed below.

2 The Majority Floor Leader. The party caucus also elects an assistant to the Speaker who will undertake the role of leading the day-to-day strategy and efforts of his party on the floor of the House. He will negotiate with committee chairmen, the Rules Committee, and minority party leaders over the timetable. When Thomas Foley became Speaker in June 1989 the former Presidential candidate Richard Gephardt of Missouri took over this role. The Republican Conference (the caucus of GOP members) elected Richard Armey of Texas as the Majority Leader in the 104th Congress.

3 The Majority Whip. The majority party elects the position of Majority Whip whose main job is to inform the leadership of the voting dispositions of members of the party on bills coming up for decision in the House. To this end the Whip will negotiate with other members to persuade them to vote the way the leadership wants. He will provide information and act generally as a communication link between leaders and ordinary members; he is the 'eyes and ears' of the majority party leadership. The Whip, however, lacks the threat of disciplinary action that the British party whip relies on to secure compliance. By the late 1980s the Democratic whip system had expanded to include 102 members: the chief deputy whip, 15 deputies, 3 task force chairmen, 64 at-large whips and 18 regional zone whips. The size and representativeness of this group not only improved communications between the leadership and members but also provided, through the whips' task forces, opportunities for junior members to participate in the legislative process beyond their own committees. In the 104th Congress new Majority Whip, Tom DeLay, had a team of 55 members involved in securing the conversion of the 'Contract with America' into legislative enactments in the House. DeLay and his chief deputy, Dennis Hastert, met regularly with the full team and even more frequently with their 13 deputy whips.

4 Republican Party Committees. The Republican Conference has two main committees in the House: the Policy Committee, chaired by Christopher Cox of California, and a new Steering Committee which replaced the Committee on Committees that had traditionally determined committee assignments for GOP members. The new committee, which also took over responsibility for proposing legislative priorities, gave the party leaders a stronger voice with the Speaker having five votes, the Majority Leader two, and four other elected positions one each, out of a total of 30 votes. Four of the most important standing committee chairmen also have one vote each.

5 The Minority Party in the House. When they became the minority party in the 104th Congress, the Democrats elected Richard Gephardt as their Leader and David Bonior as Minority Whip. Bonior had been Majority Whip from 1991–95, while Gephardt had been Majority Leader under Tom Foley.

The leadership in the Senate is provided by the following positions.

1 The President of the Senate. In the Senate the chairman of the meetings is officially the Vice-President of the United States who is called the 'President of the Senate'. He fulfils only the 'referee' role of the Speaker and only votes in the event of a tie. The Constitution gives him this formal role, although he may not, in practice, attend Senate meetings very often; as he is elected at the same time as the President and is not a Senator, the President of the Senate may be a member of the party which is in a minority in the chamber.

2 The President Pro Tempore. The Senate majority party elects a senior member to be substitute chairman when the Vice-President is not present. He will, however, be able to be an active party member and can vote in all divisions; it is a formal position with little real power.

TABLE 2.3

The Elected Leaders in the 105th Congress (1997–98)

	The Senate	
President of the Senate	Vice President Al Gore	(D)
President Pro Tempore	Strom Thurmond	(R South Carolina)
Majority Leader	Trent Lott	(R Mississippi)
Majority Whip	Don Nickles	(R Oklahoma)
Republican Conference Chairman	Connie Mack	(R Florida)
Republican Conference Secretary	Paul Coverdell	(R Georgia)
Minority Leader	Tom Daschle	(D South Dakota)
Minority Whip	Wendell Ford	(D Kentucky)
Democratic Conference Secretary	Barbara Mikulski	(D Maryland)
	The House	
Speaker	Newt Gingrich	(R Georgia)
Majority Leader	Richard Armey	(R Texas)
Majority Whip	Tom DeLay	(R Texas)
Republican Conference Chairman	John Boehner	(R Ohio)
Republican Policy Committee Chairman	Christopher Cox	(R California)
Minority Leader	Richard Gephardt	(D Missouri)
Minority Whip	David Bonior	(D Michigan)
Democratic Caucus Chairman	Steny Hoyer	(D Maryland)

Republicans gave this honour to 94 year-old Strom Thurmond, who was re-elected in 1996 to his eighth term in the chamber and is the oldest person ever to serve in the Senate.

3 The Senate Majority Leader. The Senate Majority Leader holds the most powerful elected position in the Upper House although the extent of his influence depends principally on his personality. Ability to persuade colleagues and to be a bargainer and broker of interests within the party is his main asset, and he has little patronage or disciplinary control over other independent-minded Senators. Lyndon Johnson, who was Senate Leader from 1953 to 1961, maintained a first-class communications system with all his colleagues and was scarcely ever intransigent himself on policy issues. Johnson, however, was also famous for using cajoling 'arm-twisting' tactics to build up coalitions of support. Mike Mansfield, the Senate Leader from 1961 to 1977, was a very different personality—mild mannered and unaggressive, while Senator Robert Byrd, who succeeded Mansfield, was well known for his ability to gauge correctly what the majority of the Senate wanted. He was described as a technician who made the Senate run efficiently, but who did not try to provide a lead on too many issues and policies. The Senate Majority Leader spends much of his time on the floor of the house, and one of his chief weapons in managing the Senate's business is the convention that he be recognized by the chair ahead of any other Senator. This allows him to control the day's proceedings by calling Bills and resolutions for consideration and moving motions for recess. However, the Senate Majority Leader, who has always been institutionally weaker than the House Speaker, was not given any significant new powers to deal with the more active, assertive and less predictable membership that has been evident in recent decades. Barbara Sinclair has noted:

As a result, the majority leader's control over the floor schedule is tenuous. A single senator can disrupt the work of the Senate by exercising the right of unlimited debate or objecting to the unanimous consent requests through which the Senate does most of its work. Clearly a partisan minority of any size can bring legislative activity to a standstill.[23]

The Senate Leader will also have regular consultations with both the Speaker of the House and the President on the progress of legislation.

In 1981 Senator Howard Baker became the new Republican Majority Leader and received almost universal praise for his ability in forging together a cohesive party group. Under Baker's leadership Senate Republicans showed unprecedented unity with members voting 81% of the time with their party on partisan divisions and 80% with President Reagan on roll call votes in 1981. Baker retired from the Senate

[23]Barbara Sinclair, 'The Struggle over Representation and Lawmaking in Congress', in *Remaking Congress: Change and Stability in the 1990s*, James Thurber and Roger Davidson (eds), (Congressional Quarterly Inc., 1995) pp. 105–7.

in 1985 and was replaced in the 99th Congress by Senator Robert Dole who beat four rivals to the Senate leadership. Dole stayed as Republican leader until June 1996 when, as the party's Presidential candidate, he left the Senate to concentrate on his campaign. Dole was Majority Leader from 1985–87 and 1995–96 and, during his many years in the chamber, had developed a mastery of Senate procedure and earned a reputation as a pragmatic crafter of legislative deals. As a moderate conservative, Dole had often taken an independent line from the Reagan administration and he found that, during his time as leader, the party in both houses of Congress had become increasingly more conservative.

When Dole stood down, the Republican Conference elected Trent Lott of Mississippi as its new leader. Lott, a former Majority Whip, easily defeated his fellow Mississippian, Thad Cochran, for the top job. Having also been a former member of the House and a colleague of Gingrich, he was seen as well to the right politically of Dole and benefited from the strong support of the younger and more conservative members who had entered the Senate as a result of recent elections.

4 The Majority Whip. The Senate majority leader's closest assistant is the Majority Whip who, because of the smaller numbers involved in the Senate, has an easier job in keeping contact with other members and their voting dispositions than his counterpart in the House. Trent Lott became Majority Whip and Assistant Leader in January 1995 when he defeated Alan Simpson of Wyoming, who had been the Republican Whip for the last decade, by 27–26 votes in the Conference. His election had been interpreted as a message to Dole that the newer members wanted to see a more vigorous leadership pushing a right-wing agenda, similar to that in the House. When Lott took over the leadership in 1996, Don Nickles of Oklahoma became the Majority Whip.

5 Other Positions in the Senate. The Democratic Party in the Senate had to reconcile itself to its new minority status and find a new leader in January 1995. The retirement of George Mitchell and the defeat of his expected successor, Jim Sasser of Tennessee, in the 1994 election meant that Democrats turned to Tom Daschle of South Dakota who beat the more experienced Christopher Dodd of Connecticut by 24–23 votes. Wendell Ford of Kentucky became the Minority Whip.

Institutional Change in the 104th Congress

The Republican victory in 1994 led to significant changes in the working of Congress. For the Republicans in the House, control of the chamber for the first time in 40 years gave them the opportunity to establish a new form of party government with more centralized authority in the hands of the Speaker and the party leadership than had existed at any time since the early years of the century. Even in the Senate, where the party had been in control as recently as 1987, moves were made which would lead, albeit in less radical form, to more influence for party leaders over the notoriously decentralized and individualistic body.

In examining the changes made in the House by the Republican majority it is important to place them in the context of the strengthened party leadership witnessed during the latter years of Democratic control and also the reforms made by the Republicans to their own rules while in opposition. Newt Gingrich's assertion of authority and the establishment of a dominant party leadership in the 104th Congress built on the foundations laid by these earlier developments.[24]

From the late 1940s until the mid-1980s the House Republicans had a very decentralized structure and their leader had little real power. However, in the late 1980s the House party made a number of changes which gave the Minority Leader, Robert Michel, more authority and adopted rules that mirrored those of the Democratic Caucus. At the same time a group of younger, conservative members formed the Conservative Opportunity Society and argued for a more aggressive approach as the opposition party in the House. They believed that the existing leadership was too prepared to compromise and do deals with the majority; they wanted to attack the Democrats to highlight the policy and ideological differences between the parties. Newt Gingrich who became Minority Whip in March 1989 was the effective leader of this faction and was primarily responsible for the attacks on Speaker Jim Wright which led to his enforced resignation.

The growing influence of the conservative activists led to limits being placed on the length of time ranking members (the chief spokesmen for the party on each committee) could hold their positions, and it was made clear to them that they were there to serve the Conference.

[24]William Connelly and John Pitney Jr., *Congress' Permanent Minority? Republicans in the US House* (Littlefield Adams 1994).

When Michel announced his retirement in 1994, Gingrich was the undisputed choice to take over as leader and, when the party gained control in the elections of that year, he inevitably became the Speaker. Gingrich was also principally responsible for the House Republicans adopting the 'Contract with America' as their campaign manifesto. The document was designed to provide the party with a programme that united its candidates, clearly separated the Republicans from their Democratic opponents in the public mind and turned the mid-term elections into a national campaign rather than a series of local contests, which is the way Congressional elections have traditionally been conducted. After the elections the Contract was transformed into an agenda for legislative action and the 224 candidates who were elected out of the 367 who signed it were under an obligation to support their commitment with their votes, thus creating a strong basis for party discipline in the House. The Contract included a promise to change the rules and procedures of the chamber.[25]

The Speaker and the Party Leadership

Greater party accountability for carrying out a manifesto required greater control by the party leadership. Gingrich moved quickly after the elections to establish his authority and, with President Clinton in a weak political position, he also saw the opportunity to use the Speaker's role to rival that of the Presidency itself in articulating his vision of where the country should be going. Former Presidential candidate and Senator, Eugene McCarthy, stated that, in this period, Gingrich seemed to see himself as 'a kind of Prime Minister' running 'a counter government'.[26]

Gingrich decided who the new committee chairmen would be on the basis of their ability and commitment to carrying out the party programme. Although he relied heavily on seniority, in some cases he bypassed the ranking members on committees from the previous Congress. His choices were made even before the Republican Committee on Committees was officially formed, and the Conference approved his nominations in December 1994 without dissent. A new Steering Committee, which gave the leadership more influence over assignments, replaced the Committee on Committees. In selecting members for

[25]Alan Grant, 'The New Republican Congress', *Talking Politics*, Vol. 7, No. 3, Spring 1995.
[26]*Congressional Quarterly Weekly Report*, 4 February 1995, p. 331.

committees Gingrich and his colleagues broke with convention and appointed junior legislators, and even freshmen, to important positions on committees such as Appropriations. Three freshmen even became chairmen of sub-committees. Gingrich had the loyalty of junior members; three-fifths of the Republican Conference had won their seats in the last two elections. As a gesture to those who criticized his new power, Gingrich accepted a call for an eight-year limit on anyone serving as Speaker.

Committee and Sub-Committee Chairmen

Gingrich did not inherit a group of entrenched and powerful committee chairmen and, to ensure that no independent fiefdoms developed in the future, a new rule was introduced limiting any individual to six years in any chairmanship. Despite some misgivings from senior Republicans who had waited many years to have the opportunity to chair a committee, term limits for chairmen were adopted by 355–74 in the House, with no Republican dissenters. Committee chairmen were also prevented from chairing sub-committees, although they did gain the power to nominate the chairmen of their sub-committees, with the Speaker's approval, and these bodies were brought more clearly under the aegis of their parent committees. For example, chairmen of standing committees were in future to control the appointment of sub-committee staff. These moves reversed the reforms of the mid-1970s that had decentralized power to sub-committees.

Committee Structure and Rules

Early in the transition period there were calls by some Republicans for a radical restructuring of the committee system. This opportunity was not taken and, in the event, the changes made were far less sweeping. There were two reasons for this: first, ranking members likely to succeed to chairmanships argued for the retention of particular committees and had to be placated; and, second, Gingrich saw the need to make immediate progress on his legislative agenda if the self-imposed 100-day limit for bringing bills to the floor for a vote was to be met.

Three committees traditionally tied to Democratic interests were scrapped; the District of Columbia and the Post Office and Civil Service Committees' business was transferred to a new Government Reform and Oversight Committee, while the work of the Merchant, Marine and

Fisheries Committee was split between three other panels. Approximately one-fifth of the jurisdiction of the Energy and Commerce Committee (renamed the Commerce Committee) was distributed to other bodies. Several committees were renamed to symbolize their new Republican ethos; for example, Public Works and Transportation became Transportation and Infrastructure, but their jurisdictions remained basically unchanged. Pressure from Republican interests saved the Small Business and Veterans' Affairs Committees from abolition.

As we have seen, the Democrats had recognized the dangers of fragmentation in policy-making and had already reduced the number of sub-committees in recent years, but the Republicans wanted to go further. They abolished 25 sub-committees or 20% of the total, although 13 of these came about as a result of the elimination of the three standing committees. With only a few exceptions, committees were not allowed to have more than five sub-committees and members could serve on a maximum of two main committees and four sub-committees. It was hoped that, as a result, there would be fewer scheduling clashes and better attendance would be encouraged.

Rule changes also affected the way committees worked. Among the most important was the abolition of proxy voting whereby a member could vote on behalf of an absent colleague. Chairmen had often used this practice to retain their party's majority and had been much criticized by Republicans when they were the minority. Although most committees had held their meetings in public since the 1970s, the rules had allowed them to close their sessions without explaining why. The new rules limited the circumstances in which a meeting may be held in closed session—for example, if national security might be otherwise threatened—and required a majority vote of the committee to take such a decision. In addition, radio and television coverage of all open meetings had to be allowed. In another move towards open and accountable government, committees were required to publish the names of members voting for and against all bills and amendments.

The practice of the Speaker sending a bill to more than one committee simultaneously for consideration, known as 'multiple referral', was also changed. New rules allowed him to send a bill to a second committee only after the first has finished its work or to refer different parts of a bill to separate committees.

In an effort to show the public that they were determined to cut out waste in Congress, the new majority voted to cut the staff assigned to committees by one-third. These reductions, as well as the displacement of personal staffs employed by defeated Democratic legislators, led to a large number of Democratic aides losing their jobs in 1995.

Floor Procedures

As we have seen, the Republicans promised that they would allow freer debate and introduce less restrictive rules for proposing and voting on amendments. New procedures guaranteed the Minority Leader or his nominee the right to offer a 'motion to recommit', amending the bill under debate; a vote would then take place on sending the bill back to committee to make the revisions proposed.

A number of changes were also made to the way the House operates on the floor of the chamber. Automatic roll call votes were to be required on bills and conference committee reports that make appropriations and raise taxes as well as the annual budget resolution, thus allowing the public to find out exactly how their representatives voted on these key issues. Members were also no longer able to delete or amend speeches reported in the Congressional Record, except to correct grammatical or technical errors. Remarks inserted to revise or extend a speech were to appear in a different typeface in the record of the debate. Commemorative bills honouring individuals, places or events, which had been criticized as frivolous and a distraction from substantive business, were to be banned.

The most controversial change passed on the opening day session was the requirement that a supermajority of three-fifths of members voting would be required for the passage of any bill, amendment or conference report that contained an increase in income tax rates. Republicans supported this provision on the basis that it clearly demonstrated their belief that raising taxes should not be done lightly. However, many critics argued that the House was establishing an unwelcome precedent and that the measure moved in the direction of the Senate by allowing a minority of members to thwart the will of the majority. The new rule was eventually passed by 279–152.

Administration

Republicans claimed that, under the Democrats, the internal management of the House had become sloppy and bred corruption. The Speaker was given the right to nominate, and the House to elect, a new position of Chief Administrative Officer while the Inspector General was instructed to ensure that a complete audit of the financial records of the House was carried out. In July 1995 the resulting report by private auditors listed a catalogue of abuses and concluded that the institution was plagued by overspending, inadequate records and a lack of proper financial accountability. A list of recommendations for overhauling the system was submitted and the new Chief Administrative Officer was given the responsibility for implementing them while working with the House Oversight Committee.

Funding for 28 Congressional caucuses, known as legislative service organizations, which received office space and budgets to operate on Capitol Hill, was abolished. This move caused an outcry among Democrats who claimed that these bodies performed important functions on behalf of the House, particularly those such as the Democratic Study Group which carried out research and analysis on legislative proposals. The Congressional Black Caucus and the Congressional Hispanic Caucus were particularly vocal in their opposition, claiming that the move was a Republican attempt to silence them. The majority argued that members were free to associate in such groups but that they should do so without public funding.

Impact of the House Changes

In the 104th Congress Newt Gingrich called upon all the formal and informal powers at his disposal to assert strong party leadership in the House. He saw himself principally as a visionary, articulating ideas and values, as an agenda-setter and only secondarily as a political manager. In fact, he delegated most of the day-to-day responsibility for overseeing the implementation of the party programme to the Majority Floor Leader, Dick Armey. The leadership was intent on persuading, cajoling, and sometimes compelling, specific legislative outcomes from committees on a clear timetable, whereas committees had traditionally worked to their own schedules and usually determined their own policies. Chairmen had to acquiesce in intervention in their affairs in ways that their Democratic predecessors could neither have envisaged nor would have accepted only a year before.

The Speaker made extensive use of task forces of Republican loyalists on a wide range of issues, allowing him to ensure that committees pursued policies that were consistent with the leadership's wishes. While some chairmen did complain about their loss of independence, they were forced to go along with the new way of doing business or face losing their positions altogether. Most recognized that, at least in the first period of Republican control, the passing of the Contract legislation had to take priority and that the Conference demanded that they cooperate fully with the party leaders. In only a small minority of cases did committees report out bills that did not comply with the Contract or included significant amendments. The leadership did accept some changes but, on other occasions, used the Rules Committee to remove unwelcome amendments made by a committee.

However, after the winter 1995–96 budget crisis had weakened Gingrich's personal authority, Republican members increasingly began to criticize the centralization of power within the leadership. There was also a recognition that, in bypassing committees which had subject expertise, the leadership had, on occasions, brought to the floor bills which then caused the party political trouble. During 1996, before the elections, committees became more active and helped initiate legislation which allowed the Republicans to claim that the 104th Congress had been productive. Many of the bills were compromise proposals that won both Senate support and President Clinton's backing.

In preparing for the 105th Congress the Republican Conference formally agreed to transfer more authority to committee chairmen to set the agendas in their areas and act as spokesmen for the party. Gingrich was also obliged to disband his small Speaker's Advisory Group and replace it with a broader and more representative body of around 20 members.[27] Such moves do not indicate a return to the power exercised by Democratic committee chairmen; the leadership intended to keep its right to change bills before they go to the floor and the term limits for chairmen were retained.

There is little doubt that the changes made in the relationship between party leaders and chairmen in the 104th Congress will leave a lasting mark. As Barbara Sinclair commented, 'Whatever happens, there is going to be a ratcheting effect. It won't go back completely to the way it was'.[28]

Changes in the Senate

Unlike their colleagues in the House, Republican Senators had given no commitment to make procedural changes in their chamber. Far

---

[27]*Congressional Quarterly Weekly Report*, 23 November 1996, pp. 3299–302.
[28]*Congressional Quarterly Weekly Report*, 7 October 1995, p. 3053.

from feeling an oppressed minority, they had benefited from the opportunities that Senate rules give to the opposition. In the closing months of the 103rd Congress, for example, Republican Senators had blocked a number of important bills supported by President Clinton and the Democratic majority. However, the more conservative members of the Republican Conference quickly became frustrated as they saw the Contract bills that had passed the House slow to a crawl in their own chamber. They also felt that the minority of Republican moderates in the Senate had too much influence over legislation and that those who had acquired committee chairmanships through the seniority system were too often out of touch with the views of the conservative majority within the Conference. Traditionally, committee members nominated their chairmen, on the basis of seniority in almost every case. The choice was then ratified by the Conference and then by the full Senate. The position of chairmen and their relations with the party leadership and the Conference was highlighted by the Senate vote on a proposed balanced budget Constitutional Amendment (see Chapter 1). The failure of Mark Hatfield, the Chairman of the Appropriations Committee, to support the amendment meant that it fell one vote short of the necessary two-thirds majority. Although they failed to force Hatfield to resign from his chairmanship, conservative Senators persuaded the Majority Leader, Robert Dole, to set up a task force to examine rule changes in the selection of chairmen.

The task force, chaired by Connie Mack, made a number of recommendations, and the Conference passed a package of changes, to come into operation in January 1997, which should strengthen the leadership and the party. These included a six-year term limit for chairmen, the adoption of a formal legislative agenda with positions on issues to be determined by a three-quarters majority in the Conference and the introduction of secret ballots when committee members vote for chairmen, thus allowing alternative candidates to be supported without fear of retribution if the effort failed. The full Conference would then vote on the committee's choice, also by secret ballot, and in the event of the proposed candidate being rejected, the Leader would then nominate a new chairman. Chairmen of major committees were also banned from chairing any other panel, either committee or sub-committee, with the exceptions of Appropriations, Ethics and Rules. These rule changes, combined with the influx of new members and retirements, led to nine new chairmen taking over in the 20 Senate standing committees in the 105th Congress. Power was also distributed more widely with some first-term Senators being given the opportunity to become chairmen.

Although not as radical as those in the House, the changes did indicate that the Senate Republicans were prepared to take the first steps in securing greater accountability to the party and in strengthening their leader's ability to lead. As a result, Trent Lott has been given more authority than his predecessors.

Factors Influencing Voting in Congress

Members of both houses have the opportunity of casting votes in committees and on the floor of their chambers on numerous bills and resolutions every year. As the Senate and the House of Representatives are elected by different constituencies and for different terms there can be a different party in control of each. From 1981–87 the Republicans controlled the Senate while the Democrats had a majority in the House of Representatives. The Democrats have been in control of both houses of Congress for most of the period since 1933, with the exception of the years 1947–48, 1953–54 and, most recently, since 1994. Differences between the chambers in political control were consequently not as noticeable as those which have often existed between Congress and the Presidency.

What then are the factors that influence the votes which Congressmen cast in the legislature? The process is a complex one, and there are many influences at work, some of which are more important than others on different issues and at different times.

1 Constituency Interest

One common tie that unites almost all politicians is a desire to be re-elected to one's position for another term, and retaining the support of constituents is an important consideration for any legislator. In America, the Constitution lays down that Congressmen must be inhabitants of the state which they are representing. The 'locality' rule means that not only must a legislator have a residence in the area, but he will probably also have lived in the state for a considerable time, and many Congressmen actually have been born and bred in the constituency.[29] Despite recent

---

[29]There are exceptions, and rules can be interpreted broadly. Robert F. Kennedy became Senator for New York despite residence in both Massachusetts and Virginia.

developments the decentralization of American parties means that the legislator owes his nomination and election much more to state and local party structures than to any national organization, and he will listen closely to the views of party supporters at home. This pressure is increased for House members who face re-election every two years. What is more, election campaigns will often centre on local rather than national issues and, as we have seen, voters are increasingly regarding themselves as independent, voting 'split tickets' and not always remaining loyal to traditional party ties.

The Congressman cannot afford to lose contact with his constituency; he is allowed not only an office in Washington DC but also offices and staff in his constituency so that local problems can be dealt with. Even though some Congressmen have districts or states 3,000 miles from the federal capital, they make regular visits and use Congressional adjournments for on-the-spot assessments of popular feeling, and the importance of the franking privilege in maintaining contact with the voters has already been noted. Some politicians pay for their own polls to be carried out to test opinion on sensitive issues coming before Congress. On most issues there is no clear-cut popular view and the Congressman is able to take into account other factors or use his own discretion, but sometimes letters and telegrams to his office leave little doubt as to the public's feelings.

A Congressman is expected as a good representative to take up problems that constituents may be experiencing with the federal government. He becomes an intermediary between the ordinary citizen and the maze of 'red tape' and bureaucracy in Washington. Much of his time, and particularly that of his staff, is spent trying to sort out complaints or problems that require intervention to secure an expeditious and satisfactory response from the civil servants.

Another way the Congressman can show his advocacy of his constituents' causes is by using his influence on committees. He will attempt to secure a position on a committee that deals with the sort of issues in which his constituency has an interest. A legislator from the Mid-West may well see the Agriculture Committee as his ideal assignment, while a Californian may attempt to obtain a place on the committee dealing with aeronautics and space projects. Congressmen will sometimes indulge in 'log-rolling', which means they will exchange favours and support each other's proposals. Legislators on some committees have the opportunity of passing 'pork-barrel' legislation; this allows them to obtain public works programmes, such as water projects or the building of new army installations, in their own constituencies so that they can claim to have brought new jobs and prosperity to the area. Morris Fiorina has argued that Congressmen tend to spend most of their time on matters that will help them get re-elected, such as casework and channelling federal funds and favours to their districts, and prefer to avoid policy areas that cause controversy back home, a factor which, as we have seen, has contributed to the decline in competitive elections in the House.[30]

Most Congressmen see themselves as combining the notion of a 'trustee' who votes as his conscience dictates, and the 'delegate' who follows the local views all the time.[31] In fact, many citizens do not know anything about their local representative and very few know his voting record on individual issues, although opponents in elections may well try to exploit positions taken by legislators on controversial issues. Therefore the Congressman is allowed a great deal of discretion in practice, but he must always remember 'the folks back home'.

2 Party Membership

Political parties in the US Congress do not experience the same levels of cohesion and unity in voting as those in the British House of Commons. This is partly because legislators do not have to vote to support the continuing existence of the executive as they do in a parliamentary system. The separation of powers system prevents each vote on a bill being seen as a vote of confidence in the President, as he continues in office for a set term regardless of the fate of his proposed legislation. Therefore Democrats and Republicans can examine each bill, whether proposed by the executive or not, on its merits, and vote accordingly. Local views are expected to play an important part in the Congressman's decisions, and party Whips do not expect to pressure members into voting against the expressed interests of their constituents. Whips and party leaders can only persuade, and they have virtually no disciplinary measures with which to threaten members into compliance. However, as we have seen, there have been attempts to make chairmen of committees and sub-committees more responsive to their parties with consideration being given to removing them from their posts.

[30]Morris Fiorina, *Congress: Keystone of the Washington Establishment* (Yale 1977).
[31]Roger Davidson, *The Role of the Congressman* (Pegasus 1969), p. 119.

TABLE 2.4

Party Scores in US Congress in 1995 and 1996

	1995		1996	
Party Unity	Reps	Dems	Reps	Dems
Both Houses	91%	80%	87%	80%
Senate	89%	81%	89%	84%
House	91%	80%	87%	80%
Opposition	Reps	Dems	Reps	Dems
Both Houses	7%	15%	10%	15%
Senate	9%	15%	9%	14%
House	7%	15%	10%	15%

Note: Party unity and opposition to party scores are composites of individual scores and show the percentage of time the average Democrat or Republican voted with or against his or her party majority in disagreement with the other party's majority.

Source: *Congressional Quarterly Weekly Report*, 21 December 1996, p. 3461.

Although party cohesion has traditionally been relatively weak in the American legislature, if there are no conflicting constituency interests Congressmen normally vote with the majority of their own party. Party membership is still the best single indicator of the way in which a legislator is likely to vote. There has been a tendency for partisanship to increase and the more ideological politics of the 1980s, with Democrats after 1982 reacting against the Reagan agenda, is shown in the figures in Table 2.5. In addition, political debate has been dominated by budget and deficit issues, which has also tended to polarize the parties. For example, President Clinton's budget package in 1993 was opposed unanimously by Republicans in both Houses because they rejected tax increases and argued that it did not include sufficient spending cuts. Congressmen are now voting on average approximately eight or even nine times out of ten with their party when there is a party division. This average conceals great disparities in the levels of party loyalty of individuals; some Congressmen will vote with their own party majority well over 90% of the time while some Southern Democrats have scored less than 20%. House Republicans demonstrated unprecedented levels of

TABLE 2.5

Party Unity in Congress

Year	Dems	Reps
1980	68%	70%
1981	69%	76%
1982	72%	71%
1983	76%	74%
1984	74%	72%
1985	79%	75%
1986	78%	71%
1987	81%	74%
1988	79%	73%
1989	81%	73%
1990	81%	74%
1991	81%	78%
1992	79%	79%
1993	85%	84%
1994	83%	83%
1995	80%	91%
1996	80%	87%

Note: Party unity is defined as being the average percentage Democratic and Republican Congressmen in both houses voted with the majority of their own party in party divisions.

Source: *Congressional Quarterly Weekly Report*, 21 December 1996, p. 3461.

party cohesion in 1995 with a 91% party unity score for the year (see Tables 2.4 and 2.5). A record 73% of roll call votes in that year saw a partisan split with the majority of House Democrats voting against a majority of House Republicans.

Traditionally, many Southern Democrats have aligned with the majority of Republicans to form a 'conservative coalition' in Congress. In some periods the coalition played an important role, especially in providing Republican Presidents with support for legislation so that they were successful even when nominally the Democrats had majority control. For example, in 1981 a group of mainly Southern members formed the Conservative Democratic Forum and became known as the 'Boll Weevils'; they provided the vital votes which gave President Reagan victories in the House on his tax and spending cuts package in that year. However, in recent times there have been significantly fewer Democrats elected from the Southern states as conservative Republicans have made inroads there. In the 103rd Congress Southern Democrats numbered 85 or 62% of the Southern delegation; by the time the 105th Congress met in January 1997 there were 55 or 40%. Some Democratic legislators had defected to the GOP, but the Democrats who do win in the region have increasingly had to take account of the impact of demographic changes—and the allegiance of the growing number of black voters in particular—on their chances of renomination and re-election. As we have seen, the Democratic Party in Congress is less heterogeneous than in the past and an increasing number of Southern Democrats elected in the 1990s are black; of those returned in 1997, 21 are from minority groups.

In the 104th Congress Southern conservative Democrats generally just added to the size of Republican victories rather than being crucial to their successes; with a smaller Republican majority in the 105th Congress, an alliance of 14 such members known as the Coalition, and informally as the 'Blue Dogs', was expecting to wield greater influence.[32]

The party view is the safest to go along with if the Congressman has not really had time to consider the bill fully or develop a view, and party loyalty tends to be greater in non-election years. In Congressional election years party cohesion declines somewhat as constituency concerns become more pressing (see Table 2.5).

3 Principle or Ideology

Many Congressmen consider themselves to be conservatives or liberals and this philosophy may provide them with the guidelines on which they will vote. This can lead to a consistency in decision making over a vast array of otherwise unconnected legislation. A conservative may consistently vote against bills which tend to increase the federal government's role in the domestic field, but vote for those he regards as strengthening national defence. A liberal, on the other hand, may support programmes he perceives as regulating 'big business' but op-

[32]*Congressional Quarterly Weekly Report*, 21 December 1996, p. 3438.

pose those measures cutting foreign aid to developing nations. Often the principles will coincide with the views of the majority of his party, but, for liberal Republicans (who these days prefer to be known as 'moderates') or conservative Democrats, their philosophical commitment is often more important than party ties.

4 Identification with State, Regional, Ethnic and Religious Groups

On certain issues the most important influence on a Congressman may be his personal identification with particular groups in the population or within Congress. Occasionally all Congressmen in a state delegation will recognize a common interest and support a proposal which will entail voting across party lines. In some cases regional identity will lead a larger number of legislators to work together for mutual advantage. Southern members have done this for decades, but it appears to be an increasingly familiar phenomenon. For example, in the 1977 debates on energy, the different interests of those Congressmen from oil- and gas-producing areas and those from regions where constituents were heavily dependent on cheap energy for heating (such as the North-East) were clearly reflected in the voting on proposed legislation.

The caucus of black legislators has worked hard to support new civil rights and urban aid programmes; many see their role as promoting the interests of blacks across the country and not merely those within their constituencies. Jewish members have taken particular interest in American foreign policy in the Middle East and have strenuously backed continuing aid to Israel, while Catholic Congressmen have vigorously opposed the use of federal funds for abortion operations.

5 Committee Decisions

The view of the standing committee that initially examined the proposal is an important influence on voting behaviour in the full chamber. If a bill had unanimous backing in the committee it is likely that it will pass without real opposition in the floor vote. A Congressman who has not been a member of the committee will rely, to a large extent, on what he has learnt about its details from colleagues who are members of his own state delegation or who feel philosophically as he does.

6 Pressure Groups

Many pressure groups wishing to influence legislation employ full-time lobbyists to see the legislator and persuade him to vote in a particular way; the professional persuaders usually know which Congressmen are likely to be favourable to their cause and who the waverers may be. They rarely waste their time contacting legislators they know will be in opposition to their group's objectives. Congressmen often acquire useful information and material for speeches on major bills from pressure groups, and, of course, at election times contributions from sympathetic groups to campaign funds are common. Very few Congressmen refuse to accept financial contributions from political action committees (PACs) which are frequently offered to incumbents defending their seats (see Chapter 5). Outright bribery in return for votes is probably rare but every Congressman has to ensure that his conduct, and that of his staff, is beyond public suspicion.

7 The White House

The President needs the support of Congress in order to govern effectively and therefore he will seek to influence Congressional voting on a wide range of matters that are of considerable importance to him, including bills, budget resolutions, confirmation of nominees to the executive and judicial branches, ratification of foreign treaties and the sustaining of vetoes. Nelson Polsby has pointed out that electoral results are constantly reshaping the terrain over which Presidential–Congressional relations are battled out and these electoral results must be turned by acts of institutional leadership into legislative coalitions.[33] Thus, while a President can expect the help of party colleagues in the Congress who may see it as in their mutual interest to support him, he will probably have to appeal to other legislators as well. Republican Presidents have often sought support from a coalition of Republicans and conservative Southern Democrats, especially when faced with majorities for the Democratic party in both houses.

It is inevitable that Presidents therefore have to negotiate with Congress in order to seek agreement on important issues. Charles O. Jones has analysed this process during the terms of four recent Presidents

[33]Nelson Polsby, 'Some Landmarks in Modern Presidential–Congressional Relations', in *Both Ends of the Avenue*, Anthony King (ed.) (American Enterprise Institute 1983) p. 18.

and concludes that they represent a remarkably diverse sample of conditions, styles and techniques. For example, Lyndon Johnson and Gerald Ford both were Congressional leaders themselves before becoming President. Johnson had been Senate Majority Leader and as President had very large Democratic majorities in both houses to work with following the 1964 elections. Ford had been Republican Minority Leader in the House and as President faced large opposition majorities in both houses. Despite the very different conditions they had to operate in and political resources they enjoyed, both Johnson and Ford tried to work with Congress as partners and were prepared to bargain to achieve objectives. Nixon and Carter, on the other hand, according to Jones, were uncomfortable with the politics of exchange and depended on a form of persuasion that preserved a distance between themselves and members of Congress, preferring therefore an independent or outsider model. Nixon, although a former Congressman himself, made it clear he did not trust Congress and had little interest in legislative matters, preferring to concentrate on foreign policy issues. Carter had no Washington experience at all and he had campaigned in 1976 as an 'outsider' and acted as the 'Political Layman as President'. Carter's political agenda did need the support of Congress but he was notably unsuccessful in employing the independent model for getting it.[34]

The role of the President's Congressional Liaison staff is very important in carrying out the day-to-day discussions that take place between the two branches. The Office of Congressional Relations is usually made up of a small staff of experienced lobbyists who are each expected to get to know individually a number of legislators in the hope that a favourable climate and personal relationship will lead to support for the President. President Carter's early attempts at organizing his staff on an issues basis rather than on this people-centred basis contributed to the poor relationship between the White House and Capitol Hill during his term of office.[35] Carter's problems also resulted from his failure to establish good personal relationships with the leaders of Congress and his dislike for politicking and bargaining. He also made the mistake of failing to involve Congress in the development of his legislative

[34]Charles O. Jones, 'Presidential Negotiation with Congress', in King, op. cit. pp. 96–130.
[35]Eric L. Davis, 'Congressional Liaison: The People and the Institutions', in King, op. cit. pp. 59–95. Also see Joseph D. Hogan, 'Legislative Liaison in the Reagan Administration', in *Reagan's First Four Years*, John Lees and Michael Turner (eds) (University of Manchester 1988), pp. 68–94.

proposals and then overloading the legislature with a large number of issues with no clear indication of where his priorities lay. The failure of Congress to act upon many of these initiatives early on in his Presidency resulted in his being perceived widely as a weak and ineffectual leader and this reputation handicapped him for the rest of his term.

President Reagan clearly learned the lessons of the Carter period. Despite the fact that like Carter he had run as an 'outsider' against the Washington establishment in the 1980 election, once elected he spent many of the early weeks of his Presidency on Capitol Hill getting to know Congressional leaders. He worked out a limited agenda of priorities which centred on budget and defence issues and agreed them with Republican leaders in Congress. The subsequent victories during 1981, particularly on his economic programme with reductions in federal spending and income tax cuts, established his reputation as a successful and strong President, an image that helped him in later years even when he was unable to obtain legislative support for his proposals.

The other major difference was that Ronald Reagan became his administration's own Chief Lobbyist and he obviously enjoyed meeting and talking to Congressmen. On many occasions Reagan saw personally or phoned members to persuade them to support him on issues that were of importance to the Presidency. For example, in 1981 a Senate vote of 52–48 to approve the sale of advanced warning radar planes (AWACs) was seen as a test of the President's leadership in foreign policy. Reagan personally met 75 out of the 100 Senators, 44 of them alone, to press his case and at least seven of those committed to voting against the sale and a number of waverers came down on his side. President Clinton used similar tactics, phoning and meeting personally many Democratic members, including freshmen, before the vital House vote on his budget package in May 1993; he managed to persuade sufficient waverers to win the vote by 219–213. In November 1993 Clinton scored a major victory of vital importance to his Presidency with the passage of the North American Free Trade Agreement (NAFTA) in the House of Representatives by 234–200 only days after defeat seemed probable. His party was split on the issue and 156 of 258 Democrats in the House voted against the agreement but, with Republican backing, Clinton was able to persuade sufficient members, in many cases with last-minute concessions and 'pork-barrel' projects for their districts, to win the vote.

In a 'honeymoon' period with Congress in 1981 President Reagan obtained an 82.4% success rate on Congressional votes, the highest

TABLE 2.6

Presidential Victories on Congressional Votes

Kennedy		Nixon		Carter		Bush	
1961	81.0%	1969	74.0%	1977	75.4%	1989	62.6%
1962	85.4%	1970	77.0%	1978	78.3%	1990	46.8%
1963	87.1%	1971	75.0%	1979	76.8%	1991	54.2%
		1972	66.0%	1980	75.1%	1992	43.0%
		1973	50.6%				
		1974	59.6%				
Johnson		Ford		Reagan		Clinton	
1964	88.0%	1974	58.2%	1981	82.4%	1993	86.4%
1965	93.0%	1975	61.0%	1982	72.4%	1994	86.4%
1966	79.0%	1976	53.8%	1983	67.1%	1995	36.2%
1967	79.0%			1984	65.8%	1996	55.2%
1968	75.0%			1985	59.9%		
				1986	56.1%		
				1987	43.5%		
				1988	47.4%		

Source: *Congressional Quarterly Weekly Report*, 21 December 1996, p. 3455.

since Lyndon Johnson's 93% in 1965. However, later Democratic victories in Congressional elections, particularly in 1982 and 1986, resulted in a decline in Reagan's success rate, the low point being in 1987, the year the Iran-Contra scandal weakened his administration (see Table 2.6). In 1989 President Bush's score of 62.6% was the lowest recorded for an elected President in his first year in office since *Congressional Quarterly* first analysed Congressional voting in 1953, with only the unelected Gerald Ford faring worse in 1974. Similarly, Bush's score of 43% in 1992 was the lowest of any President in 40 years. Despite the difficulties of his first period in office President Clinton achieved an 86.4% success rate in both 1993 and 1994 when the Democrats controlled Congress, the highest since Lyndon Johnson in 1965. After the Republicans' victory in the 1994 mid-term elections, Clinton was effectively marginalized and his success rate fell dramatically to 36.2%, the lowest recorded for any President. However, Clinton's fortunes improved during the next year and, with both parties seeking compromise and legislative accomplishments before the 1996 elections, his success rate rose to 55.1%, the highest one-year jump ever recorded.[36]

8 Congressional Staff

As Congress has reasserted its power and attempted to compete with the vast civil service machine of the executive branch, so its own staff have increased very substantially. By 1993 there were 14,553 Congressional staff working for individual legislators and committees. In addition, there are thousands of other officials who provide support to Congress through bodies such as the Congressional Research Service, the General Accounting Office and the Congressional Budget Office. In 1995 there were a total of 33,367 staff employed by Congress, a 11% reduction compared with 1990.[37]

Because of both the expanded workload and the increasingly technical nature of much of the legislation with which Congress deals, many of the staff employed are experts in particular fields. Congressmen, therefore, tend to become more dependent on the views of their advisers when they decide how to vote on a bill, particularly if it is in an area

TABLE 2.7

Congressional Support for the President's Proposals 1995–96

Support for the President	1995		1996	
	Reps	Dems	Reps	Dems
Senate	29%	81%	37%	83%
House	22%	75%	38%	74%
Opposition to the President				
Senate	70%	15%	61%	15%
House	76%	20%	59%	21%

Note: Percentages refer to the composite scores of all Republicans and Democrats in supporting the President's view on votes in Congress when he took a clear-cut position.

Source: *Congressional Quarterly Weekly Report*, 21 December 1996, p. 3455.

[36]*Congressional Quarterly Weekly Report*, 21 December 1996, p. 3427.
[37]*Statistical Abstract of the United States 1996*, pp. 280 and 345.

in which they have neither the time nor the interest to become involved themselves.

9 The Political Climate

Anthony King has argued that a significant influence in Congressional voting (and in the relationship between Congress and the White House) is the difficult-to-define factor of political climate or mood. This is likely to involve the widespread feeling that some political force is all but irresistible and changes in the intellectual atmosphere where, for example, a cause may become hard to defend because people have, for whatever reason, become unreceptive to the theories and values underlying it. King gives as examples civil rights in the 1960s, the dissipation in the 1980s of the pro-Israeli atmosphere that had dominated American politics since 1948 and the Reagan budget and tax cuts of 1981.[38] More recently there has been evidence that, after years of evading the consequences of rising federal deficits, politicians of both parties have begun to recognize that the public expects them to take the problem seriously and come forward with ways to achieve a balanced budget.

The Legislative Process in Congress

As only a small proportion of legislative proposals ever become law in America, the legislative process can be likened to an obstacle race with many runners or competitors falling at each of the hurdles, so that only a few actually finish the course. The filtering process that takes place means that it is often easier to prevent the passage of a bill than to ensure its success, and this is particularly true of controversial proposals or ones that directly affect the interests of important groups. It is worth considering the various stages of the legislative process, and particularly the vital points where a bill can be delayed or rejected.

1 Initiation. The inspiration or source of a bill can be individual members or their aides, pressure groups, the executive branch, or a committee in the Senate or House. Whatever the source, a Congressman

[38]Anthony King, 'A Mile and a Half is a Long Way', in *Both Ends of the Avenue* (American Enterprise Institute 1983), pp. 256–62.

must formally introduce the bill. A proposal can begin its life in either house or a joint resolution will allow concurrent consideration.

2 Committee Investigation in the House.   If a bill is first introduced into the House of Representatives it will be assigned to one of the standing committees by the Speaker. If the bill's contents overlap the jurisdiction of more than one committee, he can use his discretion to send it to the one most or least likely to be favourable, depending on his own view of the proposal. Bills may be referred to more than one committee for consideration. They are assigned to sub-committees, and those receiving approval go to the full committee for approval. If a bill is being seriously examined by the committee, there may be public hearings held to obtain evidence from interested parties. The committee stage is the main period when the bill's content will be shaped; it may be amended or combined with other bills in such a way that it is unrecognizable to the original proponents. On occasions a committee such as the Ways and Means Committee will write a bill itself, and, of course, this gives great power to the chairman. The committee decides whether to report the bill out to the full House, although on rare occasions a refusal to do so can be overruled by a 'discharge petition' passed by a majority of the chamber. The committee chairman will usually write the report to the full House on the bill's contents or appoint another member to do so.

3 The Rules Committee.   Once bills are approved by the standing committee, the Rules Committee establishes the order in which the full House will consider them and sets the terms of debate by issuing a 'rule' for each individual piece of legislation. The rules may limit debate and also determine whether amendments will be permitted. The Rules Committee in the 1960s was an independent and powerful body that was used by Republicans and their conservative Democratic allies to thwart liberal legislation, but it is now an arm of the majority leadership; its members are nominated by the Speaker who uses the committee to control and expedite floor action.

4 Discussion by the Whole House and Voting.   The debate in the full House is for a limited period and a vote is easily obtained by the cloture rule. The vote can take a number of forms: a voice vote, a roll call with tellers or electronic voting with scores shown on a scoreboard. The roll call has been used to cause delay as each member is called in turn to announce his vote.

5 Procedure in the Senate. A bill passed in the House and introduced by a Senator is assigned to a committee by an official called the Parliamentarian, who is not a Senator. The Vice-President can intervene and over-rule him if he feels an inappropriate decision has been made. The bill is considered by the Senate standing committee in the specialist area and is then assigned a place on the timetable by the majority party's Policy Committee. This body has the functions of the Rules Committee in the House. The main difference, however, is that the tradition of continuous debate without time limits allows a filibuster to be used by opponents to 'talk the bill out'. Failure to secure the necessary 60 votes on a cloture motion indicates that the bill will make no further progress for the time being.

6 Conference Committee. If a bill has passed both Houses but different amendments have been made which create two different versions, it is necessary for a conference committee, made up of members of the original Senate and House committees that considered the proposal, to meet and work out a compromise. The committee should be concerned only with resolving the areas of conflict, but in the past these bodies were often accused of rewriting whole bills. As a result of committee reforms in the 1970s, these conference committees are now open to the public, thus preventing secret deals by members, and junior members as well as senior Congressmen have been allowed to take part in conference committees. The House and Senate then have to approve the revised version of the bill without further amendment before it goes to the White House.

Conference committees have normally comprised 5–12 members from each House but, with the development of multiple referrals and omnibus and mega-bills, large conferences became common. In 1981 a record number of over 250 conferees met on the omnibus reconciliation bill to resolve over 300 matters of disagreement between the two Houses. On occasions there will also be sub-conferences established to work out agreements in specialist areas, while general conferees co-ordinate their activities.[39]

7 Presidential Action. The President has three alternatives open to him when he receives a bill that has passed Congress during a session. He

[39]Walter J. Oleszek, 'House–Senate Relations: A Perspective on Bicameralism', in Roger Davidson, *The Postreform Congress* (St Martin's Press 1992), p. 205.

can sign the bill, passing it into law with his approval. He can allow it to become law after ten working days without signing it, thus showing some reservations about its contents, or he can veto it. The President may veto only a whole bill and not specific items or sections within it, and therefore Congress sometimes exploits the inflexible veto weapon by including provisions it feels the President dare not veto, even though he may disagree with much of the content. As we have seen in Chapter 1, the 104th Congress did pass a law giving the President a line item veto over appropriations bills. If the President does veto a bill he must write a message to Congress explaining his reasons, and they can attempt to override his decision by obtaining a two-thirds majority in both Houses. A President will obviously weigh his chances of sustaining the veto when he makes his decision and sometimes he will threaten the use of the veto as a tactic to try to force Congress to make changes he wants in a bill. On occasions he will decide to go ahead on principle even though he knows Congress will probably override his veto. President Ford, for example, vetoed forty-four bills but on twelve occasions his veto was overridden by the large Democratic majorities in Congress. A President requires a minimum of thirty-four allies in Congress, a third of the Senate, to defeat an attempt to override his veto. President Bush, supported by Senate Republicans, sustained all but one of the 36 vetoes he used during his term in office. The exception was a bill that regulated cable television charges which was popular with the voters; in the run-up to the 1992 elections sufficient Senate Republicans defected to override the President's veto by 74–25. President Clinton vetoed a total of 17 bills in his first term—the lowest since Woodrow Wilson vetoed ten in 1913–17. All of the vetoes were used against bills passed by the Republican-controlled 104th Congress, and the legislature only managed to override the veto once, on securities legislation.

If a President receives the bill less than ten days before Congress adjourns, the bill dies if he does not sign it. In using the 'pocket veto' he does not have to explain his reasons for not signing it, and Congress does not have the chance to override a pocket veto. This device is important as Congress finishes consideration of many bills in a rush at the end of a session. Clinton became the first President since Franklin Pierce (1853–57) to serve a full term without using the pocket veto.

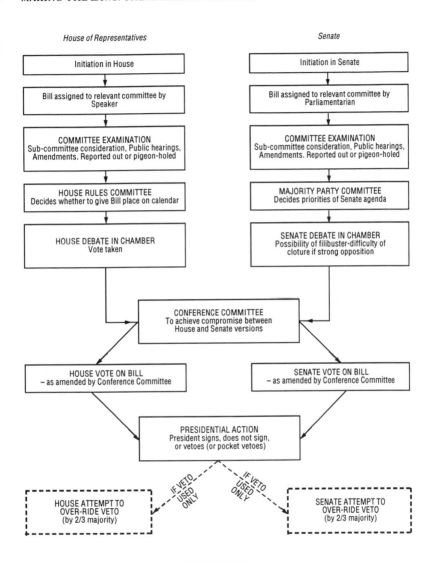

FIGURE 2.1

The Legislative Process in Congress

Financial Control by Congress

Even when a bill has passed the difficult legislative process, there is still a major problem to be surmounted; this is to obtain approval for funds so that the intention of the legislature can be implemented by government departments. The specialist committees of the House and Senate can authorize the amount of money to be spent on a purpose defined in a bill, that is 'what ought to be spent'. Within that framework, the Appropriations Committees of the two houses decide what will actually be spent. Therefore separate bills have to pass the Congress, appropriating money for particular legislation already on the statute book.[40]

The Appropriations Committees are the biggest standing committees in their respective houses and are divided into a large number of sub-committees which specialize in particular aspects of expenditure such as defence, agriculture and welfare. The Appropriations sub-committees are very important power centres because their decisions

TABLE 2.8

Presidential Vetoes 1933–97

	Regular Vetoes	Pocket Vetoes	Total Vetoes	Vetoes Over-ridden
F. D. Roosevelt (1933–45)	372	263	635	9
H. Truman (1945–53)	180	70	250	12
D. Eisenhower (1953–61)	73	108	181	2
J. Kennedy (1961–63)	12	9	21	–
L. Johnson (1963–69)	16	14	30	–
R. Nixon (1969–74)	26	17	43	7
G. Ford (1974–77)	48	18	66	12
J. Carter (1977–81)	13	18	31	2
R. Reagan (1981–89)	39	39	78	9
G. Bush (1989–93)	27	19	46	1
B. Clinton (1993–97)	17	0	17	1

[40]For a fuller discussion see Tim Hames, 'The Budget Process and Deficit Politics' in *Contemporary American Politics*, Alan Grant (ed.), (Dartmouth 1995).

on levels of expenditure are usually accepted by the full committee and eventually by the whole House.

The President's budget, which includes requests for money to cover the ongoing administration of departments, is also examined by the Appropriations sub-committees on a piecemeal basis. Traditionally Congress never debated the full implications of the whole budget on the floor of either house; parts were approved or modified, taking each separately. The President cannot necessarily expect that his requests will be granted in full. After hearings, the sub-committee may well vote substantially less than has been asked for in the departmental submission. However, it is impossible for the Congressmen, even with a substantial staff, to scrutinize properly all the detailed work of the government and assess the justification of expenditure.

The Congressional system of approving expenditure came in for a great deal of criticism in the early 1970s as President Nixon accused the specialist committees and the Appropriations Committees of approving and appropriating funds without regard for the total levels of government expenditure. He claimed this extravagance was creating large deficits and thus fuelling inflation in the country at large. The criticism was to a large degree justified, as the Congressional committees that decide how much revenue is to be raised (House Ways and Means and Senate Finance Committees) had almost no idea of what total level of appropriations they were supposed to finance until the fiscal year was almost over. In other words, the piecemeal consideration did not allow any Congressional body to consider general economic strategy.

President Nixon's answer to the problem was to impound millions of dollars of appropriated funds for particular bills he felt were unnecessary. He refused to spend the money to avoid the building up of even bigger budget deficits. Congress passed a law severely restricting the President's right to impoundment; the Impoundment Control Act 1974 provides that the President must spend appropriated funds unless both chambers consent to impoundment within forty-five days of a Presidential request. However, the controversy also resulted in the establishment of Budget Committees in the House and the Senate. These committees are supposed to provide an overall view of the financial situation that had been lacking in the appropriations procedure. The committees have a Congressional Budget Office whose economists and other specialist staff are supposed to analyse tax and spending options in all areas as well as forecasting expenditure trends. The reports from the office have certainly led to Congressmen being better informed on the consequences of their actions.

The Budget Committees fix the targets of either overall surplus or deficit by May of each year and also set the spending totals and sub-totals for different areas of expenditure. Between May and September the normal appropriations process takes place, and then a second look is taken at the spending totals in the light of developments. If the sum of individual appropriations made exceeds the total, Congress can choose to cut appropriations, raise taxation, or go further into deficit.

The reforms were heralded as another example of Congress modernizing its procedures to redress the balance in its relations with the executive branch. Critics argued that the Budget Committees were given insufficient power to enforce their spending guidelines and the jurisdictions of the Appropriations and taxation committees were left largely intact. The House Budget Committee is also weakened by having a rotating membership; no-one, including the chairman, can serve more than six consecutive years. The committees' limited success was in forcing members to consider trade-offs and the setting of spending priorities.

The budget reforms of the 1970s, while improving some procedures, did not succeed in forcing Congress to make hard choices in balancing spending and revenue. As the federal budget deficit increased in size in the 1980s, Congress voted, with President Reagan's support, to approve the Balanced Budget and Emergency Deficit Reduction Act (known after its sponsors as Gramm–Rudman–Hollings). This landmark legislation set a series of targets for reducing the deficit to zero by 1991. The original version of the legislation had given the Comptroller General of the General Accounting Office the final say over the allocation of cuts but in 1986 the Supreme Court decided that this would violate the separation of powers principle because the Comptroller General is an officer of Congress. Congress then approved a process whereby the legislature itself would pass a resolution in both houses and send it to the President to order spending cuts. As amended in 1987, the Act gave the President's Budget Director the final say in choosing the economic projections that would determine the size of the overall spending reductions. Social Security and interest on the national debt were to be excluded but cuts to meet the targets for deficit reduction would come equally from defence and domestic programmes.

Even the sponsors of the legislation admitted it was a 'bad idea whose time had come' but argued that the threat of automatic cuts

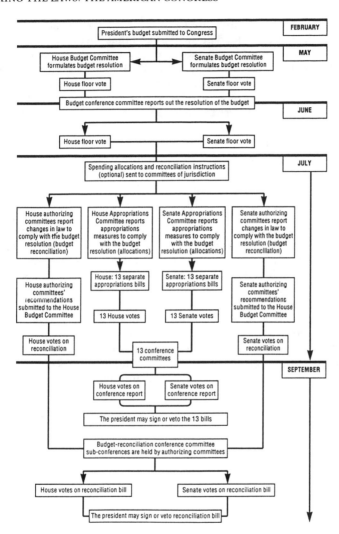

Source: House Budget Committee.

FIGURE 2.2

The Budget Process in Congress

would provide an incentive for Congress (and the President) to face the difficult choices avoided in the past and that the overriding need to reduce the deficit justified the extreme action. Although the legislation helped to stabilize the deficit at about $150 billion for three years, it failed in its stated aim of a balanced budget. When it appeared that the targets for deficit reduction would not be met, Congress adjusted them upwards. Programmes were taken 'off budget' and spending was moved from one financial year to another to make the figures look better than they were in reality.

The budget process became more centralized and in 1990 direct negotiations took place between Congressional leaders and the White House; committee hearings were effectively a sideshow while the real decisions were made in these private discussions. Congress was then presented with a budget package and, although it at first rejected the deal agreed by President Bush and its own leaders, the proposals were soon adopted after some adjustments were made and more of the tax increases were shifted from the poorer to the wealthier taxpayers. The abandonment of his 1988 election pledge, 'Read my lips, no new taxes', damaged President Bush politically, particularly as he vacillated and changed his mind several times while the negotiations were going on.[41]

The 1990 budget summit effectively, if not formally, repealed the Gramm–Rudman–Hollings legislation. The focus of the agreement, formalized in the Budget Enforcement Act, was to control increases in spending. Any new spending in three separate categories of discretionary expenditure—defence, international and domestic programmes—would have to be offset by decreases elsewhere within a category. Failure to make decisions as to where reductions would be made would lead to across-the-board sequestration within the affected categories. The deficit targets for the 1990s were also revised drastically upwards to recognize the reality of the budgetary situation, made worse by recession. The President was given authority to adjust the targets in the light of changing economic circumstances. The new procedures gave the President more budgetary power and, by locking in spending totals for five years, deprived the Budget Committees of their main functions.[42]

President Clinton therefore came to office in 1993 with an accelerating financial crisis, and his first budget included a major deficit

---

[41]David Mervin, 'George Bush and the 1990 Budget Crisis', *Talking Politics* (Summer 1991), pp. 121–5.
[42]James P. Pfiffner, 'The President and the Postreform Congress', in Roger Davidson, op. cit., pp. 218–21.

reduction package. He was forced to drastically dilute proposals made during his election campaign to stimulate the economy by increased public spending on infrastructure projects and, after months of wrangling with Democrats in Congress over the detail of tax increases and spending cuts, the budget was passed by a mere two votes in the House and with the aid of Vice-President Gore's casting vote in the Senate. The plan to cut the deficit by a total of $496 billion over five years was unanimously opposed by Republicans in Congress on the basis that it relied too heavily on tax increases and insufficiently on reductions in expenditure.

As we saw in Chapter 1, the period of Clinton's first administration saw a recovery from recession and a marked reduction in the federal deficit in 1996 due to increased economic growth. The Republican majority in the 104th Congress had eventually forced Clinton to accept the need for future plans that would bring the budget into balance by the year 2002; the bitter budget crisis of the winter of 1995–96 centred on the differences between the rival alternative proposals and projections submitted by the President and Congressional leaders, Republicans being convinced that the goal could only be achieved by tackling the escalating costs of entitlement programmes such as Medicare. Clinton had also opposed the passage of a balanced budget Constitutional Amendment, one of the central planks of the 'Contract with America', arguing that it was an unnecessarily rigid constraint on economic policy-making, particularly in a time of recession.

Congressional Oversight

One of the major roles of Congress, carried out through its committees, is that of oversight of the executive branch. The legislature has the responsibility to monitor and investigate the activities of executive agencies and personnel, including the President. Congress had been criticized for neglecting this function as executive power grew during the twentieth century, but the reassertion of Congressional authority in the 1970s saw a number of developments to improve legislative capacity in this area. These included the establishment of the Congressional Budget Office, increased staffing for committees and the use of legislative vetoes in new laws to limit executive discretion. The growing interest by Congress in this work led some critics to accuse it of 'micromanagement' and excessive interference in the implementation of policy.

Congressional oversight can be interpreted as either an ongoing activity where members are continuously reviewing executive behaviour to ascertain whether instances of maladministration have taken place or as a response to complaints received about government wrongdoing. As Peter Falconer has pointed out, generally members of Congress have many pressures on their time and they will tend to react to demands for investigation of alleged maladministration rather than actively seek out instances of such behaviour themselves.[43] Committee hearings and scrutiny will only take place when legislators feel that the problem is sufficiently serious to justify the time and cost involved and when they deem it politically profitable to do so.

Congressional oversight is a legitimate and important method of ensuring executive accountability but, with the existence of divided party control of the two branches, the majority in Congress has more of an incentive to harass and embarrass the President and his administration. As Falconer has noted, the most publicly visible instances of oversight since the 1970s have been when Democratic Congresses have acted to confront Republican Presidents: the Watergate affair and the impeachment hearings of Richard Nixon; the inquiries into maladministration in the Department of Housing and Urban Development (HUD) and the Environmental Protection Agency (EPA) in the 1980s; and the Iran-Contra hearings of 1987.

The decline of cooperation and collegiality and the rise of partisan tensions in Congress has been exacerbated by what many see as the use of legislative oversight for blatantly party political ends. It is therefore not surprising that, with the Republicans in control of Congress since 1995, a number of committees have launched investigations into alleged wrongdoing by President Clinton, his wife Hillary and the White House staff. These included allegations that the Clintons acted improperly over property transactions in Arkansas when Bill Clinton was Governor (the Whitewater affair), charges that officials responsible for organizing White House travel were dismissed to give the business to associates of the Clintons ('Travelgate') and, following the 1996 elections, accusations that the Clinton campaign had raised large illegal contributions from foreign businessmen in exchange for influence over government policies that affected them.

---

[43]Peter Falconer, 'Congressional Oversight: The Development of Legislative Review', *in Contemporary American Politics*, Alan Grant (ed.) (Dartmouth 1995).

Some Further Reading

Ross K. Baker, *House and Senate* (Norton 1989)

Roger H. Davidson (ed.), *The Postreform Congress* (St Martin's Press 1992)

Roger H. Davidson and Walter J. Oleszek, *Congress and its Members* (Congressional Quarterly Press 1989)

Lawrence C. Dodd and Bruce I. Oppenheimer, *Congress Reconsidered* (Congressional Quarterly Press 1993)

Morris P. Fiorina, *Congress: Keystone of the Washington Establishment* (Yale University Press 1989)

Michael Foley and John Owens, *Congress and the Presidency: Institutional Politics in a Separated System* (Manchester University Press 1996)

Barbara Hinckley, *Stability and Change in Congress* (Harper and Row 1988)

Charles O. Jones, *Separate But Equal Branches: Congress and the Presidency* (Chatham House 1995)

Anthony King (ed.), *Both Ends of the Avenue* (American Enterprise Institute 1983)

Steven Smith, *The American Congress* (Houghton Mifflin 1995)

James A. Thurber and Roger H. Davidson (eds), *Remaking Congress: Change and Stability in the 1990s* (Congressional Quarterly Press 1995)

3

Law Execution: The President and Administration

> I do solemnly swear that I will faithfully execute the office of President of the United States and will to the best of my ability preserve, protect and defend the Constitution of the United States.

With these words each of America's 42 Presidents has been sworn into office. However, America's Chief Executive takes over an office that has developed substantially since George Washington took the same oath two centuries ago. The Founding Fathers could hardly have conceived that the office, which was intended to avoid the tyrannies connected with hereditary monarchy, would eventually have the formidable array of powers that any modern President inherits.

The President's central position in American government is based on the fact that he is the only nationally elected politician who can claim to speak for the United States as a whole. Both in foreign policy and in domestic affairs, the President can claim to be representing the national interest as he sees it. When he meets a foreign head of state or makes an initiative on environmental conservation, he speaks for America. In contrast, the Congress can be seen, in many respects, as 535 local politicians who represent parochial interests. In a governmental system that exhibits the separation of powers, a dispersion of authority and fragmentation of influence, the President has a major role in providing some form of unity and coordination.

The perception of many people is that the President is all-powerful and that the 'Presidential system' inevitably leads to the Chief Executive getting his own way. In practice the position is far more complex.

The checks and balances principle inherent in the American Constitution often leads to frustration for the President. The reality of Presidential power is therefore something of a paradox; he is very powerful in some areas and almost powerless in others, and the effectiveness of the President will often depend upon factors over which he has no control. The problem for the President therefore is to ensure that his constitutional powers actually work for him. A President must not only use executive authority constructively and wisely in the interest of the United States, but also within the limits of the constitutional system.

The Different Roles of the President

The Presidency of the United States is one office held by one individual, but in fact the Constitution sets out a number of roles for him that can, analytically at least, be seen as distinctive. However, the Constitution has surprisingly little to say about the powers of the President, and this silence in many areas has allowed the holders of the office to 'fill in the details' by extending Presidential action in ways not necessarily foreseen by the Founding Fathers. In addition to the constitutional roles which are set out, there have evolved some political roles which are equally important for an understanding of the modern Presidency.

1 The Head of State. All nations have a head of state who welcomes foreign dignatories, represents the state abroad, and attends ceremonial functions. In this respect, the President takes on a similar role to the British monarch. The President provides a focal point for the loyalty of a very diverse society; a symbol of America that children are from their earliest experiences taught to respect. Problems do arise from this attempt to unite in one office the position of head of state and the political roles of a head of government. It is sometimes argued that the President is too busy with the administration of the country to be concerned with taking part in university graduation days, greeting astronauts after a space flight, or playing the first ball of the American baseball season. The popularity, status and publicity attached to these time-consuming duties can be utilized by the President to help him carry out his political functions. It is also true that the President's family and the Vice-President take some of the responsibilities in this area from his shoulders. A more serious criticism is the difficulty of a

President's fulfilling the roles of both national unifier and leader of a partisan government with controversial policies. This problem was seen in its most extreme form when, with the Watergate crisis hanging over President Nixon in 1974, the constitutional system provided no focus for national loyalty and unity. On the other hand, President Reagan demonstrated that it is possible to perform both these roles successfully. Paradoxically Reagan was the most ideologically committed President in the post-war era and yet he was able to maintain a distance between himself and 'politics'. Philip John Davies points out that:

> In part, this detachment has been the result of his impressive skill in the ceremonial role of the presidency ... [it] is almost always fulfilled with an air of nationalistic pride that enhanced the Presidential stature as a common man's head of state.[1]

Washington journalist David Broder comments on Reagan's performance in this role:

> When it comes to a patriotic occasion, a memorial service or a religious observance, his words, his bearing, his expressions and gestures speak eloquently for the American people and nation.[2]

President Clinton learned to play this role effectively, as was evident in the aftermath of the terrorist bombing of the federal building in Oklahoma City in 1995, and this helped to improve his overall standing with the public.

2 Chief Executive. The role of head of the executive branch of the federal system is clearly stated in the Constitution by the phrases 'The executive power shall be vested in a President of the United States' and 'He shall take care the laws be faithfully executed'. The President is thus responsible for the carrying out of policies and laws passed by the Congress; the Founding Fathers decided to have one man accountable for this operation although they recognized that he would need help. Government departments, such as State and Treasury, were quickly established, but under the control of the President. Today the President

---

[1]Philip John Davies, 'The Resurgent Presidency', in *Political Issues in America Today* (Manchester University Press 1987), pp. 18–19.

[2]David Broder, 'A Tough Act to Swallow' (*Washington Post National Weekly Edition* 30 June 1986) quoted in Davies, ibid., p. 18.

is responsible for 14 departments, numerous federal agencies and commissions, and approximately 2.9 million civil servants. The President has a major role in attempting to coordinate the many semi-autonomous parts of the government machine, and in bringing some coherence to policy making and execution. He is also responsible for formulating and presenting to Congress the federal budget which sets out the spending requirements for various parts of the executive branch. The Chief Executive can also determine how the laws are administrated by appointing, subject to Senate approval, the top officials, Cabinet Secretaries and agency directors who will make up his government.

3 Chief Legislator. The President is, of course, not part of the legislative branch, but this has not prevented Presidents from playing an increasingly important role in the legislative process. In the nineteenth century they tended to see their role as executing laws which Congress initiated and passed, but today a Chief Executive is expected to have a programme or package of measures which he will encourage the legislature to pass. Some of the most important pieces of national legislation to reach the statute book since the First World War were initiated by the White House. The Constitution says: 'He shall from time to time give the Congress information of the State of the Union and recommend to their consideration such measures as he shall judge necessary and expedient.' The President may also call emergency sessions of Congress, but he lacks the powers of dissolving the assembly and calling elections. The White House tries to influence the legislative process by the initiation of bills, by building coalitions and persuading legislators to support or oppose measures and, in the final analysis, by the use of the veto power. (See Chapter 2 and Table 2.8 on Presidential vetoes.) The President is therefore a major, if not *the* major, participant in the legislative process.

4 Chief Diplomat. The President is the Chief Diplomat for the United States, even though the Founding Fathers intended that Congress should participate in the foreign policy-making process. Congress officially declares war and the Senate can ratify treaties as well as approve the appointment of the Secretary of State and Ambassadors. The President's primacy in foreign policy developed in the nineteenth century, and in 1936 the Supreme Court confirmed that the executive branch alone has the right to negotiate with foreign states. The President should keep Congress informed of international developments, for example, by 'State of the World' messages or by officials appearing before Congressional committees, but there is little doubt that the President, in practice, is in charge of both policy making and execution in this field, although he must obtain the necessary financial support from Congress to carry out his objectives effectively.

5 *Commander-in-Chief of the Armed Forces.* Allied to the role of Chief Diplomat is that of Commander-in-Chief, because it is only by the ability to use effectively the might of America's armed forces, often known as his 'war powers', that foreign policy can be credible. The role of Commander-in-Chief gives the President extensive powers in war-time, and it has been used to justify action which would have been regarded as dictatorial if carried out in peacetime. Lincoln argued that he had the right to do anything necessary to ensure the survival of the Republic, and Roosevelt took over private companies and set up emergency boards during the Second World War. The President can also make tactical decisions on the deployment of troops and the running of a war. Truman, for example, determined to use the atomic bomb on Hiroshima in 1945 to hasten the surrender of Japan, while Lyndon Johnson decided to bomb Hanoi and Haiphong in North Vietnam. The nuclear age has made the President's power in this field both more formidable and more onerous a responsibility.

The command of the armed forces by an elected President shows the Framers' belief that civil control over the military generals was necessary for a free society to continue. The most dramatic example of this supremacy in modern times was the dismissal of General Douglas MacArthur by President Truman in April 1951. MacArthur was a national hero in his own right, but had consistently refused to follow Presidential instructions on how the Korean War should be conducted, and publicly criticized the President.

6 *Head of Party.* The five roles described above can be said to comprise the constitutional responsibilities of the President. The Founding Fathers hoped that the President would be free from the divisive influences of parties and factions, but it was inevitable that rival groups would wish to control the executive branch, and even in Washington's term of office parties began to develop. The Presidency became the major prize in the federal system and provided the most important reason why state parties combined. Patronage, in the way of jobs and favours that any President can bestow, has also helped to keep the loose American party system together.

The President can use his party identification to advantage in securing support from Congressmen for his legislative proposals, and parties have therefore helped to bridge the separation of powers, although political scientists have noted that Congressmen today do not see the same advantages of helping a President of their own party as in the past. This has come about as a result of the increasingly independent campaigns that both candidates for Congress and the Presidency run, the declining influence of party organizations over the nomination process which is carried out mainly through primary elections and the decline in straight ticket voting which has reduced the natural interdependence of the President and legislators of his own party. The President exercises great influence over the party's national organization and can play a major role in determining who his successor as the party's standard-bearer will be. He provides one of the major parties with national leadership while the absence of a 'leader of the opposition' weakens the other party. On the other hand, the President's party identification can make it more difficult for him to obtain consensus on policies and carry out his role as national leader.

Austin Ranney has noted that most Presidents have not been strongly partisan in their approach to governing as they have often needed support in Congress from the opposing party (particularly in the case of Republican Presidents) and because of the increasing anti-party tone of American political culture with the weakening of party identification and growth in the number of independents, the decline in importance of party organization in Presidential elections and an anti-politician and anti-party bias among network television broadcasters. Most Americans expect him to be a 'President of all the people'.[3]

7 Other Roles.   Clinton Rossiter has described other extra-constitutional roles for the President; as 'Voice of the People'—the national voice in American affairs; as 'Protector of the Peace'—intervening in natural disasters, race riots and other emergencies with the full force of the federal government; and as 'World Leader' because the President has become the head of a Super-Power and can be seen as a spokesman for the Western world.[4] Rossiter also calls him the 'Manager of the Prosperity' to describe the Chief Executive's responsibility for the general

---

[3]Austin Ranney, 'The President and His Party' and Anthony King, 'A Mile and a Half is a Long Way', in *Both Ends of the Avenue*, Anthony King (ed.) (American Enterprise Institute 1983).
[4]Clinton Rossiter, *The American Presidency* (Harvest 1960), Chapter 1.

management of the United States' economy. The President has a vast arsenal of weapons at his disposal for maintaining economic stability, and since the Depression of the 1930s it has been expected that the President use techniques such as changes in the tax structure, administration of the federal budget, credit controls and public works programmes to avoid the extremes of large-scale unemployment and rampant inflation. Even Republican Presidents, pledged to the maintenance of a free enterprise economy, have intervened extensively.

It is misleading to think of these different roles as being self-sufficient. They are overlapping and make up the Presidential office as a whole. Sometimes the President's performance in one area will help him achieve success in another; at other times Presidential roles may conflict and collide with one another. Only one thing is certain: the burdens placed upon a President make total success an impossibility. The President must attempt to use his constitutional and political powers to maximize advantages where he can, and minimize the risks of failures and mistakes.

The Growth of the Presidential Office

Why did the Presidency grow during the twentieth century in power and importance compared with the somewhat more passive executive office of the previous century? There have been a number of factors leading to this phenomenon:

1 The Growth in 'Big Government'

Twentieth-century experience of wars and economic crises has led to a world-wide development of strengthened executives and declining legislatures. The United States has not been an exception to this general pattern. The increasing involvement of the President in the nation's economic and social affairs as 'Chief Legislator' and 'Manager of the Prosperity' has inevitably led to a growth in the size of government itself. The bureaucracy that has expanded since the 1930s has been more difficult for Congress to control, but at the same time has not necessarily increased the power of the President personally. Frustration with the departmental organization has led to Presidents developing their own 'mini-bureaucracies' in the White House, in order to surround themselves with advisers they have felt they could trust. The main objection to this trend has been that, unlike Cabinet Secretaries and other senior departmental officials, these close aides are neither approved by nor controlled by Congress. President Nixon claimed that the doctrine of 'executive privilege' prevented these people being interrogated by legislative committees. It has been accepted that the President has a right to confidential advice from his closest counsellors, and that effective government and national security could be threatened if these officials were forced to divulge the views expressed within the White House. However, the courts did not allow such arguments to interfere with the criminal investigations arising from the Watergate revelations, and Presidential aides did eventually appear before the Senate select committee.

2 The Importance of Foreign Policy

Until the twentieth century, the United States generally followed a policy of isolationism and therefore the President's roles as Chief Diplomat and Commander-in-Chief, while not unimportant, were obviously limited in scope. With the development of America's world power and responsibilities, the two roles have grown dramatically, while the ability of Congress to supervise and participate in foreign policy has declined. 'Summit diplomacy' these days requires top level meetings between heads of governments such as those held between Presidents Reagan and Gorbachev and it has been recognized that the President must have a degree of flexibility and manoeuvre when negotiating with the former Soviet Union or other major powers. The President's ability to take initiatives, such as President Nixon's visit to China in 1972, which opened a dialogue with the Peking regime for the first time, provides him with opportunities to transform international relations and gain personal status and publicity. In an emergency the President is able to act quickly, decisively, and if necessary in secret. The Cuban Crisis of 1962 provides a good example of the sort of situation where only the President and his close advisers could make decisions; Congress is, by its nature, too cumbersome and deliberative to deal with such crises. Clinton Rossiter has written:

> Secrecy, dispatch, unity, continuity and access to information—the ingredients of successful diplomacy—are the properties of his [the President's] office, and Congress ... possesses none of these.[5]

[5]Clinton Rossiter, op. cit., p. 26.

In addition, Congress cannot provide coherence in the making of foreign policy; jurisdiction over foreign affairs is shared by dozens of committees and sub-committees. The presence of different ethnic groups within the American population and their influence within Congress can also be said to have imposed distortions on US foreign policy, for example, in the Middle East, which the executive branch has to attempt to counter.[6]

The President's degree of personal involvement in foreign policy will depend upon his own interests and experience; he may well depend heavily on the advice and recommendations of his Secretary of State, as Gerald Ford tended to when he assumed office in August 1974. Patriotic support for Presidential action when dealing with foreign powers has often led to a bipartisan approach, and the President can therefore expect more general support in Congress and among the public on foreign policy than he receives on domestic issues, although since the Vietnam War Congress has involved itself much more in the details of foreign and defence policy. Congress has also allowed the President to avoid the formal treaty-making provision in the Constitution by the use of executive agreements. These do not require the two-thirds ratification of the Senate, and with the failure of the proposed Bricker amendment in 1954 which would have required such approval, executive agreements have become a major tool of Presidential foreign policy. Between 1980 and 1985, for example, there were 1,940 such agreements covering military commitments, overseas aid and trade, while only 101 formal treaties were signed in the same period; the main distinction between the two methods seems to have been the preparedness of the President to submit them for Senate approval.

The use of American military power by the President on his own initiative was demonstrated by President Reagan's decisions to invade Grenada in 1983 and launch a bomb strike against Libya in 1986. In June 1993 President Clinton ordered a missile attack on Baghdad and Saddam Hussein's intelligence headquarters after it was claimed that evidence showed that Iraq had planned the assassination of former President George Bush while on a visit to liberated Kuwait. In October 1994 Clinton used US forces to secure the restoration to office of President Aristide in Haiti. None of these actions had long-term implications for US military involvement of the sort Congress had in mind

---

[6]David Mervin, *The President of the United States* (Harvester-Wheatsheaf 1993), p. 130.

when passing the War Powers Resolution of 1973 which limited Presidential power in this area (see below for details). The executive branch has grown in strength as America's international commitments and military power have increased.

3 Personalities and the Conception of the Office

The Presidential office has grown partly as a result of the precedents set by various Presidents during the nation's history. Sometimes the requirements of the time, particularly wars and economic crises, have necessitated strong action by the Chief Executive, while more peaceful and tranquil periods, such as the 1920s under Calvin Coolidge, have not demanded dynamic Presidential initiatives. Conservatives have tended to see less of a role for the federal government than liberals, and therefore conservative Presidents, such as William Howard Taft (1909–13), have had a fundamentally different conception of the President's role from Franklin Roosevelt (1933–45) or Lyndon Johnson (1963–69). The influence of the personalities of the individuals holding the office must also be taken into account. James D. Barber has classified the Presidents of the twentieth century according to the energy they put into the job (passive or active) and their feelings about their Presidential experience (negative or positive).[7] On this basis, for example, Dwight D. Eisenhower is categorized as 'passive–negative' while Richard Nixon was 'active–negative', John F. Kennedy 'active–positive' and Ronald Reagan 'passive–positive'.

It is likely that, with the increasing complexity of government and the industrial society within which it operates, Presidents in future will be activists rather than non-activists in their conception of the Presidential office. This applies to conservative Presidents as well as liberals. President Reagan, while renowned for not working as long hours as many of his predecessors, took a very active leadership role in attempting to reduce the role of the federal government in the nation's affairs. Another conservative, Richard Nixon, expressed this view in 1968:

> The days of the passive Presidency belong to a simpler past. The next President must take an activist view of his office ... he must lead.[8]

[7]James D. Barber, *The Presidential Character; Predicting Performance in the White House*, 3rd edition (Prentice Hall 1985).
[8]Richard Nixon, 'The Nature of the Presidency' (radio broadcast 19 Oct. 1968).

4 The Inertia of Congress and the Erosion of the Balance

The growth of the executive branch as a result of war and the Depression led to the Congress recognizing in the post-Watergate period that there was a need to reassert its authority. During the previous forty years Congress had surrendered much of its own influence, by granting the President wide discretionary powers within statutes in the domestic field, and allowing him to make executive agreements and military interventions abroad. For the major part of this period the Democratic party controlled both the Congress and the Presidency, and legislators tended to trust 'their' Presidents—Roosevelt, Truman, Kennedy and Johnson—to do whatever was right for the country. Only with the frustrations of the Vietnam War, which it originally supported, did the Democratic Congress start to criticize the Democratic President, Lyndon Johnson, on a broad basis. American liberals have traditionally supported a strong Presidency as the most likely method of securing what they see as much needed reforms; it was therefore something of a conversion when liberals in Congress started to argue for a strengthening of Congressional power in the 1970s against the 'imperial Presidency'. One writer has described this liberal support for the Presidency as follows:

> The Presidency, in the liberals' view, is uniquely equipped to authorize and give legitimacy to political and social programs which are of urgent importance but which can be counted on to meet opposition or be hamstrung if left to the inherently obstructionist procedures of the national legislature.[9]

The Supreme Court has also tended to support, by its decisions since 1937, the right of Congress to grant the executive branch large areas of discretionary power. Before that time, statutes such as the National Industrial Recovery Act, a major piece of New Deal legislation giving the President broad powers, were declared 'unconstitutional'.

5 The Mass Media

The mass media can concentrate on one national political office more easily than on the many faces of Congress, and therefore every-

[9]Paul Weaver, *Liberals and the Presidency*, from *Readings in American Government 1976–77* (Dushkin 1976).

thing the President does is news. The cameras and reporters will record him meeting foreign heads of state, electioneering for his party, signing a bill into law, and even his vacations become major news stories. The President's family also have to learn to live with endless intrusions into their private lives and they may become national celebrities in their own right. The Kennedys, for example, became a form of royal family for the American media.

The President is able to use the media to advantage in publicizing and mobilizing support for his policies. President Reagan used his experience and skill in this area with nationally televised appeals for public support in securing the passage of his economic measures through Congress in 1981. Franklin D. Roosevelt was the first President to utilize the media in this way. He recognized the importance of radio and initiated the 'fireside chats' which took him into millions of American homes. The President can today secure time on television for Presidential addresses, and there are also the regular press conferences. The Presidential press conferences have been held, since 1945, in a large hall in the White House where hundreds of correspondents can attend. John F. Kennedy initiated the 'live' press conference where the full session is seen on television without editing. The President is fully briefed by his advisers on likely questions, but he does have the opportunity to explain and justify policies, not only to the reporters present, but to the nation as well.

Until the 1970s Presidents were holding on average two press conferences a month but President Nixon made only 37 appearances in over five years. His relations with the press, which were never very good, deteriorated during the Watergate period, and his press conferences became very rare. Jimmy Carter was keen to have an 'open' administration and intended to have regular informal briefings with reporters as well as the normal conferences. Carter also became the first President to participate in a radio 'phone-in' programme when he answered questions from ordinary citizens on the air. President Reagan held only 44 press conferences during his two terms in office and was criticized for not allowing the press accessibility and for being too protected by staff who prevented journalists asking him direct questions. However, Reagan was able to use the media through 'photo opportunities' and also became known as the 'Great Communicator' because of his mastery of the prepared and recorded television address to the nation. Reagan frequently used his televised appearances to 'go public' by appealing for support for specific policies and putting constituency pressure on

legislators before major votes in Congress. James P. Pfiffner points out
that George Bush did not go public to the same extent:

> As President, Bush approached politics much more as the insider he had
> been for most of his career. His experience and personal style lent them-
> selves much more to bargaining than going public. Bush's television pres-
> ence and speaking abilities were not as suited to public appeals as were
> Reagan's, which was reflected in Bush's decision to hold ninety-one press
> conferences but only five television addresses in his first three years in
> office.[10]

President Clinton continued the use of a successful campaign technique when he came to office in 1993 by holding televised 'town
meetings', where ordinary citizens could question him on matters of
concern to them. This was in addition to regular press conferences
with the White House press corps who, early on, felt they were being
bypassed with these meetings. All Presidents have therefore been able
to use the media to increase both their public visibility and their status.

In contrast to the institution set up in 1787 by the Founding Fathers,
the US President today is stronger vis-à-vis Congress, is more involved
in national policy making, is in charge of a greatly enlarged bureaucratic machine, and is one of the world's major statesmen. The President is also elected in a more democratic fashion and is the leader of a
political party; due to the modern methods of mass media and technology, he is also the subject of far more national attention and scrutiny.

The Limits of Presidential Power

It has been clear from the examination of the checks and balances of
the American Constitution in Chapter 1 that the President does not
exercise unbridled power. It is worth considering the institutional and
political checks on the Chief Executive to obtain a balanced picture of
the Presidential office.

1 Political Culture

As we saw in Chapter 1, the political culture of the United States,
that is, people's widely shared beliefs and values about government

---

[10]James P. Pfiffner, 'The President and the Postreform Congress', in *The Postreform Congress*,
Roger Davidson (St Martin's Press 1992), p. 231.

and its relationship with them as citizens, has as one of its major characteristics a distrust and suspicion of all forms of authority. The separation of powers principle, the checks and balances and the federal division of powers have institutionalized these concerns into a fragmented and decentralized political system where power is shared among many leaders. As David Mervin has pointed out, Presidents in particular need to be aware of these sentiments, even as they are expected to provide strong and effective leadership for the nation; the anti-leadership system rooted in the American political culture continues to constrain Presidents to this day.[11]

2 Congress

The President may have increased his influence in relation to the legislature, but this does not alter the fact that no President can govern effectively for very long without Congressional support. It is required for the passage of any legislative proposals and for the appropriations to fund the executive branch. We have seen in the chapter on Congress that a President may find that his own party is in a minority in the legislature, and even when there is a majority in both houses, the President is by no means assured of success. Tables 2.6 and 2.7 illustrate this fact. A liberal Democratic President such as John F. Kennedy was constantly frustrated by opposition from a coalition of Republican conservatives and Democratic Southerners. Two years after taking office, Kennedy made this observation on the role of Congress as a check on the Presidency:

> The fact is that I think the Congress looks more powerful sitting here than it did when I was in Congress ... when you are in Congress, you are one of a hundred in the Senate or one of 435 in the House, so that power is divided. But from here I look at a Congress and I look at the collective power of the Congress ... and it is a substantial power.[12]

Since Kennedy's time, reforms within Congress in the 1970s tended to fragment power even further and made the job of Presidents even more difficult. In addition to trying to secure the support of party leaders and committee chairmen for Presidential initiatives, negotiating

---

[11]David Mervin, op. cit., pp. 88–9.
[12]'After Two Years—A Conversation with the President' (television and radio interview with John F. Kennedy, 17 December 1962).

and bargaining with groups of members and even individual legislators has now become the norm (see Chapter 2).

Congress has the right to question executive branch officials through its committees and now has the staff support and expertise to provide it with the capability of more adequately scrutinizing the administration and carry out oversight investigations.

The President is also bound to consider whether the people he nominates to executive positions are acceptable to the Senate. The condition of Senate approval acts as a check on the President's freedom of choice, although he usually secures the ratification of his nominees. In rejecting by 53 votes to 47 the nomination by President Bush of former Senator John Tower as Defence Secretary in March 1989, the Senate used its power to withhold consent from a Cabinet nominee for the first time in 30 years and only the ninth time in American history. The Senate was concerned at allegations about Tower's private life, including claims that he had developed business links with defence contractors in the period since leaving his position in Geneva in charge of strategic arms talks. The rejection of Tower was seen as throwing doubt on Bush's judgement in persevering with the nomination long after it was clear that it faced strong opposition and it also abruptly ended the new President's 'honeymoon' period with Congress. President Clinton was forced to withdraw the nomination of Zoe Baird for the post of Attorney-General in his new administration after it was revealed that she had employed two illegal immigrants and failed to pay social security taxes for them. The Senate has in recent years taken a tougher line on the many sub-cabinet level appointees the President makes. It has been concerned about potential conflicts of interest but has also rejected nominees because of their political views, particularly if they were regarded as extreme or out of sympathy with the objectives of the agency to which they were being appointed. The Reagan White House, for example, withdrew the nomination of Ernest Lefever as Assistant Secretary of State for Human Rights after the Senate Foreign Relations Committee had rejected him by 13 votes to 4. In June 1993 President Clinton withdrew the nomination of personal friend and black lawyer Lani Guinier as Assistant Attorney-General for Civil Rights, following criticism by members of the Senate Judiciary Committee, including liberal Democrats such as its Chairman Joseph Biden, of controversial articles on voting rights that she had written for a law review. Guinier's nomination was withdrawn before the official hearings by the committee had begun and this action led to strong complaints about the President's handling of the affair by civil rights groups, the Congressional Black Caucus and the media. The national legislature has made frequent use in recent years of the device known as the 'Congressional veto'. Between 1932 and 1985 over 200 pieces of legislation included some review of executive action by Congress. Whereas many legislative vetoes applied to the delegated rule-making powers of federal agencies and were seen by Congressmen as a way of checking the unelected bureaucracy, some applied to the President himself in major areas of policy. In June 1983, in a major separation of powers case, the Supreme Court decided that the Congressional veto was unconstitutional. The Court said that when Congress delegated to the executive branch the authority to issue regulations or make certain kinds of decisions it 'must abide by its delegation of authority until that delegation is legislatively altered or revoked'.[13] In March 1987 in the case of *Alaskan Airlines* v *Brock*, the Supreme Court unanimously ruled that unconstitutional legislative veto provisions do not invalidate the laws in which they appear, provided that they were not critical to the Congressional decision to pass those laws in the first place. Although the Supreme Court decision has reduced the effectiveness of the legislative veto, executive agencies have continued to respect the restrictions imposed because they have not been willing to risk Congressional anger by doing something that the legislature has clearly opposed.

Prominent examples of the principle of the Congressional veto are those included within the Impoundment Control Act of 1974, and the 1976 Arms Export Control Act which requires the President to submit to Congress major military contracts with foreign governments; if both houses vetoed the proposal it could not go ahead.

While the President has the powers of Commander-in-Chief of the armed forces, Congress has the constitutional power of declaring war. Over two centuries the United States has been engaged in over 130 significant military conflicts, whereas Congress has only formally declared war on five occasions, and in four of these cases the declarations simply recognized that hostilities had broken out. Following the Vietnam War, Congress passed the War Powers Resolution of 1973 over President Nixon's veto in an attempt to limit the President's ability to act unilaterally in this area. The resolution requires that the President consult with Congress before introducing armed forces into situations

[13]*Immigration and Naturalisation Service* v *Chadha.*

where hostilities are imminent. It also requires the President to report his actions to Congress. If, after 60 days, Congress has neither declared war nor given a time extension the President must withdraw the troops. Presidents have consistently argued that this resolution unconstitutionally impinges upon their powers as Commander-in-Chief and it has had little effect in practice. Presidents have still taken military action with little or no reference to the legislature when a brief display of force was thought to be necessary. Congress did invoke the resolution in 1983 when it authorized US marines who were in Lebanon as part of a multinational peacekeeping force to remain there for up to eighteen months.

Following the Iraqi invasion of Kuwait in 1990 President Bush moved a large American force to Saudi Arabia. Bush did not report to Congress the deployment of troops to the Gulf and Congress made no attempt to invoke the War Powers Resolution. In early 1991 the President asked Congress for authorization to use force to implement UN resolutions calling for unconditional Iraqi withdrawal from Kuwait. The House of Representatives agreed by 250–183 to his request while the Senate voted 52–47, but this was not a formal declaration of war. Opinion was divided as to whether the President required authorization for such a major military involvement. Some argued that the request effectively recognized that the President did not have the authority to wage war himself; others said that he wanted political rather than constitutional backing. However, failure to secure such support from Congress would certainly have provoked a constitutional confrontation.[14] Les Aspin, the then Chairman of the House Armed Services Committee, is reported to have told advisers that if Bush had not sought approval he would have led the move to impeach the President.[15]

Congress still retains a number of important powers in relation to foreign policy. It insists that it be presented with the texts of all executive agreements in order to avoid secret arrangements between the President and foreign states which lead to commitments of American troops and money. Congress has also shown its willingness to refuse funds for a foreign policy with which it disagrees. In 1973 an Act was passed banning the bombing of Cambodia after 15 August 1973 and in 1975 the Ford administration was denied further fi-

---

[14]James P. Pfiffner, op. cit., pp. 223–5; *Congressional Quarterly Weekly Report*, 12 January 1991, p. 65.
[15]*Time*, 5 April 1993, p. 43.

nances to help the crumbling regime in South Vietnam. President Reagan also had considerable difficulties persuading Congress to provide financial support for his policies of assisting the governments of El Salvador and the Contra rebels in Nicaragua. The Iran-Contra affair, which resulted from an attempt to provide funding for the Contras despite the lack of Congressional approval, allowed members of Congress to become even more involved in foreign policy matters. In 1987 Speaker Jim Wright took the initiative away from the White House and even appeared to negotiate with Nicaraguan President Daniel Ortega who had been refused access to the Reagan administration for over two years. Wright's intervention led to intense criticism that he was infringing the President's prerogatives in diplomatic relations and even Wright himself later conceded he may have inadvertently overstepped his role.[16]

President Clinton was forced to take account of the Republican majority in the 104th Congress in making foreign and national security policy. Conservatives and, in particular Jesse Helms, the new Chairman of the Senate Foreign Relations Committee, had strong views on issues such as the role of United Nations peacekeeping forces and relations with Cuba which conflicted with those of the administration.

Michael Foley argues that the reassertion of Congress in the 1970s created an apparently transformed institution interested not only in the development of high strategic policy, but also in the implementation of policy itself. However, its strategy is to challenge the executive branch but not to succeed to the point of having to assume responsibility itself for policy measures. He concludes:

> Congressional participation in American foreign policy is not dissimilar to taking a bus ride. Congress gets on and off at its pleasure.[17]

The power of impeachment remains as a final resort for Congress to use to remove a tyrant from the Presidency but it is a clumsy and inappropriate weapon if carried to its final stages. Andrew Johnson was acquitted, in 1868, by one vote short of the two-thirds necessary in the Senate to remove him from the office, and the Senate trial and balloting took over two months. In modern times it would lead to

[16]*Congressional Quarterly Weekly Report*, 7 January 1989, p. 12.
[17]Michael Foley, 'Congress and policy-making: can it cope with foreign affairs?', in *Explaining American Politics*, Robert Williams (ed.) (Routledge 1990), p. 91.

governmental paralysis and political uncertainty; the Watergate scandal marked the first time for over a century that such a drastic remedy had been considered.

3 The Supreme Court

The Supreme Court has the power to declare that a President has acted 'unconstitutionally' and this can severely damage his status as well as negate the particular activity. President Truman ordered the seizure and operation of the steel industry by government in his capacity as Commander-in-Chief when he regarded an industrial dispute as a threat to the war effort in Korea. The Court decided, however, in *Youngstown Sheet and Tube Company* v *Sawyer* in 1952, that the President's powers did not allow this and that he was therefore acting *ultra vires*.[18]

4 Constitutional Amendments

The Twenty-Second Amendment limits any individual to two four-years terms as President, unless a Vice-President succeeds to the office in the second half of a term. Critics of the amendment argued that this could seriously impede the bargaining powers of the President in his second term and reduce him to being a 'lame duck President', and that it was a denial of the democratic wishes of the electorate if they wanted to re-elect a popular President. The change was made after Roosevelt had been elected in four consecutive elections and seemed to be building a large personal power.

The Twenty-Fifth Amendment could be used to remove from office a man who was physically or mentally unfit to continue, and it is worth remembering that the Tenth Amendment provides for the reserved powers of the states. Although support for the 'states' rights' argument has declined outside the South, the fact that America has a federal system with 50 states that have a large degree of autonomy over their own affairs is, in itself, a check on the federal government, and thus on the President.

---

[18]For other examples of judicial checks, see Chapter 1, the section on 'Checks and Balances', 'Judicial Checks on the President'.

5 *The Mass Media*

The media may have played a part in strengthening the Presidency during the twentieth century, but it is also true that the 'freedom of the press' has been a major check on Presidential power. As a result of the Vietnam War and Watergate, the press in America has taken an increasingly critical attitude towards the executive branch. The major liberal newspapers such as the *New York Times* have led the way, but investigative journalism has become a major feature of the American press. The role of the *Washington Post* in revealing the true proportions of the Watergate affair made celebrities of its reporters, Carl Bernstein and Bob Woodward.[19] The prestige and influence of some television news personalities rivals and indeed exceeds that of many top politicians; they are seen and listened to every night by millions of Americans. Both Lyndon Johnson and Richard Nixon felt that they were dealt with unfairly by the media, and former Vice-President Spiro Agnew specifically attacked the press and television for being irresponsible.

Both President Clinton and his wife Hillary believed that they had been subjected to a barrage of unfair press attacks. Conservative critics countered by arguing that the scandals which came to light during Clinton's first term were not given the same degree of scrutiny or treated as seriously by the media as they would have been if a Republican had been in the White House because of liberal bias among journalists.

However, the abrasive criticism of the executive branch by the mass media is an essential part of a free society, and Presidents have to learn to accept it even when they feel it is unfair or ill-informed. The media have been helped in investigating government by the Freedom of Information Act, given teeth in 1974, which opens up many federal files to public scrutiny.

6 *Pressure Groups*

Any President operates as part of a political, economic and social system in which considerable power rests in the hands of private groups. Pressure groups are considered fully in Chapter 5, but it is important to note that business executives, trade union leaders, farmers and

---

[19]C. Bernstein and R. Woodward, *All the President's Men* (Simon & Schuster 1974).

professional bodies all have considerable influence on how policy decisions are made and executed. The President must take account of
these countervailing forces, particularly in the domestic field, when he
is exercising the powers of his office.

7 Public Opinion

The modern President can find out from opinion polls how the
public feels about particular policies, or about his administration in
general. Public support is important to the success of a President and,
if the indications are that a President is losing popularity, the opposition in Congress, the media and within the administration itself will
use their checking mechanisms more extensively. The Gallup Poll has
for many years regularly asked a sample of Americans, 'Do you approve or disapprove of the way [the incumbent] is handling his job as
President?' The levels of support can fluctuate and the volatility of
public opinion can be demonstrated by the responses recorded during
President Carter's years in office. His approval rating was 75% in
March 1977, declined to 39% in April 1978 and rose again after the
Camp David summit on the Middle-East to 56% in September 1978.
By July 1979 public approval of Carter had slumped to 28% but rallied
dramatically to 61% after the seizure of the US hostages in Iran.
However, with the failure to secure the release of the hostages Carter's
previous unpopularity reasserted itself and in July 1980 only 21%
approved of his performance as President, the lowest ever recorded by
Gallup Polls. President Reagan on the other hand left office in 1989
with his approval rating at 64%, a similar level to that early on in his
first term. Reagan had two relatively brief periods when the polls
showed downturns in his support, in 1982/83 when the economic
recession bit deeply and unemployment rose and immediately after
the Iran-Contra affair. Gallup recorded 63% approval in late October
1986 before exposure of Iran-Contra, a decline to 40% in late February 1987 when the Tower Commission issued its critical report on the
affair, a recovery to 53% by June and by December 1987 support levels
again above 60%, following the successful summit meeting between
President Reagan and Mikhail Gorbachev. Reagan's underlying popularity with the electorate (three-quarters of those polled still held a
high opinion of him personally and felt he was honest even at the
height of the Iran-Contra affair) allowed him to survive and recover
from short-term crises.

Following the Gulf War, in early 1991, President Bush enjoyed the highest approval rating, 89%, ever recorded for a President. However, in the run-up to the 1992 Presidential election his popularity slumped dramatically as Americans turned their attention to domestic issues and particularly the problems of the economy in recession. The deadlock with the Democrat-controlled Congress became more evident as legislators reacted to the weakness of the President and partisan differences became more strident as the election period approached.

Public opinion can therefore be a constraint as well as a source of support, because the President will be influenced by his anticipation of the next election, if he is eligible to run again, and also by the effects which public reaction will have on other actors in the political system.

8 Party Opposition

In America's two-party system the President can expect criticism within and outside Congress from the opposition party. The television networks are obliged to allow opposition replies or rebuttals to Presidential addresses to the nation. However, unlike Britain where there is a clear Leader of the Opposition and a Shadow Cabinet, the 'out' party not holding the Presidency lacks a focus and at different times a number of Congressional leaders or State Governors may take on this responsibility. The President may also find vocal opposition to his policies from factions within his own party or indeed from the Congressional leaderships of his own party. Opposition from within the party to a Presidential incumbent seeking another term in office can not only considerably reduce the chances of re-election but also weaken the President's position politically in the final year of his first term, as Presidents Ford, Carter and Bush discovered.

9 The Bureaucracy

Presidents have consistently found that the bureaucracy they formally control has expanded, but that their real powers to get things done have not. This may be due to inefficiency on the part of civil servants, or it may be the result of deliberate obstructionism or noncompliance by department heads, bureau chiefs or permanent officials. There are many semi-autonomous agencies over which the President has little or no control, and Presidents and their aides have frequently been frustrated to find that decisions taken by the White House have not been implemented by the appropriate department six months or a year later.

10 The Burdens of Office

The size and intractability of many of the problems that Presidents have to deal with, the workload and the limitations of time at their disposal also provide major constraints on Presidential power. Each new President who takes office finds a period of optimism and good will on behalf of the public and the media. However, in the past public expectations have often been too great and hopes have been disappointed, with the consequent erosion of popular support.

Dimensions of Presidential Power

Many Americans realized for the first time in 1974 the tremendous accretion of power in the hands of the President. The separation of powers principle was incorporated within the Constitution to prevent a concentration of power in one part of the government. The Watergate scandal and the revelations of abuses of power by the executive branch reminded the nation of the message spelt out at Philadelphia. A system that places the responsibilities we have described in the hands of one man must offer temptations for abuse. Arthur Schlesinger Jr has argued that the concept of the constitutional Presidency had given way by the 1970s to an 'Imperial Presidency'—a revolutionary use of power quite different from that envisaged by the Founding Fathers.[20] However, it would be a serious error to assume that the growth of executive power happened suddenly during Richard Nixon's administration; the history of the executive branch has been one of aggrandizement as people have turned to Presidential initiatives to get things done, and the President has filled the power vacuum left by the inertia or inaction of Congress, the states, or private enterprise. The growth of the Presidency has not been at a consistent pace—there were reactions to Lincoln's temporary autocracy and to governmental control in World War I. The major expansion has undoubtedly taken place since the 1930s and the excesses of the Nixon Presidency came as a culmination of forty years of executive development. Expectations of the Presi-

[20]Arthur Schlesinger Jr, *The Imperial Presidency* (Houghton Mifflin 1973).

dency increased during this period without an equivalent increase in his constitutional authority.

We have already seen how Congress in the 1970s introduced new laws and reformed its procedures in order to reassert its position vis-à-vis the Presidency. By the end of that decade many observers were sounding new alarms about the modern-day version of Congressional government. It became clear that when a President is unable to exercise authority and leadership it is difficult if not impossible for anyone else to do so with anything like the necessary drive and purpose. The Presidency seemed perilously weakened and political scientists were talking about the 'Impaired Presidency' rather than the 'Imperial Presidency'. After Nixon had resigned in disgrace, his appointed Vice-President, Gerald Ford, was left with little political power and only his veto as leverage against an increasingly assertive Congress. Jimmy Carter, despite the existence of a Democratic Party majority in both houses of Congress, appeared just as debilitated and there was an increasing feeling that perhaps the job of the Presidency had become too big for one person to handle.

President Reagan's achievement was therefore to demonstrate that the Presidency was manageable and that a popular President who knew what he wanted to do and had clear priorities could not only influence the national policy agenda but win support in Congress for his programme.

> Whether or not people believed in Ronald Reagan's policy priorities, many supported his view that the country needed a strong President who would strengthen the Presidency and make the office a more vital centre of national policy than it had been in the years immediately following the Watergate scandals.[21]

Reagan's period in office has therefore been described by some writers as the 'Resurgent Presidency' and, despite criticisms of his management of the executive branch which involved considerable delegation of authority to subordinates and of his mastery of detail, as we have seen, Reagan left office in January 1989 with a 64% public approval rate and became the first President since Eisenhower to serve two full terms in the White House.

President Bush faced large Democratic majorities in both houses of Congress during his term of office, 1989–93. Although he is credited

---

[21]James MacGregor Burns, J. W. Peltason and Thomas E. Cronin, *Government by the People* (Prentice Hall 1987), p. 359.

with successes in foreign policy, and particularly his handling of the Gulf War crisis, his lack of clear or consistent objectives in domestic policy, coupled with a generally hostile legislature, resulted in considerable public concern at the inability of divided party government to deal effectively with urgent and important problems at home. Bush made extensive use of his veto power to block Democratic initiatives in Congress while it in turn failed to act on the administration's programme or made major amendments to the President's proposals.

Bill Clinton's campaign for the Presidency centred on the need for change and an end to deadlock in Washington. He offered the hope that a Democrat in the White House could make the power of the Presidency work more effectively in cooperation with his party's majority in Congress.

However, despite what appeared to be a high success rate in Congressional votes (see again Table 2.6), Clinton's first two years in the White House were disappointing and demonstrated the difficulties and frustrations which a modern President can face even when his own party controls the legislature. As a candidate who had won only 43% of the popular vote in 1992, Clinton lacked any clear electoral mandate and could not rely on the backing from party members in Congress, grateful for helping them win their own elections. He made a faltering start in office with early problems over appointments to important positions within the administration and an ineffective and inexperienced team within the White House. There was confusion over policy priorities and he demonstrated a shaky grasp of foreign policy issues. His first budget deeply divided the Democratic Party in Congress, being passed by the slimmest of margins, and the legislature failed to act on the centrepiece of his policy agenda, health care reform. In 1994 a number of other important bills were blocked by a united Republican opposition, particularly in the Senate where the filibuster was used. Clinton was attacked for having abandoned his promise to govern as 'a new kind of Democrat' and his public approval ratings sank precipitously. Angry voters reacted by forcing him to work with a Republican-controlled Congress from 1995 and, at the beginning of the 104th Congress, an increasingly marginalized Clinton felt obliged, somewhat pathetically, to assert at a press conference that the President was still relevant in American government.

This brief survey of the Presidency since the 1970s demonstrates the pitfalls of making broad generalizations about Presidential power. Each President comes to the office in different circumstances and the political environment in which he seeks to provide leadership is in a state of constant flux. Among the most important factors affecting Presidential power are the following:

1 Personal and Political Background

Presidents arrive at the White House with substantially different personalities, experience and political backgrounds. Some have been elected in landslide victories (Johnson 1964, Nixon 1972 and Reagan 1984) while others have had only marginal victories or gained less than half the popular vote (Nixon, 1968, Carter 1976 and Clinton 1992). Some have been elected to replace a President of the other party and are expected to make a change of direction (Carter 1976, Reagan 1980 and Clinton 1992) while others have been re-elected for a second term (Nixon 1972, Reagan 1984 and Clinton 1996). Former Vice-Presidents have been elected as the heir-apparent (Bush 1988) or have replaced a President who died in office (Johnson 1963). We have even seen a non-elected Vice-President move into the Oval Office (Ford 1974). Some Presidents have won election 'running against Washington' (Carter 1976, Reagan 1980) while others have emphasized their experience as 'insiders' (Bush 1988). These differences can lead to a President adopting alternative strategies and approaches to governing and help explain their performances in office.[22] As David Mervin has argued:

> Statecraft, or governance, requires that American Presidents demonstrate the capacity to overcome the difficulties posed by a notoriously intractable political system in order to translate policy goals into policy realities. Different Presidents approach these obligations with different strategies or leadership styles derived from their personal characteristics, their view of the world and their previous experience.[23]

2 The Nature of the Times

The ethos of the period in which the President is in office can also make a difference. President-led governmental action has been more acceptable at some times than others. The post-Vietnam and Watergate era of the 1970s was a bad time to be President; Ford and Carter faced

[22]Charles O. Jones, *The Presidency in a Separated System* (The Brookings Institution 1994) pp. 282–3.
[23]David Mervin, 'Statecraft in the White House: The Reagan and Bush Presidencies', in *Contemporary American Politics*, Alan Grant (ed.) (Dartmouth 1995) p. 1.

particular difficulties in making the institutional powers of the office
work for them.

3 Fluctuations within the Presidential Term

All Presidents have ups and downs in their status and influence
during their terms in office. As we have seen, public approval ratings
fluctuate and popular and media perceptions of Presidential performance can change quite dramatically. As Charles O. Jones has pointed
out, Johnson and Nixon are dramatic examples of how political and
policy conditions can be transformed within a Presidential term.[24]
Both were elected with landslide victories and yet, within a few years,
Johnson was so unpopular that he decided not to seek a further term
while Nixon was forced to resign in disgrace. More recently, and less
dramatically, Bill Clinton recovered from the repudiation of 1994; he
enjoyed high approval ratings, increased his influence over the legislature and coasted to re-election in 1996.

4 Different Policy Areas

Presidential power will also vary in different policy areas. In general
terms Presidents have traditionally been able to exercise more independent authority and found it easier to mobilize Congressional and
public support on foreign and national security issues than in areas of
domestic and economic policy where they commonly have to share
power—particularly in the legislative process—with other political actors and there is less likely to be deference to Presidential goals. However, we have seen that, in more recent times, Congressional assertive-
ness even on aspects of foreign and defence policy has become commonplace.

5 Unified and Divided Party Government

Presidents are obliged to work within a constitutional structure where
they share powers with Congress and the balance of forces within the
legislature, between the parties and ideologically, is something over
which they have no control once the elections have taken place. This
fact of life determines the political parameters within which the Presi-

[24]Charles O. Jones, op. cit., p. 6.

dent has to operate. We have seen that, in modern times, even when a President has served at a time when his own party holds majorities in both houses of Congress (Carter and Clinton 1993–95), this has not guaranteed successful performance in office, however that may be interpreted or measured. More commonly, recent Presidents have had to face either one or both houses controlled by the other party and have had to work within a system of divided party government.

Divided party government can certainly not be described as an aberration; in the period since 1952 it has become the norm with 15 out of 23 Presidential and mid-term elections between 1952 and 1996 leading to such a balance of control. Although quite common in the nineteenth century, divided control was a rarity in the first half of the twentieth century when 22 out of 26 national elections resulted in unified control, with the Republicans dominating the first quarter of the century and the Democrats the second quarter.[25] Where divided control did occur it was a result of mid-term losses in the legislature by the party in the White House. In more recent times divided control may happen in Presidential election years, such as 1988, or in mid-term as in 1994. What is more, divided control may lead to the President's party having a majority in one house but not the other, as in the Reagan years between 1981 and 1987 (see Table 3.1).

Such election results arising from a decline in partisan attachment and split-ticket voting (see Chapter 6) may indicate a wish among a substantial proportion of the electorate to prevent one party monopolizing power and to create a form of coalition government which reinforces the checks and balances in the constitutional system. It may also reflect the impact of incumbency and the voters' perceptions of the strengths and weaknesses of the parties in dealing with different policy areas. Whatever the reasons for the phenomenon, divided party control sets even greater challenges for the modern President seeking to fashion effective leadership.

Some political scientists have seen divided party control as a major problem in governing the United States. Not only does it obscure accountability and confuse the electorate as to who is responsible for what, but it also makes the fragmented constitutional system almost unworkable. James Sundquist has argued that institutional rivalries are reinforced by clashing partisan interests so that each branch of

[25]Morris P. Fiorina, 'An Era of Divided Government', in *Developments in American Politics*, Gillian Peele, Christopher Bailey and Bruce Cain (eds) (Macmillan 1992).

TABLE 3.1

Split Party Control of the Presidency and Congress

President and Year	Type of Split Control Both Houses	One House	Time Split Control Occurred Presidential Election	Mid-term
Buchanan (D) 1858	. . .	x (H)	. . .	x
Grant (R) 1874	. . .	x (H)	. . .	x
Hayes (R) 1876	. . .	x (H)	x	. . .
Hayes (R) 1878	x	. . .	. . .	x
Garfield (R) 1880	. . .	x (S)[a]	x	. . .
Arthur (R) 1882	. . .	x (H)	. . .	x
Cleveland (D) 1884	. . .	x (S)	x	. . .
Cleveland (D) 1886	. . .	x (S)	. . .	x
Harrison (R) 1890	. . .	x (H)	. . .	x
Cleveland (D) 1894	x	. . .	. . .	x
Taft (R) 1910	. . .	x (H)	. . .	x
Wilson (D) 1918	x	. . .	. . .	x
Hoover (R) 1930	. . .	x (H)[b]	. . .	x
Truman (D) 1946	x	. . .	. . .	x
Eisenhower (R) 1954	x	. . .	. . .	x
Eisenhower (R) 1956	x	. . .	x	. . .
Eisenhower (R) 1958	x	. . .	. . .	x
Nixon (R) 1968	x	. . .	x	. . .
Nixon (R) 1970	x	. . .	. . .	x
Nixon (R) 1972	x	. . .	x	. . .
Ford (R) 1974	x	. . .	. . .	x
Reagan (R) 1980	. . .	x (H)	x	. . .
Reagan (R) 1982	. . .	x (H)	. . .	x
Reagan (R) 1984	. . .	x (H)	x	. . .
Reagan (R) 1986	x	. . .	. . .	x
Bush (R) 1988	x	. . .	x	. . .
Bush (R) 1990	x	. . .	. . .	x
Clinton (D) 1994	x	. . .	. . .	x
Clinton (D) 1996	x	. . .	x	. . .

Notes:
[a] The situation following the 1880 elections was extraordinary. The Senate was split evenly: 37 Democrats, 37 Republicans, two independents. After much manoeuvring and two Republican resignations, the Democrats appointed the officers and the Republicans organized the committees.
[b] The Republicans, in fact, won a majority of House seats (218–216), but by the time the Congress first met, a sufficient number had died to permit the Democrats to organize the House.

Source: Adapted from Charles O. Jones, *The Presidency in a Separated System* (Brookings Institution 1994), p. 13; data in Harold W. Stanley and Richard G. Niemi, *Vital Statistics on American Politics*. 3rd edn (CQ Press 1992), Table 3-17.

government has an electoral incentive to work for the failure of the branch held by the other party.[26] This heightened conflict results in immobility and stalemate as well as a failure to deal with important problems such as the federal deficit. President Bush's term is often seen as an example of this form of deadlocked government.

However, an alternative view has been put forward by David Mayhew who carried out an extensive study of legislation passed in the period 1946–90.[27] He concluded that the historical record indicates that periods of divided party control can be just as productive in terms of legislative output as eras of unified control. Although there may be periods of stalemate, both parties may demonstrate a willingness to compromise, each seeking to gain credit from the voters by finding solutions to problems. The final year of the 104th Congress when Clinton and the Democrats in Congress reached accommodation with the Republican majority, may be seen in this light. Both sides wanted to go into the 1996 election campaign being able to show the electorate some legislative achievements and major new laws were passed on, among other things, welfare reform and health. Of course, whether a President and Congressional leaders are willing and able to compromise depends upon the personalities and the issues involved as well as the particular political circumstances at the time.

Richard Neustadt in his influential book *Presidential Power* argues that, in the complex system within which he has to operate, the President's success or failure in achieving his goals depends ultimately on his ability to persuade other political actors to go along with his wishes. The President's problem is to get his constitutional authority to work for him.

> The essence of a President's persuasive task is to convince such men [bureaucrats, Congressmen etc.] that what the White House wants of them is what they ought to do for their own sake and on their own authority.[28]

The President has to be aware of the likely resistance to every step he takes, and he will find that giving orders will not necessarily result in their implementation. President Truman is quoted as saying:

---

[26]James L. Sundquist, 'Needed: A Political Theory for the New Era of Coalition Government in the United States', *Political Science Quarterly*, Vol. 103, Winter 1988–89, pp. 613–35.

[27]David R. Mayhew, *Divided We Govern* (Yale University Press 1991).

[28]Richard Neustadt, *Presidential Power* (Wiley & Sons 1976) p. 102.

I sit here all day trying to persuade people to do things that they ought to have the sense to do without my persuading them.... That's all the powers of the President amount to.[29]

Neustadt concludes that Presidential power can only be effective if the President builds up his prestige with the 'Washington Community' and with the public at large; a President can maximize his power by the choices and decisions that he has made in the past.

Whereas some studies have tended to focus on the skills and performance of the occupant of the White House and have been centred on the Presidency, Charles O. Jones has argued that this emphasis can lead to a seriously distorted picture of how the national government works. He argues:

The plain fact is that the United States does not have a presidential system. It has a separated system.[30]

Instead of a Presidency-centred, party government perspective, Jones proposes a separationist, diffused responsibility perspective where the President and Congress are genuinely equal branches of government. He sees policy-making in a separated system as being commonly characterized by 'multiple participation, mixed representation, variable institutional and partisan interaction, and diffused responsibility'.[31]

We may conclude that any proper evaluation of Presidential power must take account of the constitutional system and political environment within which the President operates and the wide range of variables that affect the exercise of that power.

Sources of Presidential Support

The Executive Office of the President

As the President's responsibilities grew it became increasingly difficult for him to do the job efficiently with the support of only a few clerks and secretaries. A committee of scholars reported in 1937 that

[29]Ibid., pp. 77–8.
[30]Charles O. Jones, op. cit., p. 2.
[31]Charles O. Jones, *Separate But Equal Branches; Congress and the Presidency* (Chatham House 1995) p. 101.

'the President needs help', and in 1939 President Roosevelt established the Executive Office of the President. As Rossiter has written:

> It converts the Presidency into an instrument of twentieth-century government; it gives the incumbent a sporting chance to stand the strain and fulfil the constitutional mandate as a one-man branch of our three-part government.[32]

The Executive Office of the President (EOP) is the umbrella under which exist a dozen or so key agencies which serve the President directly. It is his personal bureaucracy whose function is to provide the President with advice and information on top level matters and future planning. Its job is essentially to make sure the Presidency works. Michael Turner has noted four main roles for EOP under Ronald Reagan: first, to ensure coherent management of the Reagan agenda; second, to provide a policy development process which would maintain a Presidential focus; third, to obtain effective political implementation of the Reagan agenda on Capitol Hill; and, fourth, to accommodate the collegial executive style of Ronald Reagan. Turner says that Reagan avoided the criticism made of Nixon and Carter who were accused of surrounding themselves with an inner circle of home-state friends by 'the selection of his key EOP appointees on the basis of a judicious blend of talent, experience, ideological commitment and past association'.[33] Presidents have expanded the organization since the 1930s, creating new councils or offices as new problems emerged, and abolishing or reconstituting others. Staff numbers increased to well over 5,000 under Johnson and Nixon but, since the mid-1970s, the EOP has had less than 2,000 officials. In 1995, under Clinton, the total was 1,613 and the EOP had a total budget of $200 million. The main components are as follows:

1 The White House Office. The President's closest aides and staff are located in the White House Office. During the Nixon Presidency the size of the Office grew dramatically with well over 500 personnel. In 1995 there were 400 staff working in the White House Office within the sections shown in Table 3.2. In practice only a few dozen senior advisers will see the President on a regular basis. The President will

---

[32]Clinton Rossiter, op. cit., p. 134.
[33]Michael Turner, 'The Reagan White House, Cabinet and Bureaucracy', in *Reagan's First Four Years: A New Beginning?*, John Lees and Michael Turner (eds) (Manchester University Press 1988), pp. 40–41.

TABLE 3.2

Units of the White House Office under President Clinton

Office of the Chief of Staff
Office of the Staff Secretary
Office of National Security Affairs
Office of the Counsel
Office of Communications
Office of Speechwriting
Office of Research
Office of Public Liaison
Office of Media Affairs
Office of Media Relations
Office of Public Affairs
Press Secretary
Office of Legislative Affairs (formerly Office of Congressional Relations)
Office of Management and Administration
Office of Intergovernmental Affairs
Office of Policy Planning
Office of National Service
Office of Special Activities and Initiatives (Advance Office)
Office of Political Affairs
Office of the Cabinet Secretary
Presidential Personnel Office
White House Military Office
Office of the First Lady

Source: Lyn Ragsdale, *Vital Statistics on the Presidency: Washington to Clinton* (Congressional Quarterly Inc. 1996), p. 274.

have 'special assistants' on foreign and domestic affairs, speech writers, liaison officers with Congress and the departments as well as an appointments secretary and a press secretary.

The most senior aides may see their roles as protecting the President from being burdened by subordinate matters, and quite often even Cabinet Secretaries have had to have meetings 'cleared' by a 'Chief of Staff' before they have been allowed to see the President. The White House Office also works to ensure that urgent and priority matters reach the President's desk quickly. Advisers on specialist areas of policy also review the information provided by bureaucrats and experts within the President's political perspective. The other main role of the White House Office is to try to secure compliance by departments with Presidential policies, and so obtain some Presidential control over the federal administration.

The President's assistants obtain their very real authority from their closeness to the President and the trust which he places in them. By deciding whom the President should see or which issues are priority ones, these aides have a large degree of discretionary power. The danger is that the President becomes remote from the realities of the political world and is over-protected by his staff. He may also surround himself with 'yes-men' who tell him what they think he wants to hear, and thus prevent him making balanced judgements.

In President Reagan's first term three top aides were regarded as having the greatest access to the President and thus considerable power within the federal government. Edwin Meese, as Counsellor to the President, supervised the Cabinet and White House policy advisers and was the first White House aide ever to hold cabinet rank. James Baker, as Chief of Staff, was in charge of lobbying, press conferences, political liaison and personnel and also served, with Meese, on the National Security Council. Michael Deaver was Deputy Chief of Staff and concerned with the President's daily schedule, the travel office, visitors to the White House and Mrs Reagan's staff. Meese and Deaver had both served Reagan when he was Governor of California, while Baker had managed George Bush's campaign against Reagan in the 1980 Presidential primaries. This 'troika' appeared generally to work well in Reagan's first term. However, after the 1984 election Meese and Baker moved to Cabinet positions and Deaver went into private business. Donald Regan who had been Treasury Secretary took over as Chief of Staff and appeared to have a greater concentration of power in his hands than any recent predecessor; not surprisingly, during 1985 his position attracted a great deal of public attention and criticism as a number of other officials such as Robert McFarlane, the National Security Adviser, left the White House, having been denied direct access to the President. Regan's autocratic style was blamed for many of the problems afflicting the Reagan White House in his second term and in February 1987 he was forced to resign after scathing criticisms of his mishandling of the Iran-Contra affair by the Tower Commission. Former Senate Leader Howard Baker took over as Chief of Staff for the remainder of the second term in a move that was universally welcomed, and particularly on Capitol Hill.

President Bush surprised most observers when he selected the Governor of New Hampshire, John Sununu, as his Chief of Staff in 1989. Sununu's abrasive and autocratic approach soon made him extremely unpopular with the press, legislators and many within the Bush administration, but his loyalty to the President made him valuable to Bush himself. However, following allegations that he had misused government transport for personal trips, Sununu became a political liability and Bush reluctantly replaced him in December 1991.

President Clinton appointed an old school friend, Mack McLarty, as his Chief of Staff but he was severely criticized in the first few months of the administration for having failed to establish an effective management structure. A number of serious mistakes and poor staff work over appointments damaged the new President's credibility. McLarty was eventually replaced for the remainder of Clinton's first term by Leon Panetta, a very experienced Washington insider, who transferred from the position of Director of the Office of Management and Budget to which he had been appointed in 1993.

Clinton was also criticized for appointing too many young and inexperienced aides, straight from his election campaign and totally new to Washington politics, to important positions within the White House. However, one of them, George Stephanopolous, who had been in effective charge of the 1992 campaign, remained as a key policy adviser during Clinton's first term even though he lost his original position as Communications Director.

2 The Office of Management and Budget.   President Nixon reconstituted the Bureau of the Budget into the Office of Management and Budget in 1970, intending that the new body should become a major managerial instrument for the President. The main function of the OMB, which had 542 officials working for it in 1995, is the preparation of the federal budget which will be submitted to Congress, and all appropriations requests from departments or agencies must be approved by the office. The OMB therefore attempts to resolve conflicts within the executive branch over the relative shares of the fiscal 'cake' and it is the main method by which the President can exercise control over the levels of federal government spending. The Director of the Office is one of the President's principal economic advisers and his is one of the few Executive Office positions that require Senate approval. The OMB also acts as a mechanism by which the President can coordinate governmental activities and ensure, in his role as manager of the executive branch, that programmes are being carried out as efficiently as possible. Early in his first term President Reagan required that all departments and agencies systematically obtain clearance through OMB for any changes in federal regulations, thus seeking to establish tighter Presidential control over the executive branch and ensure that department and agency policies were consistent with the White House perspective.

President Reagan's Budget Director, David Stockman, became prominent in the administration during 1981 as he had the responsibility for drawing up the list of expenditure cuts which would apply to all the domestic departments of the federal government. Inevitably this led to conflicts with individual Cabinet Secretaries. Stockman, who was the youngest as well as one of the most influential of Reagan's senior staff, resigned in July 1985 after disagreements about policy on reducing the federal budget deficit. President Clinton's choice of OMB Director, Leon Panetta, had previously served as the Chairman of the House Budget Committee. Panetta's close links with Congressional Democrats were seen as being important in winning legislative support for a difficult deficit reduction package in 1993. When Panetta moved to become White House Chief of Staff, he was replaced by his deputy, Alice Rivlin, who had previously served as Director of the Congressional Budget Office.

3 The National Security Council.   The objective of this body, established in 1947, is to advise the President on domestic, foreign and military matters relating to national security. It consists of the President, Vice-President and Secretaries of State and Defense, although other officials such as the Joint Chiefs of Staff and the Director of the Central Intelligence Agency may be asked to attend. President Eisenhower met regularly the NSC and developed a committee structure beneath it. Other Presidents, such as John F. Kennedy, preferred more informal consultations with members of the Council, often on an individual basis. Dr Henry Kissinger was initially President Nixon's National Security Adviser and kept this role, when he became Secretary of State. President Carter, on the other hand, divided the two roles and chose Dr Zbigniew Brzezinski — a Warsaw-born academic — to advise on national security matters. Conflicts between Brzezinski and the Secretary of State, first Cyrus Vance and then Edmund Muskie, over policy issues and influence with the President in decision-making seriously damaged the credibility of the Carter administration both in diplomatic circles and in the media.

Under President Reagan the role of National Security Adviser was deliberately downgraded and direct access to the President was often denied. George Shultz, as Secretary of State, did not have the competition for the President's ear on foreign policy matters that his recent predecessors had had. However, the NSC and its head John Poindexter did hit the national headlines in the Iran-Contra affair when it was revealed that NSC staff, including Lieutenant-Colonel Oliver North, had been involved in clandestine operations to help the Nicaraguan opposition. The Tower Commission was of the view that there was nothing fundamentally wrong with the NSC system which had operated for over 40 years but that it required Presidential leadership to make it work. One of the members of the Tower Commission, Brent Scowcroft, a former NSC adviser for President Ford, took over the post again in the Bush administration, thus re-establishing the credibility and status of the NSC within the administration. Clinton's first term NSC adviser, Anthony Lake, played a relatively low profile role in the administration before being nominated in 1997 to become Director of the Central Intelligence Agency (CIA). However, Lake withdrew from consideration after Senate criticism of his performance at the NSC and his suitability for the new post.

4 The Council of Economic Advisers. We have seen that economic policy has become increasingly important as one of the President's responsibilities, but few Presidents have been economic experts, and therefore since 1946 there has been a three-man panel of professional economists who are appointed with the consent of the Senate to offer advice on the major decisions facing the President. These economists are usually from the universities, but incoming Presidents select professors who have a similar political outlook to their own. However, differences over policy do develop and in July 1984 Martin Feldstein, Chairman of Reagan's Council, resigned after much publicized warnings about the need to increase taxes in order to reduce the federal government's deficit were rejected by the President. The Council has a purely advisory role, unlike the OMB, whose functions are administrative, but it prepares on the President's behalf an annual economic report for presentation to Congress; this sets out the administration's view of economic trends for the next year.

The other major advisory bodies to the President in the Executive Office are shown in Figure 3.1. The President may reorganize the structure when he comes into office to suit his own needs.

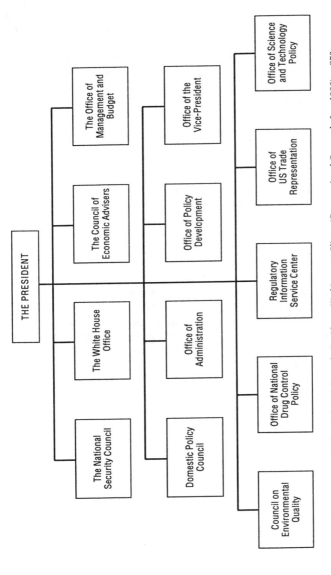

FIGURE 3.1

Organization of the Executive Office of the President under Clinton

Source: Adapted from Lyn Ragsdale, *Vital Statistics on the Presidency: Washington to Clinton* (Congressional Quarterly Inc. 1996) p. 273.

The Cabinet

In deciding upon a single man rather than a collective executive the Founding Fathers ensured that the American Cabinet would become a subordinate advisory body to the President rather than the main organ of executive decision making. The Constitution does not mention the Cabinet by name at all, and its existence rests purely on convention. The document merely says that the President may require the advice in writing of the Principal Officer in each department about their respective duties. Unlike the British Cabinet, American departmental Secretaries are the President's subordinates and are not colleagues with whom he has worked for many years in the legislature. The concept of collective responsibility does not exist; Cabinet members owe their loyalty to the President individually. Moreoever, being a Cabinet Secretary is not necessarily seen as the pinnacle of a political career as it is in the British system.

1 Appointment of the Cabinet. The selection of the heads of the executive departments is one of the first actions a President-elect takes before his inauguration, and it therefore receives great public attention as the choices give an early indication of the style and tone of the new administration. In many respects the President has a very wide choice of people to fill the top posts in his government. The individuals do not necessarily have to be in the same party as himself and there is no need for the appointees to have held any political post before. Many Cabinet Secretaries are selected for their specialist expertise or administrative capabilities and may well have previously worked in industry, commerce or the academic world.

As we have seen, Senate approval of Cabinet appointments is normally given after committee hearings but President Bush suffered a severe setback when John Tower became the first Cabinet nominee to be rejected since the Senate rejected Lewis Strauss as Eisenhower's Commerce Secretary in 1959. However, controversial appointments can lead to lengthy Senate Committee hearings and close questioning of the candidate's qualifications and views. President Reagan's nomination of Edwin Meese as Attorney-General in January 1984 was stalled by prolonged investigations into his financial dealings when White House counsellor. Over a year later Meese was approved by a 63–31 vote in the Senate.

However, there are some limitations on Presidential choice. Firstly, many members of Congress are not prepared to give up their seats and seniority in the legislature to take a temporary job in the executive branch, although President Clinton was able to persuade a number of senior members of Congress to join his Cabinet in 1993: Les Aspin, the Chairman of the Armed Services Committee in the House of Representatives, became Defense Secretary; Mike Espy was appointed as Agriculture Secretary; Lloyd Bentson, the Chairman of the Senate Finance Committee, became Treasury Secretary and, as we have seen, Leon Panetta took over at OMB. Prominent business executives will often not be prepared to make the financial sacrifices to take a position in Washington. The President will also be concerned with the loyalty of Secretaries to himself and his programmes, as his choice will have a crucial effect on how far he can influence future policy in the particular department. The President may also feel that it is necessary to reward prominent state politicians who helped him in the election campaign, and he must try to achieve some sort of geographical balance and representation of various regions within the Cabinet. The Agriculture Department, for example, is often headed by a Mid-Westerner, while the Interior Department with its interest in the management of large areas of federally owned land normally has its Secretary from the Western states. President Nixon's first Cabinet in 1969 was all-male, all-white and all-Protestant, and made up primarily of self-made businessmen. President Ford, on the other hand, tried to achieve more social balance, appointing a woman (Carla Hills, Secretary of Housing and Urban Development), a black (William T. Coleman at the Transportation Department) and two Jews (Henry Kissinger and Edward H. Levi at State and Justice) to his Cabinet. In 1988 President Reagan appointed Lauro Cavazos as Secretary of Education who became the nation's first Hispanic Cabinet member and he continued in this position in the Bush Cabinet. President Clinton came to office in 1993 with a pledge to appoint an administration that 'looked like America' and was committed to reflect this diversity by selecting more women and members from minority groups to Cabinet positions. The President's wife, Hillary Rodham Clinton, was believed to have had considerable influence on a number of appointments. Finding suitably qualified candidates for Cabinet, sub-Cabinet and other high-level posts led to considerable delays in the appointment process, particularly in the Justice Department where Janet Reno was not confirmed as Attorney-General until mid-March. Clinton's first-term Cabinet included four blacks, two Hispanics and three women; for his second term Clinton nominated three black members, one Hispanic and four women.[34] He also appointed a Republican, former Senator William Cohen, as his Defense Secretary in an attempt to broaden support for his administration following the 1996 elections. Among the female members appointed in 1997 was Madeleine Albright who, by becoming the new Secretary of State in succession to Warren Christopher, took over the most senior position in American government ever held by a woman. She had served as US Amabassador to the United Nations during Clinton's first term.

2 *The Use of the Cabinet.*   Each President can use the Cabinet as he likes; he can call it frequently in formal meetings, such as Dwight Eisenhower favoured, or he can have only irregular meetings, work with fuzzy lines of responsibility, and deal with department heads on an individual basis as John F. Kennedy preferred. Kennedy felt that full meetings tended to be a waste of time which could be better used by members in their own departments. President Nixon gradually called fewer meetings of the full Cabinet, and in 1972 held only 11 sessions.

President Eisenhower formalized the meetings for the first time with the introduction of agendas, papers for discussion and minutes. He felt that such institutionalization would result in less wasteful debate and better prepared meetings. It was hoped that Cabinet sessions would serve as useful sounding-boards for new ideas, so that the views of other departments could be heard before a policy was embarked upon, and the result would be greater administrative coherence in the diffuse system of federal government. However, the Cabinet does not really work as a team, and it is weak in terms of well informed discussion of policy alternatives for the administration as a whole. Presidents have preferred to work through bodies such as the White House Office and the Office of Management and Budget for advice and policy coordination, and therefore the influence of the Cabinet has been eroded. Recent Presidents have promised to reverse this trend by strengthening the role of Cabinet Secretaries as advisers, by having regular full meetings of the Cabinet as well as establishing sub-committees or councils of the Cabinet to confer on issues that cross departmental lines, look at long-term problems or produce option papers for the Presi-

[34]*Congressional Quarterly Weekly Report*, 21 December 1996, p. 3441.

dent. President Reagan, in particular, declared that his Cabinet would be his inner circle of advisers and likened the Cabinet to a board of directors. In the early days of his administration the Cabinet met weekly and debated issues around the table. Reagan also emphasized the importance of delegation to Cabinet Secretaries and he stated in an interview:

> When I've heard enough of the debate to satisfy my needs about knowing, then I make a decision. I believe in this because it is really the only way to execute a job this big. The trap you could fall into would be trying to keep your finger on every single detail.[35]

However, by the second year of his administration Reagan was following the familiar tendency of his predecessors by strengthening and relying more upon the White House Staff and policy advisers in the Executive Office of the President and less on Cabinet Secretaries. As Hugh Heclo has pointed out:

> It is significant that no President has ever left office extolling the virtues of cabinet government.[36]

In April 1985 Reagan announced a new streamlined system with the replacement of eight Cabinet Councils by two new bodies. The Economic Policy Council, the Domestic Policy Council and the National Security Council were to be the primary channels for advising him on policy matters. President Reagan's cabinet council system was an attempt to reinforce White House policy management and to help insulate Cabinet Secretaries from the permanent bureaucracies and from Congressional committees. As Edwin Meese, the man who devised the system, put it:

> The difference in this Presidency is that Reagan has used his system so that the Cabinet members all feel closer to him than they do to their departments. And he gives them a lot of opportunity to remember that.[37]

It is also interesting to note that during the Reagan administration there was far greater interchange of personnel than ever before between

---

[35]U.S. News and World Report, 4 January 1982, p. 26 and 29 March 1982, p. 28.
[36]Hugh Heclo, 'One Executive Branch or Many', in *Both Ends of the Avenue*, Anthony King (ed.) (American Enterprise Institute 1983), p. 26.
[37]Quoted in Heclo, ibid., p. 47.

the Executive Office of the President and the Cabinet departments. In 1983 William Clark moved from NSC to the Interior Department and Elizabeth Dole moved from the White House Office to become Transportation Secretary. At the beginning of his second term Reagan appointed Edwin Meese as Attorney-General; John Herrington, Assistant to the President for Personnel, became Energy Secretary, while William Brock, US Trade Representative, took over at the Labor Department. Meanwhile James Baker, the White House Chief of Staff and Treasury Secretary Donald Regan swapped jobs in the new administration.

3 Cabinet Secretaries and their Departments.   Each member of the Cabinet is responsible to the President for his department's affairs; there is no collective responsibility with other Cabinet members for government policy. The Secretaries may be rivals for the President's attention and for available funds, and occasionally disputes between department heads break out into public conflict. The President may have to intervene in order to maintain the appearance of a harmonious administration, as President Ford did in 1976 when he dismissed Defense Secretary James Schlesinger after a long feud with Henry Kissinger over détente policies with the Soviet Union. After giving his Cabinet Secretaries a great deal of autonomy in his first year in office President Carter became increasingly concerned about the loyalty and discipline of some members and, in an unprecedented purge in July 1979, he dismissed five department heads from their offices. However, instead of projecting an image of decisive leadership by this action Carter merely increased the scepticism about his own ability and judgement.

Sometimes the President will have to replace a Cabinet Secretary midway through the term if it becomes evident that he is failing to do the job effectively or has lost the confidence of Congress, departmental officials or important interest groups. It soon became clear that Les Aspin, Clinton's first Defense Secretary, was unsuited to running a huge executive department such as the Pentagon. His wide knowledge of security matters gained as a Congressional committee chairman did not qualify him to be an effective manager and he was replaced by William Perry, a defence technocrat who had been his deputy.

A department head is often chosen for his ability in a particular policy area and there are few interdepartmental moves during a Presidential term, although James Baker moved from the Treasury Department in 1989 to become President Bush's Secretary of State, while Elizabeth Dole who had served as Reagan's Secretary of Transportation 1983–87 became Secretary of Labor in the Bush Cabinet. Frederico Peña, who served as Clinton's Transportation Secretary during his first term, was nominated to take over as Energy Secretary in 1997 in order to ensure continued Hispanic representation in the Cabinet.

The problem for the individual Cabinet Secretary is that he is subject to a number of different pressures and often conflicting claims. He is appointed by the President and owes a responsibility to him for executing the administration's policies. He also has a responsibility to his department which has its own traditions and interests; his civil servants will expect him to represent their views at the highest level. The President's rapport with the Cabinet Secretary often declines as the latter seems increasingly to be an advocate of the department and the pressure group clientele with which it has relations. Tension also builds between the Cabinet member and the White House assistants who see him as obstructing Presidential objectives. The department head also has to take into account Congressional demands; he owes confirmation of his appointment to the Senate, and he will be expected to appear before Congressional committees to justify and 'sell' his department's policies as well as secure funds for its programmes. Richard Fenno has written:

> For his part, the President's influence over the Cabinet member becomes splintered and eroded as the member responds to political forces not Presidential in origin or direction. From the beginnings of his involvement in the appointment process, the President's power is subject to the pervasive limitations of the pluralistic system in which he seeks to furnish political leadership.[38]

The Vice-President

'My country has in its wisdom contrived for me the most insignificant office that ever the invention of man contrived or his imagination conceived.' These are the words of John Adams, the first Vice-President of the United States, but they could have been uttered with equal feeling by most of his successors. The Vice-President has a very limited number of constitutional roles, but one of them—to succeed to the Presidency in the event of death, resignation or removal from office—can be of vital significance. The Vice-President is literally 'a

---

[38]Richard Fenno, *The President's Cabinet* (Harvard University Press 1959), p. 248.

heart-beat away from the Presidency' and his main role is to wait in the wings to be called upon to take over the duties of the Chief Executive. As eight Presidents have died in office, four having been assassinated, and one has been forced to resign, there is a real possibility that such a call might come.

The Vice-President must have the same formal qualifications as the President, that is to be over 35 years old, a natural-born American citizen, and have been a resident of the country for 14 years. The voters choose, at election time, between rival teams of Presidential and Vice-Presidential candidates and there is no opportunity to 'split the ticket'. Therefore the Presidential candidates of each party have traditionally been concerned with achieving a balance in the team to make it as attractive as possible to various regions of the country, different ethnic and religious groups, and factions within the parties. John Kennedy, for example, as a Northern Catholic with strong liberal support, saw Lyndon Johnson, a Protestant from Texas who could win the votes of Southern conservatives, as an ideal choice for the Vice-Presidency in 1960. As the Presidential candidate often makes his choice in the emotional aftermath of his own nomination and in something of a hurry, the scrutiny of an individual's suitability for the office has sometimes been cursory and inadequate. In 1968 Richard Nixon selected Spiro T. Agnew as his running mate to appeal to conservative Southerners, but the former Governor of Maryland was forced to resign from the Vice-Presidency in 1973 after he was charged with tax evasion and other offences. In 1972 Thomas Eagleton was chosen by Democrat George McGovern without the Presidential candidate knowing that the Missouri Senator had undergone electric shock treatment for depression. When Eagleton's medical history was revealed, he resigned from the ticket and the first ever special convention was called to choose a new Vice-Presidential candidate. In 1988 George Bush's selection of Senator Dan Quayle of Indiana was followed by a furore over allegations that he had evaded military service in Vietnam. Although he stayed on the ticket Quayle turned out to be an embarrassment to the campaign while adding nothing to its attractiveness to the voters. On the other hand Bill Clinton's selection of Senator Al Gore, a well-respected moderate from Tennessee, was widely applauded by the party and the media; he undoubtedly added to the appeal of the Democratic ticket in the 1992 election.

The Twenty-Fifth Amendment provides for the President to nominate an individual to fill the office of Vice-President if it becomes vacant between elections. In this way, Gerald Ford became the first non-elected Vice-President to succeed to the Presidency in 1974.[39]

The Vice-President is a reserve to the President. He must be ready to take over the responsibilities of the office if the Chief Executive dies or if he is unable to carry out his duties as a result of illness. In the 1950s Richard Nixon acted on behalf of Dwight Eisenhower when the President suffered from a serious heart condition. The Vice-President will also be expected to take on some of the ceremonial duties and represent the United States on formal occasions, such as the funerals of foreign leaders.

The other constitutional duty of the Vice-President is to chair meetings of the Senate and vote in the event of a tie. On occasions this can be of crucial significance; in June 1993 Vice-President Gore used his casting vote to secure the passage in the Senate of the President's budget bill after a number of Democrats defected because of the political unpopularity in their home states of some of the tax increases and spending cuts within the package. Most holders of the office have attended as 'President of the Senate' only infrequently as, not being members of the Senate, they can rarely exert political influence but are merely 'referees' who interpret the rules. This can occasionally lead to controversy; Vice-President Rockefeller was involved in a major row in 1975 when his procedural decision led to a reform of the filibuster, thus angering many Senate conservatives.

Although he has his own staff and office in Washington, the degree to which the Vice-President will actually be involved in the administration will depend on the President. Some Vice-Presidents have felt shunned and even humiliated by the President's close advisers. Harry Truman was not told about America's development of the atomic bomb until he stepped into the Chief Executive's office, and relations between Kennedy's staff and Lyndon Johnson were notoriously cool. However, there has been a tendency in recent times to give the Vice-President more to do; he is a member of the Cabinet and the National Security Council; he may chair a Presidential Commission, as Vice-President Rockefeller did with the investigation into the CIA; he may become a 'roving Ambassador' for the United States abroad, as Hubert Humphrey did by travelling around the world, explaining America's foreign policy. Vice-President Mondale's first major responsibility in

[39]See Chapter 1, 'Amendments to Alter Government', for full details of the Twenty-Fifth Amendment.

1977 was to undertake a tour of major European capitals on behalf of the President. Vice-President Agnew saw his most important role as being that of political mouthpiece for the administration and projecting its image around the United States. He became a controversial political figure with his scathing attacks on anti-Vietnam War demonstrators and the mass media. A great deal of his time was spent at fundraising dinners and events for the Republican Party.

Vice-President Bush was given responsibility for reviewing federal regulations and made head of the Reagan administration's crisis management team. Bush was seen as an effective and influential Vice-President. He had an office in the White House, access to policy papers and played a prominent role in the National Security Council. Bush's experience in foreign affairs was of particular value to Reagan and in 1983 he won widespread acclaim for his role in helping persuade America's NATO allies to go ahead with the deployment of Cruise and Pershing missiles and for reassuring them that the administration was serious about arms control. However, loyalty to the President can also lead critics to question, as with Bush, whether the Vice-President has a clear political identity of his own, particularly when he becomes a Presidential candidate himself.

Al Gore fought the 1992 election campaign very much as part of the Clinton-Gore team and became a prominent member of the Clinton administration. He was involved in the making of key policy decisions and was given specific responsibility for reviewing the operation of the federal bureaucracy (see below).

Although in the past many able politicians found frustration and disillusionment in waiting on the side-lines of the Washington political scene, it does appear that it is possible for the modern Vice-President to play a meaningful role and hold an influential position within the administration; certainly they can help take some of the burdens of office from the shoulders of the President. It is also worth remembering that, of the 42 American Presidents, 14 had previously served as Vice-President, although George Bush became the first sitting Vice-President since 1836 to have been elected to the Presidency.

Organization of the Executive Branch

A major characteristic of the American executive branch is the way in which power is distributed among a bewildering proliferation of departments, agencies and bureaux that have developed as new problems and programmes have emerged. The Hoover Commission of the 1950s recommended a streamlining of the executive branch, and Presidents have struggled to reorganize and simplify the structure. Unlike a British Prime Minister, who can reorganize the departmental structure of government as he wishes, the President is unable to do likewise without the support of Congress even though he is nominally in charge of the executive branch in which the departments are located. The President can reorganize part of the administration if Congress does not veto the plan within 60 days, but opposition to reform has often come from vested interests within the bureaucracy, from pressure groups who are comfortable with the existing arrangements and from Congress, which hesitates about strengthening further the President's authority. The problem for all Presidents remains: to coordinate and direct the activities of the diffuse and unwieldy administrative machine.

The main elements within the federal administration are:

The Executive Departments

In 1993 there were 14 departments headed by Cabinet Secretaries— in 1789 there were three. The Defense Department has approximately half of the 2 million civilian employees who work for these departments and is easily the largest; at the other extreme the Education Department had only 5,117 staff in 1992 as policy is still mostly made and administered at state and local levels. Within some departments there are bureaux which can act almost independently of the control of the Secretary; there are, for example, the Federal Bureau of Investigation within the Department of Justice, the Food and Drugs Administration which is part of Health and Human Services and the Bureau of Indian Affairs within the Interior Department. B. Guy Peters even describes American Cabinet departments as:

> largely holding companies for a number of agencies within them.... These agencies have a legal life of their own, most having been formed by an Act of Congress or by an Executive Order, and have their own budgets and personnel allocations.[40]

---

[40]B. Guy Peters, 'Public Bureaucracy in the American Political System', in *Developments in American Politics*, G. Peele, C. Bailey and B. Cain (eds) (Macmillan 1992), p. 171.

During President Carter's term of office two new federal departments were created. In 1977 the Energy Department took over responsibilities that had previously been scattered throughout many departments and agencies. The Education Department was established in 1979 by splitting off functions from the giant Department of Health, Education and Welfare which was renamed the Department of Health and Human Services. Ronald Reagan had promised during his election campaign that he would abolish these two departments as he believed they extended federal government intervention into areas best left to the private sector or to state governments and that essential federal responsibilities could be devolved to other departments or agencies. However, suggestions to downgrade the status of the Education Department to an agency or foundation and to merge the Energy

TABLE 3.3

The Executive Departments in Order of Formation

State	1789
Treasury	1789
Interior	1849
Justice	1870
Agriculture	1889
Commerce	1913
Labor	1913
Defense	1947
Health and Human Services	1953
Housing and Urban Development	1965
Transportation	1966
Energy	1977
Education	1979
Veterans' Affairs	1989

Notes: (1) The Post Office was a Cabinet department 1872–1970, when it was replaced by the US Postal Service, an independent agency.
(2) The Department of Commerce and Labor was created in 1903 and became two separate departments in 1913.
(3) Department of War (the Army) created in 1789 and Department of Navy (1798) consolidated with the Air Force in Defense Department in 1947.
(4) Department of Health and Human Services was formerly Department of Health, Education and Welfare 1953 to 1979.

and Commerce Departments found no favour with Congressmen. In October 1988 President Reagan agreed to the elevation of the long-established Veterans' Administration to a Cabinet-level Department of Veterans' Affairs, thus making it the fourteenth federal department. President Clinton had wanted to raise the status of the Environmental Protection Agency and make it a full Cabinet department but, with disputes over appropriate departmental jurisdictions and a climate of budget cuts, Congress failed to support the change in 1994. Sometimes members of Congress itself may seek to initiate changes in structure, but conservative attempts to abolish the Commerce and Energy Departments during the 104th Congress were unsuccessful.

The Executive Agencies

A large number of agencies exist under Presidential authority which are almost indistinguishable from departments, except that they do not have the status of having Cabinet Secretaries. They are headed by Directors appointed by the President and confirmed by the Senate and examples include the US Information Agency and the General Services Administration.

Independent Regulatory Commissions

There are many commissions which have been established to regulate particular areas of economic activity that remain in private ownership. They are 'independent' in the sense that the President does not directly control their activities and their functions are administered by boards with usually five to seven members each. The President does appoint the members with the approval of the Senate, and although the requirements of staggered terms and bipartisan composition are intended to prevent Presidential control, in practice any individual President can select a majority on most of the Commissions during his term of office. Both the President and the Senate are interested in the political views of appointees, and pressure groups affected by the Commission will try to influence the selection as well. A Supreme Court decision in 1953 laid down that a President cannot, however, dismiss a Commissioner in the way he can other executive appointees (see Table 3.4).

The Commissions, which became known as 'the headless fourth branch of government', have a wide variety of powers including the

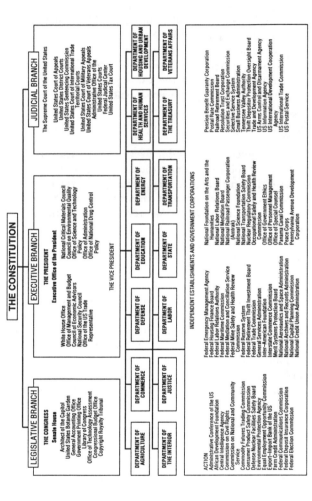

Source: *Statistical Abstract of the United States 1996*, p. 326. The structure is that as of 1 July 1993.

FIGURE 3.2

The Government of the United States

granting of licences, authorizing airline routes, approving the opening of natural gas pipelines, and regulating fares and rates on the railroads. Their functions, therefore, are quasi-legislative, quasi-executive and quasi-judicial, and do not fall easily within any of the three branches of government. These bodies have been subject to severe criticism from all sides of the political spectrum; the main charge has been that they are neither 'independent' nor 'regulatory' because they have become the captives of the industries which they are supposed to be controlling. Informal influences behind the scenes and interchangeability of personnel between the Commissions and private corporations have led many consumer advocates to argue that the boards do more to protect the industries than they do to help the public. Since 1975 politicians of both parties have supported deregulation to relax or repeal rules that have inhibited competition or kept prices artificially high.

One of the most significant agencies is the Federal Reserve Board which controls monetary policy, a vital element in economic decision making. Presidents have to learn to live with 'the Fed', knowing that, even though they do not directly control it, the Board will have important effects on the success of their economic strategies. Dr Arthur Burns, who was Chairman from 1970 to 1978, was well known for his conservative monetarist views, and disagreements with President Carter's economic advisers led to the President not renewing his appointment. His successor, Paul Volcker, became a target for many politicians who criticized the 'tight money' policies of the Fed which led to high interest rates. Alan Greenspan, the most recent Chairman of the Fed, has been praised for overseeing an effective monetary policy which produced a period of low inflation and steady economic growth in the mid-1990s.

The Federal Civil Service

Approximately 3 million Americans work for the federal government as non-military employees. In addition to the 2 million civil servants who work for the cabinet-level departments, a further million officials are employed by executive agencies and independent regulatory commissions. However, almost 800,000 of these are staff within the US Postal Service.

At the turn of the century there were less than 250,000 federal civil servants but the New Deal and the Second World War led to a vast increase in those working for the government. However, despite the growth of federal government responsibilities, regulations and expenditure the number of federal civil servants has remained remarkably stable over the last thirty years and, as William Lunch has pointed out, measured as a proportion of the population, the number of federal bureaucrats has actually declined during the historic era of government expansion.[41] However, two points are worth noting. First, the nature of employment has changed in the federal bureaucracy and there are now far more professional and technical staff and fewer

TABLE 3.4

Major Independent Regulatory Commissions

Commission	Established Jurisdiction
Consumer Product Safety Commission Five members with seven-year terms	Investigation of products' safety. Consumer protection
Federal Communications Commission Five members with seven-year terms	Television and radio stations licences. Telephones and telegraphs
Federal Election Commission Six members with six-year terms	Public funding of Presidential elections. Election regulations
Federal Reserve Board Seven members with fourteen-year terms	Monetary policy-interest rates
Federal Trade Commission Five members with seven-year terms	Unfair competition, price fixing, advertising
Inter-State Commerce Commission Five members with five-year terms (from 1 Jan. 1986)	Railroads, buses, freight, oil pipelines
Nuclear Regulatory Commission Five members with five-year terms	Nuclear power
Securities and Exchange Commission Five members with five-year terms	Registration of brokers and regulation of Stock Exchange

[41]William Lunch, *The Nationalization of American Politics* (University of California 1987), p. 178.

lower grade and manual workers, with the civil service more concerned with planning, analysing, regulating and dispensing funds than
actually carrying out direct services to the public. Second, the number
of state and local government employees has increased considerably as
grants-in-aid programmes led to programmes being administered at a
lower level but in large part financed by the federal government. It
should also be remembered that only a small minority of the federal
civil servants work in the capital, Washington DC; the others are based
in federal offices and bureaux all over the United States. There is
therefore a considerable degree of administrative decentralization in
America. 'Civil servants' include a vast range of jobs from senior advisers to Cabinet Secretaries to the most junior clerical posts. There are
also thousands of specialists such as statisticians, economists, architects
and engineers who work for the departments.

1 The Development of the Civil Service

Employment by the federal government in the early days of the
Republic was normally based on patronage; Presidents felt that they
should reward those people who had helped them win the election
and that they needed to have officials whom they trusted in key positions in the administration. Jefferson appointed supporters to government positions, but Andrew Jackson later was to institutionalize the
'spoils system' on a broad basis. He felt that a rotation of office would
prevent corruption and allow the dismissal of the lazy or incompetent.
After the Civil War, the federal government grew and the need for
more permanent and specialized staff became apparent; in addition,
the morality of the patronage system was increasingly questioned. It
was not, however, until President Garfield was assassinated by a disappointed office seeker in 1881 that Congress was persuaded to pass a
reform. The 1883 Pendleton Act established a classified Civil Service—
permanent officials to be appointed on merit—and the setting up of a
bipartisan Civil Service Commission to administer the system. Initially,
only 10% of federal posts were classified and the rest remained patronage jobs, but gradually the situation was reversed so that the Commission became responsible for the appointment of approximately 90% of
civil servants while organizations like the FBI also appoint on a 'merit'
basis through examinations and tests, leaving only a few thousand
appointments to be made by the President. In 1993 Congress passed
legislation to repeal the 1940 Hatch Act provisions that imposed

restrictions on the political activity of civil servants; new rules permitted federal employees to run for local office and participate in party campaigns outside of office hours.

2 The Permanent Civil Servants

Most civil servants are placed on one of the General Schedule grades (GS1 to GS18), according to an evaluation of the job within a unified grading system. Competitive public examinations are held at a number of centres throughout the country, and successful applicants are offered a vacancy when one occurs within a department or agency. The tests themselves tend to emphasize practical ability required in the job rather than more academic skills.

Civil Service positions became much sought after in the 1970s because they not only provided good job security, pensions and health schemes, but higher average salaries than those obtainable in private companies. However, by 1980 concern was being expressed that a pay freeze on senior administrators' salaries which Congress had imposed five years before was having the effect of draining the service of its most talented and experienced officials, many of whom were seeking early retirement or posts in private industry.

Public criticism of both the cost and the efficiency of the federal bureaucracy led Jimmy Carter to promise in his 1976 election campaign that he would reorganize the bloated Civil Service machine. He ordered the Office of Management and Budget, and his newly appointed Civil Service Commission Chairman, Alan Campbell, to put forward plans for reform. The main problems were seen to be complacency caused by high salaries and automatic pay increases, and the difficulty of dismissing, transferring or penalizing employees whose work was unsatisfactory. The Civil Service Reform Act of 1978 was the first major overhaul of the civil service for almost a century. The Civil Service Commission was abolished and a new Office of Personnel Management was established to act as the President's personnel arm handling recruitment, pay, examinations and job classifications while a Merit Systems Protection Board would review appeals against dismissal and hold investigations into alleged corruption or waste. The new law allowed some flexibility for the dismissal of employees for incompetence, although not as much as Carter had wanted, and also allowed a new system of merit pay increases for middle managers rather than automatic rises. The most significant change was the establishment of an elite corps of some 8,000 managers at the top of the bureaucracy, known as the Senior Executive Service (SES) of whom a proportion would be political appointees. They had less job security and could be transferred more easily from one department to another, but in return they were able to earn substantial bonuses for exceptional performances. Over 90% of those eligible agreed to join the SES.

The idea of introducing incentives such as those in the private sector was widely supported at the time, but Congress later restricted the number and size of the bonuses for fear that too many civil servants were being awarded them—a move which not surprisingly caused an outcry among the SES.

The Reagan administration used the provisions of the 1978 Act to give itself greater control of the federal bureaucracy and to weaken the scope for independence of action by the permanent civil service. It used its powers through the Office of Personnel Management to promote those who were sympathetic to the administration's goals and to reassign or downgrade civil servants who were unsupportive or ineffectual. Thus, 2,326 senior executives were reassigned in 1982 and 1983, while others left the civil service to avoid adverse moves.[42] Concern has been expressed about the increasing politicization of the senior levels of the civil service, both in terms of its effect on the morale of bureaucrats and the long-term effectiveness of a neutral and competent government machine. For conservative Republicans the federal bureaucracy was seen as largely unsympathetic to their policy objectives. Therefore considerable efforts were made, particularly in the Reagan years, to control it through the appointments process, to restrict it through the OMB's oversight of regulatory activity and to bypass it as far as policy initiatives were concerned.[43]

The Clinton administration's major initiative on civil service reform was the establishment of a National Performance Review under the auspices of Vice-President Gore. Inspired by the widely publicized book, *Reinventing Government*, Gore's survey of the federal government's operations found that huge potential savings in money and staffing could be made by reorganizing agencies, reducing costly regulatory activity and reforming procurement policy.[44] Its recommendations were based on the adoption of a model of government service

[42]Michael Turner, op. cit., p. 60.
[43]Robert Williams, 'Policy, process and power: understanding American bureaucracy', in *Explaining American Politics*, Robert Williams (ed.) (Routledge 1990), pp. 109–10.
[44]David Osborne and Ted Gaebler, *Reinventing Government* (Addison-Wesley Press 1992).

which moved away from the traditional bureaucratic approach to a system of more entrepreneurial management. This involves the decentralization of authority and decision-making, more emphasis on the 'customers' and the quality of services and greater use of contracting out to other providers.

Despite the general welcome given to the idea of streamlining the federal bureaucracy in an era when 'big government' has become unpopular, implementing the proposals, except on an incremental and piecemeal basis, will remain problematic given the resistance to radical change within the system. Congressional opposition to proposed cuts which might affect their constituencies or reduce the availability of pork-barrel projects, as well as legislators' wishes to scrutinize the details of administration of the executive branch through oversight activities, tend to work against the spirit of the entrepreneurial model.

3 The Political Appointees

An incoming President has the power to appoint several hundred executive schedule or 'Schedule C' posts when he forms his administration, as well as the political appointees within the SES mentioned above. A study by the General Accounting Office in 1993 showed that in 1991 there were 2,436 political appointees who did not require Senate confirmation, an increase of 414 since 1981. Of these, approximately one-quarter were Schedule C posts and three-quarters were non-career SES personnel. There were 600 or so top-level political appointees who did require Senate approval.[45] Below the rank of Cabinet Secretary there are Under-Secretaries, Deputy Under-Secretaries, Assistant Secretaries and Office Directors. These important positions are the ones likely to be filled by Presidential selection, although there may be permanent civil servants serving alongside such appointees in top grades. The President-elect himself delegates authority to his close advisers to make appointments for most of the vacancies, although he may personally interview and sift through the candidates for the top 75 to 100 jobs. The transition period between the November election and the inauguration of the new President in January is filled with frantic activity as the President-elect and his senior advisers go through dossiers and files on potential recruits. Unlike Jimmy Carter, who allowed his Cabinet Officers the power to appoint subordinates them-

[45] *Washington Post*, 1 June 1993, 'Tracking Staff Trends at the Top'.

selves, the Reagan White House exerted control of the appointment process. Michael Turner points out that:

> In consequence, whereas the Carter administration came to be character-
> ized by incoherence and contradiction, the Reagan team maintained a high
> degree of unity of purpose and commitment to the President's goals.[46]

Cabinet members were consulted about sub-cabinet posts but they did not have a free hand and many radical right conservatives were placed in these strategically important positions. It was intended that:

> the Reagan Revolution would be effected by a corps of dedicated political
> appointees willing to assert presidential goals and push for their adherence
> in the face of anticipated reluctance from a federal bureaucracy committed
> to the continuance of threatened services and programmes.[47]

Many of the temporary appointees come to Washington for short-term contracts with the government and will expect to return to private business, law practice or a university after the Presidential term ends. The Carter administration laid down the rule that these government officials, however, must promise not to take a job in a private company related to their department's affairs until two years after they have resigned from the administration. The 1978 Ethics in Government Act requires public disclosure of appointees' personal finances and was designed to prevent corruption by exposing potential conflicts of interest among high-level officials. However, President Reagan also found that the disclosure provisions acted as a significant deterrent in the recruitment of prominent people to senior posts in his administration and this was one factor contributing to delays in filling important positions. James P. Pfiffner's analysis of the appointment process showed that by the end of April 1993 President Clinton had nominated only 177 out of the top 625 appointments and, of these, just 51 had been confirmed by the Senate. In the same period in 1981, Ronald Reagan had submitted 152 names and had had 83 confirmed.[48]

There are relatively few political appointees in each department but as most of these posts are at the senior levels they have a decisive effect on the President's chances of controlling government activities. Some of the appointees will take jobs in the regional offices of departments,

---

[46]Michael Turner, op. cit., p. 57.
[47]Michael Turner, op. cit., p. 54.
[48]*Congressional Quarterly Weekly Report*, 1 May 1993, p. 1059.

exercising considerable influence on how federal policies are carried out in their areas.

4 The Advantages and Disadvantages of the Recruitment System

The American method of staffing the administration is based on the unique traditions of the Presidency: positions of party patronage existing alongside a large permanent bureaucracy appointed on the basis of competitive examinations. This piecemeal evolution has, of course, led to problems, but at the same time the system of recruitment has proved to be functional within the diffuse executive branch.

The President is able to receive political advice from people he trusts and who are committed to the administration's programmes. He is able to influence policy making and execution by appointing senior advisers and some 'middle management' positions in each department. The system combines the experience and continuity of the permanent Civil Service with the new ideas and fresh approach of temporary appointees. It can be argued that such a system prevents complacency and institutional conservatism from developing within the bureaucracy. Government can benefit from the expertise of the short-term officials who bring to their work valuable insight gained from experience in private industry or the academic world. The President also has the opportunity of rewarding the men and women who worked for his election, and although patronage has diminished considerably, it is still a factor in attracting talented people to support Presidential campaigns.

On the other hand, it can be argued that the system of recruitment causes friction between the permanent civil servants and the 'outsiders' who are immediately placed in senior positions while knowing little or nothing about the practical workings of the department. There is the problem of dislocation when there is a change of President; for several months during the transition period effective decision making is halted as the upper echelons of one administration hand over power to the new officials. Some critics feel there are dangers inherent in a system that allows the President to hear advice principally from those people who owe their jobs to him and who think politically along the same lines. There is also occasionally difficulty in attracting high-calibre staff to work in temporary positions that offer no form of job security and which may require a drop in salary. What is more, the turnover of political appointees is high. Senate hearings in May 1993 revealed that in the past decade 31% of such officials left after only 18 months and

50% had resigned within 27 months. It is clear that many of the people appointed see the post as a way of obtaining good experience before moving on to more senior and lucrative jobs, mostly outside government; Senator John Glenn, the Chairman of the Governmental Affairs Committee at the time, described this as 'résumé enhancement'.[49] Finally, there are the possibilities of corruption which inevitably exist where temporary appointees have contact with former business associates, and where interchange of personnel between government and private organizations is common.

5 The Power of the Bureaucracy

The senior civil servants in the federal government have a considerable amount of power: they cannot be seen merely as neutral administrators of policies laid down by elected politicians. Bureaucrats themselves have an essential role in the policy-making process, weighing alternatives, taking initiatives and recommending courses of action to Cabinet Secretaries. Their knowledge, expertise and skills mean that political leaders are dependent upon them in many areas.

As government intervention expanded (for example in the New Deal period and the 1960s and 1970s), new bureaucracies were created to take on new tasks such as the protection of the environment, the guarantee of civil rights, the improvement of public safety and the protection of the consumer. The legislation establishing these new agencies with regulatory and promotional functions was usually written in broad and general terms allowing the bureaucrats considerable discretion and power to interpret the laws, although in some more recent statutes legal challenges to the decisions of the agency experts have been allowed. This ability to make discretionary decisions also increased bureaucratic power.

Observers of American politics have noted the way parts of the federal bureaucracy also draw support from associated clienteles or interest groups as well as congressional committees involved in funding the agencies. Often known as 'iron triangles', this type of close relationship was seen as creating 'policy sub-governments' and criticized as working against the public interest and blurring accountability. Other writers have pointed out more recently that in Washington

---

[49]*Washington Post*, op. cit.

today there are 'issue networks',[50] more complex relationships that involve not only bureaucrats, Congressmen and interest groups but also lawyers, journalists, state governments, professors and other experts. The common denominators are the specialized knowledge about public policy alternatives related to specific issue areas. William Lunch has commented that the new networks allow for a wider variety of views than the largely closed sub-governments, but at a cost.

> Since the policy debates are frequently abstruse and obscured in a cloud of statistics, academic articles, think tank reports, and Congressional hearings, which are very meaningful to the experts but virtually impenetrable to most citizens, the capacity of the voters to follow and pass judgement on policy questions is reduced.[51]

Some Further Reading

James D. Barber, *The Presidential Character; Predicting Performance in the White House* (Prentice-Hall 1985)

Gary C. Cox and Samuel S. Kernell, *The Politics of Divided Government* (Westview Press 1991)

Fred Greenstein (ed.), *Leadership in the Modern Presidency* (Harvard University Press 1988)

Charles O. Jones, *The Presidency in a Separated System* (Brookings Institution 1994)

Louis W. Koenig, *The Chief Executive* (Harcourt Brace Jovanovich 1990)

David Mervin, *Ronald Reagan and the American Presidency* (Longman 1990)

David Mervin, *The President of the United States* (Harvester-Wheatsheaf 1993)

Richard Neustadt, *Presidential Power* (John Wiley 1980)

Richard Neustadt, *Presidential Power and the Modern Presidents: The Politics of Leadership from Roosevelt to Reagan* (Free Press 1990)

Richard Rose, *The Post-Modern President* (Chatham House 1988)

James A. Thurber (ed.), *Divided Democracy* (Congressional Quarterly Press 1991)

---

[50]Hugh Heclo, *A Government of Strangers: Executive Politics in Washington* (Brookings Institution 1977).
[51]William Lunch, op. cit., p. 184.

4

Law Adjudication: The Supreme Court and the Judiciary

On 24 July 1974, the Supreme Court of the United States announced one of its most historic and fateful decisions: it declared in a unanimous judgement that the President, Richard M. Nixon, must release tape-recordings of conversations which would reveal his involvement in the Watergate cover-up. After spending a day debating whether to obey the highest court in the land, Nixon capitulated and admitted:

> Those arguing my case, as well as those passing judgement on the case, did so with information that was incomplete and in some respects erroneous.[1]

On 9 August Nixon, faced with certain conviction in a Senate impeachment trial, became the first President to resign the office of Chief Executive.

The case of *United States v Richard M. Nixon* grew out of the Watergate scandal—the creation of the 'plumbers' unit in 1971, the break-in at the Democratic National Headquarters in 1972, and the perjury, obstruction of justice and conspiracy within the Nixon administration that followed in order to conceal from the American people the fact that the President himself was a party to the cover-up operation. The case was examined by the Supreme Court because the federal District Court's sub-poena on the President to produce 64 taped conversations was resisted by Nixon on the grounds of 'executive privilege'. The public importance of the issue meant that the Supreme Court undertook consideration of the case and bypassed the US Court of Appeals.

[1] Presidential press statement, 25 July 1974.

The Supreme Court came to the conclusion that the President had the right to confidential advice and discussions with his assistants, particularly on diplomatic and security matters. However, this right could not be extended to a general claim of 'executive privilege' to deny the production of relevant evidence in a criminal proceeding, as this was central to the administration of justice. Chief Justice Warren Burger wrote:

> The impediment that an absolute, unqualified privilege would place in the way of the primary constitutional duty of the Judicial Branch to do justice in criminal prosecutions would plainly conflict with the functions of the courts under Article 111 [of the Constitution].

He continued:

> A President's acknowledged need for confidentiality in the communications of his office is general in nature, whereas the constitutional need for the production of relevant evidence in a criminal proceeding is specific and central to the fair adjudication of a particular criminal case in the administration of justice. Without access to specific facts a criminal prosecution may be totally frustrated. The President's broad interest in confidentiality of communications will not be vitiated by disclosure of a limited number of conversations preliminarily shown to have some bearing on a pending criminal case.[2]

The Supreme Court's involvement in the downfall of President Nixon is an impressive illustration of its role in the American political system. It acted as the highest court of appeal to determine what the Constitution and the law meant when the ruling of a lower court was challenged. It was involved in the process of law adjudication, and its role as the final arbiter of the Constitution is essential as parts of the written document are ambiguous and require interpretation. In this particular case, the doctrine of 'executive privilege' is not even mentioned specifically in the Constitution, and the Supreme Court had to decide whether the independence of the executive branch, implied by the separation of powers principle, extended to an absolute privilege of confidentiality of Presidential communications.

The compliance by the President with the Supreme Court's decision on the release of the sub-poenaed tapes demonstrated the unique position which the Court had achieved. The executive and legislative

---

[2]*United States* v *Richard M. Nixon* (24 July 1974).

branches of government accept the decisions of the Supreme Court even though it has no direct way of enforcing its decisions on the other institutions. The Court has consistently found support in the popular belief that the judiciary stands apart from the elected institutions and defends the fundamental law of the Constitution, and the level of respect and confidence in the Court's integrity has been an important factor in this development.

The Nixon case confirmed once again the importance of the separation of powers doctrine and the role of an independent judicial branch in preventing an arbitrary abuse of power by the executive authority. The Supreme Court's decision effectively led to the resignation of a President who had lost the confidence of the people, but it was the culmination of a number of searching investigations by the judicial system. The District Court of John Sirica in Washington DC played a particularly crucial role in revealing the extent of the Watergate affair, and the lengthy legal procedures that went on for a couple of years after the original break-in showed the tenacity and effectiveness of the judicial process. The independence of the Supreme Court was also demonstrated by the fact that three of the eight justices who voted against the President in the case (Justice Rehnquist played no part in the discussions) were, in fact, appointed by Richard Nixon himself.

It would be wrong, however, to conclude that the Supreme Court has always enjoyed so well established a position. The Constitution of 1787 had relatively little to say about the judiciary; judicial power was vested in one Supreme Court 'and in such inferior Courts as the Congress may from time to time ordain and establish'. The judges would hold their positions during 'good behaviour' and could be removed only by Congressional impeachment. Congress could also control the Supreme Court's jurisdiction over appeals from lower courts. It was not clear exactly how important the Supreme Court would be; the Constitution did not lay down many specific powers, but neither did it actually deny or prevent the Court from assuming a central role.

Undoubtedly the major figure in ensuring the establishment of the Court's pre-eminence in judicial matters was John Marshall, who was Chief Justice of the Supreme Court between 1801 and 1835. He was a Federalist and he believed that the Union could only survive with a strong national government; under his auspices, the Court became a major influence in American politics and there was a considerable expansion of the federal government's power vis-à-vis the states. In these important formative years in the Court's history, three vital developments took place. Firstly, the danger of the President or Congress dominating and undermining the Court was avoided and the independence of the judiciary from the other branches was established. When Jefferson became President and found the courts manned by Federalist supporters it was felt that impeachment could be used to remove the incompetent or politically objectionable judges. However, the Senate failed to muster the necessary two-thirds majority to dismiss Samuel Chase from the Supreme Court. If this had been successful, Marshall himself would probably have faced impeachment and the future independence of the Court would have been severely jeopardized.

The second major achievement of the Marshall Court was the development of the role of 'Judicial Review'. This convention has led the Supreme Court to declare null and void as 'unconstitutional' any statute or action of the federal or state governments which it believes to conflict with the supreme law of the Constitution. The right of interpreting what the Constitution means has given considerable weight to the Court's opinions. The precedent for this role was set in the case of *Marbury* v *Madison* (1803).

The Federalist President John Adams appointed a large number of his party supporters to new judicial positions just before he left office himself in March 1801. The new President, Thomas Jefferson, was angry at this blatant act of packing the judiciary, and when it was discovered that some of the commissions had not been delivered he ordered his Secretary of State, James Madison, to stop the appointments. One of the aggrieved appointees, a man named William Marbury, decided to seek redress in the courts. He claimed that the Judiciary Act of 1789 gave the Supreme Court the authority to issue a writ ordering a government official to carry out his duty; he wanted the Court to tell Madison that he should secure Marbury his rightful appointment. The case placed the Supreme Court in a serious predicament. If the Court ordered the executive branch to give Marbury his job, it was likely that the President would refuse and the Supreme Court's prestige and future influence would be endangered. On the other hand, if the Court supported Jefferson and Madison it would vindicate the argument of their party that the judiciary had no power over the executive branch, as well as being politically distasteful to the Federalist majority in the Court.

Marshall's decision, in February 1803, was a landmark in constitutional history because it declared that, although Marbury had a grievance and was entitled to his commission, the Supreme Court had no power to deal with his problem. Marshall argued that section 13 of the Judiciary Act purported to give the Court original jurisdiction in this area, but that this conflicted with Article III of the Constitution, which limits the Supreme Court's original, as opposed to appellate, authority to cases in which an Ambassador, foreign Minister or state was involved as a party to a dispute. The Judiciary Act, in seeming to grant this power to the Supreme Court, was therefore unconstitutional, and the Supreme Court could not uphold an unconstitutional law. Marshall's skill had allowed him to deal with a very difficult situation, and in extricating himself he took the opportunity to set forth the doctrine of judicial review.

In the case of *Fletcher* v *Peck* (1810), the Court for the first time declared a state law unconstitutional and although it was not until the Dred Scott case in 1857 that another Congressional statute was nullified by the judges, the principle of judicial review was established as a vital part of the constitutional system despite the lack of specific authorization in the Constitution.

The Marshall Court laid the basis for the modern Supreme Court's position by claiming and securing the principle of judicial sovereignty. This has led other institutions, including the state supreme courts, to accept its decisions as binding on them. In *Martin* v *Hunter's Lessee* (1816), the Supreme Court's right to reverse the verdicts of state courts was accepted. Within a few years of Roger B. Taney's succeeding Marshall as Chief Justice, it was widely agreed that the Court was independent of the other branches of government, it had the power to declare actions of those branches 'unconstitutional', and its decisions were binding on both federal and state institutions.

The Structure of the American Judiciary

Law adjudication in the United States is carried out by two parallel systems of courts which consider a wide range of civil and criminal cases. There are fifty state systems which have been established by individual state constitutions and decide actions and settle disputes concerning their own laws. The nature of federalism has allowed differences to exist in the working and in the terminology used in the court system; for example, in about three-quarters of the states, judges are elected by a variety of methods, while in the remainder they are appointed. The vast majority of cases are settled in state municipal or justice courts in towns and cities all over the country. However, there is a right of appeal to the state appeals courts, and in a small minority of cases the state supreme court will make the final decision. Usually these are issues which require the highest court in the state to interpret the constitution of the state or involve basic constitutional rights.

There is also the federal judicial system which, as the nation has expanded and the amount of legislation passed by Congress has increased, has become relatively more important. The 'supremacy clause' of the Constitution (Article VI paragraph 2) makes it clear that the federal Constitution, and laws and treaties made under it, are supreme over state constitutions and laws, and therefore federal judicial decisions can also have a broad impact on decisions of the state courts. There are three tiers within the federal court system.[3] District courts have been established by Congress in each state to examine federal cases. The number of courts and judges may be increased when Congress feels that a growth in population or caseload justifies this. There is at least one court in each state, depending upon population, giving 94 courts in total. Most cases are examined and settled at this level but they can be reviewed by one of the US Courts of Appeals, which are set up in 12 circuits, with six to 28 judges on each circuit. The jurisdiction of a Court of Appeals therefore extends over the boundaries of states, as the number of appeal cases does not justify one circuit for each state.

Both in 1984 and 1990 Congress approved the creation of an additional 85 district and appeal court posts, bringing the total to 825. This increase in the size of the federal judiciary was necessary because of the substantial growth in the workload of the courts. The caseload of the district courts rose by 42% in the 1980s, a result of population growth, an increasingly litigious society, new federal laws and regulations and anti-crime drives, particularly against drugs.

The Supreme Court of the United States is almost completely an appellate (or appeal) court. It has original jurisdiction (that is, cases which go directly to it for consideration) only over very specialized issues mentioned in the Constitution.[4] Most of its caseload is drawn from cases that have been considered by the US Court of Appeals or from state courts where some important constitutional principle is

---

[3]There are, in addition, special federal courts for such matters as military cases, taxation, custom and patents.
[4]See above discussion on *Marbury v Madison*.

TABLE 4.1

The Structure of the American Judicial System

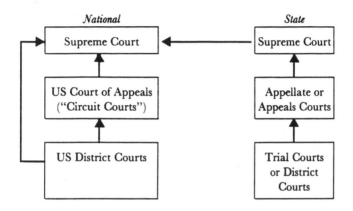

involved. The majority of the cases appealed to the Supreme Court come from petitioners who feel they have suffered a violation of constitutional rights, but the Court turns down around 95% of such applications on the grounds that no substantial constitutional question is at stake. The Court may call for a case from the lower courts for its consideration, if four out of nine Supreme Court justices feel that it is sufficiently important. Judges at district or appeal court levels may announce their views as to the constitutionality of a law in cases before them but, of course, it is the Supreme Court's opinion that is final and binding.

Each year the Supreme Court's session in Washington DC extends from October to June. The groundwork for the approximately 6,000 appeals which are filed annually with the Supreme Court is prepared by law clerks who help the justices by presenting the facts and issues in the cases so that decisions can normally be reached speedily and efficiently. These people are mostly one- or two-year appointees from the cream of the law school graduates, and they have an important role in expediting the business of the Court. The vast majority of cases will be settled by examining the written evidence and records of previous hearings, but the Court does hear oral evidence in in a certain number of cases each year. In the 1980s the Court would have a docket of up to

150 a year but, in recent times, Chief Justice Rehnquist has reduced the caseload by over a third. On these occasions lawyers have thirty minutes to argue their case, and can be interrupted for questioning during this time by the justices. The Court hears oral arguments beginning in early October and finishing in late April, with typically 12 cases being dealt with each week. All cases will be decided and the Court's opinion announced before the summer recess begins in late June or early July.

The Court normally meets on Fridays in secret conference to discuss pending cases and applications for certiorari (that is, those cases to be 'made certain'). The judges speak in order of seniority and then vote in the reverse order. Compromises may be made behind the scenes as different opinions are exchanged and discussed on the arguments and technical aspects of the law. A unanimous decision on the case tends to strengthen the impact of the Court and create an impression of unity. Chief Justice Marshall established the custom that, where there was general agreement, one justice's opinion should stand for the decision of the whole Court. On the other hand, where there is disagreement there will be a majority opinion which is the official decision of the Court and dissenting minority opinions. The Chief Justice decides who will write the Court's decision if he is in the majority; if not, it is left to the most senior ranking member of the majority to assign the writing of the Court's view. The opinions are often a result of a number of compromises so that a majority of judges are prepared to sign the final statement; it is not unusual for it to have undergone 10 drafts in a justice's chambers and 17 or 18 more drafts before it satisfies everyone. Each justice writes about 13 to 18 majority opinions a year and nearly as many dissenting and concurring views.

The views of the minority of dissenting justices are of considerable interest: at some time in the future their views may become the majority decision because, apart from a Constitutional Amendment, the only method of changing the Supreme Court's interpretation is for the Court itself collectively to change its mind. It is reluctant to make too frequent reversals on major constitutional issues but it may do so if conditions in society change or if the composition or personal views of the justices are modified.

The announcement of a Court decision, which has often laid down new rules and interpretations, is awaited expectantly not only by the plaintiffs in the particular case but by lawyers, judges, politicians, pressure groups and the mass media all over the country. The reverberations from the magnificent Grecian-style building in the nation's capital may well have a profound and fundamental effect on the lives of the American people.

The Appointment of the Federal Judiciary

1 District and Circuit Judges

All federal judges are appointed by the President with the approval of the Senate. In practice, the President is advised by the Department of Justice and the Deputy Attorney-General's office whom he should recommend for appointment to the district and appeals courts. District judges are usually selected from among local lawyers and judges who have worked in the state judicial system. When a position becomes available, members of the local community often put forward names and the Justice Department's job is to vet nominations to ensure that anyone the President eventually recommends is suitable for the position. The Federal Bureau of Investigation will check the candidate's personal background for honesty and integrity, while the American Bar Association, the legal profession's organization, will rate the nominee's training, legal qualifications and experience for the job. The ABA's 15-member committee finds that about one-quarter of the people proposed are unsuitable and this procedure usually prevents the appointment of unqualified individuals to positions in the federal judiciary.

In 1989 the ABA was involved in two controversies relating to its advisory role on judicial appointments. In a case in June 1989 brought by two public interest pressure groups the Supreme Court decided that the ABA committee could continue to conduct its business in secret; it had been argued that because the committee was an advisory one to government it should, under a 1972 statute, hold open meetings and keep a public record of its decisions. The ABA was also accused by some conservatives of being biased in its evaluation process. Attorney-General Richard Thornburgh and ABA President Robert Rowen told Senators in June 1989 that the ABA had agreed to leave out of its judicial evaluation any consideration of political philosophy; it would confine its scrutiny to candidates' professional qualifications, competence, integrity and temperament.[5]

[5]*Congressional Quarterly Weekly Report*, 24 June 1989, p. 1549.

However, there is no doubt that party politics and political views intrude heavily on the appointment process. Most judges are selected by the President from within his own political party, and although all Chief Executives maintain that they are picking the best people for the job, the records indicate that partisan affiliation is a major factor in selection. For example, 94.1% of Jimmy Carter's appointees to the district courts were Democrats while of Ronald Reagan's appointments, 95.9% in his first term and 90.7% in his second term were Republicans. Presidents have always rewarded party supporters in the states with patronage in this fashion; the posts are desirable because federal judges enjoy high public esteem, and although the salary levels have been criticized as inadequate by judges and lawyers, they generally have security for life. The President decides which particular party supporters to honour by consulting the Senator from the state to which the judge is to be appointed, if there is a member of his own party holding one of the state's two Senate seats. The convention of 'Senatorial courtesy', referred to in the chapter on Congress, arises from the Senate's right of advice and consent over Presidential appointments. In recent years Presidents have preferred to have several names submitted by a Senator from which a choice can be made. In 1990 Republican Senator James Jefford of Vermont blocked new judicial appointments from being approved in the Senate as a protest against the refusal of the Bush administration to support his nominee whom the Justice Department regarded as unacceptable for a district vacancy. Jefford claimed that this was a violation of the Senate's prerogative. If there is no Senator of the same party, the President may consult with other senior party notables such as the Governor or State Chairman, but he is likely to have more flexibility in such a situation. This is also true of Appeals Court judgeships because the circuits overlap state boundaries.

The Senate Judiciary Committee holds hearings on appointments, but if the convention of courtesy has been observed, and there are no obvious objections to the candidate's suitability, these and the vote in the full Senate have in the past usually been little more than a formality. Hearings were often so brief that one judge, an Eisenhower appointee, missed his because he was late reaching Capitol Hill. 'I walked into the committee room with my knees shaking,' he recalls, 'but the Chairman just gave me a big smile and said, "Hi, we already confirmed ya"'.[6] However, in March 1980 the Senate Judiciary Committee re-

[6]Quoted in the *Los Angeles Times*, 23 April 1975, p. 7.

jected Charles Winberry Jr, Carter's nominee for a judgeship in North Carolina, by a 9–6 vote. It was the first time since 1938 that the Committee had rejected a Presidential nomination for a district judge. In 1991 the Committee rejected the nomination of Kenneth L. Ryskamp for an Appeals Court seat after strong opposition in his home state of Florida from groups critical of his rulings in civil rights cases.

The experience of the 1980s suggests that the Senate Judiciary Committee now takes its role of scrutinizing nominees far more seriously and is no longer a rubber stamp. The Reagan years were marked by the President's commitment to appoint conservative judges and after the Democrats regained control of the Senate in 1986 they determined to play a more meaningful role in the nominating process. As Democratic Senator Patrick J. Leahy commented: 'I think the Judiciary Committee finally re-discovered the advice and consent clause of the Constitution.'[7] It is clear that the Democratic majority on the Committee were not intending to use their power to reject a Republican President's nominees unless they regarded an individual's views as extreme and unacceptable. The Committee insisted on more time to conduct investigations before having to vote on them. However, even with this more rigorous oversight President Reagan lost only two nominees at committee level and two on the floor of the Senate. Of the 66 judges confirmed by the Senate in 1992 only one, Edward Earl Carnes Jr. from Alabama, triggered a serious battle after he was criticized for insensitivity on racial issues. He was eventually approved by 62–38, following a heated debate in the Senate.[8]

During his eight years in office President Reagan had a considerable impact on the federal judiciary. He was able to appoint 48.9% of the 556 full-time district court judges and 48.1% of the 160 appeal court judges serving in November 1989. What is more, the Reagan administration made it clear from the beginning that it intended to make ideology and judicial philosophy the key factors in determining whom to nominate. Whereas this was not unusual in itself, Sheldon Goldman of the University of Massachusetts says that the Reagan administration:

> represents the most systematic, most coordinated effort at the use of the appointment power to maximize the President's agenda and to maximize the President's influence on the appointment process.[9]

[7]*Congressional Quarterly Weekly Report*, 26 November 1988, p. 3392.
[8]*Congressional Quarterly Weekly Report*, 13 February 1993, p. 317.
[9]*Congressional Quarterly Weekly Report*, 26 November 1988, p. 3393.

Reagan was looking for judges committed to 'judicial restraint' who would tend to defer to the legislative body and not intrude upon the functions of the other branches of government, as opposed to 'judicial activists' who it is claimed tend to substitute their beliefs for the intent of the legislators who wrote the law.

This emphasis on ideological qualifications goes a long way in explaining the relatively small number of minority group and women appointees during the Reagan years compared with Jimmy Carter's term of office. Carter had deliberately sought to increase the representation of these groups on the federal bench; among his 262 appointees there were 40 women, 38 blacks and 16 Hispanics. Of Reagan's 360 appointees there were only 30 women, 7 blacks and 14 Hispanics; while administration officials argued that there were relatively few qualified lawyers in these groups, it is clear that even fewer of them would pass the political qualification test. During his term in office George Bush appointed 185 district and circuit judges, almost a quarter of the total. Bush pleased conservatives by continuing the Reagan approach to judicial appointments; their main criticism was that delays in filling vacancies meant that when Bush left office President Clinton had the immediate opportunity to fill over 100 judicial positions with Democratic nominees.

During his first term Clinton appointed 198 district and appeal court judges—just under a quarter of the 837 member judiciary; with 80 vacancies to be filled at the start of his second term and four more years ahead it is possible that he will become the first President to appoint more than half of the federal bench. Almost a third of Clinton's first-term appointees were women, 19% were black and 7% were Hispanic, making him the first President not to appoint a majority of white men. Politically, most of Clinton's appointees appeared to be moderates and he seems to have wished to avoid a conflict with the Republican-controlled Senate over judicial posts, dropping some more controversial liberal nominees when the GOP took control in 1995. The administration consulted with Senate Judiciary Committee Chairman, Orrin Hatch, before sending nominations to Capitol Hill. This did not stop some conservative pressure groups arguing in 1997 that the Senate should delay the approval of Clinton nominees because they were too liberal and activist. Some conservatives wanted to alter the procedures by which judges are approved so that the President would formally have to clear nominees with the Senate in advance or reserve a certain number of positions for Republicans. A Senate sub-committee was also investigating whether the number of district judgeships should be redistributed around the states so that they would reflect populations and workloads more fairly.

As we have seen, federal judges can be removed from office by Congressional impeachment procedures: the House votes for impeachment and conviction in a Senate trial by a two-thirds majority for 'treason, bribery or high crimes and misdemeanours'. A separate provision says federal judges hold office 'during good behaviour'. In recent years there have been three cases of incumbent federal judges being impeached and removed from office (Walter L. Nixon Jr of Mississippi, Harry E. Claiborne of Nevada, and Alcee L. Hastings Jr of Florida). Claiborne became the first sitting judge to serve a prison sentence after being convicted for tax evasion and the Senate removed him from office in 1986. The other two were removed in 1988. Despite this record Hastings was elected as a Democratic member to the House of Representatives in 1992. The long and difficult process of removing judges who have been convicted of crimes before the courts has given rise to debate about whether there should be alternatives to the process. The most common suggestion has been to authorize the federal judiciary to discipline its own members, as many state courts do. Others have argued that a constitutional amendment is required to automatically remove judges upon conviction of a felony.[10]

2 Supreme Court Justices

Every American President has attempted to extend his political influence by his appointments to the Supreme Court. There are nine justices (one Chief Justice and eight Associate Justices) and they are appointed for life or until they decide to retire. In the event of a justice retiring or dying in office the President has the right to nominate his successor, therefore the number of such opportunities in any four- or eight-year period can vary considerably. Uppermost in the President's mind when he is choosing an appointee will be the political views of the candidate. It is likely that he will seek to fill the post with a judge who has a similar political disposition to himself. If he is fortunate enough to be able to appoint a number of justices he may be able to mould the Court so that it reflects his views or general outlook. Some Presidents have succeeded in changing the political balance of the

[10]*Congressional Quarterly Weekly Report*, 27 May 1989, p. 1282.

Court and thus in influencing the American political system long after they themselves have left the executive office. Franklin Roosevelt managed to do this, primarily because of his long period as President, and one of his appointees, William O. Douglas, who became a justice in 1939, was still a member of the Supreme Court thirty years after Roosevelt's death.

The Supreme Court is not merely the puppet of the executive branch and, as we have seen, judicial independence was established early in the Court's history. The life term, with no requirement for reappointments, the large salary, and effective guarantee of full pay on retirement, as well as the knowledge that removal can only be achieved by impeachment, have a wonderfully liberating effect on Supreme Court Justices. Although it can be argued that life terms could lead to out-of-touch and arrogant judges, it is generally accepted that it is a necessary prerequisite for the maintenance of judicial independence. They have nothing either to gain or to fear from the executive and legislative branches. Occasionally a President has appointed a man to the Supreme Court only to find that, once in office, the justice has acted politically in his decisions in a way very different from that originally expected. President Eisenhower selected the Republican Governor of California, Earl Warren, as Chief Justice only to find that his appointee led the Court to a new activist and liberal period of decision making. A conservative himself, Eisenhower reportedly felt this to have been his worst mistake while being President. When making decisions on controversial issues, Supreme Court Justices do not always act kindly towards the President who appointed them. We have seen that the appointees of President Nixon voted against him in *United States* v *Richard M. Nixon,* and President Truman experienced a similar rebuttal when two of his appointees declared that he had acted unconstitutionally in *Youngstown Sheet and Tube Company* v *Sawyer* (1952).

A President will be provided by his Attorney-General with a short-list of possible candidates for the vacancy in the Supreme Court from whom he will select his nominee. The Department of Justice will have provided an analysis of the alternatives, and reports on the characters of the people concerned. The ABA will also have rated the candidates on the basis of their qualifications for membership of the highest court in the land. There are four grades ('exceptionally well qualified', 'well qualified' 'qualified' and 'not qualified') and a high rating will help a candidate's chances of selection, although a low grade will not necessarily disqualify him. Richard Nixon was so annoyed about leaks of

ABA ratings, which are supposed to be confidential, that, when a candidate being seriously considered was rumoured to have been given an unfavourable grade by the ABA, the administration threatened not to consult the organization in future. The controversy over allegations of bias in the ABA's Standing Committee on the Federal Judiciary reached new heights in 1987 when the ABA's evaluation of Robert Bork who had been a Yale University law professor, US Solicitor General and a judge on the US Court of Appeals for the District of Columbia suggested it was interested not only in qualifications and ability but in philosophy, particularly in relation to his strict interpretation of the Constitution. Although a majority found Bork 'well qualified' to serve on the Supreme Court, four of the 15 members found him 'not qualified', the first time in 15 years that the ABA Committee had not awarded a Supreme Court nominee its unanimous support.[11] There is no tradition of promotion from the lower federal courts and although nominees will probably have had a legal training, they do not necessarily have to be practising judges. Politicians – legislators, Governors and, in the case of William Howard Taft, even a former President – have been appointed to the Supreme Court. However, recent nominees have been drawn from the US Courts of Appeals (see Table 4.2).

The President's nominee will therefore be chosen with all these factors in mind: ability, experience, honesty, political views, and possibly the need to reward allies from the last election campaign. Acceptability to the Senate is also an important checking mechanism on Presidential choice. The Senate Judiciary Committee, and indeed all Senators, will be very interested in the qualifications and political outlook of the nominee. The Senate takes its role of advice and consent for Supreme Court Justices very seriously and, of course, it is a matter of concern to the whole nation and not just to one state. There may well be a long and thorough investigation and interrogation of the nominee at public hearings. Pressure groups may actively campaign for and against the selection, and the President's friends and enemies will be lobbying strongly behind the scenes. The Senate has refused approval to 29 (or about 20%) of the nominations sent to it in the period to 1997.

Richard Hodder-Williams has pointed out that all nominations are made within two contexts. The White House context is created

[11]*Congressional Quarterly Weekly Report*, 22 April, p. 897.

exclusively by the President himself and reflects the goals and strategies to be achieved by nominating particular individuals. These may include the hope that the nominee will advance certain policies on the Court or that the nomination—of a woman or a member of a minority group, for example—will have symbolic significance. The Washington context is essentially outside the President's control and means that he has to take account of the balance of political forces in the Senate. The 'law of anticipated reactions' may prevent the President from submitting the name of his ideal choice because ignoring such reactions may lead to the failure of the nomination.[12] Sometimes Presidents wishing to avoid a battle with the Senate will value 'confirmability' above other factors.

When Richard Nixon became President in 1969 he entered the office pledged to use his appointment power to influence a change in the political balance of the Court, if the opportunity should present itself. Conservative Americans, angered by the judicial activism and liberal policies of the Warren Court, wanted to see the future appointment of 'strict constructionists'. These would be conservative judges who would, as far as possible, interpret the Constitution and the law, but not break into new areas which were the prerogative of Congress. Nixon, in a campaign speech in November 1968, stated:

> They would see themselves as caretakers of the Constitution and servants of the people, not super-legislators with a free hand to impose their social and political viewpoints upon the American people.

The new President had an early opportunity to fulfil the promise as two liberal justices retired. Earl Warren left the position of Chief Justice vacant and Nixon selected a conservative 'law and order' judge from Minnesota, Warren Burger, to replace him. Although his appointment was approved by the Senate without problems Nixon had much greater difficulties in filling the other vacancy, left when Abraham Fortas (a Johnson appointee) resigned after criticism of his freelance activities as a legal adviser. The President wanted to select a Southern conservative to the Court, partly as a reward to his political supporters in the region for backing him in the 1968 Presidential election. They, in turn, wanted a justice who would help moderate the Warren Court's liberal stance on civil rights and segregation. However, the majority in the Senate, made up of Democratic and Republican liberals from the

---

[12]Richard Hodder-Williams. 'The Supreme Court Nominations of Reagan and Bush', in *Contemporary American Politics*, Alan Grant (ed.) (Dartmouth 1995).

TABLE 4.2

The Composition of the Supreme Court 1997

	Birth Date	State of Origin	Party	Previous Position	Date Appointed	Appointed by
William Rehnquist	1923	Ariz.	Rep.	Ass. Attorney-Gen.	1971	Nixon
John Paul Stevens	1920	Ill.	Rep.	US Court of Appeals	1975	Ford
Sandra Day O'Connor	1930	Ariz.	Rep.	Ariz. Appeals Court	1981	Reagan
Antonin Scalia	1936	NJ	Rep.	US Court of Appeals	1986	Reagan
Anthony Kennedy	1936	Cal.	Rep.	US Court of Appeals	1988	Reagan
David Souter	1940	NH	Rep.	US Court of Appeals	1990	Bush
Clarence Thomas	1948	Ga.	Rep.	US Court of Appeals	1991	Bush
Ruth Bader Ginsburg	1933	NY	Dem.	US Court of Appeals	1993	Clinton
Stephen Breyer	1938	Cal.	Dem.	US Court of Appeals	1994	Clinton

Northern states, had no intention of approving anyone who had the slightest taint of racial discrimination in his past record, and most of these Senators were suspicious of Southern conservatives on this basis. Unfortunately for President Nixon, the Justice Department did not adequately screen the first of his appointees to the vacant post; Clement Haynsworth, from South Carolina, was rejected by the Senate after it had been revealed that he had tried some cases where he had a conflict of interest. Nixon's second nominee for the vacancy, Harrold Carswell, was rejected 51–45 by the Senate in April 1970. He was charged with showing racial bias in the Florida courts and with having a mediocre record as a judge, having been frequently over-ruled by higher state courts. Nixon was unable to count on solid support from Senate Republicans and, in the Haynsworth case, even Minority Leader Hugh Scott voted against confirmation. Having accused the Senate of bias against the South, Nixon then nominated Harry Blackmun, a moderate federal Appeals Court judge from Minnesota. The vacancy was thus filled at the third attempt, and the episode demonstrated that no President is assured of obtaining the support and consent of the Senate on Supreme Court appointments. In 1971 two other liberals from the Warren Court, Justices Harlan and Black, retired and Richard Nixon had the chance to appoint two more conservative replacements. Lewis Powell Jr, a Virginia lawyer, and William F. Rehnquist, the Assistant Attorney-General, both secured confirmation by the Senate. Therefore by the end of his first term in the Presidency, Richard Nixon had been able to shape the political composition of the Court by naming four out of the nine justices. If he had remained in office for a full second term, he would have had the opportunity of choosing the successor to William Douglas, the most outspoken liberal in the Court, and of appointing an actual numerical majority. Gerald Ford's choice of John Paul Stevens, from Illinois, received the unanimous support of the Senate in December 1975 in an unusual demonstration of political consensus. President Carter became the first President to serve a full term in office who did not have the opportunity of appointing a Supreme Court Justice as no vacancies occurred during his term. Ronald Reagan had the opportunity of filling three vacancies on the Supreme Court during his eight years in office. In 1981 he appointed Sandra Day O'Connor, an Arizona Appeals Court Judge, as the first woman Supreme Court Justice on the retirement of Potter Stewart. In 1986 Reagan named William Rehnquist, the most conservative judge on the Court, as the new Chief Justice in place of Warren Burger who stood down to preside over arrangements for the celebration of the bicentennial of the Constitution, and appointed Antonin Scalia, the first Italian-American ever to sit on the Court, in Rehnquist's position. Rehnquist was approved 65–33 votes in the Senate after a protracted debate on the nomination. The third vacancy came about as a result of the retirement of Lewis Powell, a Nixon appointee who had often joined liberals and had been the swing vote on the Court on a number of key issues. It was recognized that the filling of this vacancy would be extremely significant to the future political balance of the Court. Apart from Powell, other Republican nominees, Blackmun and Stevens, had during the 1980s moved increasingly to support the liberal judges on the Court, while Byron White, a Kennedy appointee, had moved to the right.

Reagan's first nominee, Robert Bork, was, as we have seen, in most respects well qualified to become a Supreme Court Justice. However, his personality and judicial philosophy aroused considerable opposition from liberal Senators and with the Democrats back in control of the Senate in 1987 and the Iran-Contra issue eroding Reagan's political influence, Bork's nomination was lost after the most bitter and public campaign ever seen involving a judicial appointee. Civil rights groups were successful in their lobbying against the nomination and despite an unprecedented appearance on his behalf before the Judiciary Committee by former President Gerald Ford, Bork was rejected in October 1987 by a Senate vote of 58–42, the most decisive defeat ever suffered by a nominee in American history. Reagan's second choice, Douglas Ginsberg, was forced to withdraw only days after his nomination when it was revealed that he had taken drugs when he was a college student. The President then turned to Anthony Kennedy, a Californian Appeals judge, who was confirmed by the Senate 97–0 in February 1988. Ronald Reagan was therefore able to shift the political balance of the Supreme Court decisively to the right before he left office.

In July 1990 George Bush was presented with his first opportunity to nominate a Supreme Court Justice when one of the remaining liberals on the Court, William Brennan, announced his retirement. Brennan, who was 84 years old and had been appointed by President Eisenhower in 1956, had been one of the most influential members of the Supreme Court during his 34 years of service. In nominating David Souter, a former New Hampshire state Supreme Court Judge and recently appointed member of the federal Appeals Court, President Bush was able to appoint an uncontroversial conservative to fill the vacancy without a bitterly contested confirmation process in the Senate, which was controlled by the Democrats. With the resignation of Thurgood Marshall in 1991 Bush was able to make a second nomination to the Court and he selected black conservative judge Clarence Thomas to fill the vacancy. Thomas was opposed by a number of pressure groups and given a lukewarm 'qualified' rating by the ABA (with two of the 15 committee members declaring him 'not qualified').

Despite the frustration of Democratic Senators at Thomas's refusal to answer controversial questions at the Senate Judiciary Committee hearings, his eventual approval did not seem in doubt until allegations of sexual harassment surfaced late in the process. Anita Hill, a law professor and former colleague of Thomas, testified before the committee whose televised proceedings became the focus of huge public interest. Thomas was confirmed in October 1991 by a narrow 52–48 margin, after doubt had been cast on his character and following concerted lobbying by women's groups against his nomination. What is more, the process of selection and approval of Justices itself was criticized as demeaning to the dignity and stature of the Supreme Court. *Time* magazine described the Thomas hearings as an 'ugly circus'.[13]

The Chairman of the Senate Judiciary Committee, Joseph Biden, called for more consultation between the White House and the Senate before nominations are submitted in order to try to avoid confrontation between the two branches. He also criticized extremist lobbying campaigns on appointments but defended the Senate's right to review a nominee's ideology as well as his or her character.[14]

In 1993 Byron White's retirement gave President Clinton the first opportunity a Democratic President has had since 1967 to nominate a Supreme Court Justice. After raising expectations that he was planning to propose his recently appointed Interior Secretary, Bruce Babbitt, a former Governor and Presidential candidate, Clinton eventually decided to nominate District of Columbia Appeals Court judge Ruth Bader Ginsburg to the post. She was widely perceived to be a well-qualified moderate and her nomination was approved 96–3 in the Senate in August 1993. With the retirement of Harry Blackmun, Clinton was able to appoint Stephen Breyer, another moderate whose nomination aroused no controversy, in 1994.

[13]*Time*, 21 October 1991; *Congressional Quarterly Weekly Report*, 31 August 1991, p. 2360; 12 October 1991, p. 2948; and 19 October 1991, p. 3026.
[14]*National Journal*, 4 July 1992, p. 1589.

The Supreme Court and Policy Making

The Role of Government

The Supreme Court has had a great influence on the development of American federalism. It was not clear at the beginning of the nineteenth century whether the structure of government initiated in 1787 would lead to a strong national government, or whether the powers of the states and the loyalties of peoples to their local areas would stand in the way of such a development. John Marshall, as Chief Justice, used his position to interpret the Constitution in favour of the federal government when there were jurisdictional conflicts with the states. A written constitution and a division of powers between tiers of government require interpretation and this was one of the main factors behind the Supreme Court's importance. The Civil War altered the balance of power in favour of the national government, but in the latter part of the nineteenth century conservative judges emphasized other sections of the Constitution to restrict federal and even state governments' intervention in economic and social affairs, in line with the generally accepted *laissez-faire* economic philosophy of the time. However, after 1937 and the 'New Deal' legislation in response to the Depression, the Court began to allow federal government influence in those areas previously seen as reserved to the states or those where government intervention of all kinds had been prohibited. In the economic and social fields, the Court has broadly interpreted three main sections of the Constitution and has thus enlarged the permissible areas of federal involvement in the life of the nation.

1 The 'Implied Powers' Clause. Article I Section 8 of the Constitution sets out the enumerated powers within which Congress can legislate; these are specific areas such as defence, trade and the postal services. However, at the end of this section the Constitution states that 'Congress shall have the power to make all laws which shall be necessary and proper for carrying into execution the foregoing powers'. The Court interpreted the 'necessary and proper' clause to mean that Congress can legislate on additional matters to those set out in the enumerated powers as long as these are important for carrying out the listed functions. Therefore in *McCulloch v Maryland* (1819) it was argued that the enumerated power of coining money gave the federal government the implied power to set up a bank for the United

States, even though banking is not specifically mentioned in Article 1
Section 8.

2 The 'Inter-State Commerce' Clause. One of the constitutional enumerated powers of Congress is 'to regulate commerce ... among the several
states', whereas commercial activity within the boundaries of one state
was subject only to state regulatory action. But what does 'commerce'
include? Should the phrase be narrowly or broadly construed? The
Supreme Court has, in effect, interpreted this section of the Constitution
to allow federal government regulations of almost any activity that crosses
state boundaries. In *Gibbons* v *Ogden* (1824) ferries between New York
and New Jersey were judged to be involved in commerce and subject to
federal taxes. In the twentieth century the amount of interstate, as
opposed to intra-state, commerce has increased substantially, and if a
company is involved in trading both within and outside a state it is
subject first and foremost to federal laws if there is a conflict with a state
regulatory law, because of the 'supremacy clause' of the Constitution.

3 The 'General Welfare' Clause. Congress was also given another general enabling clause which allows for a broad judicial interpretation.
This is the power to 'lay and collect taxes ... to provide for the common defence and general welfare of the United States'. The term
'general welfare' obviously requires definition and clarification. In the
1930s the Supreme Court first decided that the Social Security Act was
unconstitutional because it attempted to allow federal regulation in an
area reserved to the states. The Court then reversed its view and
decided that it was permissible because it could be seen as a 'taxing act
for the general welfare', rather than as a regulatory act.

On the other hand, the Supreme Court, at other times, has used the
Tenth Amendment specifically to prevent federal action in areas reserved to the states in the Constitution. The Court has also used the
'Due Process' section of the Fourteenth Amendment to protect industry and banking from state government regulation in such economic
matters as wages and hours of work for employees. The Amendment
says: 'No state shall deprive any person of life, liberty or property
without due process of law.'

It is clear that the Supreme Court has chosen at various times in its
history to place emphasis on one phrase or section of the Constitution
rather than another in order to justify its decisions, and retain a
flexibility which can keep it in line with public opinion.

Judicial Activism and the Warren Court

After World War II, the question of the federal government's powers in economic matters was no longer the central issue taking up the Supreme Court's time, mainly because Roosevelt's appointees and the new liberal majority in the Court made it clear by their decisions that they would not stand in the way of an expanded federal role. New issues were taken up by the Court, particularly after Earl Warren became Chief Justice. The Supreme Court examined questions which became very controversial but which had previously been dormant in American politics. Other institutions—the Presidency, Congress and state legislatures—would not act as they were too sensitive and difficult for elected politicians to handle. The Warren Court symbolized 'judicial activism' which was both applauded and condemned with tremendous emotional energy on both sides. It made a vast impact on many areas of American life where appointed judges were prepared to take up causes that were electorally unpopular. Often the issues went to the very heart of democracy—the rights of individuals, the rule of law, equal representation, and equality before the law. The Court was frequently in the position of defending minority rights against the views of a majority of the people. Many argued that the Warren Court was usurping the role of the elected legislature by making new laws and taking up new issues. Earl Warren himself admitted that the Court 'makes law' when it interprets the Constitution, but that it is not trying to take over the role of Congress. If Congress passes an act, then the judiciary has to interpret the statute; if Congress does not like the interpretation then it can pass a new law or amend the old one. However, if no statute exists in a particular area, the Court has to look at the broad language of the Constitution and see what rights exist from that document.[15]

Archibald Cox, the man Richard Nixon dismissed as Watergate Special Prosecutor and a distinguished legal authority, has written:

The appointment of Earl Warren as Chief Justice of the United States in 1953 marked the opening of a new period in our constitutional development. In the next fifteen years the Supreme Court rewrote, with profound social consequences, major constitutional doctrines governing race relations, the

---

[15]"The Warren Era: A conversation with former Chief Justice Earl Warren' (McClatchy Broadcasting, Sacramento, California). Reprinted in Charles Sheldon, *The Supreme Court: Politicians in Robes* (Glencoe Press 1970), pp. xiv–xxii.

administration of criminal justice and the operation of the political process. The extent and rapidity of the changes raise grave questions concerning the proper role of the Supreme Court in our national development—questions concerning the nature and function of constitutional adjudication.[16]

Martin Shapiro argues that:

the Warren Court took a fairly clear direction: to serve the value of equality and to incorporate that value more deeply in the Constitution. Although the structure was never completed, the blueprint was clear. ... The Warren Court was attempting to change the Constitution and impose its own will on that of other governmental bodies, particularly state legislatures. It was pretty clear that by the late 1960s nobody in the Warren–Brennan majority really cared much about anything but the policy outcomes of the cases.[17]

We shall examine four issue areas in which the decisions of the Warren Court between 1953 and 1969 had major social and political impact and where substantial constitutional questions were raised.

1 Segregation and Race Relations. Since the Civil War, equal rights for black Americans had been, in many respects, a hollow promise. In some areas, particularly in the Southern states, segregation of public facilities was practised and even written into and institutionalized in the state laws. Blacks and whites went to separate schools, ate at separate lunch counters, and had separate compartments on buses and trains. In other areas where there was no legal segregation, separation of the races took place in practice because of residential living patterns. The Supreme Court had decided in the case of *Plessy* v *Ferguson* (1896) that, as long as they were substantially equal, separate facilities were constitutional and permissible. For the next sixty years neither Congress nor the Presidency wished to step into this political minefield and intervene in such a controversial area.

The Warren Court was prepared to re-examine the principle and decided in the landmark case of *Brown* v *Board of Education, Topeka (Kansas)* (1954) that separate facilities for blacks and whites were inherently unequal under the Fourteenth Amendment. The relevant section of the Amendment says that: 'No state shall ... deny to any person within its jurisdiction the equal protection of the laws.' In this case,

---

[16]Archibald Cox, *The Warren Court: Constitutional Decision as an Instrument of Reform*, quoted in Sheldon, ibid., p. ix.

[17]Martin Shapiro, 'The Supreme Court from Early Burger to Early Rehnquist' in *The New American Political System*, Second Version, Anthony King (ed.) (AEI Press 1990), p. 58.

Oliver Brown wanted to send his daughter Linda to the school nearest his home. However, because the family was black, Linda had to travel across town to school and was not allowed to attend the all-white school a few blocks away from her home. Backed by the National Association for the Advancement of Colored People (NAACP), Mr Brown took his case to the Court, and it decided that 'equal protection' was being denied. The Court argued that the doctrine of 'separate but equal' had no part to play in state-financed schools and that separation 'generates a feeling of inferiority as to their status', thus retarding black children's educational development. The Court argued that states and school districts should desegregate their schools with 'all deliberate speed'. The Brown case was a momentous decision but it did not result in an immediate end to segregation. Direct intervention by the President with federal troops to enforce desegregation, for example, in Little Rock, Arkansas, and the Civil Rights Act of 1964, followed in the dispute between the federal government and stubborn state authorities. Fifteen years after the Brown decision, the Court, impatient at local resistance, said that authorities were obliged to desegregate their schools 'at once' (*Alexander* v *Holmes County Board of Education*, 1969).

Opponents of the desegregation decision argued against the Court on a number of grounds. They felt that the Court had accepted 'pseudo-scientific' evidence, such as psychological data and statistics on educational achievement, without allowing any challenge to the validity of this material. It was also argued that such information was not relevant to the Court's role of interpreting the Constitutional document. Others pointed to the Tenth Amendment and argued that, as education is among the reserved powers of the states, the federal authorities had no constitutional right to intervene in the running of the schools.

However, the Court's decision and the fact that it was supported by all the Supreme Court Justices, not only established the new principle but provided a firm commitment on behalf of the judiciary to the protection of minority rights.

2 Equal Representation and Reapportionment.   Each state's legislature in the United States has the right to determine boundaries for all elections within its jurisdiction. These include, as well as local government elections, contests for both houses of the state legislature itself and for the House of Representatives. In the early 1960s, most state legislatures tended to underrepresent the increasingly urban electorate and proportionally overrepresent the rural areas with declining populations.

This was a result of the failure to reapportion seats in the legislature
on a regular basis to take into account shifts in population within and
between states. There was often an unwillingness on the part of the
dominant elites in these legislatures, many of whom came from rural
areas, to make changes which would threaten their hold on the levers
of power. Consequently, there were glaring inequalities in the size of
electoral districts, with some highly populated towns and cities having
fewer representatives than sparsely peopled country areas.

The Supreme Court had been asked to investigate whether such a
situation was constitutional, but in the case of *Colegrove* v *Green* (1946)
it declined to do so on the grounds that it wished to avoid entering
what it called 'the political thicket', full of party political controversies.
By the 1960s demographic changes in America made the problem
even more urgent, and in 1962 the Warren Court reversed the 1946
decision and examined the vexed question of reapportionment. The
Supreme Court took a major initiative in the case of *Baker* v *Carr*
(1962). It said that the state of Tennessee, which had not reapportioned its legislature since 1901, was acting unconstitutionally and
denying 'equal protection' to its urban citizens as required by the
Fourteenth Amendment. A series of related cases followed and all
ended with the same conclusion: states must provide electoral districts
that are fair and equal and provide, as far as possible, a 'one person,
one vote' system. The state of Georgia tried to argue that, even if its
lower chamber was based on this principle, the upper house could be
based on unequal districts to protect the rights of minorities, just as the
US Senate was designed to do at the national level. In *Reynolds* v *Sims*
(1964) the Court dismissed the 'federal analogy' on the grounds that
the political subdivisions of a state had never been independent units
but were simply subordinate administrative areas within the unitary
structure of the state.

The Supreme Court argued that the federal courts would have to
supervise the states to ensure compliance with the 'equal protection'
clause, and the state legislature would be obliged to submit its reapportionment plans to the judges to see whether they were within the guidelines laid down. A major furore developed as many conservatives argued
that this was again an example of interference with states' rights and
angrily protested that the Constitution does not lay down anywhere that
a 'one person, one vote' principle must be used in voting.

Earl Warren has said that he regarded this area of decision making
as the most important single area examined by the Supreme Court in

his sixteen years as Chief Justice. Not only was it one that was central to democracy; he felt that if everyone had fair representation in the elected branches of government then most problems could be resolved by the political process rather than being the subject of judicial decision making.[18]

3 The Rights of the Accused. Important steps were also taken during the 1960s in protecting the rights of accused persons. The Bill of Rights includes specific mention of individual rights in criminal cases, because it was recognized that these were an essential defence against a tyrannical government. The Fifth and Sixth Amendments are particularly relevant here.

No person shall ... be compelled in any criminal case to be a witness against himself, nor be deprived of life, liberty and property without due process of law. (The Fifth Amendment)

In all criminal prosecutions, the accused shall ... have the assistance of counsel for his defense. (The Sixth Amendment)

The basic rights 'to remain silent' and to legal counsel were extended to the states by a number of Supreme Court decisions which selectively incorporated these principles into the 'due process' clause of the Fourteenth Amendment.

In the case *of Gideon v Wainwright* (1963), the Court decided that a man convicted of a felony in Florida had been denied his rights as no legal counsel had been provided by the state for his assistance. Gideon had been found guilty in his trial, having been unable to afford to hire a lawyer to help defend him. Although government provision of legal advice to the poor had been accepted in federal cases, the Gideon episode led to the widespread development of Public Defender systems in the states. The principle involved in *Gideon v Wainwright* was that the poor should not be disadvantaged in criminal cases because of their financial status, and most people accepted this as a fair and reasonable argument, even if they did not welcome the extra burden on the taxpayer.

However, the next year saw a more controversial extension of the rights of the accused. The Supreme Court ruled in *Escobedo v Illinois* (1964) that a citizen had the right to counsel *before* a trial, and that he should be provided with legal advice, if necessary by the state, when

---

[18]Earl Warren, in Sheldon, op. cit., p. xviii.

general interrogation of a suspect becomes an accusation of a criminal charge. Furthermore, any information gained by the police without a counsel being present was not admissible as evidence in court. In *Miranda* v *Arizona* (1966) the Court further limited the admissibility of confessions as evidence. To ensure voluntary confessions by defendants, the police were to be obliged to warn the suspect of his rights to remain silent and to legal counsel. In the event of a citizen's waiving these rights, it was the responsibility of the police to show that he understood what he was doing.

The introduction of these procedural safeguards by the Court was greeted with great hostility by state governments, politicians and police forces across the country. It was argued that the police were being expected to fight crime with one arm tied behind their backs, and that the guilty would go free on technicalities in court. Opponents of the Warren Court argued that it was more concerned with protecting the criminal than with protecting society from the criminal. It should be remembered, however, that the main motivation of the Court was to prevent innocent people accused of crimes from being denied their rights, and from being overwhelmed by the physical and psychological pressures of their position.

4 Religion and the State. The First Amendment to the Constitution states that 'Congress shall make no law respecting an establishment of religion, or prohibiting the free exercise thereof'. The Supreme Court, under Earl Warren, supervised how the states acted in this field by ruling against policies that seemed to represent the establishment or support of a religion by any government or public body. In doing so, the Court ran into a great deal of hostility from ordinary Americans who saw such prohibition as an interference with the free exercise of their religion. The Court's decisions could be seen, depending upon one's point of view, as upholding the 'establishment clause' and protecting minorities who do not wish to see their tax dollars supporting churches or religions, or as an unwarranted interference in the rights of the majority within a state freely to practise their faith.

In *Engel* v *Vitale* (1962), the Supreme Court declared unconstitutional a non-denominational prayer that had been written by the New York State Regents for use in the schools, on the grounds that it was intended to promote religious views. In the next year, the Court went further in *School District, Abington* v *Schempp* (1963) and declared that Bible reading in public state-supported schools was unconstitutional if it was intended as worship or as a method of advancing religious beliefs. The Bible could, however, be used in an objective study of religions. Many American Christians were incensed at what they saw as the Court's support for the arguments put forward by atheists and humanists. An Alabama Congressman, George Andrews, declared: 'The Court has put the Negroes in the schools and now they've driven God out.'

The Court argued that, although the state cannot deny anyone the right to practise his religion, it cannot conversely, through majority rule, impose any set of beliefs on all its citizens. Free exercise of religion does not mean, therefore, that people may use the machinery of the state (such as government or school buildings) or tax moneys from all citizens to further or practise their beliefs.

The Burger and Rehnquist Courts

The activism of the Warren Court led to accusations that the judges were ignoring the Constitution and substituting their own liberal views when interpreting the law. We have seen how Republican Presidents were determined to use their appointment powers to alter the political balance of the nation's highest judicial body. Under Warren Burger (1969–86) and William Rehnquist (since 1986) the Court has moved to the right and in the 1980s there was more emphasis on judicial restraint and the other political branches of government being left to assume the leadership responsibility for major initiatives and social policies. 'Federal judges—who have no constituency—have a duty to respect legitimate policy choices made by those who do', the Court declared in a 1984 case involving interpretation of the 1984 Clean Air Act and this fairly summed up the philosophy of the Court. It also based its rulings on narrow statutory or constitutional grounds and avoided making judgements of general application. The Burger Court did not reverse the major decisions of the Warren Court, as some liberals had feared in the early 1970s. It could not, and would not have wished to turn the clock back to the situation before *Brown v Board of Education*, *Baker v Carr* and *Gideon v Wainwright*. It did, however, on occasions, modify and narrow interpretations in areas where the Warren Court had taken a pioneering role. Martin Shapiro concludes:

> the Burger Court spent its early years largely in marginal readjustments of Warren Court policies.... In grappling with the record of the early Burger Court most commentators concluded that it was an activist Court but one

that tended to use balancing doctrines to reach ad hoc policy judgments in particular cases rather than announcing major new constitutional rights, except in the abortion and death penalty areas.[19]

The Burger Court was a period of considerable stability in terms of its membership and, after the initial Nixon appointees of the early 1970s, only two new members—John Paul Stevens and Sandra Day O'Connor—were appointed in the next 15 years. Like previous Supreme Courts, the Burger Court was not divided into rigid conservative and liberal blocs. There were changing alliances and majorities among its members and a shifting middle ground with various Justices holding a pivotal position at various times. The political climate also changed in the United States so that judges who may have been regarded as conservatives when appointed in the early 1970s, such as Lewis Powell or Harry Blackmun, were increasingly seen in the 1980s as moderates or even liberals on some issues. The Burger Court was often described as factionalized and criticized for lack of leadership and it was certainly true that commentators who wanted to sum up the Court's philosophy in a simple or clear-cut way were frustrated. Consistent trends were hard to establish and predictions of the outcomes of particular cases were more and more difficult to make. However, despite its generally conservative reputation, the Burger Court more often than not frustrated the Reagan administration when it called for major changes in areas such as civil rights, abortion and school prayer. Attorney-General Robert Jackman wrote in 1940, a year before he was appointed to the Court, that:

> The Supreme Court is almost never really a contemporary institution—the Judiciary is ... the check of a preceding generation on the present one.

The Burger Court, appointed largely by earlier Presidents, upheld policies adopted by earlier administrations and laws passed by previous Congresses. In doing so Justices often invoked Supreme Court decisions of the 1960s and 1970s as the basis for their actions. The Burger Court generally continued the Warren Court's tradition of enlarging the Constitution's protection for individual and civil rights, while taking a decidedly more conservative view in criminal law cases where it favoured the arguments of the police and prosecutors three or four times as often as those of defendants.

[19]Martin Shapiro, op. cit., p. 59.

After William Rehnquist became Chief Justice in 1986 President Reagan had the opportunity to replace Lewis Powell with a more conservative judge, Anthony Kennedy. Bush's appointment of two conservatives, Souter and Thomas, to replace two liberals, Brennan and Marshall, shifted the balance of the Court even further to the right. Indeed, the 1990–91 term, before Thomas joined the Court, was marked by 'a surge in conservative activism' where the Court had policy objectives, particularly in the area of criminal law, and where it was more likely to depart from precedent in its rulings. At times the Court went beyond the questions immediately before it and addressed constitutional issues that dissenters said did not need to be tackled. Some commentators argued that this was precisely the kind of judicial activism for which conservatives used to criticize the Warren and Burger Courts.[20]

During the 1991–92 term a group of moderate conservatives, O'Connor, Kennedy and Souter, were seen as significant in resisting a trend further to the right and, in a number of cases, they parted from the more conservatives Justices, Rehnquist, Scalia and Thomas. However, by the 1994–95 session, O'Connor and Kennedy were voting more consistently with the other conservatives, providing a five-member bloc that formed a majority in the most important cases that year. The conservatives were increasingly assertive both in setting out their views and in questioning recent practices in a number of controversial areas, such as the proper balance between federal and state governments and race issues. Stevens and Souter were often to be found voting with the two Clinton appointees, Ginsburg and Breyer.[21]

1 Segregation and Race Relations.   In the field of race relations, the Burger Court said that proof of intent to discriminate must be shown rather than just a demonstration of discriminatory effects in housing and jobs. The Court accepted in 1971 that bussing children was a proper means of dealing with schools that are segregated as a result of official bias, and in 1976 it broadened the ban on segregated schools to include private as well as state-financed institutions. On the other hand, the Court turned down plans to solve city school segregation by bussing children between city centres and suburbs in a number of judgements between 1974 and 1977. These were based on the grounds that no clear intention to discriminate had been proven.

[20]*Congressional Quarterly Weekly Report*, 6 July 1991, pp. 1829–31.
[21]'The Supreme Court Ronald Reagan Wanted Has Arrived', *The Washington Post National Weekly Edition*, 10–16 July 1995.

In its first attempt to influence the Court on the issue of school bussing for desegregation the Reagan administration in 1983 sought to persuade the Court to use a Nashville case as the vehicle for reconsidering its support for the practice. However, the Justices refused to do so, leaving intact a lower court decision that required more bussing of Nashville pupils.

In the same year the Supreme Court also rejected an attempt by the administration to reverse a longstanding Internal Revenue Service policy denying tax-exempt status to racially discriminatory private schools and colleges. The government argued that in the absence of explicit authorization by Congress the IRS lacked the power to deny such exemptions. The Court in a ringing declaration that 'racial discrimination in education is contrary to public policy' concluded by 8–1 that schools and colleges practising discrimination were not entitled to tax-exempt status.

In 1977 the Supreme Court considered the case of *Regents of the University of California* v *Allan Bakke*. Bakke claimed that he had been discriminated against because, as a white male, he was unable to obtain one of sixteen quota places set aside out of a hundred at Davis Medical School for ethnic minorities, despite the fact that he had achieved higher test scores than some of the students accepted for these places. He believed that he was a victim of 'reverse discrimination' and the case had broad implications for the future enrolment policies in American higher education and 'affirmative action' programmes designed to help minorities. In an important judgement in June 1978 the Supreme Court found that Bakke had been illegally discriminated against because he was white and ordered the medical school to admit him. The Court's decision, by a 5–4 majority, yielded six separate opinions. It ruled that an institution could take race into account in future admissions selection, but that this was not to be the sole determining factor. Justice Powell in the leading opinion said that the state had a substantial interest in a properly devised admissions programme 'involving the competitive consideration of race and ethnic origin'.

When dealing with job discrimination the Court decided in June 1977 that seniority systems used within many companies were not necessarily illegal even if their effect was to favour white males over others in bidding for promotions, protection from redundancies and other benefits of years in the job. This weakened the basis for further 'past discrimination' suits which had been pressed by minority ethnic groups in recent years. The Rehnquist Court gave five important rulings in the 1988–89 session that demonstrated the new conservative majority. All five decisions were settled by a 5–4 majority and narrowed the options and redress available to minorities and women facing employment discrimination. For example, in *Wards Cove Packing Co. Inc* v *Antonio* the Court held that the burden is on plaintiffs to prove that an employer has no business necessity for practices with discriminating effects whereas previously the employer had to prove the practice was necessary. In *City of Richmond* v *Croson* the Court invalidated the practice of cities setting aside a certain number of contracts for minority-owned businesses while in another case involving firemen in Birmingham, Alabama the Court changed procedures to allow challenges by white workers to affirmative action programmes. Eleanor Holmes Norton of Georgetown University said:

> The Justices are finding technical and procedural outlets for their substantive hostility to existing civil rights statutes and decisions.[22]

Congress subsequently passed the 1991 Civil Rights Act to reverse the results of the Rehnquist Court decisions on employment discrimination. The conservative majority on the Court made it increasingly clear that they were uncomfortable with government classifications based on race. They argued that at the heart of the Constitution's guarantee of equal protection lies the requirement that the government must treat citizens as individuals, not simply as components of a racial, religious, sexual or national class. Thus in the 1994–95 session, in the case of *Adarand* v *Peña*, the Court set in motion a rolling back of federal affirmative action programmes, while it rejected a federal judge's school desegregation plan for Kansas City, Missouri. Clarence Thomas, the black conservative Justice who became increasingly vocal during this session, declared that 'It never ceases to amaze me that the courts are so willing to assume that anything predominantly black must be inferior'. The conservatives' 'colour-blind' ideal was also exemplified by their striking down of 'black majority' Congressional districts (see below).

2 Equal Representation and Reapportionment. In 1983 the Court reaffirmed the importance of the 'one person, one vote' principle in the drawing of boundaries for Congressional districts. It rejected a New

[22]*Time*, 26 June 1989, p. 27.

Jersey plan in which the difference between the largest and smallest constituency was 3,674 electors, less than 1%. A year later it accepted a revised proposal in which the difference was a mere 25 voters and in doing so the Justices stressed that states must strive for perfect mathematical equality in their plans. However, despite this strict application of the principle, states have been allowed more flexibility in drawing the districts for their own legislatures. On the same day the New Jersey Congressional plan was rejected the Court allowed Wyoming to go ahead with a proposal to give its least populous county its own representative in the legislature despite the fact that it resulted in far greater population variations among the districts than that which was held impermissible among New Jersey's Congressional districts. In the 1986 decision of *Davis* v *Bandemer* the Court opened the way for future challenges of alleged political gerrymandering in the drawing up of electoral districts.

Following the 1990 census which reapportioned the 435 Congressional seats, many states redrew their district lines under the provisions of the 1965 Voting Rights Act which requires them to safeguard the influence of minority voters. A number of states, either on their own initiative or under pressure from the Justice Department, created districts in which minorities made up the majority of electors. In so doing, the boundaries were often drawn so that the constituencies lacked geographical compactness or community of interest. In *Voinovich* v *Quilter* (1993), the Court accepted the right of states to concentrate racial minorities in certain voting districts in order to secure minority representation. However, in another case in the same year, *Shaw* v *Reno*, the Justices warned that race-conscious redistricting could sometimes constitute unfair discrimination against white voters and, while it did not strike down the North Carolina districts in question, it cast doubt on 'bizarrely shaped' constituencies and said that they must be closely scrutinized. In 1995, in *Miller* v *Johnson*, the Court went further and rejected Georgia's redistricting map, and in 1996 it decided by 5–4 to strike down three disputed districts in Texas (*Bush* v *Vera*) and others in North Carolina (*Shaw* v *Hunt*), where a group of white voters were continuing with a challenge to their state's Congressional map.

The Court concluded that, in balancing the requirements of the Voting Rights Act and the constitutional provision of equal protection, states should avoid making race the predominant factor in redistricting; to do so overstepped the line and became racial gerrymandering. On the other hand, the Justices did not rule out race-conscious redistricting altogether, but said that the states had to present a compelling justification for such action. Confusion surrounding the practical implications of these rulings seemed certain to lead to further litigation on the issue.[23]

3 The Rights of the Accused. In this area more than any other the Burger Court has followed a more conservative approach than the Warren Court, and it is clear that under William Rehnquist this tendency has been even more marked.

In *Harris* v *New York* (1971), the Justices decided that confessions extracted in violation of the rule set out in *Miranda* v *Arizona* could be used for the limited purpose of helping jurors decide whether the defendant was lying on the witness stand. It also ruled that the right of counsel does not apply to a confrontation between suspect and victim, arranged by the police prior to the lodging of formal charges.

In 1984 the Court approved the first exception since 1966 to the rule set out in *Miranda* v *Arizona* that suspects must be advised of their rights before they may be questioned. The Court held that in some situations considerations of public safety may require that a police officer question a suspect first—for example, about the whereabouts of a weapon—and only then inform him of his constitutional rights. However, later that year the Court reaffirmed that the *Miranda* warnings of the rights to remain silent and to the aid of a lawyer apply to questioning of all persons in custody regardless of the seriousness of their alleged offence. Although people may be questioned briefly, for example, over a traffic violation without being informed of these rights, once arrested this must be done immediately. Also in 1984 the Court approved a relaxation of the controversial 'exclusionary rule', first enunciated 70 years before, which bans the use of illegally obtained evidence in court. The Reagan administration backed the arguments of state prosecutors that it was time to relax major Warren Court rulings denying prosecutors the use of certain evidence. The Court approved two major exceptions to the exclusionary rule: the first provided that such evidence may be used if it is clear that it would have inevitably been discovered for reasons independent of improper police conduct and later in the term the Justices gave prosecutors what they had been wanting for almost two decades, a 'good faith' exception to

[23]*Congressional Quarterly Weekly Report,* 7 October 1995, pp. 3065–7 and 15 June 1996, pp. 1679–81.

the rule. They determined that, when police conduct a search based on a warrant, only to find out later that the warrant was in some way defective, the evidence obtained may still be used in court.

The Burger Court's approach was well demonstrated by the fact that in the 1982–83 session it resolved nine cases in which searches by law enforcement agencies were challenged as unconstitutional. In seven the Court upheld the search or arrest at issue and in an eighth upheld the police practice in general while finding that in the particular case the suspect's rights had been infringed.

However, the Burger Court also extended the right of counsel for poor defendants to include those facing minor as well as serious criminal charges and in 1981 limited the right of police to question a suspect before his lawyer arrives. In 1983 it struck down as unconstitutionally vague a California law that permitted police to arrest anyone on suspicion of a crime who did not provide them with reliable identification, saying that the law left the police too much discretion. In the same session the Court also held that it was unconstitutionally cruel and unusual punishment for South Dakota to jail for life, without possibility of parole, a man convicted of seven relatively minor and non-violent crimes.

The Rehnquist Court decided in 1989 that the government may seize a criminal defendant's assets that might have been used to pay attorneys' fees. Following Congressional legislation to allow forfeiture of assets from organized crime and drug-trafficking the Court rejected arguments that defendants' rights to due process and a choice of lawyer would be violated by such a seizure. In the same year the Court decided by 5–4 that the constitutional ban on 'cruel and unusual punishments' does not forbid the execution of youths who commit crimes at 16 or 17 years of age; nor does it automatically prohibit capital punishment for people who are mentally retarded, decisions which not surprisingly aroused considerable criticism. In another case in 1989 the Court decided that the police need not use 'the exact form' of the *Miranda* warnings to inform arrested suspects of their rights. In 1991 the Court decided in *Arizona* v *Fulimante* by 5–4 that a coerced confession used at a trial does not automatically taint a conviction (reversing a 1967 decision) and by 6–3 that the impact of a crime on victims and their families could be taken into account in sentencing a person convicted of murder. In *Harmelin* v *Michigan* it ruled by 5–4 that a state may require life in prison without parole for a first-time drug offence without violating the Constitution's ban on 'cruel and unusual punishments'. However, Justices did agree in the 1993 case of *Helling* v *McKinney* that an inmate in a Nevada state prison who was forced to share a cell with a heavy smoker was exposed to an unreasonable health risk and that his Eighth Amendment rights had been infringed. Overall the record clearly demonstrates the strong law and order emphasis of the Rehnquist Court.

4 Religion and the State. The relationship between church and state again became a prominent issue in American politics in the 1980s. President Reagan on many occasions expressed his view that the saying of prayers in America's public schools should be permitted and he backed a proposed Constitutional Amendment that would have reversed the Supreme Court decisions of the 1960s. The Burger Court dealt with a number of cases in this area including the use of public buildings for religious groups, school prayers, and so-called 'parochaid' cases which involve the question of public money supporting private parochial or religious schools.

Generally the Burger Court maintained the view of its predecessor that the Constitution requires a 'high wall' of separation between church and state and that government should demonstrate a neutrality to religion, neither promoting nor hindering a particular faith or faith generally. The Court reviewed at least a dozen different forms of aid to parochial schools and in only one or two cases did it find such support from the public purse permissible. For example, in 1985 the Court ruled that it was unconstitutional for New York City and Grand Rapids, Michigan to pay teachers who went into private parochial schools to teach remedial classes or provide counselling services on the basis that such arrangements fostered 'an excessive entanglement between church and state'. One of the exceptions which the Court allowed in the 1982–83 session was a Minnesota law which provided for a state tax credit for tuition fees, transport and textbooks for parents of children at *both* private and public schools. In a major departure from previous practice, the Rehnquist Court allowed the provision by a public authority of a sign-language interpreter for a deaf student who was attending a religious school (*Zobrest* v *Catalina Foothills School District* 1993).

In another major case in 1985 the Court declared unconstitutional an Alabama law authorizing a moment of silence for meditation or voluntary prayer in public schools. Advocates of school prayer felt that the concept of silent prayer might have been more acceptable to the Court than the recital of prayers by a class, which the previous year the

Court had reaffirmed as unconstitutional, but the Justices still insisted that it infringed their neutrality rule.

On the other hand, the Court in 1981 did rule that Missouri State University had violated the freedom of religion of its students by denying the use of its campus buildings to student religious groups when allowing such use by other student groups. Other decisions in the 1990s have widened public access by church groups in the use of school buildings for meetings outside school hours. In 1993 the Court decided that prayers may be said at high school graduation ceremonies if they are organized and led by the students, rather than by a member of the clergy, which they had ruled impermissible the previous year. In 1995 the Justices allowed government funding for a student Christian journal at the University of Virginia, thus lowering the wall between Church and state. In 1984 the Court permitted the City of Pawtucket, Rhode Island to include a Nativity scene in its Christmas holiday display, overruling a lower court's ban on such a display, saying that the creche simply depicted the historical origins of Christmas and whatever benefit accrues to one religion or all religions 'is indirect, remote and incidental'. In 1993 the Justices ruled unanimously that a Florida city had acted unconstitutionally in banning animal sacrifices because it was a direct attack on the religious practices and free exercise of religion by adherents of Santeria, most of whom were Cuban immigrants. Anthony Kennedy wrote for the Court:

> Legislators may not devise mechanisms, overt or disguised, designed to persecute or oppress a religion or its practices.[24]

5 Other Major Issue Areas. The Supreme Court under Burger and Rehnquist has sometimes belied its conservative reputation in its rulings on a range of other social issues. It has declared unconstitutional statutes that treat men and women differently (for example, in the work place in relation to medical coverage and retirement benefits) and in 1984–85 the Court supported a federal law banning employment discrimination based on age. It has held that mental patients cannot be confined by a state if they can survive safely in the community and it has ensured that inmates have procedural safeguards in prison, such as the right to a hearing before being disciplined.

In the area of First Amendment freedoms the Justices rejected a federal law which banned editorial comment on public broadcasting

---

[24]*Church of the Lukumi Babalu Aye* v *Hialeah.*

television channels as an infringement of freedom of speech of broadcasters and also struck down a $1000 limit on the independent expenditures by pressure group political action committees in Presidential election campaigns. Justice Rehnquist writing for the Court wrote that this was 'like allowing a speaker in a public hall to express his views while denying him the use of an amplifying system'. In 1996 a 7–2 majority in *FEC* v *Colorado Republican Federal Campaign Committee* ruled that political parties could spend as much money as they wished in Congressional races, so long as they acted without coordinating their contributions with candidates' campaigns, thus giving them the same rights as pressure groups in making independent expenditures.

In two controversial 5–4 decisions in 1989 and 1990 the Court supported the right of a member of the Revolutionary Communist Youth Brigade to burn the American flag, saying that the action was protected under the First Amendment's freedom of speech provision. The judges struck down as unconstitutional federal and state laws prohibiting desecration of the flag; what was surprising was that the two most recent Reagan appointees, Scalia and Kennedy, voted with the majority in these cases. The Supreme Court also decided unanimously that a 1988 federal law banning so-called dial-a-porn telephone messages was drawn too widely and also violated the First Amendment.

In 1997 the Court struck down a central part of the 1996 telecommunications legislation which banned the use of the Internet or online services to disseminate indecent or patently offensive material which might be seen by minors. In *Reno* v *ACLU* the civil liberties group argued that such restrictions were an unconstitutional infringement of the First Amendment.

The conservative view on 'states' rights' was not generally supported by the Supreme Court until the 1990s. Although the states have won major victories before the Court, it refused to resurrect as a guarantee of states' rights the Tenth Amendment which reserves power to the states or the people. The Justices rejected the state of Wyoming's argument that the 1974 federal law barring age discrimination against state employees infringed too far on states' rights. Moreover in 1985 the Court overturned its 1976 decision that Congress could not constitutionally tell state and local governments how much to pay their employees. Both the 1976 and 1985 decisions were settled by 5–4 votes and Justice Harry Blackmun's change of mind was enough to settle the issue. However, in 1992 in *New York* v *United States* the Supreme Court struck down part of a 1985 nuclear waste law which held that states were liable for waste generated by commercial nuclear reactors. More-over, in 1995 the Court's decision in *US* v *Lopez* supported the Tenth Amendment rights of the states and cited the limits on the commerce clause as a way of justifying federal intervention, something that had not been done since the New Deal era. The Justices ruled that a law banning the possession of guns near school playgrounds was an unac-ceptable extension of federal authority in the area of law and order— traditionally the preserve of the states. A challenge to the 1993 Brady law on gun control, requiring a waiting period for police checks to be made on the background of purchasers, was supported by the Court in 1997 in a 5–4 ruling, on the grounds that the background check was a federal mandate in violation of the Tenth Amendment. These cases demonstrate that the conservatives on the Court led by Chief Justice Rehnquist were much more willing than in the past to question the constitutional basis of Congressional acts.

Advocates of states' rights were, however, disappointed in 1995 when the Court ruled by 5–4 votes in the case of *Thornton* v *Arkansas* that the states had exceeded their powers by setting term limits for federal legislators. In a decision that effectively struck down laws passed by voters in 23 states, the majority argued that the relationship between citizens and the federal government was a distinct one and could not be regulated by states imposing additional qualifications for member-ship of Congress to those specified in the Constitution.

One of the most constitutionally significant decisions for many years came in the 1983 case of *Immigration and Naturalisation Service* v *Chadha* when the Court declared the use of the legislative veto weapon by Congress 'unconstitutional', thus potentially altering the delicate bal-ance of power between the legislative and executive branches of gov-ernment (see Chapter 3 for details).

In 1997 the Supreme Court was asked to determine the limits of Presidential immunity against civil actions. Paula Jones, a former employee of the Arkansas state government, accused Bill Clinton of sexual harassment while he was Governor, and her lawyers argued that she had the right to an early hearing of her case. President Clinton's counsel countered that a sitting President should have pro-tection from such suits until after his term of office has ended, on the basis that civil court cases of this type would be distracting and dam-age the President's ability to carry out his official duties. The Court, in a unanimous decision, found in favour of Ms. Jones and against the President.

In the case of *Roe* v *Wade*, a major decision in 1973, the Court declared that government must not interfere with the right of a woman to have an abortion in the first three months of pregnancy if she so wishes, but the effectiveness of this decision was restricted by a subsequent ruling in June 1977 that state and local governments could choose whether to finance the abortions of needy women when their health was not endangered.

In 1983 the Court reaffirmed a woman's constitutional right to an abortion and made it clear that state and local efforts to curtail this right would continue to be strictly scrutinized. The Reagan administration had urged the Court to withdraw from the abortion controversy and leave the issue to elected legislators to resolve. In 1989 the Supreme Court upheld a Missouri law in *Webster* v *Reproductive Health Services* that banned the use of state facilities and prohibited state employees from performing abortions on the ground that it 'leaves a pregnant woman with the same choices as if the state had chosen not to operate any public hospitals at all'. In *Rust* v *Sullivan* (1991) the Court upheld federal regulations barring workers at publicly funded clinics from counselling pregnant women about abortion (rules that were reversed by the new Clinton administration in 1993). In the 1992 case of *Planned Parenthood of Southeastern Pennsylvania* v *Casey* Justices took the middle way on the abortion issue by upholding restrictions by the state of Pennsylvania as legal, while at the same time affirming a woman's right to have an abortion. These decisions stopped short of reversing the *Roe* v *Wade* decision and while it indicated that a Court majority may exist in the future for such a course of action observers also felt that the first woman Justice, Sandra Day O'Connor, did not relish being the swing vote in a decision to completely reverse *Roe* v *Wade*.

The Political Nature of the Supreme Court

Robert McCloskey has pointed out that the Supreme Court is neither completely a judicial body nor completely a policy-making and political body; it has managed to blend both in a complex mixture.[25] It has been apparent that politics play a crucial role in the appointment, working and decision making of the American Supreme Court and many of its judgements have had broad policy implications. What is

[25]R. McCloskey, *The American Supreme Court* (University of Chicago Press 1960), p. 20.

more the federal judiciary has been forced to become involved in detailed regulation by devising remedial actions, drawing up electoral boundaries and supervising the actions of other government bodies in order to ensure that the rights it has asserted are actually granted in practice. However, the Court is limited in a number of important ways. It does depend in the main on the executive branch to enforce the law it has interpreted. The Court can also only wait and react to cases that are brought into the judicial system. Unlike the President and Congress, the Supreme Court cannot, by itself, initiate policy making. Therefore the Court may find itself dealing with such matters as family or lifestyle issues because cases on these matters are brought before them and they are too significant to be refused judgement. This may be so, even at a time when the conservative majority tries to disclaim such an intrusive role in everyday life.[26]

Finally, the Justices are aware that they are appointed to their positions and must use their powers sparingly, so that wherever possible direct confrontation is avoided with the democratically elected branches of government. The judges are part of the society within which they are working and they are subject to many of the same influences and prejudices as elected politicians, but the Court's high standing with the public would be threatened if it resisted for long periods clear trends in public opinion. The Court's friends and enemies depend upon the nature of its decisions at any one time; it has been attacked in turn by conservative and liberal politicians. Its decisions have often been controversial and it has been in the centre of the political arena precisely because the questions it examines are in important areas of vital interest to society and democracy. Professor Archibald Cox explains why the Court has managed to command general support for its judgements as follows:

> The Court must know us better than we know ourselves … the roots of its decisions must already be in the nation. The aspirations voiced by the Court must be those the community is willing not only to avow but in the end to live by, for the power of the constitutional decisions rests upon the accuracy of the Court's perception of this kind of common will and upon the Court's ability, by expressing its perception, ultimately to command a consensus.[27]

Richard Hodder-Williams has argued that the legitimacy of the Court, in the sense that people accept its judgements as authoritative and its

---

[26]*Congressional Quarterly Weekly Report*, 19 September 1992, pp. 2813–16.
[27]Archibald Cox, *The Role of the Supreme Court in American Government* (Oxford: The Clarendon Press 1976), pp. 117–18.

role as proper, has been threatened by three factors in recent times: the division in partisan support in the executive and legislative branches preventing a dominant political consensus in Washington on the right judgements of the Court; the increasingly open way that interest groups use litigation as part of their overall political strategy and embroil the Court in the most contested controversies of the day; and the extent to which the Reagan administration set out publicly to influence the judicial branch as a whole and the Court's jurisprudence in particular. He concludes:

> These developments appeared to pose a very real threat to the mythic role of the Supreme Court as the impartial guardian of the Constitution and thus offered a real challenge to its legitimacy.[28]

Despite these difficulties and that of finding consensus in a society that is deeply divided on many of the issues that come before it today, the role of the Supreme Court is to maintain the Constitution as a living document by interpreting it in the light of the needs of a complex modern industrialized society. The Founding Fathers could not have predicted, for example, that one day the Fourth Amendment's prohibition of 'unreasonable searches and seizures' would be used to prevent, in most cases, the police invading the privacy of the individual by the use of electronic bugging devices on telephones (*Katz v United States,* 1967).

The Supreme Court is, by its nature, the one institution set up at the Philadelphia Convention that can take the long term into account as it has no elections or constituents to worry about, and for similar reasons it can protect minority rights from the prospect of a 'tyranny of the majority'.

Some Further Reading

Henry J. Abraham, *The Judicial Process* (Oxford University Press 1986)

Henry J. Abraham, *The Judiciary: The Supreme Court in the Governmental Process* (Allyn and Bacon 1987)

Henry J. Abraham, *Justices and Presidents* (Oxford University Press 1992)

---

[28]Richard Hodder-Williams, 'Constitutional Legitimacy and the Supreme Court', in *Developments in American Politics*, Gillian Peele, Christopher J. Bailey and Bruce Cain (eds) (Macmillan 1992), p. 139.

Sheldon Goldman and Thomas P. Jahnige, *The Federal Courts as a Political System* (Harper and Row 1985)

R. Hodder-Williams, *The Politics of the US Supreme Court* (George Allen and Unwin 1980)

William Lasser, *The Limits of Judicial Power: The Supreme Court in American Politics* (University of North Carolina Press 1989)

Robert McKeever, *Raw Judicial Power? The Supreme Court and American Society* (Manchester University Press 1993)

Thomas R. Marshall, *Public Opinion and the Supreme Court* (Unwin Hyman 1989)

David M. O'Brien, *Storm Center: The Supreme Court in American Politics* (Norton 1993)

H. W. Perry, *Deciding to Decide: Agenda Setting in the Supreme Court* (Harvard University Press 1991)

Elder Witt, *The Supreme Court at Work* (Congressional Quarterly Press 1990)

Bob Woodward and Scott Armstrong, *The Brethren—Inside the Supreme Court* (Secker and Warburg 1980)

5

Pressure Group Politics

We have observed already that politics in the United States can be seen as a continuous process of different groups competing to persuade the formal institutions to reflect their interests and objectives in the official policies of the nation, state or locality.[1] Having examined the working of the three branches of the federal government, it is now time to consider how these groups operate, what contribution they make to the political process, and how the political system provides checks on their power.

Pressure groups and political parties are often described as 'informal' political institutions, because although they are not mentioned in the Constitution as official bodies, an understanding of their role in the system is essential for a proper appreciation of policy making. Indeed, in our consideration of the formal institutions the importance of these bodies should already have been clear. Pressure groups are organized attempts to influence government policy rather than institutions which try to control the government and enter candidates in elections for office. In this respect they are different from parties, which are examined in the next chapter. Pressure groups should also be distinguished from the many social groups that exist to promote objectives that have no political content—sports clubs, operatic societies, rotary clubs, parent-teacher associations and private charities are formed by groups of people who have similar interests, but their common activities do not normally involve government or attempts to influence its policy. On the other hand, if there is the danger of a major highway being built across the sports club's field, or if the

[1]See Chapter 1, p. 1.

government proposes to change the tax status of a charity, then even these groups may enter the political arena.

Pressure groups have an important role in the political system; they are conveyors of demands from the ordinary American citizens to the decision makers, intermediaries that can provide both ideas and reactions to government policies. In a democratic system, the importance of such bodies in the two-way process of political communication can hardly be overemphasized.

FIGURE 5.1

Pressure Groups in the Political System

The American System and Pressure Group Activity

It has often been said that the American political system is particularly open to pressure group influence, and even in the early nineteenth century Alexis De Tocqueville commented:

> Better use has been made of association and this powerful instrument of action has been applied to more varied aims in America than anywhere else in the world.[2]

What was evident to a European visitor to the United States in those days has continued to be a factor of major political importance as a result of a number of social, cultural and institutional influences.

1 The Diversity of American Society.   In Chapter 1 it was emphasized that America is a country of rich social diversity. The many ethnic and national backgrounds of its people, the different interests of its regions

---

[2]Alexis De Tocqueville, *Democracy in America*, Vol. 1 (Fontana 1968), p. 232.

and the complexity of its economy have all contributed to making the United States a country ripe for the development of competing pressure groups. Since De Tocqueville wrote his major works, America has had widespread and heterogeneous immigration, a tremendous growth in its territory, and the movement from a fairly simple agrarian society to a vastly more complicated industrial and technological nation. With greater division of labour and economic specialization, and with increasing government intervention which has accompanied industrialization, the number and variety of groups affected by public policy who wish to protect their interests have grown dramatically. Groups formed to represent both the recipients and the providers of public services in areas such as health and welfare have a strong interest in the continuance and possible expansion of those services.

2 The Political Culture. The American political culture has encouraged the growth of pressure groups as legitimate methods of free expression in a democracy. The constitutional guarantees of free speech and press and, most particularly, freedom of assembly are of vital importance to the development of such associations, and in states which do not allow these rights pressure groups have been effectively curtailed. The acceptance by Americans of pressure groups is based on the belief that private groups have a right to be heard as long as they work within the law and the constitutional system. There is little support for the view that such groups are inimical to the public interest and are destructive of national unity, an approach which finds support in many countries where pressure groups are discouraged or work only under severe social and legal constraints.

3 The Decentralized Nature of American Government. The organization of the formal governmental institutions also provides many opportunities for pressure groups to exert influence in the policy-making process. Pressure groups inevitably seek contacts with those decision makers who have the power to affect their particular interests, and the decentralized and diffuse nature of American government has led to there being many 'access points' which are open to these organizations. The separation of powers means that the legislature, executive and judiciary, as well as bodies such as independent regulatory commissions, can all have a crucial role in particular areas of policy. The federal structure entails possible approaches to the national or state authorities, or to a variety of local government bodies. The multiplicity of official positions at various levels in America has resulted in there being more 'access points' than in other political systems, but they are not all of equal importance to pressure groups. Those interested in defence or foreign policy will obviously see that most decisions in these areas are made in Washington, and therefore they will concentrate on the Defence and State Departments and on Congressmen who have seats on the relevant House and Senate committees. On the other hand, groups interested in education will find that access to local authorities, such as school boards, will probably be as important, if not more so, than contacts in the state capital or in Washington. Changes in Congress in the 1970s and 1980s made the legislative process both more open and more complex. The opening up of committee sessions to public scrutiny and the televising of both chambers means that groups can monitor the activities of legislators more closely. At the same time decentralization of authority to sub-committees and overlapping jurisdiction on matters such as environmental or foreign and trade policy within Congressional committees (as well as executive departments and agencies) has provided more access points for groups to approach. However, it has also made the task of influencing policy more complicated and uncertain in terms of outcome achieved, as they have to spread their efforts across a number of decision makers.

Not only are there thousands of official decision makers: many of them are elected to their positions and this provides a further opportunity for direct contact between candidates and pressure groups.

The American system is particularly vulnerable to pressure group influence partly because of the large number of potential office-holders who require financial resources to fight elections. Officials such as judges, sheriffs, attorneys and coroners, who are appointed in most countries, continue to be elected to their positions in most parts of the United States. In addition at state and local level issues may be determined not by elected representatives at all but by popular vote in referenda. The campaigns on such propositions are normally organized and financed by pressure groups which have a direct interest in the issues involved.

4 The Weakness of Party. One other side-effect of the separation of powers system and localized politics is that party cohesion among Congressmen and state legislators has tended to be weaker than in centralized parliamentary systems, although we have seen in Chapter 2 that partisan voting has increased in recent times. Legislators in

TABLE 5.1

'Access Points' in the American Political System

	Legislature	Executive	Judicial	Other Agencies
Federal	House of Representatives, Senate, Committee members and chairmen	President, Cabinet Secretaries, Civil servants	Supreme Court, Other federal courts	Independent Regulatory Commissions
State	State legislature (two houses),* Committee members and chairmen	Governor, Department heads, State officials	State supreme court, Courts of Appeals	State commissions and agencies
Local	Councils, School Boards, Other local boards	Mayors, Other elected officials, Local government officials	Other state courts	Local commissions

*Except Nebraska.

America are able to take independent stands on policy issues, knowing that their votes will not affect the existence or future of the executive, and this freedom means that they are more useful to pressure groups. Parties cannot dictate to legislators how they must vote on major issues: neither can pressure groups, but they do have the opportunity of influencing the direction of those votes.

American political parties are relatively weak in terms of both organization and discipline and this also provides opportunities for pressure groups. The use of primary elections to nominate candidates for office has taken power away from the party leaders and activists and broadened participation to a wider electorate. The need for candidate-centred organizations to obtain finance and the relatively small percentage of the electorate who use their votes in primary elections gives well organized single-issue pressure groups a good opportunity to make their presence felt.

Different Types of Pressure Group

The literature on pressure groups, particularly in America, has often been somewhat confused by the lack of an agreed terminology among the political scientists who have studied this form of political activity. However, we shall find it useful to apply the term 'pressure group' to all those organizations concerned with political objectives, while attempting to subdivide these groups into two major categories. Those pressure groups who are primarily self-interested, and whose goals are to protect, defend and promote the interests of their own members are known as 'interest groups'. Frequently such groups have important economic power and generally they comprise the most influential pressure groups in the United States. They tend to have a clearly defined clientele which is often restricted to those with specific occupations, financial interests or qualifications. Examples of 'peak' business interest groups which seek to represent a wide range of commercial organizations include the *National Association of Manufacturers* and the *US Chamber of Commerce* which speaks for some 180,000 businesses, many belonging to local, state and regional chambers. They have been joined by the *Business Round Table*, representing the largest corporations, and the *National Federation of Independent Business* which puts forward the interests of small businesses. There are also numerous trade associations such as the *American Petroleum Institute* which speaks for the major oil companies, and the *National Association of Realtors*, the estate agents' group, as well as individual corporations that lobby on their own behalf.

The *AFL–CIO* (American Federation of Labor–Congress of Industrial Organizations) is an alliance of trade unions established in 1955 from the craft-based AFL and the industrially based CIO. The influence of organized labour has declined in recent times with only 15% of the workforce belong to trade unions, less than half the proportion of the 1950s. Unions have failed to win support in the Southern and Sunbelt states and there are concentrations of membership in the traditional heavy industries of the North East. However, while unions in the private sector have been in decline, public employee unions, such as the *American Federation of Teachers* and the *American Federation of State, County and Municipal Employees*, have grown rapidly in the last two decades.

Professional bodies are prominent among the ranks of interest groups; the *American Medical Association* is the main organization representing doctors and has had a long history of lobbying on health issues, while we have already seen in Chapter 4 the importance of the *American Bar Association*, the lawyers' professional body, and how it has influence within government, particularly over the appointment of judges. America's farmers traditionally had considerable political influence in states where agriculture was a major part of the economy but this has reduced as the numbers working on farms have declined. The *American Farm Bureau Federation* is the largest of the general membership or peak groups but its influence and that of the *National Farmers' Union* has declined as the number of specialist commodity associations has increased. Examples include the *Associated Milk Producers*, the *National Wool Growers' Association* and the *American Cattlemen's Association*.

The largest pressure group in America is the *American Association of Retired Persons*. Founded in 1958, its membership increased from one million in 1968 to 33 millions by 1991, that is more than half of all Americans over fifty years of age. The 'grey lobby' has not only formidable voting power but the ability to organize immediate and effective grassroots campaigns whenever it sees a threat to, for example, social security or Medicare services. It employs a legislative and policy staff of 125 as well as 18 specialist lobbyists in Washington.

The second category of pressure groups includes those who are attempting to secure political objectives which are in the interests of people other than themselves, or are concerned with promoting a cause which in their view will help society as a whole. These associations are often called 'promotional groups' or citizens' groups based around an idea and at times a single issue with no occupational basis of membership. About a third of these groups have been formed since 1975 and have contributed to a huge expansion of pressure group activity. Burdett A. Loomis and Allan J. Cigler claim that a 'participation revolution' has occurred as large numbers of citizens have become active in an increasingly diverse range of protest groups, citizens' organizations and specialist associations.[3] In addition to those who wish to play an active role in such bodies, increased affluence has created a large potential for 'cheque book' membership, where people can make an expressive statement of support for a group at the cost of a relatively small subscription without incurring other time-consuming obligations. Loomis and Cigler note that it has been mainly white, educated, middle-class voters who contribute to citizens' groups.[4]

[3]Allan J. Cigler and Burdett A. Loomis, 'The Changing Nature of Interest Group Politics', in *Interest Group Politics*, Loomis and Cigler (eds) (Congressional Quarterly Books 1991), p. 10.
[4]Allan J. Cigler and Burdett A. Loomis, ibid., p. 22.

Common Cause, 'a national citizens' lobby' of approximately 250,000 members has advocated liberal reforms in the governmental and electoral systems, having been a particularly strong proponent of changes in the seniority system for Congressional chairmanships and for statutory limits on campaign expenditure and public funding in elections. *Common Cause* was one of the most prominent 'public interest' groups that were particularly active in the 1970s and 1980s in trying to influence policy in areas such as consumer protection, the environment, health and minority rights, often opposing the views of business corporations and government agencies. Ralph Nader, the best known public interest lobbyist, is head of an umbrella organization called *Public Citizen* which has contacts with more than a dozen organizations such as *Congress Watch,* the *Health Research Group* and the *Center for Auto Safety. The League of Women Voters* has also been interested in government, but on a less partisan basis; its main concerns have been to promote civic responsibility and participation in politics. *The American Civil Liberties Union* has taken up the cause of accused persons and has advocated reforms in the administration of justice and strongly opposed the use of capital punishment. The *Sierra Club* and the *Friends of the Earth* have been organized across the country to campaign for conservation of the environment while the *National Organization of Women* has been very vocal in advocating the passage of the 'Equal Rights Amendment' to the Constitution, the greater representation of women in government, and equal treatment in employment, housing and other areas. *The National Association for the Advancement of Colored People* and the *National Urban League* have been active in civil rights and racial desegregation campaigns while the 'religious right', through groups such as *Christian Coalition,* has emphasized 'family issues' with its strong opposition to abortion, bans on prayers being said in state schools and what it regards as pornographic literature and television programmes. In recent decades there has also been the growth of 'think tanks' and policy institutes such as the *Heritage Foundation* and the *American Enterprise Institute* which have submitted arguments on a range of issues. There are also a variety of ideological groups ranging from the left-wing *Americans for Democratic Action* to many of the 'new right' groups such as the *Free Congress Foundation*

There has been a very significant increase in the number of 'single issue' groups active in American politics in recent years. They are intensively organized for or against particular policies such as abortion or gun control and have caused concern by their campaigns to unseat politicians who disagree with them on one emotional issue. They have been able to use appeals for money carefully directed at those who have been identified as sympathizers and to raise substantial funds for their cause. Many organizations are principally interest groups but have a promotional aspect which helps them justify their objectives to the public at large. In this way they can claim that they are not merely self-interested but are concerned with the welfare of the community. Other groups are 'hybrids' in the sense that some members join to defend an economic interest while others advocate the same cause but on ideological grounds. For example, the *National Rifle Association* numbers among its membership those who have a direct commercial interest in selling guns and who therefore object to attempts by government to regulate the trade. However, it also has considerable support from gun owners and political conservatives who argue that the Second Amendment to the Constitution guarantees the right of citizens 'to bear arms'. These people argue that such a right is fundamental to the maintenance of a free society, that any monopoly of arms by the government could lead to a tyranny, and that regulation would take away the right of citizens to defend themselves against criminal attacks. In the mid-1990s attacks on the extremist positions taken by the NRA led to the resignation of former President George Bush and thousands of other members. However, it still exerted considerable influence on many members of the Republican-controlled 104th Congress.

Methods of Pressure Group Influence

The American political system provides numerous opportunities for pressure groups to influence the official decision makers, but the methods used by a particular group will depend upon the objectives it is seeking to achieve and its position with regard to size, finance and the strategies of its leaders.

1 Electioneering

Clearly any group has an advantage if decision makers in the relevant areas are sympathetic to the organization's interests, and many pressure groups attempt to influence the outcome of elections by advancing the campaigns of friendly politicians or trying to bring about the defeat of hostile opponents.

Fighting elections can be very expensive and many pressure groups, particularly wealthy interest groups, provide campaign contributions. The election finance reforms of the 1970s put limits on the amounts any one contributor could give but provided a vehicle—the political action committee—to circumvent the new spending restrictions. Federal law limits direct PAC contributions to 5,000 dollars to each candidate for each election, primary or general, but there is no limit on the number of PACs that can be formed or their own independent expenditures on campaigns. Independent expenditures are those made without the knowledge of or consultation with the candidate or his managers. The great bulk of money from political action committees goes to Congressional candidates who, unlike Presidential candidates, are not eligible for public campaign financing (see Chapter 7).

Congressional candidates are not limited in the overall amount of money they can accept from PACs. While many pressure groups are eager to support their friends at election time they are also finding that they themselves are subject to a form of reverse lobbying in which legislators do the wining, dining and cajoling for campaign contributions. The outcome of these factors is that in 1993–94 PACs dispensed $189.4 million to candidates in Senate and House races of which 62% went to Democrats. Not surprisingly, the Republicans received a higher proportion of PAC money after they won control of Congress in 1994 and held the levers of legislative power.

There has also been a tremendous growth in the number of PACs since the campaign finance reform of 1974 which followed the Watergate scandal. In that year 608 PACs were registered with the new Federal Election Commission; by the end of 1995 there were 4,016. Most of the growth was in the 1970s and the peak year was 1988 when 4,268 PACs were registered. Business corporations' PACs have soared from 89 to 1,674 in 1995. Their largesse is shared by both parties' candidates but with some bias to the Republicans. The 334 Trade Union PACs are far more partisan with almost all their contributions going to Democratic candidates.[5] The percentage of PAC contributions going to incumbents seeking re-election rose from 57% in 1978 to 79% in 1989–90, but fell to 72% in both the 1991–92 and 1993–94 election cycles. This was explained by the larger number of open races in those years. PACs contributed 18% of their donations to candidates in open elections, but gifts to those challenging incumbents

[5]Figures from Federal Election Commission reports, November 1995 and January 1996.

fell to 10% of the total. PACs are therefore tending to try and keep in office the members they know and with whom they feel comfortable. In 1992 only 11 incumbent Congressmen refused to accept PAC contributions. However, the actual percentage of PAC contributions to campaign funds varied widely. The average House incumbent fighting for re-election obtained 44% of his total funds from PACs compared with 30% for the average Senate incumbent.[6] Critics express concern at the amounts of special interest money involved in American election campaigns and bills have been presented to Congress limiting spending by both candidates and PACs at elections. This has been exacerbated by the large amounts of 'soft money' given by pressure groups to political parties, which has no limits placed on it and is not regulated by law.[7]

In June 1989 President Bush outlined a plan that he said would 'free our electoral system from the grips of special interests'. He proposed to eliminate corporate, union and trade association PACs which contributed $136 million or 29% of the $476 million raised by Congressional candidates in 1988. His plan would retain PACs formed by single issue or ideological groups but reduce the maximum contribution by half to $2,500. Congress took no action on the President's proposal but House and Senate Democrats overcame their own differences on the issue and passed the 1992 Campaign Finance Bill, while knowing that President Bush would find it unacceptable and would veto it. The legislation was designed to limit spending on Congressional campaigns within the framework of the 1976 Supreme Court decision in *Buckley* v *Valeo* which ruled that mandatory restrictions on campaign expenditure were an unconstitutional infringement of free speech. The bill thus provided incentives for compliance in the form of federal financial benefits. Spending in primary and general elections campaigns would be capped at $600,000 for House seats and between $1 million and $9.5 million for Senate races, depending on the size of the state. House candidates would receive matching public funds for the small donations they raised, while Senate candidates would receive federally funded vouchers to buy television advertising time. PAC contributions would be limited as well. While House candidates could still receive, as now, up to $5,000 from individual PACs, they could not receive more than $200,000 in aggregate from such groups. Senate candidates would be restricted to $2,500

[6]*Congressional Quarterly Weekly Report*, 27 March 1993, pp. 723–7.

[7]See Alan Grant, 'Financing American Elections', *Politics Review*, November 1995; Alan Grant, 'The 1996 Elections and Campaign Finance in the United States', *Talking Politics*, Autumn 1997.

from individual PACs, with an overall cap of 20% of their total campaign limit from this source. President Bush vetoed the bill as he had warned he would if it contained what he saw as objectionable features: spending limits on campaigns which Republicans argued would hurt challengers more than incumbents, public funding through the use of taxpayers' money ('foodstamps for politicians' as critics labelled it), different rules for the House and Senate elections and the continued role of 'special interest', as opposed to issue-oriented, PACs.

In May 1993, after prolonged discussions with Democrats in Congress, President Clinton proposed a bill with similar provisions to that which Bush had vetoed a year before, saying that the $150 million cost of public funding would be met by a tax on pressure groups' lobbying expenses. The Senate passed a bill in June 1993 which differed in a number of ways from the President's plan and included a total ban on PAC contributions. The House version passed in November 1993 retained the $5,000 limit on PAC donations. However, after a long delay during which Democratic Congressional leaders tried to reach agreement on a compromise, the bill was finally reported out with a provision for a $3,000 limit. By September 1994, with the elections approaching, Republicans were intent on blocking legislation which they described as pro-incumbent, partisan and unconstitutional. In the Senate a filibuster meant the bill fell eight votes short of the 60 necessary for cloture. President Clinton was criticized for failing to campaign publicly for the bill and exerting insufficient influence on Democratic legislators to reach an early compromise. Bipartisan proposals for campaign finance reform in the 104th Congress also included a ban on PACs but, in the face of hostility from the Republican leadership, they failed to win sufficient support.

The debates on election campaign reform show that there are sharp differences of view concerning PACs, their role and impact on American politics. Opponents have argued that their gifts come with strings attached and that the legislative process is tainted by the buying of Congressmen's votes. PACs are also criticized for being internally undemocratic and unaccountable for their actions, for undermining the role of political parties and for the growth of divisive and negative single-issue politics. Supporters of PACs, on the other hand, argue that they are merely the modern method of channelling money to pay for expensive election campaigns, that limits and public disclosure of contributions prevent corruption and that the banning of PAC funding would simply lead to rich individuals having more influence, with more undisclosed gifts. They claim that the range of PACs reflects the diversity of American society and competition between them prevents the dominance of any particular groups. It is also argued that PACs have increased political awareness and participation among the electorate. PACs claim that their contributions at most help them to gain access to legislators and an opportunity to make their case on issues of concern to them.[8] Given the range of factors that influence Congressional voting decisions (see Chapter 2), political scientists have found it very difficult to identify causation, as opposed to correlation, between PAC donations and the votes of legislators on bills.

Groups who contribute to campaign funds hope that in return they will receive a sympathetic hearing after the election but it should be noted that big money does not necessarily guarantee success at the polls for the candidate. Pressure groups can also provide something else at elections which is occasionally even more important than money—voluntary manpower. Organizations with large memberships, such as trade unions, can provide an invaluable source of campaign workers, people who will actually mobilize the voters by knocking on doors, delivering publicity or providing transport to the polls. Christian Coalition regularly distribute millions of voter guides to churchgoers, informing them of candidates' positions on issues important to the organization. It is also worth remembering that large numbers of individuals who identify with, or belong to, particular groups, such as Hispanics, gays or the elderly, may comprise a substantial proportion of the electorate in particular districts or states. Candidates will have to take account of the views of pressure groups that claim to speak on their behalf. The endorsement of a candidate by a group leader may also be helpful if the group has a large following, but such support from extremist or minority groups can be an embarrassment and more of a hindrance than a help to the candidate.

2 Lobbying

Most large pressure groups either employ full-time lobbyists in Washington or hire lobbyists on a part-time basis to represent their interests. Lobbying is the institutionalized form of the traditional right of petitioning government, and the 'professional persuaders' work permanently in

[8]Alan Grant, 'Political Action Committees in American Politics', in *Contemporary American Politics*, Alan Grant (ed.) (Dartmouth 1995).

Washington and the fifty state capitals, as well as communicating with
local government when necessary. To be effective, a lobbyist must know
the workings of the political system very well and have personal contacts with decision makers in the relevant policy areas. It is not surprising that many lobbyists are former government officials, Congressional
aides who have the expertise and have built up these relationships
over a number of years, or are members of prestigious Washington law
firms. The number of lobbyists has increased substantially in recent
years and concern has also grown about their influence. The annual
publication *Washington Representatives* listed more than 5,000 people in
1979 and by 1991 this had increased to 13,500. In November 1989
Congress passed a new restriction on Cabinet members, White House
staff and Congressmen from lobbying former colleagues until one year
after leaving office. This followed the much publicized case of Michael
Deaver, the former Reagan aide, who was accused of exploiting his
contacts with the White House on behalf of clients immediately after
leaving the administration. In 1995 Congress passed new regulations
tightening the rules on lobbying and banning members or their staffs
from accepting gifts from pressure groups (see 'The Checks on Pressure Group Influence' below).

In recent years it has not been only domestic pressure groups that
have employed lobbyists in Washington. Foreign governments increasingly seek representation in this way: former Senate Foreign Relations
Committee Chairman William Fulbright, and former Attorney-General
Richard Kleindienst were acting on behalf of Arab states during 1977.
The exposure of the so-called 'Koreagate' scandal showed that Tongsun
Park, a South Korean businessman, was attempting to buy influence
on Capitol Hill in the hope of affecting American foreign policy. Park
was said to have paid large sums of money to individual Congressmen
in prominent positions.

The White House and federal government departments also employ
a number of full-time officials whose job is to persuade Congressmen
to support particular programmes. Many state and city governments
maintain permanent representatives in Washington to look after their
interests. Therefore, although it would be misleading to describe such
formal governmental institutions as pressure groups, they do lobby on
behalf of their policies.

It should be emphasized that, for private pressure groups, lobbying
does not merely mean trying to persuade legislators; often it is even
more important to contact and persuade civil servants, administrators

of state governments, or officials of regulatory agencies who formulate and execute policy. Lobbyists are communication links between pressure groups and politicians and officials. They let government know the views of the group they represent, hoping to persuade decision makers to promote these policies. They also inform the group's headquarters of any moves or developments in government circles which may affect the organization's position, so that leaders have an 'early warning system' and do not suddenly find themselves facing the prospect of hostile policies which have already been formulated and are too far advanced to change. Lobbyists can provide legislators with information and drafts of legislation, and their hope is that by being helpful and constructive they will be able to build a relationship of trust and mutual convenience which will pay dividends in the long term. Lester Milbrath, in his book *The Washington Lobbyists*, showed that most Congressmen feel that they obtain useful information from pressure groups on both legislation and administration, and that few felt that lobbyists tried to exert an unreasonable pressure on them.[9] Robert H. Salisbury argues that the increasing number of pressure groups and today's complex world of interdependent interests and policies means that it may often be unclear what the 'true interests' of a group actually are. Lobbyists have been forced to shift much of their energy and activity from advocating policies and influencing government officials to information gathering and analysis. He concludes that organizations in Washington:

> are engaged in a never-ending process of learning, assessment and calculation; and timely information, much of it available only from government, is the sine qua non of this process.[10]

Salisbury suggests that we should not ignore the extent to which pressure groups have come to Washington out of need and dependence rather than because they have influence.

3 Use of Court Litigation

The American judiciary has an important role in interpreting the Constitution and the law, and pressure groups occasionally attempt to

[9]Lester Milbrath, *The Washington Lobbyists* (Rand McNally 1963).
[10]Robert H. Salisbury, 'The Paradox of Interest Groups in Washington – More Groups, Less Clout', in *The New American Political System, Second Version*, Anthony King (ed.) (AEI Press 1990), pp. 225–9.

use the courts as a method of influencing policy. An organization can seek a court injunction as a tactical manoeuvre, for example, to delay a decision until further pressure can be exerted on the legislative and executive branches, and can also help finance and provide legal counsel for a defendant or plaintiff in a court case. The tradition of *amici curiae* (friends of the court) allows a pressure group's spokesman to give evidence to the court, thus publicizing the objectives of the group. In *Brown* v *Board of Education,* the National Association for the Advancement of Colored People saw the case as a test of the constitutionality of segregation laws in general. The American Civil Liberties Union also backed the attempt to challenge the 1974 federal election funding laws by obtaining a Supreme Court ruling that the regulations were 'unconstitutional'.

Many business organizations have retained prestigious law firms to represent them in the courts whenever it is necessary. Business groups tend to be frequent users of the courts because the vast amount of regulatory legislation, such as tax and anti-trust law, can often be challenged on technical or narrow legal grounds. Public interest groups have also been active in pursuing class actions and other lawsuits through the courts. We have seen in Chapter 4 the way that pressure groups increasingly use the judicial system as part of their overall political strategy.

4 Grass-Roots Pressure by Members

Although many of the tactics used by a pressure group require initiative and action by the elite of the organization, the leaders are aware that it can often help their cause if the feelings of the ordinary members in support of the group's policies can be demonstrated. They can then avoid the charge that they are not representative of the mass membership, and elected politicians are impressed by the size or strength of popular support or opposition to particular policies. Pressure groups frequently urge their members to write to their Congressmen, although legislators can easily distinguish between the spontaneous messages from individual citizens and a large mailbag of similar letters which are part of a carefully orchestrated pressure group campaign. The technology of direct mailing has had a considerable impact on pressure group politics and there are companies which specialize in orchestrating telephone and mail blitzes to drum up constituent support for an issue in key Congressional districts.[11] Groups have also encouraged the use of mod-

[11]*National Journal,* 27 March 1993, 'Green Green Grass', pp. 754–7.

ern technology, with e-mail and fax messages to legislators complement-
ing traditional means of communication.

Occasionally associations will organize demonstrations and marches
in Washington or in state capitals to show the strength of feeling
among their members. A large turn-out will draw attention to the
group's aims and television coverage will provide publicity to the wider
electorate as well as obtaining the notice of the policy makers. The
marches and peaceful protests of the civil rights movement in the
Southern United States attracted considerable publicity and contributed to the atmosphere of reform which eventually led to the passage
of the Civil Rights Act in 1964. However, demonstrations that are
poorly organized or attended, or which spill over into violent confrontation can do the group's objectives far more harm than good.

Promotional groups, which may have less funds but more active members, find it more difficult to use other more direct methods and tend to
use the tactic of grass-roots pressure more frequently than do interest
groups who see it as a supplementary device to their more important
lobbying activities, or as a last resort when they have failed to convince
the decision makers by use of other channels. Indeed single-issue groups
such as the *National Right to Life Committee* rely upon the zealotry and
commitment to the cause of their members to pursue the whole range of
grass-roots methods available to influence decision makers.

5 Publicity and Advertising

Pressure groups use public relations campaigns in order to inform
the nation of their objectives and to create a favourable, or at least
neutral, climate of opinion so that it will be more difficult for government adversely to regulate their activities. Although the public does
not decide directly what legislation or policies are adopted at the
national level, no pressure group can afford to face generally hostile
public opinion for any length of time as this will eventually be reflected
in the decisions of government. However, in states that allow referendums and initiatives on important issues direct appeals to the public
have even greater significance.

The extent and actual methods of publicity will inevitably depend
upon the financial position of the group. Publicity in newspapers and
journals is common but television commercials are very expensive and
only wealthy pressure groups are able to afford this kind of publicity.
While TV advertising may be used to promote a positive message

about the group and its goals, in recent years there has been a huge growth in 'issue advertising', much of which has been negative in tone. The insurance companies' television campaign helped to kill President Clinton's health care proposals by stirring up opposition to the plan and portraying it as an expensive, bureaucratic nightmare that would restrict patients' choice of doctors. In 1994 Americans for Limited Terms were credited with helping to defeat the then Speaker, Tom Foley, in his Washington district, by attacking his strong opposition to legislative term limits.

In 1996 pressure groups made extensive use of advertising attacking a law-maker's record in office or his stand on particular issues while not specifically calling for the election or defeat of a candidate. The Supreme Court has determined that, unless the adverts do so, they are not covered by campaign finance laws and expenditure on them is not regulated. The AFL–CIO was estimated to have spent $20 million on commercials targeting particular Republican legislators and attacking their stands on issues such as Medicaid and the minimum wage.[12]

6 Relations with Political Parties

Most pressure groups try to avoid too close an identification with a particular political party so that they may more easily work with whichever government is in power and with Congress, whatever its political composition. However, many promotional groups in particular appear to be increasingly involved in seeking to influence the platforms of one or both of the major political parties which are drawn up at the national conventions every four years. Groups for and against abortion, feminists for ERA, the gay rights lobby and those supporting the disabled are just some of those in evidence at recent party gatherings. They realize that their presence at these events will provide them with a great deal of media publicity and that if a plank advocating their cause is included in the party programme this may well strengthen their position. However, party platforms in America are not firm policy commitments in the way that British parties often treat their election manifestoes and therefore inclusion does not by any means guarantee eventual legislative success.

Although Democratic candidates rely a great deal on trade union contributions for their campaign funds there has not been the close

[12]*National Journal*, 15 June 1996, 'Air Strikes', pp. 1313–15.

historical and institutional links that one sees in Britain between the
Labour Party and the trade union movement. Organized labour (or
individual unions) do on occasion support Republican candidates.
During the 1990s the Christian Right, and the Christian Coalition in
particular, has become an influential force within the Republican Party,
having supporters in leading positions in many state parties and an
estimated 25% of the delegates at the 1996 national convention in San
Diego as members. It spent $1 million on phone banks, advertising
and direct mail to drum up support for the House Republicans' 'Contract with America' and was particularly influential in pressing legislators to enact a proposal in the document to cut tax for families with
children. The Coalition was also active in ensuring that the party
platform's commitment to a pro-life position on abortion was not diluted in 1996.

7 Violence and Disorder

All the tactics we have examined so far are accepted as the normal
ways in which pressure groups can influence policy so long as they stay
within the law and avoid, for example, bribery or illegal industrial
action. However, there are occasionally incidents when groups with
extreme political opinions, or those who have been frustrated by their
lack of progress through the normal channels, resort to promoting a
violent demonstration or disorder so that their views may be brought
to the attention of politicians and the public in a dramatic way. In a
society where the mass media immediately reflect any violent confrontation or crisis, it is a certain way of obtaining publicity, if not the
successful implementation of the group's goals. Militant Indians in
the American Indian Movement, for example, took over and occupied the Bureau of Indian Affairs in November 1972, and a few
months later seized the village of Wounded Knee in South Dakota, as
protests against poverty, the federal government's policy towards the
Indians, and the fact that the Bureau was run almost exclusively by
white officials. In the last occupation a battle ensued between Indians
and federal marshals during which two people were killed, before the
Indians surrendered in May 1973. Since the 1980s there have been a
number of incidents where extreme opponents of abortion used physical intimidation and violence against clients and staff of abortion clinics. In some cases the clinics themselves have been destroyed and
hospital staff murdered. The bombing of the federal office block in

Oklahoma City in 1995 highlighted the clandestine activities of extremist militia groups that have been formed in certain parts of the country. Their conspiracy theories and hostility to the federal government in all its forms raised concern about the dangers of domestic terrorism being used as a political weapon.

The Role of Pressure Groups in the American System

Pressure groups are accepted by most political scientists and politicians as being an inevitable and necessary part of the democratic process, but it is also true that they generally have a bad image with the general public who often feel that pressure groups can be harmful to representative government. What are the reasons for this apparent contradiction?

Political scientists feel that, although there are certainly defects in the way the pressure group system operates, on balance these organizations fulfil important functions for the working of American government which cannot be satisfactorily performed by other formal or informal institutions. Pressure groups carry out the function of 'interest articulation', which means that they express the views and represent the interests of specialized sections of society. Political parties inevitably have to appeal very broadly to a large number of groups and a cross-section of society in order to win elections, and consequently their programmes often tend to be a series of rather vague compromises. Pressure groups, it is argued, are not seeking power for themselves, and they can afford to give voice to special interests without having to worry about offending voters or other groups, even though they may take these factors into account when formulating their own policies. Pressure groups not only complement the activities of parties in representing more exclusive interests, but also supplement the official geographical system of representation by an expression of functional or ideological interests and ideas. Congressmen are elected from compact geographical territories within one state and have to attempt to articulate the views of a heterogeneous population within their constituencies. It can be argued that often a section of the population who wish to give vent to their feelings or protect their common interests do not live neatly within one constituency or state. Pressure groups therefore speak on behalf of these people and provide an additional, if subordinate, tier of representation that intersects with and overlaps the official system. Trade unions, professional bodies, business associations, farmers, ethnic minorities and environmental protection groups have members all over the country and they seek to speak on behalf of interests that cut across geographical boundaries.

Pressure groups also provide, as we have seen, a great deal of information and specialized knowledge which is put at the disposal of the formal institutions. Pressure groups make a positive contribution to policy making and administration by meeting legislators and officials on a regular basis, by submitting proposals for examination and by appearing before Congressional hearings to provide evidence on specialized areas. They also act as intermediaries between government and the public, and relate the reactions of various sections of the community to official policies and current issues. Pressure groups are channels of communication by which government is kept permanently responsive to public opinion between election campaigns, as they ensure that all the 'access points' of the formal structure are fully informed on the state of the body politic.

If these positive benefits result from pressure group activity, what explains the continuing suspicion among the public? Even the name, 'pressure' group, implies to some people the use of undue or illegitimate influence, and others feel that these organizations are invariably selfish and must be advocating policies which conflict with the general or public interest, however that is construed. Perhaps the most trenchant criticism of pressure group politics is the fact that, unlike the formal system of democracy, in which there are equal voting rights, there is often grossly inequitable representation. A major problem of the pluralist system is that those groups with large memberships or financial resources tend to have a much more powerful voice and more open access to the decision makers. Large interest groups, such as business organizations and trade unions, have, it is often argued, a disproportionate amount of influence, while others, such as the disabled, the ethnic minorities, the unemployed and low-income groups, are difficult to organize into effective pressure groups, have insufficient financial support, or are inarticulate and unable to promote and defend their interests as well. One consequence of this has been, of course, the establishment of many promotional groups so that these less powerful elements of society do not go totally unrepresented.

A second major criticism of the working of pressure group politics in America is that the diffuseness of the formal structure of government and the checks and balances in the system provide major built-in advantages to those groups who wish to preserve the *status quo* and prevent change. The possibilities of delay and obstruction in the legislative, administrative and judicial processes provide opportunities for pressure groups intent on blocking social reforms desired by the majority of the nation.

Some groups are thought by the public to be too powerful, and often criticism is levelled at the leaders of such groups not only for threatening to control an area of policy making but also for being unaccountable to society for the way in which they exercise their authority. Elected representatives have to stand for renomination and re-election, and they can be defeated if they have used their official positions unwisely or irresponsibly. But many citizens feel that pressure group leaders are elected or appointed by a small minority of the organization's membership and that they frequently become self-perpetuating oligarchies with little accountability to their own members, let alone the general public.

Some critics argue that America's economic performance has suffered from the increasing burden of government regulations and mounting public expenditure commitments which Congress and the executive branch have implemented as a result of pressure group influence. What is more, attempts to deal with the federal budget deficit have been hampered by special interests anxious to protect their particular programmes and privileges, no matter the cost to the overall public interest.

Finally, it can be said that there is fairly widespread feeling among the American public that the methods used by pressure groups to influence government are often immoral, if not actually illegal. There is much disquiet about pressure groups' large electoral contributions to candidates; even though there may be no bribery intended, the relationship between donor and recipient is liable to be the object of suspicion. The secrecy involved in pressure group lobbying activities, where negotiations take place behind closed doors in a legislator's office or a government department, also arouses fears. The public is understandably concerned about behind-the-scenes deals from which everybody apart from the decision makers and special interests is excluded.

Although only a small minority of pressure groups ever resort to the use of violence, direct action or law breaking to promote their goals, the great publicity which accompanies these tactics also helps to create a bad impression in the minds of the public. A riot or demonstration that leads to violence tends to linger in the memory, whereas daily consultations between government and pressure groups either are not reported by television which seeks news with a visual impact, or are easily forgotten.

The Checks on Pressure Group Influence

Although there may be some substance to public anxiety in America about the influence and methods of major interest groups, it should not be assumed that these organizations are free from political constraints and enjoy an unlimited and uncontrolled power. The system of checks and balances works not only to dilute the power of formal institutions but also to restrict the influence of pressure groups.

Firstly, there is a decentralization within the formal decision-making bodies created by the separation of powers system and the federal structure. Although these factors provide numerous access points and opportunities to influence government, they also act as checks on pressure groups achieving their goals. Groups find that, even if they have mobilized support in the Senate by lobbying, they may well fail to marshal sufficient votes in the House or one of its committees; if they do obtain Congressional approval, a Presidential veto or a government department's administering the statute in a particular way may thwart the group's objectives.

There are also a number of legal restrictions on pressure groups. The Federal Regulation of Lobbying Act (1946) required registration of lobbyists and a record of who employs them, although many groups by-passed this control by claiming that lobbying was not their 'principal purpose'. Some state governments have enacted stricter regulation laws, and there are also penalties for bribery, exerting unlawful influence on politicians and breaking election contribution laws. The general unwillingness of politicians to enact even more stringent regulation of pressure groups has stemmed from the fact that they feel that most of these organizations are generally helpful to the efficient government of the country, the difficulty of imposing meaningful restrictions without infringing on the constitutional rights of free speech, press, assembly and petition and the highly effective opposition of lobbies. Some members may also wish to keep open for themselves the possibility of a future lobbying career.[13] However, public pressure and

---

[13]Tougher Lobby Disclosure Bills failed to pass during the 95th and 96th Congresses (*Congressional Quarterly Almanac*, 1980, p. 19).

concern about the role of special interests spurred Congress to pass tougher lobbying registration and disclosure legislation in 1995. Under the new statute those who spend at least a fifth of their time meeting with top executive branch officials, members of Congress or their staff have to disclose the names of their clients, the issues on which they are lobbying and the amounts they are spending. The legislation exempts all grass-roots lobbying and that of tax-exempt religious organizations from the disclosure requirements in order to meet the objections that helped kill a similar bill in the 103rd Congress. Congress also adopted a $50 value limit on gifts—including meals and entertainment—that members or staff could accept from individuals or organizations and a total of $100 from any one source in a year. The previous limit had been $250 but had not included meals.

It should also be remembered that most pressure groups do not have an unrivalled influence with government. There is often the countervailing pressure of other groups with conflicting objectives: women's movements such as the National Organization of Women, who wish to see the passage of the 'Equal Rights Amendment', are opposed by those women who see it as a threat to their existing position in society; those wishing to ban nuclear energy plants are resisted by the energy and power companies. This does not mean that in all political issues the pressure groups on each side or the resources they control are equally matched. Where a threat to a section of the population exists, either from another group or from government, there is likely to be the mobilization of that interest into a new pressure group.

Opposition from other organizations is an obvious check on pressure group influence; less obvious, perhaps, are the constraints operating within the group itself. Not all pressure groups are united and cohesive forces working in an efficient manner and taking every opportunity to advance their causes. Many organizations suffer from divisions within their membership, possibly on functional, ideological or tactical lines, which weaken the effectiveness of the groups. Internal conflicts can be enhanced by rival leaders struggling to control the group's policy or by a large and disparate membership that causes difficulties in coordination. Pressure group members may also have overlapping membership with other groups and this tends to dissipate their loyalty and dedication. Lack of money, experienced leadership or efficient administration will also be major constraints on the activities and effectiveness of a pressure group.

The mass media, of course, also provide an invaluable check on the power of pressure groups. Journalists and investigators are vigilant for any scandals, evidence of corruption or the use of intimidation by pressure groups in pursuing their goals. A pressure group uses the media to advance its cause, but all its efforts and expenditure can be wasted if there is a revelation which tarnishes the group's image in the eyes of the politicians or the public.

Public opinion can act as a constraint on the power of even the most deeply entrenched and influential pressure groups. Public suspicion means that groups' claims are often regarded with scepticism and their motives and policies are constantly being examined and questioned. Pressure groups may be able to delay action for a while, but if there is widespread public support for a particular policy, as evidenced by opinion polls and legislators' constituency soundings, it may prove impossible to prevent legislation or the execution of a policy indefinitely. The American Medical Association spent millions of dollars in their campaign against federal 'socialized medicine' but the strength of public support ensured the eventual passage of Medicare legislation in 1965.

Some Further Reading

Jeffrey M. Berry, *The Interest Group Society* (Scott Foresman/Little Brown 1989)

Allan J. Cigler and Burdett A. Loomis (eds), *Interest Group Politics* (Congressional Quarterly Press 1991)

Lester Milbrath, *The Washington Lobbyists* (Rand McNally 1963)

Larry Sabato, *PAC Power: Inside the World of Political Action Committees* (Norton 1984)

Kay Lehman Schlozman and John T. Tierney, *Organized Interests and American Democracy* (Harper and Row 1986)

Mark Petracca (ed.), *The Politics of Interests* (Westview 1992)

Graham Wilson, *Interest Groups in the United States* (Oxford University Press 1981)

B. Wolpe, *Lobbying Congress* (Congressional Quarterly Press 1990)

6

Party Politics

Political scientists have frequently emphasized that democratic government in a modern industrial society would not be possible without political parties. Parties are not simply appendages of representative government; they are central to its effectiveness and play a positive role in it. They are organized attempts to select candidates for official positions, promote certain goals and objectives, and gain government power. The Constitution of the United States does not mention these informal institutions and George Washington warned against the 'baneful effects of the spirit of party'. Since that time an American political culture has developed which has traditionally been suspicious of strong parties and concentrations of authority, but political parties have been an integral and essential part of the American political system since its early days. In examining the workings of the three branches of the federal government, we have already seen the importance of party for an understanding of American politics. American political parties have to operate within a very diverse society and a federal system of government; they therefore tend to be broadly-based coalitions of interests organized in a decentralized way rather than tightly disciplined hierarchical structures. In this chapter we shall examine some of the characteristics of American parties and the party system.

The Structure of American Parties

A number of diffuse elements make up what is usually known as the American party 'organization'. Discussion of political parties can be complicated by the fact that they generally do not have fee-paying or card-carrying members. We therefore have to distinguish between the vast array of people with different sorts of connection and relationship to the Democratic or Republican parties. Parties comprise the following groups:

1 The Party's Voting Support. Every election there are millions of Americans who vote regularly or sporadically for one of the parties' candidates. These people, therefore, include both hard-core supporters and 'independents' who have decided to vote for the party in that specific year.

2 Registered Party Supporters. In identifying on a regular basis with one of the major parties, millions of voters are prepared to register themselves on the electoral list as 'Democrats' or 'Republicans'. Although they pay no subscription to the party, these registered supporters are the closest to being party 'members'. In return for this public expression of support, they usually receive the right to participate in the selection of party candidates in primary elections.

3 Party Activists. A much smaller number of Americans regularly play an active role in party politics. These people provide the voluntary labour at elections to mobilize voters, contribute money to campaigns, and may hold local committee positions. Party activists may also attend party conventions as delegates.

4 Party Leaders Outside Government. In both parties there are leadership positions at local and state level as well as within the national organization which are sought by the most dedicated activists. These leaders are often referred to as the party 'professionals' and they often exert considerable influence over the party's administration and finance.

5 Party Leaders Holding Government Positions. For many Americans political parties are, in practice, the government office-holders who carry the party label at elections. The President is, of course, the national leader of one of the parties, but there are also many important Governors and Congressmen who are seen as the party leaders within their own states and who can exercise control over the running of state and local parties. What is more, the voters' image of the parties is, to a large extent, shaped by the personalities of its best-known political and governmental leaders.

Political parties are often subject to very detailed regulation of their affairs by state laws, mostly originating from the Progressive era at the beginning of the twentieth century when there was considerable concern about political corruption. Many local elections, as well as those for Nebraska's unicameral legislature, are required by law to be nonpartisan.

As a result of the federal system and the plethora of elections that are fought on a state and local basis, American party organizations have traditionally been very decentralized and have lacked a strong central authority. Power over nominations for office, finance and policy making has been the prerogative of state and local party organizations, and any attempts by the national party headquarters to interfere in these areas have been greatly resented. This decentralization, diffuseness of authority and lack of clear hierarchy of command has led to party organizations that have been described as 'confederative' rather than federal, although in recent years the national party organizations' roles have been strengthened, as we shall see later.

The main functions of political parties, nominating candidates for the thousands of elected offices and mobilizing voter support to secure victory and the control of government, dictate the structure of the institutions. V.O. Key Jr described the organization as a system of layers with each successive layer having an individual concern with elections within its geographical jurisdiction. For each higher level of the party to accomplish its ends there had to be collaboration with the lower layers of the organization. However, the cooperation came from a common sense of purpose rather than from the execution of commands from national to local units in the structure.[1] American parties therefore have not been disciplined armies but rather loose coalitions of state and local organizations which have their own followings and areas of independent action free from external control.

As parties are primarily electoral structures, it is not surprising that the main organizational units develop within electoral constituencies. There may be a dozen or so top officials who are elected at the statewide level, such as the Governor, Treasurer, Attorney-General, Lieutenant-Governor and the two US Senators, but there are hundreds of politicians who represent districts within the state. These include the US Congressmen, state legislators, county and city council members, mayors and sheriffs.

[1]V.O. Key Jr, *Politics, Parties and Pressure Groups* (Crowell 1964), p. 316.

Formal organizational structures can vary considerably from state to state owing to local traditions and electoral laws. They can also be misleading as guidelines to the actual distribution and control of political power, and official positions may be more or less important depending upon the personalities, energies and leadership qualities of the holders. In some areas party organization may not exist or be in skeleton form only, with many official positions being left unfilled through lack of volunteers. All state parties have state committees and there are almost always county committees, but these may be elected by primaries among all the registered party voters or selected by conventions of activists.

The most local units of organization are normally the precincts which are administrative subdivisions of cities and counties. Meetings of all party supporters who care to attend elect *precinct chairmen* (or 'captains') who have the responsibilities of directing local fund raising and mobilizing voters at election time. Ward caucuses meet in many areas to select a *ward committee* to run the party's affairs over a number of precincts; wards are also usually the electoral constituencies for city or county council members.

The *county committee* has an important coordinating role in local party administration and its members select a county chairman who will probably become a major figure in state as well as local politics. In some parts of the country there are separate committees for geographical areas which form, for example, Congressional districts or state senate constituencies, and these overlap with the county organizations. At the state level conventions are held which usually last for two or three days and are major political events. Party platforms may be adopted, candidates for state-wide office and for the *state party committee* either endorsed, if chosen by primaries, or selected by the delegates representing county and ward areas. A smaller executive committee and the state party chairman will often act in the name of the state committee as this body may be too large and unwieldy to be an effective decision-making institution in practice. In those states which do not have Presidential primaries, the state conventions and caucuses also select the delegates to attend the party's national nominating convention.

One of the formal roles of the national convention is to select a *national committee* with overall administrative responsibilities. In practice, each state party determines who its representatives will be and these are endorsed by the full convention. National committees are made up of one man and one woman from each state, plus a number of additional members. The Democrats have included representatives of the party's Governors and Congressmen and the Republicans have added state party chairmen. The effect has been historically to make the committees far too large to fulfil any function other than a symbolic unifying one. The national committees are concerned with overseeing the Presidential campaign as well as selecting the site and making the arrangements for the next convention. However, the national party chairman and the office staff in Washington carry out most of the functions and are involved in fund raising, publicity and administration. The national chairman is formally selected by the committee but it ratifies the choice made by the Presidential nominee of the party. If the Presidential candidate suffers a heavy defeat in the November election, the national committee may decide to replace the chairman with one of its own choosing. However, if the candidate becomes President, despite his lack of a formal role in the national committee, his informal control over its leaders and activities is nearly total and if he wants to change the national chairman the committee will promptly elect his choice, usually without dissent.[2]

Until the last decade American national parties could be said only to come into practical operation once every four years when there was a Presidential election. The rest of the time the state parties had no real reason to cooperate and the national committees' Washington offices were run by small skeleton staffs. The national parties have now taken steps to develop their organizations and roles so that they can make a difference in national politics. The Republican National Committee, particularly during the chairmanship of William Brock between 1977 and 1981, took the lead and was involved in raising money, recruiting candidates against Democrats thought to be vulnerable and conducting centralized polling and advertising campaigns, while the Congressional Campaign Committees have provided funds, advice and support to favoured Republican candidates in legislative elections. The RNC has also sought to coordinate business and corporate PAC contributions to Republican candidates. These roles came about as an indirect result of the weak position of the Republican Party in the mid-1970s and the RNC's determination to improve both its financial and technical capacity as well as the fact that the party has become more ideologically unified.

[2]Austin Ranney, 'The President and His Party', in *Both Ends of the Avenue*, Anthony King (ed.) (American Enterprise Institute 1983), p. 133.

Large amounts of money, raised principally by direct mail solicitation of supporters, allowed the Republicans nationally to become involved in party-building activities and in strengthening the organization in the country. The Democrats began the process later and also concentrated on fundraising to develop their organization. By the early 1990s, concern was being expressed about the large amounts of 'soft money' being raised and spent at national and state levels by the parties that was not subject to the regulations and limits of election campaign law (see Chapter 7).

The Democratic National Committee has also gained power over state parties by the establishment of binding party rules on the composition of delegations to the national convention. Starting in 1964, when it resolved a challenge to the seating of an all-white Mississippi delegation in favour of a compromise that bound all future Democratic delegations to a rule of non-discrimination, the party has determined acceptable delegate selection procedures. The rules have actually been very unstable with new ones set for every recent convention. The McGovern-Fraser Commission in 1969 emphasized the greater participation of minorities, women and young people and dramatically changed the nature of delegations to the 1972 convention which selected George McGovern. More recently, after the poor results in Presidential contests the party moved in the opposite direction by requiring the representation of so-called 'super delegates' comprising elected officials who would bring experience and political realism to the conventions, while still requiring state delegations to reflect the demographic profile of the states.

Whether the party organization at state, county and ward level works hard to secure the election of the party's Presidential candidate depends on how local activists feel about him. With the increasing tendency for voters to be willing to 'split their tickets' when voting for the Presidency and other offices, the 'coat-tails effect' has been reduced with the effective uncoupling of Presidential from other elections (see Chapter 2).

On the other hand, the activists would obviously prefer to have a popular Presidential candidate such as Ronald Reagan in 1980 and 1984 at the head of the party's ticket than one who seems destined to lose such as George McGovern in 1972, Walter Mondale in 1984 and Robert Dole in 1996. Party workers at state and local level will then concentrate on securing positions of their Gubernatorial, Congressional and local candidates and distance themselves from a Presidential candidate who is unpopular in their state. The Democratic party has had particular problems in this regard because its national conventions have often selected Presidential candidates who are far more liberal than the candidates the state and local parties, particularly in the South, often select themselves.

While examining American party organizations it should also be noted that, in many respects, parties are becoming less important than they used to be in the actual running of campaigns. Party nomination and the party label will be necessary for election to most offices, but candidates for positions ranging from the Presidency to local sheriff are increasingly relying on personal organizations to run their campaigns. We are now in the age of candidate-centred campaigns; activists often prefer to work on behalf of individual men and women and are concerned solely with their victories rather than with the success of the party ticket as a whole. The main reason for this phenomenon is that increasingly primaries are being used to nominate party candidates; this weakens the influence of the party organization, the committees, the chairmen and the 'professionals'. It also means that aspirants for office inevitably have to set up their own organizations in order to win the party's nomination. They have their own offices, staff, fund-raising and campaign workers and they are likely to hire independent campaign consultants, pollsters, direct mail specialists and media advisers. The cost of hiring highly paid political consultants has fuelled the mounting expenditure levels in recent campaigns; in the 1990 cycle this growing industry earned $188 million from Congressional candidates. These consultants are usually responsible for strategy and are heavily influenced by opinion poll findings on what issues to emphasize and what approach to take to the opposition. Candidates are increasingly political entrepreneurs who will keep this campaign structure in operation during the general elections because they feel they can trust it as well as exercise greater control over it. Philip John Davies concludes:

> It is not so much a case of candidates being chosen to represent the party line by party loyalists, as it is of candidate organizations capturing the party nomination, thereby eliminating some competitors, and gaining the use of party assets, on the way to a personal victory.[3]

[3]Philip John Davies, 'Shifting Sands: Developments in Party Politics', in *Political Issues in America Today*, Philip John Davies and Frederic A. Waldstein (eds) (Manchester University Press 1987), p. 79.

Therefore one may find a large degree of overlap and duplication of work by personal and party organizations, and occasionally friction and conflict between the two. The decline of American party organization has been the result of a number of other factors. Earlier in the century American parties, particularly in the cities, were famous for their tight and well disciplined organizations. Precinct captains and ward chairmen would be proud of their capacity to know the inhabitants in their areas and to get out the vote on election days. 'Machine politics' became a common phenomenon in many Eastern cities and organized local politics, often under the influence of a political 'boss', became as much a tradition as the unorganized national party system. Tammany Hall in New York was the best known of these local machines; machine politics itself was really the result of dense urban populations, the fragmentation of city government, and the democratic right to vote of large numbers of people, particularly new immigrants to the United States, who had no tradition of political participation. The machines acted as intermediaries who would help provide informal welfare services, such as jobs and housing, in return for electoral support. In recent decades the system has disintegrated because patronage jobs are no longer so easily available, there has been closer vetting of city funds, and the introduction of government welfare programmes has meant that the poor are no longer dependent on local party politicians. The trading of votes has also largely ended with changing political morality and the end of mass immigration to American cities. The importance of the mass media as a basis of communication and a method of campaigning has reduced the impact of the door-to-door contacts made by the local machine. What is more, increasing mobility and the growth of the sprawling suburbs and the decline of the cities as residential areas have also contributed to the breakdown of the city machines. The death in 1976 of Mayor Richard Daley of Chicago, often seen as the last of the old-style city bosses, marked the end of an era in the history of American party organization.

The American Two-Party System

1 The Historical Development

There are two major parties which operate successfully within the American political system, as indeed there have been for most of the nation's history. This does not mean that there are only two parties or that the same two parties have continued to contest elections with each other since the Union was created. In fact there are, and have been, many minor parties, most of which had a fleeting and transitory existence, and there have been several party systems over the last two centuries of American political life. V.O. Key Jr has observed:

> A salient characteristic of the American party system is its dual form. During most of our history power has alternated between two major parties. While minor parties have arisen from time to time and exerted influence on governmental policy, the two major parties have been the only serious contenders for the Presidency. On occasion a major party has disintegrated but in due course the biparty division has reasserted itself.[4]

The first American two-party system lasted a relatively short time after 1787. Despite Washington's and Adams' dislike of party politics, it was inevitable that in a free society groups would coalesce to try to obtain control of government and, in particular, of the Presidency. The Democratic-Republicans led by Thomas Jefferson formed an alliance of agrarian and business supporters and created a party organization to challenge the Federalists, the supporters of Alexander Hamilton, and the idea of a strong national government. The Federalists sank into oblivion within a couple of decades because of their restricted elitist appeal to the well-to-do in society and their opposition to political democracy. For some time after the demise of the Federalists, the United States experienced the 'Era of Good Feelings' when the Democratic-Republicans were the only viable party; but the strong reaction to the policies and personality of Andrew Jackson led to the eventual formation of an opposition party known as the Whigs. The Whigs lasted from 1832 to 1852 but had no real hope of long-term survival because they were, in Rossiter's words:

> The coalition to end all coalitions, a patchwork party with few premonitions of immortality, a loose alliance of every section and interest that was sure to crack under the first hard blow.[5]

The traumatic question of slavery nearly led to the dissolution of the Union, but it actually did lead to the disintegration of the party system and the destruction of the Whigs. The Democratic Party came under the control of Southern interests dedicated to the preservation

[4]V.O. Key Jr, op. cit., p. 205.
[5]Clinton Rossiter, *Parties and Politics in America* (Cornell 1960), p. 78.

and expansion of slavery. The Republican Party emerged from the confusion of the 1850s as a grass-roots democratic movement which managed to bring together an alliance of smaller parties as well as disillusioned Whigs and Democrats. The Republican Party's origins were radical and its opposition to the extension of slavery to the territories destined it to be a sectional Northern party. The antipathy in the South to the Republican Party has had its political repercussions for well over a century after these events.

After the Civil War the Democratic Party made a recovery and in the period 1876–96 there was intense competition between it and the Republicans for control of both Congress and the Presidency. However, social changes in America inevitably were reflected by modifications of the party system. With rapid industrialization, the growth of big business and the increasing pressure of large-scale immigration, there was growing agrarian discontent which was articulated by small parties like the Populists. In 1896 the Democrats moved to absorb the Populist movement's ideas while their candidate, William Jennings Bryan, ran on a 'free silver' Presidential platform. The Republicans, under William McKinley, emerged victorious from the election and were strengthened as a result of becoming a coalition of businessmen, urban workers and Mid-Western farmers. The Republicans became recognized as the more conservative and business-oriented party and managed to dominate American politics until 1932. They controlled both the White House and Congress and the only real Democratic success was achieved when Woodrow Wilson was elected twice to the Presidency in 1912 and 1916. Even this was mainly as a result of a split in the 'Grand Old Party' (as Republicans call it) between the conservative supporters of William Howard Taft and the progressive followers of Theodore Roosevelt.

The onset of the Great Depression in the period 1929–31 had as disastrous an effect on the fortunes of the Republicans as the Civil War had had on the Democratic Party. Herbert Hoover suffered a massive defeat in the 1932 Presidential election and Franklin D. Roosevelt began the first of three full terms in the White House. Roosevelt died in 1945 after being elected a fourth time to the office, but his establishment of the 'New Deal Coalition' was to have repercussions on American politics long after his death. It seems that only major national crises lead to the widespread reassessments of loyalties and attitudes that result in large numbers of Americans changing their party identification on a long-term basis, but the Depression and the New Deal era led to the transformation of the traditional Republican majority in the country into a normal Democratic one.[6]

The period of Democratic dominance meant that the party controlled both houses of Congress from 1932 to 1980 with the exception of only four years—the 80th (1947–48) and 83rd (1953–54) Congresses. Between 1981 and 1987 the Republicans had a majority in the Senate and there was split control of the two houses of Congress. After a further eight years with Democratic majorities in both houses, the Republicans at last gained control of the House and the Senate in 1994 and retained their majority status in 1996. The opportunity to consolidate their position and make further gains in 1998 is helped by Democratic control of the White House, as historically the President's party generally loses Congressional seats in mid-term elections. Democratic dominance of the legislature, which in effect lasted from 1932 to 1994, now appears to be at an end, with the Republican breakthrough in the South being a key factor.

Between 1932 and 1996 the Democrats won ten Presidential elections to the Republicans' seven, but it is noteworthy that the Republican victories have included five out of the last eight, the exceptions being when the Democrats nominated Southern moderate candidates in 1976, 1992 and 1996.

The American two-party system has therefore experienced periods of one-party dominance. The national party system is normally described as a 'two-party system' because, although in any period one party may control government, the other party continues to draw large support in terms of both popular votes and Congressional seats. At Presidential elections the two main parties normally share well over 90% of the popular vote, although in 1992 and 1996 between 10% and 20% of the voters opted for alternative candidates. Congressional representation is still shared almost exclusively between the two parties. Despite the decline of voter identification and commitment to the parties and the rise in the number of 'Independents', the parties have demonstrated remarkable durability.

[6]See Table 6.1. For an interesting analysis of the emergence of the New Deal Coalition and its effects, see Samuel Lubell's *The Future of American Politics* (Harper & Row 1965).

TABLE 6.1

The Party Composition of Congress 1959–98

	President		Congress	The House		The Senate	
				Maj. Party	Min. Party	Maj. Party	Min. Party
1959–60	Eisenhower	(R)	86th	D 283	R 154	D 66	R 34
1961–62	Kennedy	(D)	87th	D 263	R 174	D 64	R 36
1963–64	Kennedy	(D)	88th	D 258	R 176	D 68	R 32
1965–66	Johnson	(D)	89th	D 295	R 140	D 67	R 33
1967–68	Johnson	(D)	90th	D 248	R 187	D 64	R 36
1969–70	Nixon	(R)	91st	D 243	R 192	D 58	R 42
1971–72	Nixon	(R)	92nd	D 256	R 179	D 55	R 45
1973–74	Nixon	(R)	93rd	D 243	R 191	D 57	R 43
1975–76	Ford	(R)	94th	D 291	R 144	D 62	R 38
1977–78	Carter	(D)	95th	D 292	R 143	D 62	R 38
1979–80	Carter	(D)	96th	D 276	R 159	D 59	R 41
1981–82	Reagan	(R)	97th	D 243	R 192	R 53	D 47
1983–84	Reagan	(R)	98th	D 269	R 166	R 54	D 46
1985–86	Reagan	(R)	99th	D 253	R 182	R 53	D 47
1987–88	Reagan	(R)	100th	D 258	R 177	D 54	R 46
1989–90	Bush	(R)	101st	D 260	R 175	D 55	R 45
1991–92	Bush	(R)	102nd	D 267	R 167	D 56	R 44
1993–94	Clinton	(D)	103rd	D 258	R 176	D 57	R 43
1995–96	Clinton	(D)	104th	R 230	D 204	R 53	D 47
1997–98	Clinton	(D)	105th	R 227	D 207	R 55	D 45

Note: The 102nd to 105th Congresses included one independent from Vermont in the House of Representatives. Republican strength in the 104th Congress was increased by Democratic defections. Before the 1996 elections the Republican lead was 236–198 in the House. In the Senate, Richard Shelby (Alabama) and Ben Nighthorse Campbell (Colorado) also defected to the Republicans in November 1994 and March 1995 respectively.

2 Patterns of State Party Competition

In addition to the national party system, the United States has fifty other state party systems in which there is a great variety of partisan competition. In the vast majority of states, the two major parties contest most important political offices and the extent of competition depends upon the particular traditions and social composition of the individual states. In some areas there is a close struggle for power, with Democrats and Republicans both winning at various times the Gubernatorial elections and control of the state legislature. In other areas there is uneven competition, where one party usually controls the legislature for long periods but is not permanently in a majority. Elections for Governor are more competitive and are often won by the party in the legislative minority. In other states there is a virtual monopoly, where one party has long-term dominance of the legislature and the minority may, on occasions, win the Gubernatorial race. As at national level, divided party control of the legislature and executive has become more common. Whereas in 1960 only 37.5% of states had different parties in control of the two branches, by 1990 this had risen to 61%.[7]

The other main trend in the 1990s has been the growing Republican strength at state level. Table 6.2 demonstrates that the party has made considerable gains in both Gubernatorial and state legislative elections. With the large swing to the Republicans in 1994, the GOP held the governorships of 30 states, including the largest and most popular states in the Union such as California, New York and Texas.

In those Southern states which until recently could be described as 'one-party systems' and had been solidly Democratic since the Civil War, the Republicans historically put up only token resistance in most state elections or did not compete at all. The reasons for the overwhelming domination of one party were historical and social. In recent years there has been a weakening of sectionalism and one-partyism due to the increasing urbanization and pluralism of social groups and interests even in these areas. This has been demonstrated both by the tendency of the Southern states to support Republican candidates for the Presidency in preference to liberal Democrats, and also by the increasing number of Republican Congressmen and Governors elected in Southern states. In 1984 71% of Southern whites voted for Ronald Reagan and 59% for Republican Congressional candidates. Demo-

[7]Dean McSweeney and John Zvesper, *American Political Parties* (Routledge 1991), pp. 80–82.

TABLE 6.2

Party Control of the States 1980–97

Governors

	Dem.	Rep.	Ind.
1980	31	19	–
1985	34	16	–
1987	26	24	–
1990	29	21	–
1993	30	18	2
1995	19	30	1
1997	17	32	1

State Legislatures

	Dem.	Rep.	Split control/tie
1981	28	15	6
1985	27	11	11
1987	28	8	13
1990	29	9	11
1993	25	8	16
1995	18	19	12
1997	20	18	10

Note: Nebraska's unicameral non-partisan legislature is excluded. 1997 figures exclude Texas where position in legislature undecided at time of compilation.

Sources: *Statistical Abstract of the United States 1996*, pp. 281 and 283, and *Congressional Quarterly Weekly Report*, 9 November 1996, pp. 3240–44.

cratic strength in the South has suffered severe erosion and it appears that more voters have accepted that their conservatism fits more comfortably with the Republicans than a regionally-based Democratic ideology. This has led not only to ordinary voters, but politicians themselves, switching party; in the 104th Congress five Southern Democrats in the House and one in the Senate defected to the Republicans.

In 1961 Republicans held only nine (7.5%) of the 120 House seats in the 13 Southern states. In 1993 these states had 137 House members, of whom 52 (38%) were Republicans; by 1997 Republicans had won 82 or 60% of the Southern seats. Similarly in the Senate, the GOP's share of the seats rose from 7.7% in 1961 to 42% in 1993 and 69% (with 18 of the 26 members) in 1997. In 1961 all the Governors in the South were Democrats; by 1993 there were three Republicans, whereas in 1997 nine of the 13 statehouses were controlled by the GOP.

3 Why a Two-Party System?

When one considers the heterogeneity of the United States and the diversity of social, ethnic and regional interests, it is perhaps surprising that there are only two major parties. Multi-party systems are, in fact, more common in liberal democracies than two-party structures, and one could reasonably expect that America would exhibit the former pattern of competition. The explanation is not to be found in one factor, but rather in the historical, cultural, constitutional and social experience of the country.

V.O. Key Jr has argued that the circumstances that happened to mould the American party system into a dual form at its inception had a long-term effect because there is a tendency in human institutions for a persistence of initial form.[8] There was the great debate about the adoption of the Constitution which was an issue that was bound to divide the country into two blocs. There was the rivalry between agrarian and commercial interests that tended to unite in two broad coalitions, and there was, of course, the slavery issue and the Civil War which reinforced a dual division.

The electoral system used in the United States for Congressional and state elections encourages the persistence of a two-party system. With a 'simple plurality' or 'first past the post' system, representatives are elected in single-member constituencies by winning more votes than any opponent. Minor parties may be said to be at a disadvantage in that they may contest a large number of elections but not finish at the top of the poll in any constituency and thus remain unrepresented in the legislature. Under a proportional representation electoral system, used by many European democracies, these parties would obtain a number of seats roughly equivalent to the proportion of the popular vote they acquired overall. Minor parties in the United States have therefore found it virtually impossible to beat both the major estab-

[8]V.O. Key Jr, op. cit., pp. 207–8.

lished parties and win seats in Congress. The system of electing the President encourages the same tendency to dualism. An absolute majority of Electoral College votes is required to win the Presidency outright and therefore a pressure exists on voters to coalesce around two main candidates. When further serious contenders do compete in the Presidential election, there is the danger of a deadlock in the Electoral College and the decision being thrown into the House of Representatives. In addition, the very nature of the single-man executive makes it impossible for coalitions of more than one party to win control of the government, as can happen with a Cabinet system.

Further institutional problems exist for minor parties because there is a great diversity of state laws and regulations concerning elections and the qualifications that have to be met before a candidate's name can go forward for the ballot. Perhaps even more important than the complexity of election laws is the actual cost of campaigning. In elections where large campaign expenditure is necessary to secure television, radio and press advertising, candidates and parties with few financial backers and meagre resources of their own are obviously at a grave disadvantage in attempting to break into the system.

While not running as a party candidate, Ross Perot was backed by a mass movement of volunteers who successfully worked to place his name on the ballot paper for the 1992 Presidential election in every state. Perot used his personal wealth to finance his campaign, but even though he won 19% of the popular vote he did not come close to winning any state's Electoral College votes. In 1996 Perot ran again, but this time as the candidate of the Reform Party. On this occasion he won only 8.4% of the popular vote, but the new party will be eligible for some public funding in 2000.

The United States also does not have the class-conscious or ideological style of politics so common in many countries that experience multi-partyism. The nature of American political culture means that there is a large degree of consensus on the fundamentals of the political and economic systems. Despite the social and ethnic diversity there is basic support for the Constitution and the principles of liberal democracy based on a private enterprise or capitalist economic structure. This means that traditionally the two major parties have existed with differences of style and approach but with no deep ideological divisions between them. The Democrats and Republicans have been flexible and prepared to adapt themselves to social change, where necessary by broadening their coalitions to absorb any minor parties that have arisen. The absence of a major socialist party dedicated to the transformation of the social and economic order has also been a factor in the creation and persistence of parties which exhibit 'dualism in a moving consensus'.[9]

4 The Democratic and Republican Parties

One commonly heard complaint about American parties over the years has been that they fail to offer a real choice to the electorate and that voters are in practice often asked whether they prefer 'Tweedledum' or 'Tweedledee'. The existence of a broad national consensus and the absence of strong class divisions have meant that American parties have reflected those social facts of life by not exhibiting such clearcut ideological differences as most European party systems. Political parties in attempting to win control of government, particularly at national level, are obliged to appeal to broad coalitions of interests and win votes from all sections of society. Both parties have tended to try to move to the 'middle ground' in order to win the support of independent voters who do not identify with either party and the result has been that both parties have usually offered broad and moderate policy proposals, often with a great deal of similarity.

American experience has indicated that, when parties have chosen candidates, formulated policies or projected images that could be criticized as 'extreme' or 'outside the mainstream', they have suffered heavy defeats at the hands of the voters. Barry Goldwater, a conservative Republican who promised to provide 'a choice not an echo' in his Presidential campaign of 1964, and George McGovern, a Democrat on the left wing of his party who was nominated as his party's standard-bearer in 1972, were both tagged as 'extremists'. Both challengers, who were fighting incumbent 'safe' Presidents, were decisively defeated. Jimmy Carter tried unsuccessfully to use this tactic in his 1980 campaign against conservative Republican challenger, Ronald Reagan.

There can be little doubt that in the 1980s the two parties moved further apart politically than for many years and that in Ronald Reagan the Republican Party and the American people had a President who was far more ideologically committed than any of his recent predecessors. The differences in 1984 between the avowedly right wing platform of the Republican Party and the essentially liberal programmes

---

[9]V.O. Key Jr, op. cit., p. 222.

adopted by the Democratic convention were more clearcut than they probably had ever been. Many of the activists in both parties and the pressure groups associated with them appeared to be far more strident and in some cases more extreme than has traditionally been the case in American politics. However, opinion polls do not indicate that the nation as a whole is necessarily more ideologically committed and many voters from a wide range of social groups who supported President Reagan were attracted to him on personality grounds rather than because they supported his conservative policies and they continued to vote for Democratic candidates elsewhere on the ticket.

American parties have always had their differences and their own distinctive bases of support even though they have had to appeal to the country at large and have generally been moderate and non-ideological. After the Great Depression, the Democratic Party managed to become the majority party by winning the regular support of a disparate and heterogeneous coalition of groups. The very nature of this alliance meant that there were constant threats to its stability, but the enduring nature of voter identification and a mixture of good luck and judgement enabled it to survive. The Democrats have gained most support from people in the lower socioeconomic groups; the New Deal programmes enabled the party to project the image of caring for the security and welfare of the poor, the unemployed and the ordinary worker. Roosevelt managed to add the votes of the cities, the recent immigrants, the minority ethnic groups and small farmers to those of the traditional Southern white electorate, the unions and liberal academic establishment in the universities. With upward social mobility, many Americans have obtained middle-class status since the 1930s but retained their Democratic Party identification.

Until the 1980s the Republican Party's dilemma was that it had become very much the second party in terms of voter identification. The party was therefore more homogeneous than the Democratic Party in terms of social support. It tended to draw votes from nonmanual workers and their families and particularly the upper middle classes, the business community, large farmers and college graduates. Republican support came primarily from WASPs (White Anglo-Saxon Protestants) rather than other ethnic groups. Despite the fact that more Americans were working in non-manual jobs and living in the suburbs, the Republicans did not seem to be benefiting to the extent one would have expected. This is at least partially explained by the image of the two parties that the voters tended to have. The Republican

Party was often identified as 'the party of the rich' and this rather exclusive image deterred many middle-class Americans. The Democrats were more often seen as 'the party of the ordinary or working people' and, although Americans are less class-conscious than European voters, most do see themselves as 'working people'.

However, the Reagan years enabled the Republican Party to project an image of being the party of peace and prosperity and to improve its position in terms of voter identification. In 1980 the Democrats outnumbered Republicans by 22% but in a Gallup survey in July 1989 the gap had narrowed to 4%.[10] Apart from the changing fortunes of the parties it is also worth noting the large percentage of voters who say they are 'Independents' and do not identify with either party on a regular basis. In 1992, of those voting in the Presidential election, 38% identified themselves as Democrats, 35% as Republicans and 27% said they were Independents and in 1996 the proportions were almost identical: 39%, 35% and 26%. Interestingly, of the Independents in 1992, only 30% voted for Perot, while 38% backed Clinton and 32% Bush.[11] Other studies have further sub-divided the electorate according to their degree of attachment to the parties. In 1994, according to the University of Michigan's Center for Political Studies, 15% were Strong Democrats, 19% Weak Democrats, 13% Independent Democrats (or leaning to the Democrats), 16% Strong Republicans, 15% Weak Republicans, 12% Independent Republicans (or leaning to the Republicans) and 10% Independent of both parties.[12]

During the 1980s and 1990s there has also been a marked increase in the number of voters identifying themselves as conservatives when compared with those who say they are liberals. In the 1996 exit poll, 33% were conservatives, 20% liberals, while 47% declared themselves to be moderates; these figures have been fairly typical since the mid-1980s, but are very different from the post-war period when liberalism was more attractive.

The two main parties have differences of emphasis in their policies and programmes which have been inevitably interrelated with their traditional sources of social support in the country. The Democrats have tended to favour government regulation of the economy, large spending programmes such as Social Security, Medicare, federal aid to education and welfare, as well as legislation supported by the trade

[10]*Congressional Quarterly Weekly Report*, 11 November 1989, p. 3098.
[11]Exit poll data from Voter Research and Surveys; see Table 7.5.
[12]*Statistical Abstract of the United States* 1996, p. 285.

unions and ethnic minorities. They have advocated reform and change initiated by a strong federal government, where necessary pushing state and local governments to implement interventionist policies. They have seen an activist President and executive branch as the main mechanism for experimentation and social change. Democrats have seen themselves as 'the party of progress', being prepared to look to the future and attempt bold new methods of achieving welfare, security and national prosperity. The Republican Party, on the other hand, has advocated a far more limited role for the federal government in the economic and social affairs of the country. It has opposed large and inflationary spending programmes, particularly in areas that it regards as being much more suitable for state and local policy making, while resisting intervention in the economy and regulation of business activity. Republicans have often opposed Democratic legislation since the 1930s and then had to accept the major programmes as they have become part of the *status quo* supported by the American consensus.

One of the prices of unity in obtaining support for Presidential candidates is the tolerance of diverse shades of opinion within both parties and this overlapping of political orientations has tended further to blur the differences between them. However, it is fair to say that the 'centres of gravity' within the parties are distinct. The Republican party today can be fairly described as principally a conservative party. The orientation among its Presidential candidates, its Congressional representation and its active supporters has been to the right of the political spectrum and the influence of Ronald Reagan in consolidating the influence of conservatism within the party in the 1980s has been very significant. It is notable that all six of the potential Republican successors to Reagan in the Presidential primaries of 1988 were conservatives of various shades; the last liberal Republican to seek the Presidential nomination, John Anderson in 1980, left to run an Independent campaign after failing in the primaries. It was not always this way; until the 1960s the party's liberal wing with its supporters based in the big cities of the Eastern United States and the 'Eastern liberal establishment' of the GOP succeeded in dominating the party's Presidential conventions. The nomination of Arizona Senator Barry Goldwater in 1964, over New York Governor Nelson Rockefeller, was a landmark in the wresting of control of the party by the conservative wing. The death of Rockefeller big government liberalism was also witnessed in Congress, and gradually the ranks of moderate Republicans have also been depleted. The remaining moderates, around 30–40 in the House and 7–8 in the Senate during the 104th Congress, mostly represent constituencies in the North-East. Their ranks have declined as retirements have led to more conservative replacements, by defeats in primaries and by Democratic successes in the region. Overall, the House and Senate Republican Conferences have become far more conservative, with many more members from the West and South and far fewer from the North-East and Mid-West.[13] With the collapse of communism and the Soviet threat which had been a uniting factor for Republicans, factional fights in the 1990s have been principally between those supporters of the Christian Right who have wanted to emphasize social and moral issues and traditional family values, and those free market conservatives who believe the party's main attraction to the electorate is its stands on economic policy, less government and reduced taxes. Although some observers have argued that the conflicts between social conservatives and the libertarian wing of the party would lead to damaging disunity and electoral disaster, this does not appear to have been borne out by events, with Republican successes in Congressional and state elections in the mid-1990s. Nigel Ashford suggests that the Republican Party is capable of managing these disagreements and can unite around the themes of less government, a free economy and the removal of government obstacles to the promotion of traditional values, such as reform of the welfare system.[14]

The Democratic Party has been more heterogeneous in ideological terms and remains so today. The New Deal coalition put together by Roosevelt consisted of a wide variety of groups with sometimes mutually inconsistent political views. The general orientation of the party among its Presidential candidates, Congressional representation and party activists outside the Southern states has been liberal and interventionist. The party's conservative wing has been based mainly in the South and it has remained within the Democratic Party even though it has often been opposed to the policies endorsed by the Congressional leadership and its Presidential candidates. George Wallace became the main spokesman for the distinctive Southern segregationist viewpoint of the 1960s, articulating a 'states' rights' doctrine and opposition to federal government intervention in social matters, particularly those

[13]See Nicol Rae, *The Decline and Fall of the Liberal Republicans* (Oxford University Press 1989).

[14]Nigel Ashford, 'The Right After Reagan: Crack-Up or Comeback?', in *Contemporary American Politics*, Alan Grant (ed.) (Dartmouth 1995).

pertaining to civil rights and race relations. In the 1980s Democratic candidates in the South moderated their views on these issues, reflecting both the changing socioeconomic position of the South and the recognition that they need the votes of the increasingly significant black electorate there. In 1986, for example, the Democrats won back control of the Senate partly because of the influence of black voters in the South in a number of key elections. The nomination and eventual election in 1976 of Jimmy Carter, the former Governor of Georgia, was the result of a calculated appeal to both liberals and conservatives within and outside the party. He managed to project the image of the 'moderate liberal Southerner' when campaigning in the North, while convincing his fellow Southerners that he was really a 'moderate conservative'! Edward Kennedy's challenge to Carter in the 1980 primaries was based on the claim that the President had failed to continue in office the liberal New Deal traditions of the party. The Democratic Party's candidates in the Presidential primaries have tended to cover a wider spectrum of views than the Republicans but the nomination process generally has favoured liberals consistent with the philosophy of most Democratic Party activists (although not, it appears, most voters or even those who identify with the Democratic Party).

Following the defeats of Walter Mondale in 1984 and Michael Dukakis in 1988, the influence of the Democratic Leadership Council, a group within the party comprising moderate and mostly Southern politicians, increased considerably. The DLC argued that the party could only win a Presidential election if it moved towards the centre, distanced itself from 'old-fashioned liberalism' and nominated a candidate who could appeal to the growing populations of the Southern and Western states, which had been won by the Republicans in recent campaigns. Two prominent members of the DLC were Governor Bill Clinton of Arkansas and Senator Al Gore of Tennessee. In 1992 Clinton campaigned as a 'new kind of Democrat', drawing a distinction with the 'tax and spend liberals' of the past. He argued for welfare reform to increase individual responsibility, supported a tax cut for the 'forgotten middle class' and favoured capital punishment. By stressing the need for job training and an industrial strategy, he also appealed to the 'neo-liberals' within the party who, during the 1980s, had emphasized the necessity of the American economy adapting to the technological revolution. The neo-liberals, such as Gary Hart who ran in the 1984 primaries, argue for a tough-minded and non-ideological approach to dealing with problems, which recognizes the fiscal and other limits on government action, while seeking to promote greater equity and social justice.[15]

In the Democratic primaries in 1992 the candidate most associated with 'New Deal liberalism', Senator Tom Harkin, did very poorly and was forced into an early withdrawal from the race. The radical wing of the Democratic party has had its most effective and charismatic spokesman in Jesse Jackson, who campaigned in the 1984 and 1988 primaries. Jackson argued that a more determined attempt to appeal to the disadvantaged groups in American society and the creation of a 'rainbow coalition', most of whom are currently alienated and do not vote, would pay greater electoral dividends than trying to appeal to white middle-class voters by forsaking traditional Democratic policies. In 1992 Jerry Brown, in the absence of Jackson, represented the most radical faction in the Democratic primaries. Nicol Rae's typology of contemporary Democratic party factionalism identifies the New Left/ Minorities (the radicals); the Neo-Liberals; the New Deal Regulars and the Southern Democrats.[16]

The Democratic and Republican parties, therefore, do differ in their approaches to the central political question of how much government should do in a modern industrialized society and at what level. There are also internal divisions within each party on doctrinal and geographical lines. It is worth noting that there are greater differences between the leaders and activists of the political parties on policy questions than exist between the ordinary voting supporters of the parties. The leaders and activists, not surprisingly, hold more ideologically consistent views than the general population.

Party leaders are aware that the general public are not deeply divided on ideological lines and therefore often make efforts to moderate internal doctrinal differences in order not to risk offending large sections of the electorate.

[15]Kenneth M. Dolbeare and Linda J. Medcalf, 'The Rising Stars? Neoliberalism and Neoconservatism', in *Political Issues in America Today*, Philip John Davies and Frederic A. Waldstein (eds) (University of Manchester Press 1989), p. 93.

[16]Nicol Rae, 'Clinton and the Democratic Party: the 1992 Election and Beyond', in *Contemporary American Politics*, Alan Grant (ed.) (Dartmouth 1995).

Minor Parties and Independent Campaigns

We have already examined some of the underlying reasons for the dominant dualism of the American party system. Minor parties have had great difficulty achieving success in terms of gaining government office because of the electoral system, the cost of campaigning, the enduring nature of party identification and, perhaps most of all, the flexibility of the two main parties in being prepared to modify their own policies and programmes. Support for minor parties has at various times demonstrated the lack of appeal and failure to aggregate interests by the two major parties. Republican and Democratic party leaders have tended to react to such movements in a typically pragmatic fashion; they hate to see much needed electoral support going to minor parties.

> One of the persistent qualities of the American two-party system is the way in which one of the major parties moves almost instinctively to absorb—thus to be somewhat reshaped by—the most challenging third party of the time.[17]

In some states there have been local parties that have enjoyed some measure of success, such as the Progressives in Wisconsin and the New York Liberal and Conservative parties. At the national level, there have been two types of minor party. There are the ideological or doctrinal parties that have a long history of competing in elections, and there are the transient third parties that have a rapid rise and decline.

Doctrinal parties tend to operate on the fringes of the political consensus and advocate consistently ideologies or principles that do not find broad support among the electorate. They are therefore not prepared to compromise their basic policies in order to appeal to the voters; they would rather wait for the voters eventually to see the futility of supporting the two main parties and for them to desert in large numbers to an ideologically pure and consistent alternative. They do not seek or expect to govern immediately but think in the long term. Their candidates, therefore, often obtain a derisory percentage of the vote and have no real hope of winning elections. Examples of these parties would include the Socialist Party, the Prohibition Party and the Peace and Freedom Party. The Libertarian Party which was founded in 1972 argues for a massive reduction in the powers of

[17]Clinton Rossiter, op. cit., p. 5.

government at all levels. Its candidate, Ed Clark, won almost a million votes in the 1980 Presidential election while in 1996 Harry Browne obtained 485,120 votes or 0.5% of the total. In 1996 the new Green Party, with a campaign based on environmental issues and the dangers of corporate power, had the well-known consumer advocate, Ralph Nader, as its candidate. Nader secured 684,871 votes—0.7% of the total —despite raising little money, campaigning only intermittently and being on the ballot in only 21 states. More than half his votes came from the three Pacific Coast states of California, Oregon and Washington.

The transient third parties, on the other hand, can be seen as part of the two-party system, as their national prominence is usually as a result of the inadequacies of that system and their speedy decline is due to their reabsorption within one or both of the major parties. They may be parties of economic protest such as the Populists in the 1890s or the Progressives in the 1920s whose rise was a reaction to increasing unemployment. They may be secessionist parties who have broken away from one of the two main parties because of dissatisfaction with the majority coalition's policies or candidates. In 1912 the Progressive 'Bull Moose' movement split from the Republicans because former President Theodore Roosevelt mobilized opposition to President Taft's conservative policies. In 1948 some Southern Democrats refused to support Harry Truman's Presidential campaign and broke away to launch the 'Dixiecrat' candidacy of South Carolina's Strom Thurmond. Twenty years later an even more serious division within the Democratic coalition led to the formation of George Wallace's American Independent Party. Wallace obtained 45 Electoral College votes in the South in 1968 under the AIP banner. The flexibility of the American party system is demonstrated by the fact that four years later he was back in the Democratic Party, and was shot in an assassination attempt while seeking its nomination in the primaries. The 1968 vote was, in effect, a personal vote for George Wallace and most of these supporters returned to the two-party system, leaving the American Independent Party to continue as a right-wing segregationalist doctrinal party. John Schmitz, the party's candidate for the Presidency in 1972, obtained approximately 1% of the popular vote, compared with Wallace's 13.5% in 1968, and former Georgia Governor Lester Maddox fared even more disastrously in 1976, obtaining a mere 170,673 votes across the nation. In 1988 the AIP candidate polled only 27,818 votes.

In addition to minor party campaigns for the Presidency there have also been two independent candidates in recent elections who polled substantial numbers of votes. In 1980 John Anderson, a liberal Republican Congressman from Illinois, ran as an Independent, having failed to win his party's nomination. He obtained 5.6 million votes or 7% of the total. As we have seen, 19.7 million Americans, or 19% of the total voting, backed Ross Perot in 1992. Perot formed an organization of activists in every state, United We Stand America, with the stated intention of influencing Congressional races by defining the issues and possibly by endorsing candidates. Perot established the Reform Party and, not surprisingly, won its nomination, beating former Colorado Governor, Richard Lamm, at its convention. Perot's vote was down in every state compared with 1992. His best performances in both elections were in New England and in sparsely populated states in the West.

TABLE 6.3

Minor Party and Independent Candidates in the 1996 Presidential Election

Candidate/Party	Popular Vote	%	Best Showing
Ross Perot (Reform)	8,085,285	8.40	Maine 14.19%
Ralph Nader (Green)	684,871	0.71	Oregon 3.59%
Harry Browne (Libertarian)	485,120	0.50	Arizona 1.02%
Howard Phillips (US Taxpayers)	184,359	0.19	Virginia 0.57%
John Hagelin (Natural Law)	113,659	0.12	Montana 0.43%
Monica Moorehead (Workers World)	29,082	0.03	Ohio 0.24%
Marsha Feinland (Peace & Freedom)	25,332	0.03	California 0.25%
Charles Collins (Independent)	8,899	0.01	Colorado 0.19%
James Harris (Socialist Workers)	8,463	0.01	DC 0.14%

Source: *Congressional Quarterly Weekly Report*, 18 January 1997, p. 187.

Political Parties in the 1990s

Much of the academic debate about political parties has been over their declining influence within the political system, particularly noticeable in the 1960s and 1970s, and how far there have been signs of revival in the last decade or so. It has been argued that the political parties have traditionally carried out important functions, and they

have been regarded by political scientists as essential tools of democratic government. There has therefore been concern that a decline in
political parties would damage their ability to perform these roles
within the political system. What then are the functions that parties
have fulfilled to make representative government viable?

Firstly, the peaceful transfer of power from one administration to
another, which is one of the characteristics of a stable democracy, is
helped by the existence of parties. One President and his staff leave
the White House as a new Chief Executive and his party move in. The
transition requires cooperation but the new President can find people
to take over the vacant offices by rewarding party notables and supporters. In this sense, the parties are huge personnel agencies to be
drawn on for filling government posts, judicial appointments and Congressional offices.

Political recruitment of potential government leaders also occurs
through the political parties. Candidates for local, state and federal
offices normally have been active in party politics and emerge as people with leadership qualities. Although it is possible in American politics to become a government leader, and even President, without close
ties and a long history of party connections (as Dwight D. Eisenhower
did), the vast majority of the political elite, elected and appointed,
have risen through the party system.

Parties, therefore, find potential leaders, nominate them for office
and provide choices of candidates for the electorate. They also simplify
the choice by providing party labels as a frame of reference and guideline for the voters. Fred Greenstein has pointed out that the majority
of American citizens' actual information and knowledge about issues
and government policies are very vague and that political party labels
allow the voters to respond to complex events by simple criteria. Without such a structuring of the choices, detailed research on the issues
and the candidates' backgrounds would be necessary for a meaningful
choice.[18] It is also worth remembering that American voters are required to select candidates for dozens of federal, state and local positions on the same ballot and that, without the party guideline to help
them sort out the vast array of hopefuls, most electors would be totally
lost. The effect would be to reduce voting turnout and increase the
importance of less relevant criteria such as the names of the candidates
or their positions on the ballot paper. It can be argued, therefore, that

[18]Fred Greenstein, *The American Party System and the American People* (Prentice Hall 1970), p. 39.

parties encourage both electoral participation and accountability of government office-holders to the voters.

The American parties also provide a series of programmes and policies in their platforms and documents. They may not be as specific and clearcut in terms of sharp differences as some critics would like, and may not be able to be carried out as effectively as party manifestoes in a parliamentary democracy where the government can count on the support of a disciplined legislative majority (although the House Republicans' 'Contract with America' came close to it in 1994–95), but the parties do perform the function of interest aggregation by putting forward coherent programmes of broad appeal. By doing so they can help reconcile the interests of conflicting groups in a diverse society. Parties organize voters into coalitions whose interests are loosely but perceptibly linked to policies proposed by groupings of politicians under the same party label. As we pointed out in Chapter 1, parties also may help to bridge the institutional gaps created by the separation of powers and the Constitution.

Evidence of the decline of political parties occurred in a number of different areas.[19] In organizational terms there has been a declining number of activists and official positions in the party structures remained unfilled. The parties have lost direct control of the nominations process as more candidates were selected by the primary process. American parties cannot even exclude from their nomination process candidates who are totally outside the mainstream of the party's beliefs or who have run against party nominees in the past. Racist politician David Duke not only campaigned for the Republican nomination for state office but also entered the 1992 Presidential primaries, to the embarrassment of party leaders who roundly condemned his extreme views. Duke, who had been the Populist Party's Presidential candidate in 1988 when he received almost 47,000 votes, appeared in 16 Republican primaries and won over 10% of the votes in Mississippi, although few elsewhere. As the use of primaries increased so did the number of candidate-centred organizations actually running election campaigns. PACs have taken a bigger role in funding candidates, further reducing the influence of parties. The role of grass-roots activists carrying out traditional electioneering declined, to be replaced by campaigns conducted increasingly through the use of television.

[19]For a detailed discussion of these trends, see Dean McSweeney, 'Is the party over? Decline and revival in the American party system', in *Explaining American Politics*, Robert Williams (ed.) (Routledge 1990).

As far as the electorate is concerned, there is considerable evidence pointing to partisan dealignment, that is the weakening of identification with and attachment to a political party. More voters have said they were independent of party; of those who do identify with one of the parties there has been an erosion in the commitment of many to their party and a marked increase in split-ticket voting. For example, the percentage of voters who are ticket-splitters increased from 12% in 1952 to 28% in the 1988 Presidential election.

Split-ticket voting has had a direct effect on the working of government with more frequent occurrences of divided party control of the legislative and executive branches at state as well as at national level, thus making it more difficult for parties to bridge the gap created by the separation of powers system. In the 1970s parties also declined within Congress, as we saw in Chapter 2, with party cohesion weakened and greater independence among legislators making governing more problematic for both party leaders in Congress and for the President.

Despite these trends there have been signs of party renewal and revival in the 1980s and 1990s. We have seen that the Republican Party led the way in strengthening the capacity of its national organization. In doing so, it offered services to candidates in competition with political consultants and other providers while, at the same time, it built up grass-roots structures at state and local level. Although they may not act as governing bodies over the rest of the party organization in the country or exert disciplinary control over candidates, political scientists such as Larry Sabato believe that the national parties are stronger than they have ever been in their history.[20] Most voters still do identify with parties and support their candidates for office and, as we saw in Chapter 2, party cohesion in Congress increased markedly in the 1980s. As Dean McSweeney has pointed out, many of the features of party decline and their causes are also evident in other political systems and may be seen as the characteristics of post-industrial societies rather than as uniquely American phenomena.[21]

James W. Ceaser sees the parties as being flexible bodies that are able to adapt by using the new technology and campaign methods that have often been said to have been instrumental in their decline. He believes that parties could be strengthened by developments in areas

[20]Larry Sabato, *The Party's Just Begun* (Scott, Foresman 1988), p. 90.
[21]Dean McSweeney, op. cit., pp. 161–2.

where political leaders can have influence: by changing the prevailing opinion among elites and the public about the proper role for parties, particularly in their relationship with candidates, and by altering party rules and election laws at state and federal level that bear on how the parties function, especially with regard to the financing of campaigns. He concludes:

> A consideration of parties today reveals a number of tendencies and countertendencies at work at the same time. In different ways, parties are declining, stabilizing, and resurging. The fluidity of this situation is reinforced by forces driving party development, which leave a great deal to human choice.... The future of the American political party depends greatly on what people decide its future should be.[22]

In recent years the parties have raised large amounts of 'soft money' to spend in support of their Presidential campaigns as well as on party-building activities at state level, the use for which it was originally intended. In 1996 this money was used extensively to support Congressional campaigns as well (see Chapter 7). A Supreme Court decision in 1996 also allowed parties to raise and spend unlimited amounts to support their Congressional candidates so long as these expenditures were not coordinated with their campaigns. It is possible that this condition will be removed in a future judicial decision, leaving the political parties free to play an even more influential role in elections.

Some Further Reading

William J. Keefe, *Parties, Politics and Public Policy in America* (Congressional Quarterly Press 1991)

Dean McSweeney and John Zvesper, *American Political Parties* (Routledge 1991)

Nelson Polsby, *Consequences of Party Reform* (Oxford University Press 1994).

Larry Sabato, *The Party's Just Begun* (Scott, Foresman 1988)

Frank J. Sorauf and Paul Allen Beck, *Party Politics in America* (Scott, Foresman 1988)

Martin P. Wattenberg, *American Parties in Decline* (Harvard University Press 1990)

[22]James W. Ceaser, 'Political Parties – Declining, Stabilizing or Resurging', in *The New American Political System*, Anthony King (ed.) (AEI Press 1990), p. 137.

7

Elections and Voting

No nation in the world has as many elections as the United States. In a Presidential election year, American voters across the country select a total of over half a million officials in addition to the President, the members of the House of Representatives and a third of the Senate. Altogether there are over a million elected positions, the vast majority of which are at the local level for school boards, county boards of supervisors, sheriffs, and so on. As well as electing politicians to national, state and local offices Americans in many states are asked to vote on a wide range of issues in state and local referenda when propositions are submitted to the electorate for approval in accord with state constitutions. Before these general elections there are also primary elections which in many states determine who will represent the parties in the November contests.

Elections are not only a method of deciding who shall govern and hold office but are also important in the process of political communication. Candidates and parties have to attempt to identify the interests of the people in their campaigns; not only do they speak about what they intend to do if elected, they are also obliged to listen to the views of the voters. Politicians who seek election or re-election need to be responsive to public opinion and American legislators are well aware of the 'folks back home'. Elections allow ordinary citizens to participate in politics in a number of ways besides voting. If they are sufficiently interested they can work on behalf of a candidate or contribute money to his campaign funds, and the right to take part in these ways reinforces the feelings of Americans that they live in a liberal democracy.

Who Runs for the Presidency?

The President's roles and limitations have already been examined in Chapter 3, and it is clear that not only Americans but people throughout the world have an interest in how he is selected and what kind of individual is given legitimacy by the electoral process to control the powers of the Presidency. For the parties the Presidency is the big prize; it is the only nationally elected office (along with the Vice-Presidency), and each party hopes not only that one of its members will lead the nation in order to determine domestic and international policy priorities, but also that the future will in addition bring the fruits of office in the shape of appointments and favours to state and local organizations.

James Bryce said in 1910 that American parties were more concerned that their nominee for the White House should be a good candidate than that he should turn out to be a good President. What sort of person makes a 'good candidate' and who actually runs for the Presidency of the United States? The formal qualifications are clearly stated in the Constitution: the President must be 35 years of age or over, must have been a resident of the country for 14 years, and must be a natural-born American citizen. This last condition excludes several million Americans who are immigrants and naturalized citizens as well as the many aliens who live and work in the country. Henry Kissinger, the former Secretary of State, an American citizen born in Germany, was excluded from the Presidency on this basis although not, of course, from having considerable influence within the White House. However, there are many more millions of Americans who technically are qualified to become President, but who in practice are ineligible because they lack the 'political' qualifications.

Firstly Presidential candidates are almost always male and white; certainly all the 42 Presidents have had these characteristics. In 1984 and 1988 the Rev. Jesse Jackson made a major impact in the Democratic party's nomination process. After winning two primaries and 18% of the votes cast in 1984 primaries, Jackson extended his support in 1988 beyond black voters in the cities and came top in seven primaries and won a total of 29.1% of the votes cast, second only to the eventual nominee, Michael Dukakis.

The high regard with which Margaret Thatcher is held in America has almost certainly helped to prepare the electorate for the possibility of a woman in the White House and in 1984 Geraldine Ferraro was the first woman Vice-Presidential candidate.

Presidential candidates are normally middle-aged. Americans are thought to want a mature and responsible individual as President, and therefore the candidate will preferably be in his middle to late forties or fifties. He cannot be too young or he will be accused of being inexperienced, and if he is over 65 there will be doubts as to whether he is too advanced in years to stand the strains of the office. Ronald Reagan, who was 69 years old in 1980, defused the 'age issue' by vigorous campaigning throughout the Republican primaries. Four years later the issue surfaced briefly after a stumbling performance by the President in the first television debate against challenger Walter Mondale, but Reagan was enjoying a huge lead in the opinion polls at the time and a better showing in the second debate limited the damage. Subsequently he won an easy re-election victory to become America's oldest ever President. In 1996 Robert Dole was 73 years old and, if elected, would have become America's oldest ever first-term President; although fit and appearing younger than his years, the generational gap between him and the 50 year-old President Clinton became an issue during the campaign. No matter what his age, the candidate should be in good health mentally and physically—his fitness for the office may otherwise become a campaign issue later. A wife and family are also generally prerequisites for the aspiring candidate; not only do they provide him with a settled family image but they can also become useful campaigners in their own right, as Jimmy Carter's wife, Rosalynn and his sons showed in the 1976 Presidential race. Governor Jerry Brown of California who campaigned in 1976, 1980 and 1992 was unusual in being both relatively young (at 39 in 1976) and a bachelor.

The scrutiny by the media of the suitability of candidates for the Presidency, including their past personal lives, reached a new level in 1988 when Gary Hart, who had been the frontrunner for the Democratic nomination, was forced to withdraw from the race after allegations about extra-marital affairs. Although he tried to make a comeback his chances were ruined by the issue. Bill Clinton managed to survive similar allegations in the early stages of the 1992 campaign. He and his wife Hillary were forced to go on television to discuss their marriage and assure voters that any problems they might have had in the past were behind them. Stories about Clinton's personal life continued to circulate during his first term, and a sexual harassment suit brought against the President by Paula Jones, a former Arkansas state employee, caused embarrassment in the run-up to the 1996 campaign. Despite a number of personal, financial and political scandals leading to Clinton's character and integrity being questioned, voters in 1996 largely appeared to ignore such issues and the President enjoyed high public approval ratings for his overall performance in office.

Inevitably Presidential candidates tend to be politicians with considerable practical governmental experience. There can be no completely adequate preparation for the Presidency as there is no other office quite like it, but perhaps the nearest approximation to the duties of the American Chief Executive is those of the state Governors. Governors of states are, therefore, often candidates for the Presidency, although their concerns in the state capitals are purely domestic and they have no responsibility for the vital area of foreign affairs. Leading Senators may also aspire to the Presidency even though the legislative responsibilities of a Senator are quite different from those of the head of the executive branch. The Vice-President may also hope to have the opportunity of heading his party's ticket, and members of the House of Representatives and Cabinet Secretaries also occasionally run. To be serious contenders they will all have to convince the party activists that they can extend their electoral base from the local and state to the national level.

There have been candidates whose main claim to leadership potential was not in the political but the military field. Dwight D. Eisenhower is the most recent example to make it to the White House, but in the nineteenth century several Presidents established their names initially as military heroes. In 1996 the popular former Chairman of the Joint Chiefs of Staff, Colin Powell, was under pressure to declare as a candidate for the Republican nomination but he eventually ruled himself out of the race. Candidates are likely to be drawn from business and professional backgrounds; even though they may have been brought up in modest family circumstances they are likely to have become fairly wealthy in their own right. In 1996 billionaire businessman Steve Forbes sought the Republican nomination in a self-financed campaign that was based principally on promoting the merits of a flat-rate income tax system. Presidential candidates, like Congressmen, have often been lawyers, although Jimmy Carter had been a Georgian peanut farmer and businessman, and Ronald Reagan was a Hollywood actor before becoming Governor of California. In 1988 two church leaders were prominent candidates although neither Jesse Jackson nor Pat Robertson, the right-wing evangelist, had any experience of public office.

It seems that the religious background of a candidate is much less important today than it has been in the past. It was often said that a

Presidential candidate had, in practice, to be a Protestant to be successful; John Kennedy became the first Catholic President in 1960 and
disposed of that argument. Jimmy Carter's Baptist religion was discussed in the 1976 election and may have had a marginal effect on
voting behaviour, but it was not a major problem for his campaign.
Serious candidates for the Presidency normally strive to win the nomination of one of the two main parties; minor party candidates may
exert an influence on the eventual outcome of the election, although
this is rare, but they have little real chance of winning themselves. Ross
Perot's candidacy in 1992 was the most successful independent or
third party campaign since 1912; he obtained 19% of the popular vote
nationally, although he failed to gain any Electoral College votes.

Any Presidential aspirant has to win two main contests to take occu-
pancy of the White House: firstly, the nomination of his own party in
competition with other potential candidates, and then the Presidential
'general' election against the other party's nominee. Together these
contests make for a long and arduous struggle, a battle that will tax the
energies and finances of even the most dedicated and ambitious politician. They will test his stamina, his nerve and the loyalty of his family
as he criss-crosses the nation in order to build the foundations of a
party and electoral coalition. In recent years many well-qualified potential candidates have decided not to seek the Presidency because of
their reluctance to submit themselves and their families to the intrusive scrutiny of the media which involves making public personal,
financial and even medical records. The rigours of a long campaign
and an unwillingness or inability to raise the large amounts of money
necessary to make a viable run have also been factors. The battle for
the party's nomination can almost be seen as a four-year process,
because as soon as one election is resolved speculation starts among
the politicians and pundits as to who will be the candidates at the next
election. As election year itself approaches the guessing game reaches
new heights as a field of candidates emerges when declarations are
made, disavowals of interest stated and organizations are developed in
those states holding early Presidential primaries. Some politicians prefer to sound out opinion in the country by personal tours before
formally announcing that they are in the running, and those who have
retired from office the previous year have more time and opportunities to do this and make earlier campaign sorties than those currently
in government. Both Jimmy Carter and Ronald Reagan ceased to be
Governors in January 1975 and used the next year marshalling sup-

TABLE 7. 1

The Presidential Election Timetable

Before election year	Candidates sound out opinion, prepare organizations and declare interest
January	Campaigning begins in those states with early primaries and caucuses
February to mid June	State primaries and caucuses select delegates
July–August	National conventions—formally nominate party candidates
September to early November	Election campaign between parties' candidates
First week in November	Presidential election day
January	Inauguration of new President

port and travelling in readiness for the 1976 campaigns. Table 7.1 shows the main dates on the timetable leading to the election.

The Nomination Process

The objective for any candidate in the nomination process is to obtain the support of a simple majority of the delegates to the party's national nominating convention that is held in the summer of election year. For example, in 1996 the Republican candidates required 996 votes and at the Democratic convention 2,145 was the magic figure for victory. Each state party has the right to send a number of delegates to represent its views and this will be approximately proportional to the population size of the state. However, some states may be given extra delegates as a reward for supporting the party's candidate for Governor or Presidency at the last election. The delegates at national conventions tended to be overwhelmingly white, middle-aged and male until the 1960s and pressures grew from minority groups for fairer representation. Challenges against some Southern Democratic states' delegations on the basis of racial bias led to protest walk-outs. In 1972 the Democratic Party adopted a 'quota system' and demanded that each state delegation reflect the proportions of women, young people, blacks and other minorities in the population at large. After the

disastrous 1972 McGovern defeat the system was dropped and a compromise formula established which lays down only that state parties
must seek to achieve a fair cross-section of social groups within their
delegations.

The Democratic Party's emphasis on the representation of grass-
roots activists at the national convention and the increasing use of
primaries for delegate selection in 1972 and 1976 resulted in the
exclusion from the convention of many leading party figures in Congress and state politics as well as the charge being made that delegates
were out of touch with the views of ordinary Democratic voters. In
1982 the National Committee accepted the recommendations of a
party commission chaired by North Carolina Governor, James Hunt,
that about 14% of the delegate votes in the 1984 Convention (566 out
of a total of 3,933) would be elected office-holders uncommitted to any
candidate and this would renew the national party's ties with its es-
tranged Congressional wing.[1]

In subsequent elections the Democratic Party increased the number
of so-called 'super-delegates' to around 750 to include members of
Congress, state Governors, the Democratic National Committee and
elder statesmen, such as former Presidential candidates. In 1992 almost one in five of the delegates to the New York convention were
super-delegates. When this change was first made there was speculation that these delegates might hold the balance of power at the convention in a race where no candidate secured a clear lead in the
primary elections, but this has not proved to be the case so far.

There are two main methods for electing delegates to the national
conventions:

1 State Caucuses and Conventions

Until the 1970s the caucus-convention method of selecting delegates
was the dominant form. It provided for the election of delegates by
rank and file party activists from one level of the party to the next—
from precinct caucuses to county conventions to the state convention
and from there to the national convention. During the 1970s the
number of states using this process declined so that by 1980 only one-
quarter of the delegates to the national convention coming from 17 or

---

[1] For an analysis of changes in the nomination process, see Dean McSweeney, 'Parties and
Presidential Nominations', in *Contemporary American Politics*, Alan Grant (ed.) (Dartmouth 1995).

18 states were selected in this way. In 1988 675 out of 4,160 Democratic delegates were selected by the caucus method while 471 Republican delegates out of 2,277 were chosen this way. In 1992 Democrats in 17 states and Republicans in 14 used caucuses. In 1996 Republicans in 12 states held caucuses wholly, or in conjunction with primaries, to select delegates.

State caucuses tend to reflect the more clearly defined doctrinal views of interested grass-roots supporters and local politicians. They also favour candidates who have a long record of working for the party in the country and whose efforts have been appreciated by party workers.

State caucuses do not obtain as much media attention as Presidential primaries but since 1976, when Jimmy Carter first came to public notice in the Iowa caucuses, held even before the first primary in New Hampshire, more interest has been focused upon them. The Iowa caucuses have now become the first major battleground of the nominations process, with some candidates spending months of their time and considerable resources in personally wooing the relatively small number of activists who attend the party meetings. They do so in the hope that a good performance in Iowa will give them an early breakthrough and the momentum to succeed in the New Hampshire primary. Caucuses are mass meetings of active party supporters who gather on a precinct basis in schools, village halls and private homes to express their preferences for the Presidential nomination. In 1992 the estimated attendance at Democratic meetings varied from around 1,100 in Alaska to 60,000 in Minnesota and Washington. Candidates try to ensure that there is a maximum turnout of their own supporters at these caucuses and the effectiveness of the candidates' organizations in the state is often the key factor in determining success.

2 The Presidential Primaries

In 1968 Presidential primaries were used by Republicans in 16 states and Democrats in 17; by 1980 this had grown to 32 and 33 respectively with three-quarters of national convention delegates selected in this way. In 1992 around 20 million voters took part in the 40 Democratic primaries while 13 million people voted in the 39 Republican primaries, including the District of Columbia and Puerto Rico. A small number of states combined the use of primaries and caucuses. In 1996 the Republicans held 42 primaries in which 13.8 million people participated, while 8.6 million took part in the Democratic contests even though President Clinton was unopposed.

The rules for primaries vary considerably, are complicated and for-ever changing, particularly in the Democratic Party. Voters elect del-egates by casting ballots directly for them or by expressing a preference for a particular candidate. In some states delegates' names appear on the ballot and are elected directly; any preference vote for a candidate is non-binding on the delegates. In closed primaries registered party vot-ers only may participate in their party's election. In open primaries party registration is not a factor and electors can vote in either party's event. In other states registered party voters may only take part in their own party's primary and independent voters can participate in either.

As far as the allocation of delegates is concerned, the Democratic Party now insists upon proportional representation, with all candidates who reach a threshold of 15% in a state obtaining a share of the delegates. The Republicans allow a greater variety of approaches. States may use a 'winner-takes-all' system, with the leading candidate statewide acquiring all the at-large delegates and other delegates going to the top candidate in each Congressional district.

The increasing number of primaries has led to several significant developments. Candidates are obliged to develop personal organiza-tions in a large number of states, making them more independent of the formal party hierarchy. Primaries, therefore, tend to weaken the influence of the state party elders and 'bosses' and there is little or no scope for the 'smoke-filled room' decision making at the party conven-tion, as in the past. The tactic that has been used in the past, of avoiding the primaries and hoping that a deadlocked convention will allow one's emergence as the compromise candidate, is also very un-likely to be successful. Candidates who are serious Presidential con-tenders now have to enter the primaries at the beginning to pick up delegate support because generally one candidate builds so great a lead that he is impossible to stop.

Primary campaigns traditionally began in the cold North-Eastern state of New Hampshire in late February and went on to the climax in sunny California, the largest state with the most delegates, in June. The increasing number of primaries stretched candidates' resources, particularly as they may be fighting in a number of different states on the same day. In 1988 an important development took place in that 16 states, mostly in the South, agreed to hold their primaries on 8 March and this became known as 'Super Tuesday'. The move had been initiated by Southern Democrats who had hoped that by establishing a regional contest on the same day the candidates would be obliged to take more notice of their interests and that their influence would be strengthened in relation to the Northern liberal states. If it was intended to prevent the eventual nomination of a liberal Democrat it was a failure because Michael Dukakis won in Texas and Florida and thus established himself as a broad-based candidate, while Jesse Jackson won five Southern states. Senator Albert Gore of Tennessee also won in five Southern border states after a concentrated campaign in the area but failed to do well elsewhere in the country. George Bush swept the Super Tuesday primaries to virtually assure himself of the Republican nomination while his rival Robert Dole failed to win a single primary on 8 March.

In 1992 a number of states, particularly in the West, moved their caucuses and primaries to the week before Super Tuesday in an attempt to increase their own influence on the nomination. In practice, the results of 'Junior Tuesday', as it became known, proved to be indecisive on the Democratic side and it was not until Super Tuesday on 10 March that Bill Clinton, by winning throughout the Southern states, emerged as the clear frontrunner. Therefore, although Super Tuesday in 1992 was reduced to eight primaries and four caucus states, its influence was considerable. In 1996 each Tuesday throughout the month of March saw a number of primaries clustered in a particular region: on 5 March New England; 12 March the South; 19 March the Mid-West; and, finally, 26 March the Western states.

In recent elections there has been an increasing tendency to 'frontloading' in the delegate-selection process. Approximately a third of all Democratic delegates in 1992 were chosen in the eight-day period of 3–10 March and half of the total were selected by the end of March (compared with 38% in 1984). This trend was developed further in 1996 when two-thirds of the Republican delegates were selected by the end of March. The effect of this development is that, once a frontrunner does emerge from the pack, he appears to be unstoppable. Candidates also have to build a very substantial warchest of campaign funds before the primary season starts; there is now little chance of building on the momentum from early successes and raising money later in the process because the vital contests are concentrated into such a short period. Voters in states which hold their primaries at the end of the season, have often understandably complained that they are virtually disenfranchised in the process because most of the candidates

have withdrawn by then and they are left only to endorse the pre-
sumed nominee or to cast what is effectively a protest vote. Disagreements on alternative dates, requirements of state laws and the need to
hold primaries for state and local offices have prevented these potentially powerful states from having more influence, although California
did move its primary in 1996 from June to the end of March.[2]

The trend of holding larger numbers of primaries earlier in the year
also means that, after months of personal campaigning in the small
states of Iowa and New Hampshire where there is both massive media
coverage and also the opportunity to meet voters and address meetings to gain momentum from early victories, the frenetic pace of the
campaign thereafter inevitably leads to most of the states being fought
principally through the use of television and advertising.

Presidential primaries serve a major purpose apart from the selection of delegates; they demonstrate something which the parties are
clearly concerned to discover before entrusting the nomination to a
candidate: who can and who cannot win votes. Victory in a primary
can remove fears about a candidate among the party 'professionals'
and activists. John Kennedy's win in the mainly Protestant state of
West Virginia in 1960 showed that his Catholic religion was not as
much a handicap as his opponents had forecast. Jimmy Carter's victory in Pennsylvania, a Northern industrial state, allayed suspicions
that he was merely a Southern regional candidate, while Clinton's
victories outside his own region, in Illinois and Michigan, a week after
Super Tuesday consolidated his position as the Democratic frontrunner in 1992.

The early primaries play an important role in weeding out those
contenders who have little real public support within their own parties.
Candidates tend to enter the primaries in which they feel they can do
quite well, and victory or a second place showing in a large field can be a
major boost to an individual's chances and enhance the morale of his
supporters. Perhaps most importantly, it will impress party leaders and
voters in other states. On the other hand, a poor showing in one of the
early primaries may lead to a candidate dropping out of the race altogether as his organization crumbles and his financial resources dry up.

The media here is important, not only in reporting campaign news
and events, but also in their interpretation of what is happening.

[2]Ryan J. Barilleaux and Randall E. Adkins, 'The Nominations: Process and Patterns', in *The
Elections of 1992*, Michael Nelson (ed.) (Congressional Quarterly Press 1993), p. 26.

Journalists tend to focus on the 'horse race' aspects of the nomination process: who is in the lead, who is behind and so on, but they do so through the lens of expectations.

> Expectations of candidate performance are crucial to interpreting the evolution of the race. Primary and caucus results are reported not just in terms of raw data but in terms of how the candidates performed against what was expected of them.[3]

It is a remarkable aspect of American Presidential politics that a man who is virtually unknown nationally at the beginning of election year can have an unassailable lead and become his party's nominee within a few months. In 1992 Governor Douglas Wilder of Virginia withdrew from the Democratic race even before the primary season had begun, while Senator Bob Kerrey of Nebraska and Senator Tom Harkin of Iowa dropped out after disappointing early results. Former Senator Paul Tsongas of Massachusetts, who had been the first Democrat to declare his candidacy in 1991 at the height of George Bush's popularity, bowed out after the Super Tuesday contests, having run out of money and energy. Only former California Governor Jerry Brown who, in the absence of Jesse Jackson, sought to appeal to the party's radical wing and those disillusioned with orthodox party politics, continued his lonely campaign against Clinton to the convention in July. Although the party establishment may have less control of the nominations process as a result of popular involvement through the primary system, it may still influence events. In 1996 the Republicans had an original field of nine candidates, although only five (Dole, Buchanan, Forbes, Senator Phil Gramm of Texas and former Tennessee Governor Lamar Alexander) could be said to be serious contenders. Dole suffered some early setbacks with defeats in New Hampshire (to Buchanan) and in Delaware and Arizona (to Forbes) but, with the party hierarchy rallying to his cause and opposing what they saw as the dangers of the extremist Buchanan gaining further success, he won the vital South Carolina primary on 2 March and throughout that month went on to sweep the remaining primaries to secure the nomination. Overall, Dole won 59% of the total votes cast in the primaries and 1,477 convention delegates. Pat Buchanan continued to campaign after all the other candidates had dropped out, amassed 21% of the popular vote and received 141 delegates.

[3] Ibid., p. 29.

The party that already controls the White House usually has fewer problems in finding a candidate if the President is eligible and wishes to run again. No incumbent President who actively sought it has been denied his party's nomination since 1884. Therefore in some cases the primary elections and state caucuses are merely formalities with either no opposition or purely token resistance from a minor faction within the party; Johnson in 1964, Nixon in 1972, Reagan in 1984 and Clinton in 1996 were all renominated in conventions that were uncontested. However, the strength of the opposition to an incumbent President in an early primary may lead him to decide not to fight again. President Truman in 1952 and Johnson in 1968 both determined to retire from politics rather than face a struggle for their own party's nomination. The opposition to the Vietnam War policies and the support for Eugene

TABLE 7.2

Presidential Candidates and Presidential Primaries 1996

	Total vote	%	Best Showing	
REPUBLICANS				
Robert Dole	8,147,882	59.0	New Jersey	82.3%
Pat Buchanan	2,944,117	21.3	Wisconsin	34.0%
Steve Forbes	1,396,766	10.1	Arizona	33.2%
Lamar Alexander	498,626	3.6	New Hampshire	22.8%
Alan Keyes	436,262	3.2	New Jersey	6.7%
Richard Lugar	126,723	0.9	Vermont	13.7%
Phil Gramm	69,788	0.5	N. Dakota	9.4%
Robert Dornan	38,854	0.3	New Mexico	1.2%
Maurice Taylor	20,888	0.2	New Hampshire	1.4%
Others/uncommitted	127,072	0.9		
Total	13,806,978			
DEMOCRATS				
Bill Clinton	7,482,656	87.3	Georgia	100%
Others/uncommitted	1,090,813	12.7		
Total	8,573,469			

Source: *Congressional Quarterly Weekly Report*, 15 June 1996, p. 1704.

McCarthy in the first primaries in 1968 were undoubtedly major factors in Johnson's decision. A consequence of the increasing importance of primaries in the nomination process is the greater political vulnerability of Presidential incumbents seeking a second term in office. In 1976 the incumbent but non-elected President Gerald Ford suffered a number of humiliating defeats at the hands of his rival, Ronald Reagan, and neither emerged as the clear victor from the primaries; it was only at the Kansas City convention itself that Ford's slender majority of delegates was confirmed. In 1980 the challenge by Senator Edward Kennedy to President Carter's renomination was carried to the convention itself. Carter won 24 primaries to Kennedy's ten, giving him an eventual majority of 2,123 to 1,150 in the roll call of delegates. In 1992 President

TABLE 7.3

Presidential Incumbents and Re-election Contests

Nomination Contest		Incumbent's Primary Vote	Percentage of Convention Delegates	General Election Result
Minor or No Opposition				
William McKinley	(1900)*	—	100	Won
Theodore Roosevelt	(1904)	—	100	Won
Woodrow Wilson	(1916)*	99%	99	Won
Calvin Coolidge	(1924)	68	96	Won
Franklin D. Roosevelt	(1936)*	93	100	Won
" "	(1940)	72	86	Won
" "	(1944)	71	92	Won
Harry S. Truman	(1948)	64	75	Won
Dwight D. Eisenhower	(1956)*	86	100	Won
Lyndon B. Johnson	(1964)	88	100	Won
Richard M. Nixon	(1972)*	87	99	Won
Ronald Reagan	(1984)*	96	100	Won
Bill Clinton	(1996)*	87.3	100	Won
Major or Significant Opposition				
William H. Taft	(1912)*	34%	52	Lost
Herbert Hoover	(1932)*	33	98	Lost
Gerald R. Ford	(1976)	53	53	Lost
Jimmy Carter	(1980)*	51	64	Lost
George Bush	(1992)*	73	98	Lost

*Presidents completing first full four-year-term when seeking re-election.

Source: Modified from: *Congressional Quarterly Weekly Report*, 4 February 1984, p. 224.

George Bush was challenged for the Republican nomination by right-winger Patrick Buchanan. The fact that Buchanan won 37% of the vote in the New Hampshire primary and between one-fifth and one-third of the vote in 17 other states demonstrated Bush's potential vulnerability. Although he only won 18 delegates in the convention his attacks on the President, particularly over taxation and the economy, damaged Bush's standing and developed themes the Democrats were able to capitalize on later in the campaign.[4] In 1996 Bill Clinton was unchallenged for his party's nomination despite the fact that he had been very unpopular during much of his first term, and was widely blamed for contributing to the Democrats' disastrous performance in the 1994 mid-term elections. He achieved this by first building up a huge campaign fund that deterred internal challengers and, second, moving to the centre politically and confronting the Republican-controlled Congress over budget cuts, thereby securing rising approval ratings in the opinion polls. The record of twentieth-century Presidential elections shows that a smooth path to renomination is essential for incumbents seeking re-election. Those Presidents who were unopposed or faced relatively weak opposition within their own party have all won another term, but those that faced significant opposition for renomination all ended up losing in the general election, as Table 7.3 demonstrates.

The National Conventions

The climax of the nominations process is the national party convention which takes place in July or August and formally selects the party's candidate for the Presidency. Both parties have succeeded in nominating a candidate on the first ballot in every convention since 1956; the last occasion when more than one ballot was needed was in 1952 when the Democrats required three votes before finally choosing Adlai Stevenson. Although there have been hotly contested conventions, for example, the Republican one in 1976 referred to above—in recent times the nominations process has led to one candidate emerging with a substantial majority of the delegates, and the conventions have merely endorsed the verdict of the primaries and caucuses.

[4]Alan Grant, 'The US Presidential Election of 1992', *Parliamentary Affairs*, April 1993, pp. 238–54 and 'The 1992 Presidential Election' in *Contemporary American Politics*, Alan Grant (ed.), (Dartmouth 1995).

The conventions are important political events insofar as they demonstrate that parties do exist on a national basis and they provide rare opportunities for party activists to meet fellow supporters from other parts of the country. Delegates spend much of the four days in social as well as political gatherings with meetings of state, ethnic and other caucuses. Pressure groups will use the opportunity to lobby on issues of importance to them as many delegates hold influential positions in their own states. A site committee selects a city to host the convention which can accommodate not only the delegates and other guests but also the media commentators, journalists and television crews from all over the world. In 1996 the Democrats met in Chicago, while the Republicans convened in San Diego.

A platform committee draws up a set of policy statements which the convention can endorse. The party platform is made up of various 'planks' on different issue areas; sometimes these have been vague and non-specific, but on other occasions they have been more ideologically defined, indicating the strength of the faction that has control of the convention. Austin Ranney has pointed out that most delegates and party leaders, including Presidents running for office, take the platform seriously because it serves two important functions. One is the external role of appealing to as many voters and offending as few as possible and the other, more important function in recent years is the internal one of helping to unite the party's various factions behind the ticket so that they will support it enthusiastically.[5]

Party conventions offer great opportunities for national exposure of the party's candidate and policies to the electorate with free publicity in the national media in a system that requires other political messages to be paid for. In many cases the proceedings have appeared as well-choreographed events played out for the benefit of the television cameras rather than as conferences where real debates take place and important decisions are made. Delegates become spectators and cheer-leaders while the coronation of the candidate takes place. Slick video presentations celebrating the life and achievements of the candidate, short speeches by the party's leading politicians and celebrities, an emphasis on entertainment and the avoidance of controversy have become the order of the day, with the 1996 conventions of both parties particularly exemplifying this trend. As a result, the national television

[5]Austin Ranney, 'The President and His Party', in *Both Ends of the Avenue*, A. King (ed.) (American Enterprise Institute 1983), p. 136.

networks have reduced their coverage, the number of viewers has declined and it has been suggested that the conventions should be reduced to two or three days in future.

Party managers have increasingly wished to prevent conflict and the appearance of disunity because they recognize that the image of a divided party will stay in the voters' minds and will diminish the chances of success in November. In 1968 the violence outside the convention centre in Chicago as anti-war protestors clashed with police was mirrored by ugly scenes of rancour and hostility between delegates inside the convention itself. Hubert Humphrey's campaign was severely damaged in the general election as a result. In 1992 the divisive issue of abortion and the emphasis on 'family values' promoted by the Christian Right dominated much of the media coverage of the Republican convention, giving the impression of a narrow and exclusive party that was not reaching out to the wider electorate. Pat Buchanan, who had made a controversial and extreme speech in 1992, was refused an opportunity to address the convention in 1996 by Republican leaders, intent on avoiding a repeat of the public relations disaster of four years before.

The selection of the Vice-Presidential candidate is eagerly awaited, even though the convention merely endorses the choice of the Presidential nominee. In 1992 Bill Clinton, and in 1996 Robert Dole, both named their potential running mates, Al Gore and Jack Kemp respectively, before the convention actually met. The announcement had usually been made during the convention, partly to increase interest in its proceedings. In 1980 there was considerable speculation at the Republican convention in Detroit that Ronald Reagan would invite former President Gerald Ford to become his Vice-Presidential nominee. In the event negotiations broke down as Ford appeared to be demanding too powerful a role in a future Reagan White House and the candidate turned instead to George Bush, who had been his main rival for the Presidential nomination. Many candidates have sought to 'balance the ticket' so the Vice-Presidential candidate has attractive and vote-winning qualities, which they themselves lack, in areas of the country or among particular groups.

Sometimes the eventual choice of Vice-Presidential nominee has mired the campaign in controversy and embarrassment, diverting media attention from the candidate while raising questions about his political judgement. In Chapter 3 we noted the examples of Thomas Eagleton in 1972 and Dan Quayle in 1988. In 1984 Walter Mondale decided to take the bold step of selecting a woman as his Vice-Presidential candidate in an attempt to revive his lacklustre campaign. Although his selection of Rep. Geraldine Ferraro of New York initially heightened interest and support for the Democratic ticket, subsequent press stories about Ferraro's financial affairs and her husband's business connections created further problems for the Mondale campaign and considerably reduced the impact of her presence on the ticket. However, the effect can also be positive. In 1992 Bill Clinton announced his selection of Senator Al Gore as his running-mate before the convention began. Gore in many respects mirrored Clinton: both were in their mid-forties, both were from the South and were centrists within the party as well as sharing the same religious and ethnic background (WASP). However, Gore also complemented Clinton by being a Vietnam veteran, someone with direct experience of Washington politics and an acknowledged specialist on environmental and defence policy. Gore was also able to reinforce the image of generational change and his nomination was well received by both the party and the media.

All that remains for the convention to do is to hear the acceptance speeches of the candidates which are important in setting the tone and the agenda of the general election campaign and to give rapturous applause to the party standard-bearers and their families on the platform. This emotional moment is the reward for the Presidential candidate and his supporters after the long months of work and planning. Hopefully the party is not too divided at the end of the convention and the losers accept their defeat gracefully. This factor may well decide the ultimate success or failure of the party at the next stage of the process—the Presidential election campaign itself. In both 1976 and 1980 incumbent Presidents' hotly disputed victories led to their parties being divided and weakened during the election campaigns. On the other hand, as challengers, Jimmy Carter in 1976 and Ronald Reagan in 1980 led remarkably united parties to victory in the November elections. In 1992 the Democratic delegates left their convention in New York in high spirits with their candidate enjoying a substantial lead in the polls. They had put on a display of public unity and projected a positive image to the public of the Clinton–Gore ticket. The Republicans, in contrast, left their convention in Houston a month later knowing that the convention had damaged the party in the eyes of uncommitted voters and with Bush still trailing in post-convention polls. Normally a candidate received a 'bounce' in the polls following the near-monopoly of media coverage he has received during convention week. In 1996 Robert Dole, who had lagged well behind Clinton since the beginning of the year, reduced the lead to around 7% after the San Diego convention and a well-received acceptance speech but, following the meeting of the Democrats in Chicago in late August, the margin again widened to double that figure.

Traditionally the two parties' nominees took a short vacation following the conventions and began their general election campaigns in earnest after the Labor Day holiday in early September. However, in recent elections campaigning is almost continuous and voters are not treated to even a short break in hostilities. The Democrats learned the lesson from the Dukakis campaign in 1988 when the candidate frittered away a large post-convention lead and disappeared from public view for several weeks, while the Republicans were able to monopolize the media. In 1992 Clinton and Gore were determined to capitalize on their successful convention and set out immediately on one of a number of 'meet the people' tours by coach, thus ensuring that they remained in the public eye throughout the summer and consolidating their poll lead by the time the Republicans met in Houston.

The Presidential Election Campaign

1 Strategies and Organization

American Presidential campaigns therefore last for several months, and with hundreds of meetings, speaking engagements and television appearances it may seem an unnecessarily long time. However, the sheer size of the country, the need for the candidates (particularly a challenger) to become known nationally and the problem of defining more specifically the issues and the candidates' policies within the broad party platforms are determining factors. There is also a need for the cracks in party unity which may have been opened during the nomination process to be papered over, as well as for the coordination of the party and candidate organizations, and all these things can take considerable time.

A Presidential candidate has to recognize that the winning of the party's nomination, often achieved by factional support within the party, and achieving success in the actual election, when all the nation's voters are entitled to participate, are two different propositions. He will therefore often try to modify his positions on the issues or change his image so that he can broaden his appeal to the mass electorate. A candidate who fails to move to the centre and win the support of the 'middle ground' risks being labelled an 'extremist' or 'radical'. At the same time a candidate must avoid the other pitfall: if he moves too clearly away from the positions he supported in the primaries he may alienate and disillusion his original supporters whose backing helped him win the nomination. The activists, who have clearer ideological preferences than the majority of the electorate, dislike any watering down of commitments or fuzziness on the issues but those candidates who maintain only this factional party support are doomed to defeat in November. In 1988 Michael Dukakis was attacked by George Bush for his 'liberal' positions which Republicans calculated were unpopular with the majority of voters. It was only in the last stages of the campaign, by which time Dukakis had lost his early lead in the polls, that the Massachusetts Governor tried to turn this charge to his advantage by admitting that he was in the 'New Deal' tradition of the Democratic Party. He thus enthused and motivated Democratic activists in a way that he had noticeably failed to do until that point.

The objective of the Presidential campaign is to win an absolute majority of the nation's Electoral College votes. Each state is allocated a number of votes equivalent to its number of Congressmen (that is House members plus two Senators) and the candidate who wins the majority of the popular vote in each state takes all the Electoral College votes of that state. There are, in practice, 50 separate Presidential elections (51 if we include the District of Columbia which has three votes) and the Electoral College is a device to record the preferences of each state electorate. There are 538 Electoral College votes and the candidate has to obtain 270 to win. With this system it is inevitable that the largest states with the biggest number of College votes (California 54, New York 33, Texas 32, Florida 25, Pennsylvania 23, Illinois 22 and Ohio 21) are the most valuable prizes as even a narrow victory in the popular vote in these states will give the winning candidate a sizeable bloc of votes. Therefore this factor will help determine where the candidates and their organizations concentrate their efforts; the Presidential aspirants, the running-mates and the candidates' families will spend a great deal of their time in the larger states, and particularly in the big cities, with the objective of winning these 'swing-states'. Bill Clinton made numerous visits to California, not only during the 1996 campaign but during his first term in the White House, in order to consolidate his support in this key state which he had won by a large majority in 1992. Under the 'winner-takes-all' Electoral College system, there is little point in campaigning extensively in areas that are either safe or hopeless for a particular candidate or party; it is in the marginal states that the election will be won or lost. The weakness of George Bush's campaign in 1992 was demonstrated by the fact that he had given up California and its 54 votes as hopeless early in the summer, despite the state's record of having supported Republican candidates in every Presidential election since 1968. On the other hand, candidates do not want to appear complacent, and to show that they are not neglecting any one section they will probably make at least fleeting visits to all areas of the nation. Harry Truman's famous 1948 'whistle-stop tour'—a nationwide campaign by train stopping at small towns and villages to visit the voters in the country as well as the big cities—added the personal touch to the normal canvassing for support, but in modern elections candidates usually fly by jet plane from one major city to another to give speeches to party rallies where they are assured of a good reception.

Perhaps the most significant development in the method and style of campaigning, however, is the use made of television by all candidates in modern Presidential elections. A personal appearance is often made to appeal not simply to the voters who are present in the stadium or hall where the meeting is held, but principally to the millions who will see extracts of it that evening on the television news. In 1988 George Bush proved to be far more effective in obtaining this sort of coverage than his opponent, Michael Dukakis; the 'soundbites' of a few seconds taken from his comments often summed up in a sentence a theme or issue he wanted to develop that day in the news programmes. In 1988 the average direct quote from a Presidential candidate on news programmes was a mere 8.9 seconds, compared with 43.1 seconds in 1968.

Television today is the main method by which Americans find out about politics, and therefore the candidates not only try to obtain as much news coverage as possible, but also spend a very large proportion of their total budgets on television advertising. The organizations buy commercials of a few seconds' to several minutes' duration at very expensive rates in order to reach the peak viewing time audiences. As the campaign goes on the number of commercials increases steadily with saturation coverage in the large states immediately prior to election day itself. Inevitably in the short slots that are mostly used there is very little that can be said about policies, and the campaign public relations advisers try to project an image of the candidate to which the electorate will respond favourably. They emphasize the man's honesty, integrity, strength of character, concern for the needy and other perceived virtues. The candidate is filmed while campaigning, talking to voters, working in his office or relaxing at home with his family. Occasionally the intention of the commercial will be to communicate a short sharp message on an issue (for example, a brief clip of film or some statistics on criminal offences with the accompanying indication that the candidate favours a strong 'law and order' policy) or to launch an attack on the other candidate's policies. The most famous (and criticized) Bush commercial in 1988 featured the case of a black murderer, Willie Horton, who had been released on a prison furlough programme in Massachusetts and had committed further crimes. The commercial implied that Governor Dukakis was 'soft on crime' and it appeared to be effective with the voters. In 1992 Bill Clinton's team were prepared for similar campaigning and were determined not to repeat the mistake the Dukakis campaign made in allowing such attacks to go unanswered, which enabled the Republicans to paint a very negative image of the Democratic candidate. A number of officials were commissioned to issue immediate rebuttals of any charges they felt distorted Clinton's record or position on the issues so that the news media would feel obliged to present their side of the story, if indeed the story was used at all. Frequently campaign managers like to encapsulate the main theme of their candidate's appeal to the voters by the use of an easily identifiable slogan. Gerald Ford, for example, claimed that among his achievements in office he had rescued America from the nightmare of Watergate and restored decency to and trust in the Presidency. His television commercials and campaign literature repeated the slogan 'He's making us proud again'.

The 1992 election saw several developments in the way the media covered the campaign and in how they were used by the candidates. Many broadcasters, stung by criticisms that they had trivialized recent elections by their coverage, did attempt to spend more time analysing issues and in critically examining the claims and counter-claims made by the candidates. Candidates themselves sought new and alternative ways of getting their message across. They appeared for longer interviews on morning and late evening news programmes, as well as on talk shows with more relaxed formats than the traditional political interview programmes and which often included audience participation. By the end of the campaign the three major candidates had made more than a dozen appearances on 'Larry King Live', a CNN talk show. Bill Clinton often led the way, for example, by appearing on MTV, the cable music channel, to appeal to younger voters, and even playing his saxophone and wearing dark glasses as a guest on the Arsenio Hall late night show. He answered voters' questions directly at dozens of 'town hall meetings' across the country which were each carried live by local television stations, while his staff distributed hundreds of thousands of videocassettes about the candidate and his policies. Ross Perot spent over $60 million of his own money to pay for his campaign which included half-hour 'infomercials', in which he lectured millions of television viewers about the federal budget deficit and poured scorn on his opponents. The diversity of the new or 'alternative' media, including cable and satellite channels, enabled the candidates to some extent to bypass the major television networks which had dominated election coverage in the past. It has been said many times that in the last two decades America has experienced the era of 'market politics', and critics have drawn attention to the dangers of selecting a man for the most powerful national office on the basis of 'images' created by Madison Avenue public relations and advertising people who package and sell candidates as if they were dealing with a new soap powder or soft drink.[6] However, it would surely be unrealistic to expect Presidential candidates not to make maximum use of the modern media which can so easily take them into millions of American homes. By 1996 both the Clinton and Dole campaigns were using the Internet extensively to communicate with the increasing number of voters with access to personal computers. However, the network television news programmes cut the time devoted to covering the campaign by half, reflecting the general lack of interest and excitement among the public for the candidates or the issues raised in the election.

Television can be used by voters in a mature, responsible way to help them decide on the respective merits of the contenders for the Presidency. In 1960, there was a series of television confrontations between Republican candidate Vice-President Richard Nixon and Democratic Senator John Kennedy, and these programmes dealt with policy issues in a number of important areas. Kennedy was able to use these occasions to convince the voters that he was not as inexperienced as his opponent had suggested, and Nixon not only did not 'win' the debates

[6]See e.g. Joe McGinniss, *The Selling of the President 1968* (Trident Press 1969), a critical study of Richard Nixon's campaign.

as he had confidently expected but also projected a rather shifty appearance that did not help his image. In every election since 1976 televised debates between the main contenders have become part of the ritual of Presidential elections. In 1992, with greater public interest in the election, it is estimated that 92 million Americans tuned in to the final televised debate, compared with 71 million in 1988. For President Bush the debates were seen as the most important opportunity to make a breakthrough in the campaign. However, his team managed to give the impression that they were afraid of letting their man in the ring with Clinton (the 'Oxford debater' as Bush called him) by refusing for weeks to agree the number of debates, rules and procedure. Eventually, three 90-minute programmes featuring the Presidential candidates were arranged, with one featuring the Vice-Presidential contenders, all to take place over a ten-day period in mid-October.

In the past, over-rehearsed candidates, constrained by a format of questions and answers from hand-picked journalists within rigid time limits, have restricted the opportunity for real debate. The contrived drama, the prepared one-liners and effective sound-bites tend to stay in the memory. In 1992 the first debate was based on the traditional pattern. The main winner was Ross Perot. Appearing on the same platform with the two main party candidates raised his stature, and his good humoured folksy wisdom played well with the viewers. In addition, it was noticeable that in all three debates Bush and Clinton concentrated their fire on each other and at times seemed to defer to the independent candidate in the hope of not alienating Perot supporters and with an eye to eventually winning them over to their own cause. A *Newsweek* poll after the first meeting reported that 43% felt Perot had won, 31% Clinton and only 19% backed Bush. Perot's support in the opinion polls jumped from 7% to 14% almost overnight.

The second debate provided a welcome variation in format with a talk-show setting and the candidates being questioned by an audience of uncommitted voters. Candidates could move around the platform while answering questions in a more informal style, an approach that had been suggested by Clinton and suited him well as he set out specific proposals to deal with the wide range of issues raised by the voters. Bush, who was chastened by a voter chiding him for negative attacks on his opponent, appeared ill at ease and on several occasions was caught by the camera glancing at his watch. Viewers began to tire of Perot's hectoring style and lack of specific answers, and a CBS poll showed that 53% judged Clinton to be the winner, 25% Bush and 21%

Perot. It was only in the third debate that Bush gave a combative and forceful performance with a focus on the main themes of his campaign; even then, polls indicated Clinton was judged to have performed better. The Vice-Presidential debate was notable for the fact that Dan Quayle surprised many observers by being a match for Al Gore and for what ranks as easily the most embarrassingly inept performance ever in such confrontations, by Perot's running-mate, retired Admiral James Stockdale.

In 1996 the bipartisan Commission on Presidential Debates agreed with an advisory panel chaired by political scientist, Professor Richard Neustadt, that Perot should be excluded from participation on the basis that his poll ratings indicated that he did not have a realistic chance of winning the election, in contrast to 1992 when, at one point, he was neck and neck with the two major party candidates. The Dole campaign also wished to deny Perot exposure, believing that any improvement in his fortunes would be likely to be at the expense of the Republican candidate. As predicted, the 1996 televised debates allowed Clinton to exploit his superior communication skills and Dole's last real opportunity to make a breakthrough was lost.

Another feature of recent Presidential campaigns is the growth in the number of opinion polls which are carried out and published. Whereas there were 16 national polls in the peak campaign months in 1960, there were more than 70 in the comparable months of 1988, all gaining wide news coverage and helping to shape the campaign itself. In 1992 Bill Clinton's 15% lead in the opinion polls following the Democratic convention was reduced by a few points after the Republican meeting in Houston, but Bush did not achieve the 'bounce' of the 1988 campaign when he overtook Dukakis after his party's convention and remained in the lead until polling day. Clinton's advantage in the polls remained remarkably consistent from early September until the last week of the campaign, when it appeared to narrow dramatically. It seemed as if Bush's attacks on Clinton's character and the issue of 'trust' were at last paying off, but in the last few days the momentum was lost as the personal abuse became more shrill and unpresidential. Final polls indicated Clinton's lead had widened again to 5–8%; on election day his winning margin in the popular vote was 5%. All but one of the polls underestimated Perot's final tally by 2–5%.

During 1996 every opinion poll published during the year showed Clinton enjoying a substantial lead over Dole and helped to create a feeling of inevitability that the President would secure a second term.

However, as in 1992, Clinton's lead shrunk in the final days of the campaign; of those making up their minds in the last week, Dole won 47% to Clinton's 35%. It appears that revelations of campaign finance abuses may have damaged Clinton, while Dole made a final 96-hour campaign swing that seemed to mobilize many Republican supporters and helped prevent a Clinton landslide, as well as secure vital votes that enabled the party to retain its control of Congress. Almost all the final polls failed to identify this late trend sufficiently well and gave Clinton a much larger lead than the 8% he actually secured in the election (see Table 7.4).

In terms of campaign planning, the candidate's personal organization set up during the primary contests will have to work alongside the official party organization which is headed by the party chairman at

TABLE 7.4

Final Opinion Surveys in 1992 and 1996 Presidential Election

1992	CLINTON	BUSH	PEROT
ACTUAL POPULAR VOTE	43%	38%	19%
Gallup/CNN/*USA Today*	44	37	14
Lou Harris	44	38	17
CBS News/*New York Times*	45	37	15
Washington Post	43	35	16
ABC News	44	37	16
NBC News/*Wall Street Journal*	44	36	15
Battleground Poll	40	36	19

1996	CLINTON	DOLE	PEROT
ACTUAL POPULAR VOTE	49%	41%	8%
Reuters/Zogby	49	41	8
Gallup/CNN/*USA Today*	52	41	7
Lou Harris	51	39	9
CBS News/*New York Times*	53	35	9
ABC News	51	39	7
NBC News/*Wall Street Journal*	49	37	9
Hotline/Battleground	45	36	8

Source: *Congressional Quarterly Weekly Report*, 7 November 1992, p. 3550 and 9 November 1996, p. 3193.

TABLE 7.5

Portrait of the Electorate 1988, 1992 and 1996

% of 1996 total		VOTE IN 1988		VOTE IN 1992			VOTE IN 1996		
		Bush	Dukakis	Clinton	Bush	Perot	Clinton	Dole	Perot
—	TOTAL	53%	45%	43%	38%	19%	49%	41%	8%
48	Men	57	41	41	38	21	43	44	10
52	Women	50	49	46	37	17	54	38	7
83	Whites	59	40	39	41	20	43	46	9
10	Blacks	12	86	82	11	7	84	12	4
5	Hispanics	30	69	62	25	14	72	21	6
66	Married	57	42	40	40	20	44	46	9
34	Not married	46	53	49	33	18	57	31	9
17	Aged 18–29	52	47	44	34	22	53	34	10
33	30–44	54	45	42	38	20	48	41	9
26	45–59	57	42	41	40	19	48	41	9
24	60 and older	50	49	50	38	12	48	44	7
6	Not a high school graduate	43	56	55	28	17	59	28	11
24	High school graduate	50	49	43	36	20	51	35	13
43	College graduate or more	56	43	44	39	18	47	44	7
46	White Protestant	66	33	33	46	21	36	53	10

TABLE 7.5 *continued*

29	Catholic	52	47	44	36	20	53	37	9
3	Jewish	35	64	78	12	10	78	16	3
23	Trade union household	42	57	65	24	21	59	30	9
11	Family income under $15,000	37	62	59	23	18	59	28	11
23	$15,000–$29,999	49	50	45	35	20	53	36	9
27	$30,000–$49,999	56	44	41	38	21	48	40	10
39	over $50,000*	56	42	40	42	18	44	48	7
9	over $100,000*	62	37	36	48	16	38	54	6
23	From the East	50	49	47	35	18	55	34	9
26	From the Mid-West	52	47	42	37	21	48	41	10
30	From the South	58	41	42	43	16	46	46	7
20	From the West	52	46	44	34	22	48	40	8
35	Republicans	91	8	10	73	17	13	80	6
39	Democrats	17	82	77	10	13	84	10	5
26	Independents	55	43	38	32	22	43	35	17
20	Liberals	18	81	68	14	18	78	11	7
47	Moderates	49	50	48	31	21	57	33	9
33	Conservatives	80	19	18	65	17	20	71	8
9	First-time voters	51	47	48	30	22	54	34	11

*The 1988 and 1992 figures are based on the income ranges $50,000–$74,999 and over $75,000 respectively.

Sources: Exit polls from 1996 Voter News Services, 1992 Voter Research and Surveys and 1988 *New York Times*/CBS News.

the national level. It is important for the smooth running of the campaign that these two structures—one with loyalty solely to the Presidential candidate and the other with interests in elections at all levels— should be able to integrate their efforts into a coordinated and harmonious relationship. President Nixon's 'Campaign to Re-elect the President' (CREEP) in 1972 did virtually nothing to help other Republican candidates and was resented by many of the party regulars; probably the most that can be expected is a *modus vivendi* and the avoidance of open squabbling. The candidate's personal office will probably organize press and television coverage, brief him on the most important issues in particular areas of the country, draft speeches and research areas for new policy statements. It will also be responsible for ensuring that his meetings are well publicized in advance and attended by large enthusiastic audiences. The leading members of the successful candidate's campaign staff will often be given important positions in the new administration.

An incumbent President who is running for a second term in the White House clearly has some major advantages over his rival. He can claim to be experienced in the job, is a recognizable national figure at the beginning of the campaign and can appeal to the voters' respect for and trust in the Presidential office. He can make strategic policy moves, such as President Nixon's visit to China, or his peace initiative in the Vietnam War in 1972, which can influence the campaign issues and to which the challenger can only respond without shaping events. He usually has to campaign less and can argue that he is getting on with the job of being President while staying in the Oval Office. The media will report whatever he does anyway, because the President's actions are always news. On the other hand, if the nation's economic position is not healthy the President may take the brunt of public dissatisfaction, as George Bush clearly did in 1992. The 'hostage crisis' in Iran was a continuing problem for President Carter during 1980 and a constant reminder to the voters of foreign policy failures. The challenger to an incumbent will probably have to make the running in his strategy and attack the Presidential performance, at the same time convincing electors that he has the ability and experience to do better. In some cases Presidents have succeeded in turning the tables on the challenger and making *him* the major issue. Barry Goldwater and George McGovern both found their own suitability for the Presidency seriously questioned, and Bill Clinton's character and experience were also themes in the 1992 election. Perhaps the worst position a Presidential candidate can be in is when he is attempting to follow a President of his own party, if the administration has seriously declined in popularity. Hubert Humphrey, the Democratic nominee in 1968, had been Johnson's Vice-President and thus was connected with the government's unpopular Vietnam policy. He was therefore in a position of either having to defend policies for which he was not personally responsible, or seeming to be disloyal to the President if he criticized them. What is more he could not claim the experience of an incumbent President. Vice President George Bush's problem in 1988 was rather that of establishing his own identity after serving eight years in the shadow of a popular President. Although opponents tried unsuccessfully to connect him with the Iran-Contra scandal in the minds of the public, Bush had to establish a new image as his own man with his own ideas and policies. On the other hand, being Ronald Reagan's heir-apparent undoubtedly helped him both in securing the Republican nomination and in the election campaign itself.

2 Voting in Presidential Elections

Any campaign manager planning the strategy for achieving a majority of the Electoral College votes will bear in mind the factors that influence the American electorate in deciding how to vote in Presidential elections. The three main criteria are issues, the candidates and party identification.

For an issue to be significant in electoral choice it requires knowledge and feeling on the part of the voter: he has to know about the issue, care strongly about it and know the positions of the candidates on it. Relatively few voters are likely to decide how to vote on the basis of one single issue but a general disenchantment or contentment with the policies of the existing government may have their effects, although in the American system, where the President and Congress are separate and often divided in party control, determining who is to blame or whom to credit with achievements is more difficult for voters. In 1992, however, the state of the economy was clearly the key factor; 43% of electors said that jobs and the economy were the major influences on their vote, and the budget deficit was named by a further 21%. President Bush, successively battered by Buchanan, Clinton and Perot, took the lion's share of the blame from the electorate with fewer than one in three approving of his handling of the issue. In 1996, with rising prosperity, low inflation, falling unemployment and a reduced federal deficit, Bill Clinton undoubtedly benefited from the return of the 'feel good factor' among a substantial proportion of the electorate. It is quite natural that voters should consider the personalities and characters of the individuals who aspire to become President of the United States. Given the importance of the office to the nation—and the world's security—voters are particularly interested in the candidate's experience, competence and emotional stability. They are also concerned with the honesty and integrity of the candidates, particularly in the post-Watergate era although it appears that many voters in 1996 were prepared to ignore questions about Clinton's character. Relatively few candidates have had the vote-winning qualities that Roosevelt and Reagan demonstrated in being able to draw support from almost all sections of society, even when in some cases voters did not agree with the candidate's stand on particular issues. Sometimes a candidate wins support because of a negative reaction by voters to the personality of the other candidate. With voters being increasingly willing to split their tickets at Presidential elections and the candidates running their own campaigns separately from party organizations, the importance of the individual contenders for the Presidency has grown.

Party identification is, however, still a significant factor in Presidential elections. Around three-quarters of those voting do think of themselves as Republicans and Democrats although the number of 'Independents' who do not attach themselves to a party at all has grown. Partisan commitment has also weakened and the incidence of split-ticket voting has increased. However, most electors who identify with a particular party support its Presidential candidate even in a year when the party does badly. In 1992 73% of Republican identifiers voted for Bush while in 1996 80% supported the party's candidate, Robert Dole, despite the fact that his defeat seemed inevitable.

The Democratic Party used to enjoy a substantial lead over the Republicans in voter identification and therefore its candidates had to concentrate principally on obtaining a full turnout of the party's supporters, while the Republicans, with a narrower base, had to appeal to independents and disillusioned Democrats in order to win the Presidency. Democrats faced the challenge of mobilizing voters from social groups who have traditionally had low turnout rates, while the Republican white middle-class voters were more likely to go to the polls. During the 1980s the gap in partisan support narrowed substantially: among white voters it was non-existent in 1984 and just three points in 1986. Only the solid support of the black electorate kept the Demo-

crats from slipping to an even position with their opponents nationwide. According to Martin P. Wattenberg, the Republican strategy for
Presidential elections has therefore changed dramatically from need-
ing to win Democrat and independent votes to simply maintaining
their own base.[7] In 1996 Dole actually enjoyed a 3% lead over Clinton
among white voters but, in many states huge leads among blacks and
Hispanics provided the President with the popular majorities sufficient to secure their Electoral College votes.

The factor of party identification probably explains why a very large
group of voters—42% in 1980, for example—reported that they decided how to vote before the party conventions officially decided who
the candidates would be. However, a further 40% said they made up
their minds during the campaign itself and clearly undecided voters
hold the key to victory in close elections.[8]

We have already seen in Chapter 6 that certain social groups in the
nation tend to support one or the other of the major parties. A candidate for the Presidency knows the traditional supporters of his party
very well and has to attempt to preserve this base and preferably also
attract 'Independents' and those who are undecided at the beginning
of the campaign. Between 1968 and 1988 the Republicans won five of
the six Presidential elections. Their successes came about as the traditional New Deal coalition cracked and Nixon, Reagan and Bush made
inroads into areas of the country and among social groups which had
historically supported the Democratic Party. In 1992 and 1996 Bill
Clinton succeeded in winning back many of these voters and, in so
doing, became the first Democratic President to win re-election since
Franklin Roosevelt. If we analyse the vote in Presidential elections we
can see that the following factors are significant:

Region.   Republican victories in the 1980s were built on an electorally
solid base of Western and Southern states, many of which were growing economically and expanding in population, thereby increasing
their Electoral College votes. Reagan and Bush swept these regions,
although in 1988 Michael Dukakis did win Oregon and Washington in
the Pacific West. However, in the 1990s Bill Clinton won a number of
important Western and Southern states, breaking GOP dominance in

[7]Martin P. Wattenberg, 'From a Partisan to a Candidate-centered Electorate', in *The New American Political System, Second Version*, Anthony King (ed.) (AEI Press 1990), pp. 158–60.

[8]William H. Flanigan and Nancy H. Zingale, *Political Behaviour of the American Electorate*, 5th edn (Allyn and Bacon 1983), p. 159.

these areas. In both 1992 and 1996 he won California with large pluralities of the popular vote. The South was the only region in the country in which Dole obtained a majority of the Electoral College votes (104–59) but the Democratic ticket headed by the two Southerners did win in Louisiana, Florida and Kentucky, as well as in their home states of Arkansas and Tennessee.

Democratic strength in the North-East has been consolidated in the 1990s, and in 1996 Clinton swept every state in the region, winning all 127 Electoral College votes. All these states, with the exception of Pennsylvania, gave Clinton at least a ten-point margin of victory over Dole. Dole's only successes in the Mid-West were in sparsely populated areas such as his own home state of Kansas and in Indiana which has remained loyal to the Republicans in the 1990s.

Occupation and Income. Republican successes were based on the party's traditional support among white collar professional and managerial voters, complemented by winning over large numbers of blue collar manual workers in the 1980s. In 1984 Reagan had a 9% lead among this group while in 1980 and 1988 the parties attracted this key part of the old Democratic coalition in equal numbers. The votes of blue collar 'Reagan Democrats', particularly those of skilled workers, were crucial to the Republicans' victory in a number of large industrial states in the North-East and Mid-West, but in 1992 this group went back to the Democrats by a margin of two to one. Suburban and middle income voters also moved decisively to Clinton, while low income groups remained solidly Democratic. In 1996 only the highest income groups gave Dole a majority of their votes.

Ethnic and Religious Minorities. The Democratic Party's traditional coalition included many ethnic and religious minorities, but the Republicans made inroads among a number of these groups in the 1980s. For example, Catholic voters, including Italian, Irish and Polish Americans, supported Reagan by 9% in 1984 and Bush by 5% in 1988. However, many returned to the Democrats in the 1990s: in 1992 Clinton enjoyed an 8% lead among Catholics and increased this to 16% in 1996. In contrast, Jewish voters have been loyal to the Democrats throughout, even giving Mondale two-thirds of their votes in the Reagan landslide year of 1984. In 1996 Clinton led by a massive 62% among Jews. Hispanic and black voters have also provided solid and consistent support for Democratic candidates in every Presidential election.

Age. One of the most remarkable aspects of Reagan's 1984 victory was that the nation's oldest ever President enjoyed a huge 19% lead among younger voters between 18 and 29 years in age. This Republican lead was reduced to 5% in 1988, and Clinton secured large majorities among younger voters in the 1990s. Older voters over 60 supported Reagan overwhelmingly in 1984, split their votes almost evenly in 1988 and in the 1990s backed Clinton, although in 1996 his lead over Dole was only 4% compared with a 12% margin four years earlier.

Gender. Political scientists have been particularly interested in the phenomenon known as the gender gap that opened up in the 1980s and has become a significant feature of voting behaviour. Women are a larger proportion of the electorate and have a longer life expectancy than men. Female voters are much more willing to support Democratic candidates: Reagan's lead over Mondale in 1984 was 25% among men, but only 12% among women; in 1988 Bush gained 16% more of the male votes than Dukakis but only 1% more of the female vote. In 1992 Clinton had a 3% lead among men but a 9% margin among women, while in 1996 the most dramatic display of the gender gap took place: 1% more men voted for Dole than Clinton, while the President had an overwhelming 16% lead among women. This dominance was particularly notable among unmarried women (62%–28%) and younger women (58%–31%).

The explanation for these differences seems to lie in the issue areas that have been of most concern to men and women. Male voters were attracted to Republican candidates in the 1980s because they gave priority to defence, patriotism and law and order; females put more emphasis on social issues, such as health care and education, and perceived the Democratic candidates as better equipped to deal with them. In recent times the Republicans have also been seen as hostile to abortion, affirmative action programmes, increases in the minimum wage and being in favour of cuts in welfare programmes, all of which are viewed as threatening by many women. More women than men are in low paid or part-time employment, and this economic factor helps explain women's greater tendency to support the Democratic Party in elections.

FIGURE 7.1

The Electoral College Votes in the 1996 Presidential Election

The Electoral College

As soon as the polls close on election evening in the Eastern United States, the count begins, even though voters are still casting their ballots in the Western states. Owing to the time differences across the country, the first tentative returns will be announced before all the polling stations have shut.[9] The major television networks use their computers to make predictions as to which candidate will win particular states on the basis of the returns from a few 'representative' precincts, and they can usually tell the nation who the next President of the United States will be well before all the votes are counted. Despite the fact that the decision of the people will be known that night or early next day, the actual formality of casting Electoral College votes does not take place until several weeks later. Since 1789, the election of President has taken place using a constitutional procedure designed to help preserve the rights of the individual states. When voters mark their ballot paper for Presidential and Vice-Presidential candidates, they are really endorsing a list of electors picked by the candidate's party in that state. These party dignatories are authorized to cast all their state's Electoral College votes for their candidate if he wins the majority of the popular vote in the state. In most states the names of the candidates only and not the list of electors appear on the ballot paper. Electors meet in each of the state capitals and register their votes which are transmitted to Washington, but the nation's Electoral College never meets as a body.

As a candidate can win all the state's Electoral College votes by a very small plurality of the popular vote, there is a tendency for the Electoral College result, which is what really matters, to exaggerate the margin of victory indicated by the national popular vote. There are also three main criticisms that are frequently made about the Electoral College:

(1) There is the possibility that the candidate who wins most votes in the country will actually lose the election because his rival has accumulated his support in such a way that he wins more Electoral College votes. This has happened three times—John Quincey Adams (1824), Rutherford B. Hayes (1876) and Benjamin Harrison (1888). In 22 of the nation's Presidential elections the winner has had an

---

[9]A bill to provide for all polling stations in the continental United States to close at the same time in Presidential elections passed the House on the 99th and 100th Congresses but died each time in the Senate. West coast politicians claim that projections of the winner before polls have closed in the West discourages electors from voting.

uncomfortably close victory and even Jimmy Carter, who had a 1.7 million vote plurality, would have lost in the Electoral College if a mere 9,245 votes in Ohio and Hawaii had gone to Ford.[10]

(2) It is necessary for a candidate to win an overall majority of Electoral College votes to become President. If no such clear majority is obtained because of the intervention of a strong minor party candidate, then the House of Representatives has the constitutional right to decide, voting in state blocs with one vote each. Many critics see such an eventuality as a threat to the democratic wishes of the people. The House had to resolve the issue in 1800 and 1824, and there were fears that George Wallace's 1968 campaign might also produce a deadlocked situation. However, Wallace did not obtain sufficient Electoral College votes to deny Nixon victory (see Table 7.6).

(3) Although the party officials who become state electors are supposed to vote for their own party's candidate they are not legally bound to do so, and sometimes an individual will go against the popular wishes of the state's electorate and vote for a different candidate. For example, in 1972 a Virginian Republican voted for the Libertarian party's John Hospers rather than for Richard Nixon and in 1976 one Republican elector supported Ronald Reagan rather than Gerald Ford.

There have been hundreds of proposals for constitutional amendments that would either modify the rules of the Electoral College or abolish it altogether. Early in his own Presidency, Jimmy Carter threw his weight behind the reform movement by stating that he would like to see the archaic system replaced by direct popular election. The best-supported proposal in recent times has been put forward by Senator Birch Bayh of Indiana, who suggested direct elections of the President with a run-off election between the two top contenders if no-one secured more than 40% of the popular vote in the first poll. In July 1979 the Senate passed a proposal for a constitutional amendment on these lines by 51–48 votes but this was well short of the two-thirds majority necessary. There have been less radical suggestions to modify the 'winner-takes-all' nature of the Electoral College; there could be a system of dividing the Electoral College votes of a state in proportion to the popular vote attained by each individual, although this would make it more difficult for one candidate to secure an absolute majority.

[10]*Time*, 4 April 1977.

TABLE 7.6

Electoral College and Popular Votes

	Electoral College Votes	Popular Vote	
1968			
Nixon (R)	302	37,770,237	(43.4%)
Humphrey (D)	191	37,270,533	(42.7%)
Wallace (A I P)	45	9,906,141	(13.6%)
1976			
Carter (D)	297	40,827,394	(50.0%)
Ford (R)	240*	39,145,977	(47.9%)
McCarthy (Ind.)	—	745,042	(0.9%)
Others	1	965,505	(1.2%)
1984			
Reagan (R)	525	54,455,093	(59.0%)
Mondale (D)	13	37,567,331	(41.0%)
1988			
Bush (R)	426	48,881,278	(53.4%)
Dukakis (D)	112	41,805,374	(45.7%)
1992			
Clinton (D)	370	44,908,233	(43.2%)
Bush (R)	168	39,102,282	(37.7%)
Perot (Ind.)	0	19,741,048	(19.0%)

*Ford won 27 states with 241 Electoral College votes, but one of the Republican electors in Washington voted for Ronald Reagan. (See the third criticism of the Electoral College.)

Why has the present system survived so long? This is most easily explained by the lack of consensus behind any particular method of reform. Direct popular election across the nation would take away from the states their role in Presidential elections; the federal Constitution was designed to safeguard their interests and reform would remove the influence of small states and less populated areas. Other opponents of popular election argue that the big cities which now often determine the direction of their states' Electoral College votes would lose power, and the influence of minority groups would be less. Some people also fear that popular election would further weaken the two-party system and encourage minor party candidates. For all these reasons reform of the

TABLE 7.7

Number of Electoral College Votes and % of Popular Votes for Clinton, Dole and Perot in 1996

Clinton (Dem.) 379 EC Votes; 49% popular vote

	EC	Clinton	Dole	Perot	Other
Arizona+	8	46.5	44.3	8.0	1.2
Arkansas	6	53.7	36.8	7.9	1.6
California	54	51.1	38.2	7.0	3.7
Connecticut	8	52.8	34.7	10.0	2.5
Delaware	3	51.8	36.6	10.6	1.0
District of Columbia	3	85.2	9.3	1.9	3.5
Florida +	25	48.0	42.3	9.1	0.5
Hawaii	4	56.9	31.6	7.6	3.8
Illinois	22	54.3	36.8	8.0	0.8
Iowa	7	50.3	39.9	8.5	1.3
Kentucky	8	45.8	44.9	8.7	0.6
Louisiana	9	52.0	39.9	6.9	1.1
Maine	4	51.6	30.8	14.2	3.4
Maryland	10	54.3	38.3	6.5	1.0
Massachusetts	12	61.5	28.1	8.9	1.6
Michigan	18	51.7	38.5	8.7	1.1
Minnesota	10	51.1	35.0	11.8	2.2
Missouri	11	47.5	41.2	10.1	1.2
Nevada	4	43.9	42.9	9.5	3.7
New Hampshire	4	49.3	39.4	9.7	1.6
New Jersey	15	53.7	35.9	8.5	1.9
New Mexico	5	49.2	41.9	5.8	3.2
New York	33	59.5	30.6	8.0	1.9
Ohio	21	47.4	41.0	10.7	1.0
Oregon	7	47.2	39.1	8.8	5.0
Pennsylvania	23	49.2	40.0	9.6	1.3
Rhode Island	4	59.7	26.8	11.2	2.3
Tennessee	11	48.0	45.6	5.6	0.8
Vermont	3	53.4	31.1	12.0	3.6
Washington	11	49.8	37.3	8.9	3.9
West Virginia	5	51.5	36.8	11.3	0.5
Wisconsin	11	48.8	38.5	10.4	2.4

TABLE 7.7 continued

Dole (Rep.) 159 EC Votes; 41% popular vote

	EC	Clinton	Dole	Perot	Other
Alabama	9	43.2	50.1	6.0	0.7
Alaska	3	33.3	50.8	10.9	5.0
Colorado *	8	44.4	45.8	6.6	3.2
Georgia *	13	45.8	47.0	6.4	0.8
Idaho	4	33.6	52.2	12.7	1.5
Indiana	12	41.6	47.1	10.5	0.8
Kansas	6	36.1	54.3	8.6	1.0
Mississippi	7	44.1	49.2	5.8	0.9
Montana *	3	41.3	44.1	13.6	1.1
Nebraska	5	35.0	53.7	10.5	0.9
North Carolina	14	44.0	48.7	6.7	0.6
North Dakota	3	40.1	46.9	12.2	0.7
Oklahoma	8	40.4	48.3	10.8	0.5
South Carolina	8	44.0	49.8	5.6	0.7
South Dakota	3	43.0	46.5	9.7	0.8
Texas	32	43.8	48.8	6.7	0.7
Utah	5	33.3	54.4	10.0	2.3
Virginia	13	45.1	47.1	6.6	1.1
Wyoming	3	36.8	49.8	12.3	1.1

Note: Table based on official election returns.
+ indicates states that switched from supporting Republican George Bush in 1992.
* indicates states that switched from supporting Clinton in 1992.
In 1992 Clinton won 370 EC votes (43.2% popular vote), Bush 168 EC votes (37.4% popular vote) and Perot no EC votes (19% popular vote).

electoral system is assured of strong opposition in Congress and the state legislatures, which have to approve any constitutional changes.

Participation in Elections

At the national level the voting turn-out in Presidential elections has not been impressive when contrasted with many European democracies. The 1960 figure of 62.8% in the Kennedy–Nixon election was very good by American standards. In the 1992 Presidential election

FIGURE 7.2

Voting in Presidential Elections 1960–96

55.2% of qualified Americans of voting age turned out—the highest since 1968 with a record increase in new voters (nearly 13 million) and the largest ever total (over 104 million). However, in 1996 only 49% went to the polls, the lowest turn-out since 1924 when women first had the right to vote. In the mid-term Congressional elections, when there is no Presidential election to stimulate voter interest, 30–40% of eligible voters usually take part.

Evidence suggests that groups given the right to vote do not immediately exercise that right. After the passage of the Nineteenth Amendment in 1920 many women were slow to use their new right and, since the early 1970s, turn-out rates have been affected by the low participation rate of young voters, always well below 50%, following the ratification of the Twenty-Sixth Amendment in 1971.

The most important factor in America appears to have been the effects of registration laws. The United States is the only democracy in the world where voter registration is initiated by the individual; in other countries the Government (in whole or part) draws up the list and usually makes efforts to obtain as complete a register as possible. In most states each individual has the responsibility of registering himself as a qualified voter well before election day. Those who fail to do so by a specific date are ineligible to vote on election day even if they are technically qualified to vote in other ways. The turn-out rate for those who are actually registered was approximately 70.5% in 1988 compared with 50.1% of adults of voting age.

In 1993 Congress passed and President Clinton signed into law a measure that became known as the 'motor voter' bill because its main provision requires states to allow people to register to vote when applying for a driving licence. The law, which came into effect in 1995, also requires states to provide registration through the mail and at state offices that assist the disabled and distribute welfare payments. Despite easier procedures resulting in an additional 5 million people being registered, the 1996 election saw almost 10 million fewer citizens exercising their right to vote than in 1992. Although voter turn-out in general was down, the number of blacks voting was greater and they comprised 10% of the voting electorate compared with 8% four years earlier.

In the 1984 election 92.6 million people did vote and a further 84 million Americans of voting age did not. After the election the Gallup poll issued a breakdown of non-voters and the reasons they gave for not voting, with the percentages from sample projected into numbers of people. This is shown in Table 7.8.

Some of the reasons given for non-voting would undoubtedly be similar to those in other countries, although the mobility of American society with up to 20% of the population moving home each year is likely to exacerbate the trends. Institutions that have traditionally mobilized voters such as political party organizations and trade unions have been in decline, and campaigns that were once principally conducted at grass-roots level by party activists are now waged through the more impersonal medium of television. A number of variables may apply to a particular election: in 1972, 1984 and 1996 the result was in many people's minds a foregone conclusion and it may not have seemed worth voting. In 1988 and 1996 there was a lack of feeling that the election was a really important choice between two clear and divergent philosophies; in 1996 Clinton ran on what, in many respects, was a conservative programme that made the differences with Dole seem minimal. The campaigns stimulated little voter interest, and the negative tone of much of the advertising may well have acted as a deterrent.

TABLE 7.8

Reasons for Non-Voting in the 1984 Presidential Election

54 million were not registered.
17.4 million did not like the candidates.
14 million were not interested in politics.
14 million had no particular reason.
12 million were ill or disabled.
12 million said they could not leave their jobs.
12 million said it was inconvenient.
10.4 million were not American citizens.
10.4 million were not residents in their community and had not met
    residence requirements.
8.7 million were travelling and away from home.
5 million had no way to get to the polls.
1.7 million had not obtained an absentee ballot.
1.7 million mentioned a variety of other reasons.

Source: Gallup Poll press release, 9 December 1984. As some people gave more than one reason,
the number of responses is greater than 84 million not voting.

At the same time the lack of major issues worrying the electorate also
seems likely to have depressed turn-out levels. A former US Census
Bureau Director said:

> Peace and prosperity can generally operate to keep the vote down as well as
> to help the incumbent. In a sense low turn-out is consent. A pool of discon-
> tent may be valuable for a democracy.[11]

In 1992 the increased turn-out resulted from a number of factors.
Polls indicated that 79% of respondents said they were interested in
the Presidential race compared with 64% in 1988. The efforts made by
candidates to use new and alternative methods of communication with
the electorate, the recession and the intervention of Ross Perot all
helped stimulate interest. A number of states had also eased their
registration rules since 1988, while many states had controversial issues on their ballots as referendums which also encouraged a higher
turn-out.

[11]*Congressional Quarterly Weekly Report*, 21 January 1989, p. 135.

Education seems to be the most significant factor in determining voter turnout. For example, in a survey on the 1980 election almost 80% of college-educated adults reported they had voted compared with 58.9% of those with four years of high school and 42.6% of those with grade school education.[12] Income, education and occupation are closely related and the higher the level in all these categories the more likely the person is to vote. The greater people's sense of political effectiveness, in that they feel they can understand and influence politics, the more likely they are to vote. The non-voting citizen is more likely to be very young or very old, have only elementary education, live in a rural area, be a Southerner, have a manual occupation, be black and have little interest in politics.

Congressional Elections

Although there is a tendency in the media, particularly outside the United States, to focus almost exclusively on the Presidential election, it is important to remember that the political landscape in Washington DC depends as much on the results of the Congressional elections and which party secures a majority of seats in the House of Representatives and the Senate as who occupies the White House.

We have seen in Chapter 2 the importance of incumbency in legislative elections and noted the trend in recent elections of more members deciding to stand down voluntarily, with a consequent higher turnover of membership within Congress and more open races for vacant seats. All 435 House seats and one-third of the Senate are elected every two years and members, particularly in the House, are constantly keeping a wary eye on the next election.

A legislator will try to establish a solid record of achievements and a reputation as an effective constituency representative so that voters will be inclined to return him regularly to Washington. Many members play down their party attachment in their campaigns in order to appeal to as wide a cross-section of voters as possible. Name recognition and seniority in Congress are important and many Congressional elections have been fought on what are essentially local issues and have focused on local personalities. Opinion polls that ask a generic question about which party voters will support in Congressional elections

[12]US Bureau of the Census, *Current Population Reports*, April 1982, p. 3.

have been notoriously unreliable indicators of actual results because they do not take account of these local factors.

The 1994 mid-term elections were therefore unusual insofar as the Republican House candidates, led by Newt Gingrich, ran a more coordinated national campaign based on the 'Contract with America' which most of them signed. The document became a manifesto of commitments and was designed to draw out differences between the parties. The Republicans' campaign attacked the record of the Democrats who had been in control of Congress and exploited the current unpopularity of Bill Clinton. Gingrich believed that the traditional locally-based campaigns enabled Democratic members to exploit their incumbency advantages while avoiding accountability for their actions as the majority party. The sweeping Republican victories, with 52 net gains in the House and an additional eight seats in the Senate, gave them control of Congress for the first time in 40 years. No Republican incumbent lost his seat while Democratic leaders such as Speaker Tom Foley (Washington), Dan Rostenkowski (Illinois), Jack Brooks (Texas) and Senator Jim Sasser (Tennessee), who had hoped to become the new Senate Majority Leader, were swept from office.

In 1996 the Democrats attempted to turn the tables on their rivals by running a nationally-oriented campaign exploiting the unpopularity of Speaker Gingrich and voters' concerns about Republican plans for cuts in social programmes. Vulnerable Republicans, especially those freshmen who had won their seats in 1994 by small majorities, were targeted and their association with, and support for, Gingrich highlighted. Although neither party produced a campaign document similar to the Contract, the Democrats' 'anti-Newt' message was projected nationwide. Republican candidates generally emphasized their records in serving their constituents and distanced themselves from the Speaker, who concentrated on fighting his Georgia district and was almost invisible as a national campaigner, in stark contrast to two years earlier.

With Dole's defeat appearing inevitable and concerns that he might drag down many Republican Congressional candidates with him, the national party decided to take a gamble late in the campaign and run commercials that emphasized the need to re-elect a Republican Congress to act as a check on Clinton during a second term. In the event, the late swing to the Republicans meant that, of the party's 73 House freshmen, only 14 were defeated and the GOP retained control of Congress, albeit with a reduced majority in the House. The GOP share of the national vote in House elections was down 3.5% compared with

1994 and at 48.9% was the lowest for a party winning a majority of seats since 1938; their lead over the Democrats in the popular vote was only 0.33%. Despite the closeness of the elections, the Republicans actually improved their position by two seats in the Senate where the party won 2.3% more of the votes than their rivals.

Financing Elections

Traditionally, American elections have been financed by private donations, both large and small, to a candidate's campaign or by a combination of such gifts with the candidate's own money. In 1974, after the Watergate scandal and revelations that illegal and undisclosed contributions had been made to the Nixon campaign, Congress passed amendments to the Federal Election Campaign Act of 1971 and, in so doing, introduced the most sweeping reforms of campaign finance in American history. The major components of the bill included limits on campaign contributions and spending by candidates, a system of public funding for Presidential elections and the establishment of a new regulatory agency, the Federal Election Commission, to enforce the law. A challenge to the constitutionality of the Act led to the Supreme Court upholding some parts of the law but overturning others in the case of *Buckley* v *Valeo* in 1976.[13]

The Supreme Court argued that, while there had to be safeguards against corruption of the electoral system with the improper use of money, this had to be done without infringing the constitutional freedoms of both candidates and citizens. In modern elections candidates need money to pay the costs of communicating with the voters through the media. It therefore ruled that it was unconstitutional to impose mandatory expenditure limits on campaigns, to restrict the amounts candidates could spend of their own money or prevent independent campaigns for or against particular candidates. However, the Justices did accept that voluntary spending limits could be established as a condition for receiving public funding, that public financing of elections by taxpayer contributions was legal and that it was permissible to place limits on the amounts which individuals and groups could donate. The law restricted individual citizens to a maximum of $1,000

[13]See Alan Grant, 'Financing American Elections', *Politics Review*, Vol. 5, No. 2, November 1995; Alan Grant, 'The 1996 Elections and Campaign Finance in the United States', *Talking Politics*, Autumn 1997.

to any campaign with an overall annual limit of $25,000; political action committees (PACs) could give up to $5,000 to a particular candidate but no aggregate limit was imposed. These figures have not been raised to take account of inflation over the period since 1974 and their real value therefore has depreciated by two-thirds.

In Presidential elections the scope of public financing available has led to candidates, with the exception of the very wealthy Ross Perot in 1992 and Steve Forbes in 1996, accepting money from the taxpayer check-off fund set up by the 1974 legislation, and, in so doing, they are technically obliged to comply with the 'voluntary' spending limits laid down. These have been index-linked to reflect the effects of inflation. Candidates in the nomination process raise money from private contributors and, once they demonstrate they can do so on a broad basis, they become eligible for matching public funds. This condition was included so that only serious contenders on a national basis could receive taxpayers' money. Public funding was made available to the parties to pay for their national conventions and to the candidates to provide the bulk of their spending in the general election campaigns. In 1996 Clinton and Dole each received $62 million and their parties were restricted to spending $12 million on their Presidential campaigns.

However, in recent Presidential elections both major parties have routinely circumvented these limits with the use of so-called 'soft money' to supplement the public funding. In 1979 Congress passed legislation designed to help political parties revive their grass-roots activities, such as registration drives and 'get-out-the-vote' efforts, by allowing them to raise and spend money for general campaigning outside the limits on federal contributions. Individual, corporate and trade union donors can give large sums to party committees and bypass the limits on contributions to campaigns. Critics claim that this allows the return of 'fat cat' influence in the electoral process that the post-Watergate reforms were supposed to have prevented. Since 1980 party committees have used this soft money to support their Presidential candidates. In the 1990s the extent of this spending has increased so dramatically that the official limits have been effectively ignored altogether, giving rise to new demands for reform of the legislation applying to election funding. In 1996 party committees raised $264 million in soft money— three times more than in 1992 and more than 13 times what they raised in 1980. The Democratic Party raised $102 million in soft money in 1996, 232% more than in the previous Presidential election. Revelations that President Clinton had encouraged his fundraisers with promises to meet wealthy donors personally, even allowing some of them to stay overnight at the White House as a reward for their generosity to the Democratic cause, coupled with allegations that illegal contributions had been received from foreign businessmen who may have sought to influence American trade or foreign policy, highlighted the way this type of election funding has been abused.

Some commentators have argued that soft money has become important in Presidential elections because the official limits for spending are set unrealistically low. In 1996 Robert Dole spent practically all his permitted funds in the early months of the nomination process fighting off the challenge of Steve Forbes who was not restricted in the amounts he spent as he was not in receipt of federal funds. Subsequently Dole was left without official funding for many months until the start of the general election campaign, at a time when Clinton was spending freely, particularly on television advertising. Dole was therefore forced to rely on spending by Republican committees to keep his name before the public in the period up to the convention.

In Congressional elections there are no overall statutory limits on the amounts candidates may spend on their campaigns and, as there is no public funding available, there are no 'voluntary' limits either. Candidates are able to raise and spend as much as they feel they require to run a winning campaign or as much as they can persuade contributors to give them. Wealthy candidates can spend their own resources without constraint, although Michael Huffington's 1994 Senate campaign in California demonstrates that this does not necessarily guarantee success. Having used over $26 million to pay for his campaign, the Republican candidate still lost the race to incumbent Democratic Senator, Dianne Feinstein.

Congressional candidates draw money from individual supporters, from party committees and from PACs. There has been concern over the increasing costs of running for Congress and the growing gap in the funding available to incumbents and challengers. This has been a major factor in explaining the high success rate of incumbent members and the decline in competitive elections. In 1974 the average House incumbent spent $56,000 and the average challenger $40,000, a gap of only $16,000. By 1992 the figures were $580,000 and $180,000 respectively, a margin of $400,000. After remaining fairly static during the 1980s, overall campaign expenditure in Congressional elections rose sharply in 1992 to $678 million and in 1994 totalled $725 million, a trend partially explained by the increased number of open races (see Chapter 2).

In 1996 political parties extended the use of soft money to support Congressional campaigns as well as their Presidential candidates. A Supreme Court ruling in June 1996 also paved the way for additional party funding of legislative races; the Justices decided that parties could spend as much as they wished in Congressional campaigns, so long as they acted independently of the candidates. One consequence of this ruling was that parties were given the green light to spend large amounts on negative advertising. This is because such commercials are generally felt by the parties to be safer than spending money on positive messages on behalf of their own candidates which may be claimed to have been coordinated with their campaigns and thus count as illegal expenditure.

Proposals to reform Congressional campaign finance have tended to focus on introducing limits on spending with some form of public finance or subsidy as the inducement to candidates to comply, as well as restrictions on the contributions from PACs. All efforts to pass such legislation have failed as a result of deep divisions both between and within the political parties in Congress as well as differing priorities between House and Senate members (see Chapter 5). Public and media pressure for some reform legislation seemed likely to increase during the 105th Congress, following the exposures of the obvious inadequacies of existing regulations in the 1996 elections. However, finding agreement, let alone consensus, on this vexed and complicated issue is likely to remain problematic.

Some Further Reading

M. Margaret Conway, *Political Participation in the US* (Congressional Quarterly Press 1991)

Philip John Davies, *Elections USA* (Manchester University Press 1992)

Paul Herrnson, *Campaigning for Congress: Candidates, Parties and Political Action Committees* (Congressional Quarterly Press 1994)

Gary Jacobson, *The Politics of Congressional Elections* (Harper Collins 1992)

Michael Nelson (ed.), *The Elections of 1992* (Congressional Quarterly Press 1993)

R.G. Niemi and H. Weisberg, *Controversies in Voting Behaviour* (Congressional Quarterly Press 1993)

Nelson Polsby and Aaron Wildavsky, *Presidential Elections* (Scribner's 1991)

Gerald M. Pomper (ed.), *The Election of 1992* (Chatham House 1993)

Gerald M. Pomper (ed.), *The Election of 1996* (Chatham House 1997)

A. James Reichley (ed.), *Elections, American Style* (Brookings Institution 1987)

Byron Shafer (ed.), *The End of Realignment? Interpreting American Election Eras* (University of Wisconsin Press 1991)

Frank J. Sorauf, *Inside Campaign Finance: Myths and Realities* (Yale University Press 1992)

8

Federalism and Regional Diversity

The Federal Principle

The Founding Fathers established a system of government at the Philadelphia Convention in 1787 which was the result of the compromises necessary to reconcile the conflicting political and economic interests present. Federalism was in fact a 'half-way house' between the concept of a centralized unitary state that was unacceptable to the thirteen states jealous of their own independence and that of a confederation which was a weak association of autonomous states of the kind that had proved unsatisfactory between 1776 and 1787. Federalism arose out of a desire to bolster national unity while at the same time accommodating regional diversity. The Constitution itself does not mention anywhere the terms 'federalism' and 'federation' but the United States has been recognized ever since as the major example of this compromise form of unity. Many other nations later attempted to adopt the federal principle which K.C. Wheare describes as:

> The method of dividing powers so that the general and regional governments are each, within a sphere, co-ordinate and independent.[1]

Wheare says that the fundamental characteristic of the United States as an association of states is that the Constitution establishes an arrangement whereby powers are divided between a general (that is national or federal) government, which in certain matters is independent of the governments of the associated states, and state governments, which in certain matters are independent of the general government.

[1]K.C. Wheare, *Federal Government* (Oxford University Press 1961), p. 10.

Both national and state governments operate directly upon the people and each US citizen is subject to two governments.

The American federal system should not be seen therefore as a pyramid structure with the federal government at the apex, the states below it and the local governments as the base, because in constitutional terms at least the federal and state governments are of equal status with their own distinctive areas of authority. What is true, however, is that local government units are subordinate bodies and creatures of the states; their boundaries and powers can be altered as the state determines, because the 50 states are unitary systems in their own right.

There are certain institutions and practices which are essential for a federal system to exist and operate as an effective policy-making and administrative structure. Firstly, a written constitution has to be accepted as supreme so that the terms of the division of power are binding upon all governments. The 'supremacy clause' makes it clear that the American Constitution and the laws of the United States shall be the supreme law of the land. Therefore, particularly in areas where concurrent legislative powers exist, the Constitution provides that federal statutes shall prevail in the event of a conflict with state laws.

It is also important that a single body be recognized as being able to settle disputes which arise about the division of powers. The US Supreme Court has developed this function of constitutional adjudication and, after some early opposition, its judgements have been accepted as binding upon both federal and state governments.

If federalism is to work satisfactorily, the power of amending the Constitution cannot be left exclusively to either tier of government; to do so would, of course, lead eventually to the subordination of one to the other. In the United States, both Congress and the state legislatures (or conventions) are involved in the amendment process. The federal relationship also entails the acknowledgement that states may not secede unilaterally from the Union, and that a state cannot be expelled from the association against its will. In most federations, the interests of the smaller states are protected either by equal representation or by additional members to those warranted by the size of their population in the upper house of the legislature. The US Senate was a very important part of the federal compromise at Philadelphia and was established to secure the support of the less populated states.[2]

[2]See Chapter 1, 'The Historical Framework: From Independence to Philadelphia'; for a discussion of the nature of federalism, see Wheare, ibid., Chapters 4 and 5.

As the Founding Fathers assumed that the states would continue to perform the major domestic roles of government, such as the maintenance of law and order, the Constitution does not deal in any detail with the functions of the states. The document is more specific on what the states could not do—the limitations on their freedom of action which was the price of greater national unity—and what the newly created federal government could and could not do. The powers of government can therefore be described in the following ways:

(a) The 'Enumerated' Powers of the Federal Government. Congress was given the right to legislate in certain specific areas in Article 1 Section 8, such as defence, currency, the Post Office and naturalization of citizens;

(b) The 'Inherent' Powers of the Federal Government. The federal government has the right to do certain things because these are 'inherent' in its role as a national government; most important are the rights to conduct foreign relations and wage war;

(c) The 'Implied' Powers of the Federal Government. Having listed specific areas where Congress may legislate, Article 1 Section 8 of the Constitution says that it has the right to make all laws that are 'necessary and proper' for carrying into execution the enumerated powers;

(d) The 'Concurrent' Powers of Federal and State Governments. In some fields, such as taxation, both federal and state governments can legislate simultaneously;

(e) The Powers Specifically Denied to the Federal Government. There are constitutional prohibitions on the Congress, for example, taxing exports, creating titles of nobility or favouring the ports of one state over another (Article 1 Section 9);

(f) The Powers Denied to the States. Article 1 Section 10 restricts the activities of state governments in certain fields; they cannot, for example, enter into treaties with foreign powers, or impose import or export duties;

(g) The 'Reserved' or 'Residual' Powers of the States. The Tenth Amendment was included as part of the Bill of Rights as the price for the

ratification of the Constitution. It provides that anything not delegated to the federal government or denied to the states be left to the authority of the states or to the people.

It has not always been easy to say which matters in practice are within the spheres of the federal or state governments because, as new issues have arisen, there have been disputes over the meaning of words in the constitutional document. The Supreme Court has had to interpret the Constitution and settle disputes in individual cases, but, as Wheare has noted, once it is granted that a government is acting within its allotted sphere that government is not subordinate to any other in the United States.[3]

The Development of Modern Federalism

In the early days of the Republic, there was a major political controversy concerning the nature of the federalism which had been created at the Philadelphia Convention. The Jeffersonian Democratic-Republicans wanted to see a restricted national authority and were concerned to protect the rights of the states against encroachment and centralizing tendencies. The Hamiltonian Federalists were equally convinced of the need to strengthen the powers and status of the national government if America was to avoid the dangers of disintegration.

Although most Americans would have accepted the view that the Constitution established a relationship between independent and coordinate federal and state authorities, an important body of opinion argued that the federal government was not an equal partner, but was rather the creation of the states and thus subordinate to them. In the Southern states particularly, it was frequently asserted that the state legislatures had the right to nullify any Act of Congress with which they disagreed, and that if this was done the statute would have no force of law within their boundaries. Only after the Civil War was this view discredited. With the defeat of the South, Chief Justice Samuel Chase stressed the permanence of the Union:

> The Constitution, in all its provisions looks to an indestructible Union, comprised of indestructible States.[4]

[3] Wheare, op. cit., p. 2.
[4] *Texas* v *White* (1869).

In the period since the Civil War, government regulatory activity has expanded at all levels, but the most striking development has been the increasingly important role of the federal government in its relationship with the states. A number of underlying social and economic factors have influenced the growth of responsibilities in Washington and contributed to the shift in the balance of power in the federal system. Firstly, there has been the development of a strong national identity, which has helped provide the cultural background making the national government's expanded role acceptable. There are also much better communications and a greater degree of geographical mobility than ever before, so that, despite the size of the country, Americans are far more aware of social conditions in other parts of the nation. One of the effects of the modern mass media has been to provide further pressures towards uniformity of standards and provision of services.

The federal government's influence has also been considerably strengthened by the United States' twentieth-century role as a world super-power. This had led to vast increases in its budget and an expansion of its personnel in both civilian and military capacities and, because it is a major contractor and provider of jobs in private defence-related industries, the government's decisions vitally affect the economic well-being of the states and their people. The Great Depression of the 1930s also increased the expectation that the federal government would intervene to deal with the major social and economic ills of the country. Washington's attempts to ameliorate the problems by direct works programmes and unemployment insurance schemes filled a vacuum left by many state governments, which either were unable to act themselves as a result of the pressures on their own finances or seemed unwilling to do so. Some of the unreformed and rurally dominated state legislatures tended to neglect urgent problems afflicting the nation's urban areas. It is not surprising that city administration which found the state authorities unprepared to help looked instead to the federal government. The lack of a positive approach by some state governments to the crisis of the cities has been an exacerbating factor encouraging centralization. Indeed, the very nature of the problems in a highly complex industrialized society provides a challenge to the federal system. The federal government has often stepped in to co-ordinate governmental programmes when the problems cut across state and local boundaries.

These social and economic factors have led to pressures over the last two centuries for changes in the constitutional and political relationships within the federal system. A number of different methods have been adopted by reformers to bring about this transformation.

1 Constitutional Amendments

The most obvious way of changing the constitutional relationship is by altering the written document, and some of the amendments passed since 1787 have significantly affected the federal system. After the Civil War, the Fourteenth Amendment gave the federal government the power to ensure that the states provided 'due process of law' and 'equal protection' of the laws to all their citizens. The Bill of Rights, initially a restriction on the federal government, was from that time on to apply to the states as well, and the federal government had the duty to enforce these provisions, a responsibility which would allow direct intervention in the affairs of the states.[5]

The Sixteenth Amendment, passed in 1913, was possibly the most important constitutional change in shaping the modern federal system. The federal government was given the right to raise a graduated tax on individual incomes, and this transformed its financial position. Without this lucrative source of revenue, the federal government would have found it increasingly difficult to raise sufficient money to pay for its defence and foreign policies and would have been unable to take action in the social and economic spheres. It might have had to approach the states for grants or subsidies to cover its expenditure. In practice, the federal government tended to squeeze the states out of the income tax field as its own demands on the taxpayers grew, and eventually state legislatures were obliged to accept grants from the federal government.

2 Judicial Interpretations of the Constitution

The decisions of the Supreme Court also have led to important changes in the federal relationship. Although at various times in its history the Court has restricted the powers of the federal government by stressing the provisions in the Tenth Amendment, in modern times it has allowed a considerable expansion of national intervention by its emphasis on the broad permissive clauses of the Constitution. The three most relevant sections have been:

[5]See, in Chapter 1, 'Amendments to Advance Individual Rights'.

(a) the 'necessary and proper' clause;
(b) the Congressional power to 'tax for the common defence and general welfare' of the United States;
(c) the 'inter-state commerce' clause.[6]

3 The Financial Relationship

As the Sixteenth Amendment allowed the federal government to raise income taxes there was a considerable improvement in its tax base after 1913 and this led to a great expansion in the size of its budget and the scope of its activities. In 1913 federal government spending had been just over a third of the total outlay of state and local governments. In 1929 public spending in the United States totalled $10.2 billion[7] of which the federal government spent $2.6 billion and state and local governments $7.6 billion. Fifty years later, in 1979, total public expenditure amounted to $764.5 billion; the federal government spent $507 billion while state and local governments paid out $257.5 billion from their own funds.[8] By that time federal spending made up about two-thirds of all public spending and the American people paid 60% of their total taxes to Washington, 21% to the states and 19% to local governments.

As demands for more health and welfare services, education, police protection and environmental services fell heavily on the states and local authorities, the federal government increased the amounts of financial aid from its treasury to make up the cost of performing these functions. Over the two decades to 1978 federal grants had been increasing rapidly and at a faster rate than the state and local governments' own source revenues. In 1964 federal aid comprised 15.4% of state and local governments' outlays; by 1978 this had grown to 26.5%. The last years of the Carter administration saw the beginnings of a reversal of this trend and Ronald Reagan's period in office continued that process. Federal aid as a percentage of total state and local expenditure dropped from 25% in 1981 to approximately 18% in 1990.[9]

---

[6]See, in Chapter 4, 'The Supreme Court and Policy Making: The Role of Government', for a detailed examination of this development.

[7]The American billion (a thousand millions) is used throughout, as figures are from US sources. (In the UK the billion is a million million.)

[8]*Significant Features of Fiscal Federalism* (Advisory Commission on Intergovernmental Relations 1980), p. 7.

[9]*Statistical Abstract of the United States* 1992, p. 282.

However, the dependence of the states on federal financial resources to support their services has inevitably coloured the relationship. The main form of federal finance since the Great Depression has been the 'grants-in-aid' system. Although six such programmes were established before 1900, it has been since the 1930s that the major development has taken place. The balance of aid has shifted from supporting programmes for places, such as urban renewal or highways, to assistance directly to individuals in the form of programmes such as Medicaid and food stamps. In 1995 almost two-thirds of the $225 billion in federal aid was dedicated to programmes to persons, compared with approximately a third in the 1970s. The system has led to federal government supervision in areas which would otherwise not be within its powers, because these categorical grants, the most common form of aid, have strings attached to them. The states and local governments may only spend the money on the conditions laid down and must make matching funds available themselves in order to receive the federal finances. The actual proportion or percentage which Washington pays will depend upon the programme, but the system is designed so that state and local governments have to commit their own money to the schemes. The federal government also has the right to approve the plans, lay down minimum standards and inspect the results of any programme to which it has contributed. The grants-in-aid system has led to more government activity at all levels because, although they are not compelled to take part, a refusal by the states to do so would mean that they were, in effect, cutting themselves off from the tax money raised from their own citizens. As John Lees wrote:

> The key to the acquisition of funds is ... intensive state activity. The more a state is prepared to develop programmes, the more it is likely to receive national funds or contracts.[10]

Despite its longevity and established status as part of the modern federal relationship, cogent political criticisms are made of the grants-in-aid system. Conservatives do not like these programmes for a number of reasons. It is argued that they stimulate a considerable amount of unnecessary government regulatory activity and encourage the states to initiate schemes that they do not really need simply to obtain federal funds that are on offer. What is more, conservatives feel that the system has led to widespread federal government intervention in the

[10]John Lees, *The Political System of the United States* (Faber 1975), p. 57.

affairs of state and local authorities and has resulted in the decline of the states as coordinate and independent units of government. Grants-in-aid therefore encourage centralization and the abridgement of states' rights under the Tenth Amendment. Critics also point to the high costs of administering the system and argue that grants-in-aid have led to wasteful and inefficient bureaucratization. They feel that revenues could be better raised and spent at the state and local level rather than have the federal government collecting and redistributing the funds, with the attendant problems and delays. Finally, it is argued that the system developed as a response to the crisis of the Depression and that there is no real justification for Washington's retaining and expanding these powers in the different circumstances of today.

However, supporters of the grants-in-aid system are convinced that, far from destroying the federal relationship and eroding the responsibilities of the states, it has rescued federalism from the verge of collapse and put it on a sounder basis. They feel that the alternative would have been the direct control by the federal government of services and functions, whereas under the grants-in-aid system the states are heavily involved in planning and administering the programmes and a great deal is left to local initiative. Liberals who have promoted the grants-in-aid system also argue that it has encouraged the reactionary or backward states to meet their responsibilities in providing services for all their people as well as ensuring basic minimum standards throughout the country. They believe that without some safeguards the resulting inequalities would threaten the stability and unity of the American nation. The system, therefore, allows a certain redistribution of wealth and helps the poorer areas of the country whose state governments would otherwise be unable to pay for satisfactory public services. It also allows the federal government to promote social objectives such as the elimination of discrimination in public services and to meet problems without apparently increasing the size of the federal bureaucracy.

Dual Federalism and Cooperative Federalism

The arguments between conservatives and liberals about the value of grants-in-aid can be broadened to demonstrate two different approaches to the workings of modern federalism. The popular view of the federal system before the New Deal, and still supported by many conservative

Americans, is that of 'dual federalism'; this is a belief that the Constitution created two separate tiers of government which should be independent, with their own clearly defined areas of responsibility. In such a system there would inevitably be a certain amount of tension and competition, and the Supreme Court would have the role of arbiter in cases of conflict and would protect the constitutional division of powers. It is argued that the Supreme Court abandoned this responsibility and has since allowed considerable encroachment by the federal government into the areas reserved for the states. Grants-in-aid have been mechanisms for extending this intervention, a process which conservatives would like to see reversed. They feel that, for the constitutional division of powers to become a reality once again, the federal government must give up many of its present responsibilities and return the powers of effective decision making and revenue raising to the states.

Since the New Deal an alternative approach has been articulated by supporters of the expanded federal government role. 'Cooperative federalism' emphasizes the partnership between the different levels of government providing effective public services for the nation.

> The various levels of government are seen as related parts of a single government system, characterized more by co-operation and shared functions than by conflict and competition.[11]

Some writers have argued that dual federalism not only does not exist today, but in fact never did exist in a pure form, because even in the early nineteenth century the federal government provided some grants to the states for internal improvements such as new roads. Morton Grodzins said that the national, state and local governments have always shared activities, powers and responsibilities. He did not see American government as symbolized by a neat 'layer cake' of three distinct and separate planes but rather as a 'marble cake', an inseparable mixture of differently coloured ingredients.[12] Daniel Elazar, Grodzins' associate, argued that, given the existence of a national economy in which people and goods flow freely across boundaries, state governments are simply unable to cope with certain problems without federal assistance. Major highways construction, water pollution control and unemployment insurance, for example, could not be

---

[11]M. Cummings and D. Wise, *Democracy Under Pressure*, 5th edn (Harcourt, Brace, Jovanovich 1985), p. 69.
[12]M. Grodzins, *The American System* (Rand McNally 1966), pp. 3–4.

undertaken alone, even by those states that can afford to support
them. He summed up this theory by saying:

> In the years since the establishment of the Republic, inter-governmental co-
> operation has been progressively expanded to include virtually every func-
> tion. From public welfare to public recreation, from national defense to
> local police protection, the system of sharing has become so pervasive that it
> is often difficult for the uninitiated by-stander to tell just who is doing what
> under which hat. The highly institutionalized system of federal–state co-
> operation that has developed has become part of the nation's constitutional
> tradition. Under this co-operative system, the federal government, the states
> and the localities share the burden for the great domestic programs by
> making the larger governments primarily responsible for raising revenues
> and setting standards and the smaller ones primarily responsible for admin-
> istering the programs.[13]

The proponents of cooperative federalism argued that in the nature
of the relationship the role of the federal government is to supplement, stimulate and assist the states, not to pre-empt their functions
and act as a superior partner. Therefore the states have considerable
discretion as to how they administer programmes such as welfare
schemes that are financed by both federal and state authorities. Apart
from federal–state cooperation, grants-in-aid programmes which
involve Washington directly with the local governments also developed,
as well as those which are jointly administered by federal, state
and local agencies. The officials of all three tiers of government had
frequent communications with one another, and it is worth remembering that almost 90% of federal civil servants work outside the capital
and administer policy in regional offices. There is also a great deal of
informal cooperation between different governments and formal contracts also exist for cooperative action by different governments.

During the 1960s, particularly as a result of President Johnson's
'Great Society' legislation, there was an official recognition of the existence of cooperative federalism and a marked expansion of the role of
the federal government in not only initiating programmes but also
using various forms of pressure to ensure state and local government
compliance with its wishes. Johnson described this relationship as 'crea-
tive federalism', but in fact the vast proliferation of various forms of
grant programmes resulted in large-scale confusion and over-
bureaucratization. States and local governments found it difficult to

[13]D. Elazar, *American Federalism* (Cromwell 1972), p. 47.

decide which programmes would be valuable to them and many opened offices in Washington to represent their interests before federal government departments. This presence was particularly valuable in securing project grants, a special form of categorical grant, designed to handle specific problems and made selectively to those states and cities which submit proposals for developments within federal guidelines and then successfully lobby for their approval by the department concerned. There were also complaints that some federal agencies tried to reduce the areas of state discretion and increase the degree of national uniformity in administering policies. There were long and frustrating delays before states obtained decisions from federal offices, and also direct contacts between Washington and local governments which bypass the states have tended to create tension and worsen relations between the states and the cities. Therefore those who saw cooperation and partnership as being the key to the federal relationship recognized that all was not harmony and that 'squeak-points', as Grodzins called them, existed. One student of the federal system, Michael D. Reagan, went further than the proponents of 'cooperative federalism' by saying that the growth of federal aid to the states has created a 'nationally dominated system of shared power and shared functions'.[14] With his colleague, John G. Sanzone, he argued that a new label should be given to the system as it operated in the 1980s—'permissive federalism'.

> That phrase conveys the notion that there is a sharing of power and authority between the national and state governments, but that the states' share rests upon the permission and permissiveness of the national government ... The national government unquestionably possesses the legal authority to impose whatever degree of restrictiveness it wishes. It should be clear at once that this is not federalism at all in its classic conception. Federalism in that sense is dead.[15]

The New Federalism, Revenue Sharing and Block Grants

In the late 1960s there was a reaction against the continuing expansion of the federal government's activity and expenditure. Despite the vast amounts of money spent by Washington it appeared that the

[14]Michael D. Reagan, 'The New Federalism' (Oxford University Press 1972), p. 145.
[15]Michael D. Reagan and John G. Sanzone, 'The New Federalism', 2nd edn (Oxford University Press 1981), p. 175.

problems of the cities in particular were actually getting worse. President Nixon, in his first year of office, declared that there was a need
for a 'new federalism' so that the proper balance of power between the
state capitals and Washington could be restored. He looked forward to
a decade of decentralization when power would be shifted away from
the centre and handed back to the state and local governments. He
argued on nationwide television:

> For a third of a century, power and responsibility have flowed towards
> Washington, and Washington has taken for its own the best sources of
> revenue.
> We intend to reverse this tide and to turn back to the states a greater
> measure of responsibility—not as a way of avoiding problems but as a better
> way of solving problems.[16]

Nixon was a managerial conservative who was not against increasing
federal government authority in principle but believed that improving
the efficient implementation of programmes was the most important
priority. Nixon's principal legacy in the development of federalism was
the introduction of revenue sharing as a way of distributing aid to
other levels of government and which was a major initiative designed
to begin the process of decentralization. The plan was that Congress
should assign a set proportion of revenues from its taxes to be passed
back to the states with scarcely any restrictions on how the money
should be used, and a certain percentage of these funds should be
channelled directly to the local governments. The philosophy of this
approach was that state and local authorities knew how to deal with
their own problems better than the more remote federal bureaucracy,
and that these funds should not have the strings attached to them that
traditionally accompanied grants-in-aid. Nixon found that his original
proposals ran into opposition in Congress. Liberals were opposed to
giving unconditional grants to the traditionally conservative state legislatures, while committee chairmen, such as Wilbur Mills (Ways and
Means), were reluctant to give up their own discretionary powers on
how federal taxes should be spent.

However, in 1972 Congress did eventually pass a Revenue Sharing
Act which provided for $6 billion a year of federal revenues to be
distributed to state and local governments. By 1975 revenue sharing
accounted for 14.3% of total federal aid and a number of extensions of

[16]President Richard Nixon, television address, 8 August 1969.

the legislation were passed until the late 1980s when the Reagan administration, having reduced the funds over the years, cut out the programmes as part of its reductions in federal government expenditure. Treasury Secretary James Baker, referring to the federal deficit, said that there was 'no revenue to share'. The programme, which was never very popular on Capitol Hill, was easy prey when the search for spending cuts became an urgent priority.

Another development in the financing of the federal relationship which allows the states more discretion was the introduction of block grants as a form of grant-in-aid programme. In 1966, categorical grants with their many conditions made up 98% of all federal aid, but by 1975 this had declined to just under three-quarters of the total amount. There were about 600 categorical grant programmes in operation that year costing approximately $40 billion. Block grants, on the other hand, are sums of money with few strings attached but which must be spent by the states in one of five broad subject areas (community development, manpower services, law enforcement, social services or health). The block grant system was first tried in 1966 but was expanded greatly in the period 1972–75, so that by 1975 over $5 billion (approximately 10% of total federal assistance to state and local governments) was transferred in this form. Block grants have developed either as new programmes with broad functional aims or through the merging of separate categorical grants. By 1985 'flexible funding' through revenue sharing and block grants accounted for about one-fifth of total federal aid.

President Reagan and New Federalism

Ronald Reagan, unlike Nixon, was an ideological conservative, and opposition to government intervention at all levels, but particularly by the federal government, was the cornerstone of his political philosophy. His eight years of experience as the Governor of California had reinforced his belief that Washington's interference in state and local affairs was not only undesirable and led to inefficiency but was also in many cases unconstitutional. For him, government was more often the cause of a problem rather than its solution. Taking up the theme of the need to re-establish a form of dual federalism, President Reagan vowed in his inaugural address to 'demand recognition of the distinction between the powers granted to the federal government and those reserved for the states or to the people'. In April 1981 he established an advisory committee chaired by Senator Paul Laxalt of Nevada to draft legislation to 'restore a proper constitutional relationship' between the three levels of federal, state and local government. Demands for a realignment of powers had been developing for several years; the Advisory Commission on Intergovernmental Relations and the National Governors' Association were among the bodies urging a review of the federal system which most agreed had shifted too much power and decision making to Washington. They argued that state and local governments could manage programmes more effectively and efficiently than the federal administration. In his first year in office Reagan announced that the federal departments of Energy and Education would be dismantled (although this did not happen in practice because of opposition within Congress) and that there would be major reductions in the number of federal regulations. He established the Office of Information and Regulatory Affairs within OMB to evaluate proposed federal regulations, and departments and agencies were required to justify any new orders as well as an assessment of costs of implementation. The administration also restricted the power of federal civil servants in reviewing the activities of state and local governments, insisting that they defer to states' own policies on standards wherever possible, rather than imposing uniform national standards of provision.

The President's budget cuts led to a decline in federal aid to state and local governments from $95.9 billion in 1981 to $86.8 billion in 1982, the first reduction in federal grants since 1946. In the decade up to 1988 the money transferred in grants-in-aid fell by a quarter and, as a proportion of state and local revenues, by more than a fifth. The number of government employees at federal, state and local level also fell in 1981 for the first time since the First World War. Congress voted to establish nine block grants to replace 57 individual grants-in-aid in the areas of education, social services and health care, thus devolving more discretionary powers to the states.

In his state-of-the-union address in January 1982, President Reagan called for the creation of a 'New Federalism' which would lead to a major upheaval in the administration of many government programmes. The major proposals were:

(a) From October 1983 the federal government would take over completely Medicaid, the health cost programme for the poor, at present shared with the states. At the same time the states would assume full responsibility for the costs of the major welfare programmes, Aid to Families with Dependent Children and food stamps.

(b) Federal excise taxes and part of the tax on oil profits would be put into a trust fund. Approximately $28 billion a year from the fund would go to state and local governments to finance 43 additional programmes currently funded by the federal government. These programmes include vocational education, local transport and water and sewage services.

(c) The trust would be phased out by 1991 and states and localities would have to increase their own taxes or discontinue the services.

It was immediately evident that the President would encounter many obstacles in obtaining the coalition of support necessary to ensure passage of these radical proposals in their original form. Many politicians at all levels sympathized with the general philosophy of shifting power and responsibility to the states and localities but there was concern about the detailed implementation of the policy.

The National Governors' Association was particularly opposed to taking over the very costly welfare programmes and was also worried about having the responsibility for other social services without sufficient revenue to pay for them. Many Democrats argued that the New Federalism proposal was bound to be given a cautious reception as it was part of the Reagan administration's overall retrenchment in social policy. There was also the familiar concern among liberal politicians that many state legislatures would be insensitive to the needs of the urban areas, ethnic minorities and the poor and would not support the continuation of services at present financed by the federal government. Some Republicans were worried about the complexity of services such as the food stamp programme being administered by fifty separate authorities and also that large variations in state welfare benefits might prompt mass migration of recipients seeking more generous provision. Many observers also questioned whether Congressmen would be prepared to give up the power implicit in the Reagan plan, particularly as it would reduce the scope for legislators to claim that they had brought federal funds and favours to their constituencies.

The administration's $21 billion legislative package consolidating 34 programmes into four 'mega-blocks' was never reported out of committee on Capitol Hill and a consensus on the major swap of health care and welfare responsibilities did not materialize. In practice the problem of the federal budget deficit in the 1980s meant not only a

reduction in federal aid to state and local governments but a reluctance at the national level to initiate programmes that would lead to
greater federal expenditure on activities that could be considered to be
basically state or local matters. In this respect there was a movement
towards a de facto sorting out of responsibilities. As John Shannon, the
former executive director of the US Advisory Commission on Intergovernmental Relations, has said:

> The creation of a fiscal environment that forces state and local officials to
> become more self reliant stands out as the primary impact the Reagan
> administration has had on our federal system ... Federal policymakers are
> being forced by fiscal and political realities to allocate an increasing share of
> their resources for strictly national government programs: defense, social
> security, medicare and interest on the $2.4 trillion debt ...[17]

Shannon describes this as a return to the competitive 'fend-for-yourself' federalism of the pre-'Great Society' kind.

The 1980s were therefore a decade during which there was considerable discussion about the future of American federalism. The Reagan
administration frequently stated that it wished to recast the roles and
responsibilities of the federal government and, in May 1986, the President signed a statement of federalism principles developed by his
Domestic Policy Council. However, because this policy occasionally
came into conflict with Reagan's overall commitment to the deregulation of business, pressure groups representing business interests managed to persuade the administration that it would be preferable to
have one national regulatory standard with which they had to comply
rather than a patchwork quilt of 50 different sets of rules. The Reagan
administration used the pre-emption powers given to the federal government under the Supremacy Clause of the Constitution (Article VI)
to set national policies in such areas and to short-circuit more demanding state laws passed by liberal Democrats. The regulation of truck
weights and sizes, the enforcement of the national 55 mph speed limit
and the withdrawal of highway funds from those states failing to adopt
a minimum drinking age of 21 years were all examples of the Reagan
administration ignoring its own federalist objections to regulation by
Washington.

---

[17]John Shannon, 'A Return to Fend-For-Yourself Federalism: The Reagan Mark', in *State
Government 1988/9 (Congressional Quarterly Guide to Current Issues and Activities)*, Thad T. Beyle
(ed.), pp. 216, 218.

Reagan left his mark on American federalism but did not succeed in securing the fundamental shift he was seeking, principally because of political opposition in Congress, among state officials nervous of the consequences and because public opinion was not yet prepared for such radical reformation of the post-New Deal governmental system. Reagan's New Federalism did have the overall effect of reversing the trend towards the nationalization of the federal system by restraining, to some extent, the intervention of government in Washington and stimulating the revitalization of the states. State governments, which had reformed and professionalized their activities in recent decades, were usually willing and able to play a more activist role. Whether conservatives, who wished to see less government at all levels, were happy with the effects of their federal budgets cuts, the results were more state spending and tax increases to replace much of the federal funding and many of the programmes. Richard Nathan has argued that the period of conservative retrenchment in Washington led to a 'ratcheting up' effect with more liberal activist government promoted by Democratic administrations at state level.[18] By 1990 the states and local governments were raising $1 trillion in taxes, on a par with the federal government, according to Census Bureau figures.[19]

While this increase in state activity was possible during the growth years of the 1980s, the effects of recession, the rising costs of programmes and voter resistance to further tax increases forced many states to make spending cuts of their own in the early 1990s in order to balance their budgets, as required in state constitutions.[20] The phasing out of direct federal aid to local governments during the Reagan years made the local authorities more dependent on support from the states which were responsible for the distribution of federal block grants.

Federalism in the 1990s

In the continuing debate about the nature of contemporary federalism, John Kincaid, the Executive Director of the US Advisory Commission on Intergovernmental Relations, has written that it is marked by a seeming paradox: federal dominance coexists with the resurgence of the

[18]Richard Nathan, 'Federalism—The Great Composition', in *The New American Political System*, Anthony King (ed.) (The AEI Press 1990).
[19]*National Journal*, 3 October 1992, 'Rethinking Federalism', p. 2256.
[20]*National Journal*, 2 January 1992, 'Just Saying No', p. 18.

states.[21] He argues that, in the early 1990s, the federal government was exercising more power over more aspects of domestic policy than ever and, although the states occupied the leading position in fiscal and administrative areas, they did so within a significant regulatory framework established at national level. Increased federal intervention has been accompanied by increased activity at state and local levels as all governments have broadened their involvement with society and, as we have seen, many federal programmes are in practice implemented by other tiers of administration in a complex system of intergovernmentalism.

Kincaid states that the system has become less cooperative and more coercive since the 1960s because Washington has sought to harness state and local capacities to its own policy ends. He argues that 'coercive federalism' has a number of key characteristics. Among these are the reduction in total federal aid and the change in the balance of aid from programmes based on location to those supporting persons, to which reference was made earlier in this chapter. He points out that, despite the encouragement of block grants with more discretion for the states during the Reagan years, Congress still prefers to attach conditions to federal money. In 1993 almost 90% of all aid took the form of categorical grants with Congress funding 578 such programmes, compared with only 15 block grants. The federal government has also imposed numerous mandates so that state and local officials must perform functions laid down in statutes or face criminal or civil actions. However, these regulations are usually unfunded, and no federal money is provided to enforce compliance with the mandates.

Furthermore, Congress has passed many laws which pre-empt state authority; over half of all the explicit pre-emption laws enacted by Congress from 1789 to 1991 were passed after 1969. Federal laws overrode state legislation in areas such as commerce, health and safety, banking and finance, civil rights, natural resources and taxation. Other features of coercive federalism have included the intrusion of the federal government in the traditional tax bases of state and local governments, the decline of genuinely cooperative programmes, the role of the federal courts in requiring state or local action or institutional changes and the federalization of criminal law—traditionally a state preserve—with over 3,000 federal crimes being established.[22]

---

[21]John Kincaid, 'Governing the American States' in *Developments in American Politics 2*', Gillian Peele et al. (eds), (Macmillan 1994).

[22]See Chapter 4 for discussion of the Supreme Court's impact on federalism and the Lopez case in 1995 based on the Tenth Amendment rights of the states.

Federalism and the 104th Congress

It was against this background that the Republicans won control of both houses of Congress in the 1994 mid-term elections with the commitment to reshape the federal relationship and devolve power back to the states. The elections were widely interpreted as a rejection by the public of 'big government'; public opinion had swung in recent years against federal institutions, and confidence in the federal government had declined. President Clinton's ambitious health care initiative in 1994 failed to progress largely because of fears that Washington would not be able to run an efficient health care system. Clinton himself had recognized the need to streamline federal bureaucracy and create a more responsive and efficient national government and had placed Vice-President Gore in charge of the 'Reinventing Government' initiative (see Chapter 3). In 1996 the President declared in his State of the Union address that 'the era of big government is over'.

The Republican-controlled 104th Congress developed plans for a radical restructuring of federalism, balancing the federal budget over a seven-year period with huge cuts in expenditure at the national level in many areas and the scrapping or reduction of many programmes and agencies. Although the ultra-conservatives within the party did not achieve all they wanted in the period up to the 1996 elections, particularly in terms of the dismantling of government departments, they were able to go a great deal further than Reagan had managed. This was a result not only of the Republicans' legislative majority and the transformation of public opinion in the intervening period but also because Republican Governors now controlled the majority of the state houses around the country, including the largest states. Republican politicians at state level were enthusiastic in their support for devolution, were regularly consulted by Congressional leaders and involved in developing legislative proposals.

One of the first acts of the new Congress was to pass legislation restricting the federal government from imposing new 'unfunded mandates'. A consensus had developed during the previous session that this practice had to be checked and President Clinton, a former Governor himself and aware of the resentment they caused at state and local levels, signed the bill into law in March 1995. The statute requires the Congressional Budget Office to signal when any bill creates mandates involving more than minimal expenditure by states, localities or the private sector and forces Congress to debate the merits of such requirements. While providing exemptions in the areas of conduct relating to civil rights, disability and discrimination and not banning unfunded mandates altogether, the new law was expected to curb the tendency of Congress to impose expensive new regulations and pass the costs on to others. Congress also repealed all national speed limits, leaving it to the states to decide the most appropriate rules for their own areas and, in overhauling the Safe Drinking Water Act, it gave states and local governments more flexibility in implementing the policy and ended the requirement that the federal government create new regulations every three years.

The most important legislation devolving power was the welfare reform bill, reluctantly signed by President Clinton in August 1996, which ended the federal government's 61 year-old guarantee to provide welfare cheques to all low income mothers and children and instead gave the states considerable discretion over eligibility and benefits. It was the first time that a major individual entitlement programme had been transformed into a block grant to the states. The Republicans argued that capping the federal government's commitment on welfare expenditure was essential if their objective of a balanced budget was to be achieved; the new law was expected to save $54.1 billion in the period up to the year 2002, mostly by cutting the food stamps programme and denying a variety of benefits to legal immigrants. However, the Republican proposal to turn Medicaid, the federal–state health insurance system for the poor, into a similar block grant programme and to end the guarantee of coverage for all those who qualify, failed to pass into law, despite the eagerness of Republican Governors to exercise more control of the policy which is more costly to the states than welfare. Clinton and the Democrats were more resistant to ending individual entitlement to Medicaid coverage, which enjoyed wider public support, than in ending entitlement to welfare payments.

However, in other areas the Republican majority, as in the Reagan era, confounded expectations and consolidated authority in Washington when it appeared to be the best way to implement their political agenda. Legislation passed in the 104th Congress established national criteria for state-issued drivers' licences, ended state registration of mutual funds, created national food safety standards, nullified state laws that had restricted telecommunications competition and extended federal criminal penalties to cover certain violent crimes.[23]

[23]*Congressional Quarterly Weekly Report*, 5 October 1996, pp. 2824–5 and 2 November 1996, pp. 3117–22.

Political pressure from voters encouraged conservative legislators to take at least symbolic action in areas such as crime and education, even though they generally argue that these are issues which rightly come under state and local jurisdiction. At the same time as they were giving states more authority in social and environmental policy, Republicans also found that their efforts to reduce government interference in the marketplace and protect business from a variety of state regulations more stringent than the federal one resulted in them designating the federal government as the sole regulator in a number of areas.

It is clear that in the 105th Congress there will be a continuing debate over the extent of future devolution of power to the states in areas such as highway funding, environmental protection programmes and health care insurance.

The Organization of State and Local Governments

The states in the American federal system have therefore been widely perceived as resurgent in the last decade. Far from being the poor relations with low public visibility and having a reputation for being backward and less concerned for the well-being of the people than either the federal or local governments as they were in the past, John Kincaid claims that today they are largely seen as 'competent, innovative and fiscally responsible'.[24] The states have acted as laboratories of experimentation, finding new ways of dealing with problems, and the new generation of Governors have earned a reputation as pathfinders for the federal government. It is also important to note that state and local government revenues grew faster than those of the federal government in the 1980s, while in 1993 there were 4.6 million staff working for the states, 11.2 million in local governments and a total of 3 million federal civilian employees.[25]

1 The States

All the states have 'republican' forms of government with the separation of powers principle written into their constitutions. All but Nebraska have bicameral legislatures (usually called the Assembly and the Senate) and all have state Governors in charge of the administration and

[24]John Kincaid, op. cit., p. 200.
[25]*Statistical Abstract of the United States 1996*, p. 319.

separate judicial systems. The 50 states have written constitutions which are on average three times the length of the federal Constitution, and many are very detailed and restrictive of government initiative and spending powers. Frequently power is divided not only between the three branches of government but also between numerous agencies and commissions, which exacerbates tendencies to fragmentation of authority.

Despite these similarities of structure, there has been a considerable diversity in the actual workings of state politics. The position and powers of the Governor vary considerably from state to state. 'Weak' Governors typically have had short terms, cannot succeed themselves in office and share executive power with a number of other elected officials such as the Lieutenant-Governor, Treasurer and Attorney General. They also have had little power in formulating the state budget and very restricted appointment powers. In other states the Governor is in a much better position to influence policy if he has a four-year term, is able to seek unlimited re-election to the office, has strong appointment and budgetary powers and shares executive authority with few other elected officials. The Governor in all states except North Carolina has a veto power over legislation and in forty-three states has the right to an 'item veto' over single parts of appropriations bills; in three states the item veto extends to other bills as well.

Since the 1960s there has been a trend for the modernization of state governments to take place so that they may more adequately deal with the responsibilities they have acquired. Constitutions have been reformed to allow state legislatures to have longer and more frequent sessions to study legislation. The legislatures themselves have streamlined their committee structures, have become more professional, taken on more support staff and have reapportioned their constituency boundaries. The tight control of state legislatures by rural elites has been broken and city dwellers and minorities are better represented. There has been a tendency to strengthen the executive powers of the Governor, by lengthening his term of office, by allowing him to succeed himself, strengthening his veto power, and by improving his control over the budget and administrative reorganization. This has led to what David B. Walker calls 'the remarkable and largely unheralded renaissance of the states'.[26]

The moves towards the professionalization of government and the growth of career politicians led to a backlash in the 1990s, with many

[26]David B. Walker, 'American Federalism in the 1990s', in *Political Issues in America: the 1990s*, Philip John Davies and Frederic A. Waldstein (eds) (Manchester University Press 1991), p. 130.

states adopting term limits for legislators as well as for executive officials where they did not already exist. In contrast to the federal level
where the Supreme Court ruled that such restrictions on service were
unconstitutional, state constitutions have been amended or interpreted
to allow term limits, which supporters hope will lead to the return of
'citizen legislators'. The impact of such developments on the working
of state government will only become fully apparent over the next
decade.

2 Local Governments

Local governments have those powers which the states delegate to
them and they carry the responsibility for much of the day-to-day
administration of major services. Although they are elected in their
own right, they are subordinate governments and are essentially the
administrative agents of the states. Each state is free to organize its
local governments as it wishes and there are differing patterns throughout the nation. The main units are:

(a) The Municipalities.   These include cities, villages, boroughs and some
towns. Most cities elect a council which makes policy and a mayor who is
responsible for carrying out the administration of the area, or elect a
council that employs a professional 'city manager' to run the city.

(b) The Counties.   Outside the city areas, the county is the basic unit of
organization within the states. The number, size and powers of the
counties vary from one state to another, but in the majority of counties
there are elected 'Boards of Supervisors' which make policy, and also
elected executive officials such as the Sheriff, Treasurer and Coroner.
The council-administrator system, in which an elected commission
passes laws and appoints an administrator to carry out policy, is used
in some areas and the remaining counties have an elected administrator who acts as chief executive and a council that determines legislative
policy.

(c) Special Districts.   These districts have been established to deal with
one particular service which, it is argued, may be more efficiently
administered through separate functional areas. Therefore elected
'Boards of Trustees' run, for example, special park, harbour, school
and college districts. They are the fastest growing form of local govern-

ment. Excluding school districts the number of units has risen from 8,299 in 1942 to 31,555 in 1992, and critics have argued that the fragmentation of local government in this way hinders effective coordination and administration of services.

The Roles of State and Local Governments

In 1993 state and local governments in America spent a total of $1,207 billion in providing public services. Education was by far the most expensive function with $342.6 billion allocated for its administration. The states normally are responsible directly for running the universities and higher education institutions, while local governments administer the schools and other colleges. Public welfare, which includes payments to the elderly, the poor and the handicapped, as well as unemployment insurance and the maintenance of institutions, accounted for $167 billion, while highways cost $68.1 billion and hospitals and health $62.5 billion. The other major areas of state and local government spending are police and fire protection, sewerage, prisons and the administration of justice, parks and recreation, housing and urban renewal.[27]

To finance these services there are a number of different sources of revenue. We have already seen that federal aid to state and local governments, while still a significant factor, has been declining as a proportion of their overall revenues. In 1980 18% of state and local governments' income came from Washington; by 1990 this had been reduced to 13%. The most lucrative independent forms of income raised within the states are property taxes and sales taxes. Property taxes are levied normally by local governments to pay for their services but revenues have not always kept pace with inflation and the pressures of increasing demand, while many states have given way to public pressure for property tax relief to home owners.[28] In 1994 state

---

[27]Figures for state and local government expenditure taken from *Statistical Abstract of the United States* 1996, p. 298.

[28]In June 1978 the voters of California passed the Jarvis-Gann initiative or Proposition 13. This showed the growing resentment among citizens at the spiralling costs of public services and had the effect of cutting their property taxes by almost two-thirds. These taxes are based on the annually assessed capital value of the property and with house prices soaring in California many home owners were hard-pressed to pay these costs. The tax rebellion was repeated in other states later in the year. The Californian state legislature transferred revenues to the local governments from its own surplus so that many local services could continue despite the loss of considerable property tax revenues.

	Units
Federal	1
States	50
Total local governments	84,955
Counties	3,043
Municipalities	19,279
Townships	16,656
School districts	14,422
Special districts	31,555
Totals	85,006

Source: *Statistical Abstract of the United States* 1996, p. 295.

FIGURE 8.1

Government Units in the United States 1992

governments raised $373.8 billion in taxes. Of these revenues half came from sales taxes, either in the form of a general levy on all goods and services, sold within the state (88% of the total) or specific taxes on gasoline, alcohol and tobacco and fees for motor vehicle and operators' licences. State income taxes accounted for 31% of total revenues and corporation taxes a further 7%, although these are at lower rates than the equivalent federal taxes. Additional income in some states come from running public utilities, lotteries and liquor stores.[29]

[29]Figures from the *Statistical Abstract of the United States 1996*, p. 292.

TABLE 8.1

State Government Finances in 1994 (figures in $ millions)

Revenue, Total	844,897
Taxes, Total	373,824
From Federal Government	191,829
Insurance Trust Revenue	144,978
Charges & Miscellaneous Revenue	114,361
Expenditure, Total	779,931
Education	230,791
Public Welfare	185,125
Insurance Trust Expenditure	83,541
Health and Hospitals	56,995
Highways	53,849
Corrections	23,135
Natural Resources	11,878
Financial Administration	11,376
Utility Expenditure	7,214
Police	6,000

Adapted from *The Book of the States 1996–97*, p. 241.

The Problems of Modern Federalism

The United States has changed beyond all recognition in the two centuries since the original thirteen states formed the federal union in 1787. Many of the developments that have taken place since that time, such as the expansion of the federal government's domestic functions, the increased activity of state and local governments, and the development of grants-in-aid and 'cooperative federalism', have been responses to the industrialization and urbanization of the nation. More than three-quarters of the population now live in cities, towns or the suburbs and urbanized living has brought new problems with which governments have to deal.

Today the United States really has too many governments for effective policy making. In addition to the federal government and the fifty states, there are over 80,000 local government units (see Figure 8.1), each with its own territorial area and jealous of its own jurisdiction.

This hotch-potch of cities, townships, counties and special districts with overlapping boundaries and responsibilities complicates considerably the coordination of policies designed to deal with these twentieth-century problems. The separate jurisdictions of police forces in an area can hinder effective crime fighting, while individual local and even state governments often have inadequate resources or are insufficiently broad in area to deal with the issues of pollution control or transportation policy.

However, even with more active and well-financed state governments, sources of tension between state legislatures and city administrations still exist, and these lead not only to difficulties in executing policy efficiently but also to the cities looking to Washington for more sympathy and assistance. Not least of these conflict areas is the question of how the cities should be financed. American cities have found themselves in an increasingly precarious financial situation. Their populations have steadily become socially unbalanced so that racial ghettos have developed. Demands on the city services, particularly welfare provision, housing and police protection, have grown dramatically at a time when their tax bases have declined. Property taxes have provided insufficient revenue and, with the middle class flight to the suburbs, the deterioration of the city centres has led to even fewer resources. In some cases the cities have found themselves almost bankrupt although, as in the most famous case of New York City, this may be partially the result of profligate and extravagant spending programmes.

In the mid-1990s the city of Miami in Florida ran into severe financial difficulties, while Washington's long history of mismanagement by city administrations led to a serious crisis affecting basic public services. There were calls for the federal government to take over the running of the police force as crime figures escalated and to provide billions of dollars of additional support for the nation's capital. The cities have traditionally looked to the states to provide more funds, but the legislatures controlled by politicians representing suburban and rural areas have often been reluctant to vote any more aid for the city services. The resistance to providing revenues for the cities occasionally overlooks the fact that many of the suburban voters actually commute to and work in the cities during the day and therefore derive benefit from better facilities in the downtown areas.

Another alternative which is often vigorously opposed by county residents is that the city's boundaries be extended to incorporate within its area the surrounding suburbs. In this way the city would have a broader and more lucrative tax base, but suburban residents have generally fought against 'incorporation' on the grounds that it would not only force them to pay higher taxes but would also integrate their school systems with those of the city centres. Many of the white suburbanites feel that the standards of education for their children would be irreparably damaged by such a move. Consolidations between cities and counties are rarely carried out because they usually require the approval of the voters. It is somewhat ironic that, whereas minority ethnic groups have obtained political control of some of the major cities through the demographic changes of the last decade, incorporation of suburban areas into the cities would almost certainly weaken and dilute this influence. Incorporation is in many parts of the United States not merely a question of reforming and making more efficient the organization of local government, it is also an issue that arouses intense feelings on all sides because it affects political control and the distribution of resources.

Some Further Reading

Timothy Conlan, *New Federalism* (Brookings Institution 1988)

Thomas R. Dye, *American Federalism* (Lexington Books 1990)

Daniel J. Elazar, *American Federalism: A View from the States* (Harper and Row 1985)

Richard P. Nathan and Fred C. Doolittle (eds), *Reagan and the States* (Princeton University Press 1987)

Lawrence J. O'Toole Jr, *American Intergovernmental Relations* (Congressional Quarterly Press 1992)

Alice Rivlin, *Reviving the American Dream* (Brookings Institution 1992)

Carl E. Van Horn, *The State of the States* (Congressional Quarterly Press 1992)

Joseph F. Zimmerman, *Contemporary American Federalism* (Leicester University Press 1992)

Appendix I

The Constitution of the United States

PREAMBLE

WE THE PEOPLE of the United States, in order to form a more perfect Union, establish justice, insure domestic tranquillity, provide for the common defense, promote the general welfare, and secure the blessings of liberty to ourselves and our posterity, do ordain and establish this Constitution for the United States of America.

ARTICLE I

SECTION 1. All legislative powers herein granted shall be vested in a Congress of the United States, which shall consist of a Senate and House of Representatives.

SECTION 2. The House of Representatives shall be composed of members chosen every second year by the people of the several States, and the electors in each State shall have the qualifications requisite for electors of the most numerous branch of the State Legislature.

No person shall be a representative who shall not have attained to the age of twenty-five years, and been seven years a citizen of the United States, and who shall not, when elected, be an inhabitant of the State in which he shall be chosen.

Representatives and direct taxes shall be apportioned among the several States which may be included within this Union, according to their respective numbers, which shall be determined by adding to the whole number of free persons, including those bound to service for a term of years, and excluding Indians not taxed, three-fifths of all other persons. The actual enumeration shall be made within three years after the first meeting of the Congress of the United States, and within every subsequent term of ten years, in such manner as they shall by law direct. The number of representatives shall not exceed one for every thirty thousand, but each State shall have at least one representative; and until such enumeration shall be made, the State of New Hampshire shall be entitled to choose three, Massachusetts eight, Rhode Island and Providence Plantations one, Connecticut five, New York six, New Jersey four, Pennsylvania eight, Delaware one, Maryland six, Virginia ten, North Carolina five, South Carolina five, and Georgia three.

When vacancies happen in the representation from any State, the executive authority thereof shall issue writs of election to fill such vacancies.

The House of Representatives shall choose their Speaker and other officers; and shall have the sole power of impeachment.

SECTION 3. The Senate of the United States shall be composed of two senators from each State, chosen by the legislature thereof, for six years and each senator shall have one vote.

Immediately after they shall be assembled in consequence of the first election, they shall be divided as equally as may be into three classes. The seats of the senators of the first class shall be vacated at the expiration of the second year, of the second class at the expiration of the fourth year, and of the third class at the expiration of the sixth year, so that one-third may be chosen every second year; and if vacancies happen by resignation, or otherwise, during the recess of the legislature of any State, the executive thereof may make temporary appointments until the next meeting of the legislature, which shall then fill such vacancies.

No person shall be a senator who shall not have attained to the age of thirty years, and been nine years a citizen of the United States, and who shall not, when elected, be an inhabitant of that State for which he shall be chosen.

The Vice-President of the United States shall be President of the Senate, but shall have no vote, unless they be equally divided.

The Senate shall choose their other officers, and also a President pro tempore, in the absence of the Vice-President, or when he shall exercise the office of President of the United States.

The Senate shall have the sole power to try all impeachments. When sitting for that purpose, they shall be on oath or affirmation. When the President of the United States is tried, the Chief Justice shall preside: And no person shall be convicted without the concurrence of two-thirds of the members present.

Judgment in cases of impeachment shall not extend further than to removal from office, and disqualification to hold and enjoy any office of honor, trust or profit under the United States: but the party convicted shall nevertheless be liable and subject to indictment, trial, judgment and punishment, according to law.

SECTION 4. The times, places and manner of holding elections for senators and representatives, shall be prescribed in each State by the legislature thereof; but the Congress may at any time by law make or alter such regulations, except as to the places of choosing senators.

The Congress shall assemble at least once in every year, and such meeting shall be on the first Monday in December, unless they shall by law appoint a different day.

SECTION 5. Each house shall be the judge of the elections, returns and qualifications of its own members, and a majority of each shall constitute a quorum to do business; but a smaller number may adjourn from day to day, and may be authorized to compel the attendance of absent members, in such manner, and under such penalties as each house may provide.

Each house may determine the rules of its proceedings, punish its members for disorderly behaviour, and, with the concurrence of two-thirds, expel a member.

Each house shall keep a journal of its proceedings, and from time to time publish the same, excepting such parts as may in their judgment require secrecy; and the yeas and nays of the members of either house on any question shall, at the desire of one-fifth of those present, be entered on the journal.

Neither house, during the session of Congress, shall, without the consent of the other, adjourn for more than three days, nor to any other place than that in which the two houses shall be sitting.

SECTION 6. The senators and representatives shall receive a compensation for their services, to be ascertained by law, and paid out of the Treasury of the United States. They shall in all cases, except treason, felony and breach of the peace, be privileged from arrest during their attendance at the session of their respective houses, and in going to and returning from the same; and for any speech or debate in either house, they shall not be questioned in any other place.

No senator or representative shall, during the time for which he was elected, be appointed to any civil office under the authority of the United States, which shall have been created, or the emoluments whereof shall have been increased during such time; and no person holding any office under the United States, shall be a member of either house during his continuance in office.

SECTION 7. All bills for raising revenue shall originate in the House of Representatives; but the Senate may propose or concur with amendments as on other bills.

Every bill which shall have passed the House of Representatives and the Senate, shall, before it becomes a law, be presented to the President of the United States; if he approves he shall sign it, but if not he shall return it, with his objections to that house in which it shall have originated, who shall enter the objections at large on their journal, and proceed to reconsider it. If after such reconsideration two-thirds of that House shall agree to pass the bill, it shall be sent, together with the objections to the other House, by which it shall likewise be reconsidered, and if approved by two-thirds of that House, it shall become a law. But in all such cases the votes of both Houses shall be determined by yeas and nays, and the names of the persons voting for and against the bill shall be entered on the journal of each House respectively. If any bill shall not be returned by the President within ten days (Sundays excepted) after it shall have been presented to him, the same shall be a law, in like manner as if he had signed it, unless the Congress by their adjournment prevent its return, in which case it shall not be a law.

Every order, resolution, or vote to which the concurrence of the Senate and House of Representatives may be necessary (except on a question of adjournment) shall be presented to the President of the United States; and before the same shall take effect, shall be approved by him, or being disapproved by him, shall be repassed by two-thirds of the Senate and House of Representatives, according to the rules and limitations prescribed in the case of a bill.

SECTION 8. The Congress shall have the power to lay and collect taxes, duties, imposts and excises, to pay the debts and provide for the common defense and general welfare of the United States; but all duties, imposts and excises shall be uniform throughout the United States;

To borrow money on the credit of the United States;

To regulate commerce with foreign nations, and among the several States, and with the Indian tribes;

To establish an uniform rule of naturalization, and uniform laws on the subject of bankruptcies throughout the United States;

To coin money, regulate the value thereof, and of foreign coin, and fix the standard of weights and measures;

To provide for the punishment of counterfeiting the securities and current coin of the United States;

To establish post offices and post roads;

To promote the progress of science and useful arts; by securing for limited times to authors and inventors the exclusive right to their respective writings and discoveries;

To constitute tribunals inferior to the Supreme Court;

To define and punish piracies and felonies committed on the high seas, and offenses against the law of nations;

To declare war, grant letters of marque and reprisal, and make rules concerning captures on land and water;

To raise and support armies, but no appropriation of money to that use shall be for a longer term than two years;

To provide and maintain a Navy;

To make rules for the government and regulation of the land and naval forces;

To provide for calling forth the militia to execute the laws of the Union, suppress insurrections and repel invasions;

To provide for organizing, arming, and disciplining the militia, and for governing such part of them as may be employed in the service of the United States, reserving to the States respectively the appointment of the officers, and the authority of training the militia according to the discipline prescribed by Congress;

To exercise exclusive legislation in all cases whatsoever, over such district (not exceeding ten miles square) as may, by cession of particular States, and the acceptance of Congress, become the seat of the Government of the United States, and to exercise like authority over all places purchased by the consent of the legislature of the State in which the same shall be, for the erection of forts, magazines, arsenals, dockyards, and other needful buildings;—And

To make all laws which shall be necessary and proper for carrying into execution the foregoing powers, and all other powers vested by the Constitution in the Government of the United States, or in any department or officer thereof.

SECTION 9. The migration or importation of such persons as any of the States now existing shall think proper to admit, shall not be prohibited by the Congress prior to the year one thousand eight hundred and eight, but a tax or duty may be imposed on such importation, not exceeding ten dollars for each person.

The privilege of the writ of habeas corpus shall not be suspended, unless when in cases of rebellion or invasion the public safety may require it.

No bill of attainder or ex post facto law shall be passed.

No capitation, or other direct, tax shall be laid, unless in proportion to the census or enumeration herein before directed to be taken.

No tax or duty shall be laid on articles exported from any State.

No preference shall be given by any regulation of commerce or revenue to the ports of one State over those of another: nor shall vessels bound to, or from, one State, be obliged to enter, clear, or pay duties in another.

No money shall be drawn from the Treasury, but in consequence of appropriations made by law; and a regular statement and account of the receipts and expenditures of all public money shall be published from time to time.

No title of nobility shall be granted by the United States: And no person holding any office or profit or trust under them shall, without the consent of the Congress, accept of any present, emoluments, office, or title, of any kind whatever, from any King, Prince, or foreign State.

SECTION 10. No state shall enter into any treaty, alliance, or confederation; grant letters of marque and reprisal; coin money; emit bills of credit; make any thing but gold and silver coin a tender in payment of debts; pass any bill of attainder, ex post facto law, or law impairing the obligation of contracts, or grant any title of nobility.

No state shall, without the consent of the Congress, lay any imposts or duties on imports or exports, except what may be absolutely necessary for executing its inspection laws: and the net produce of all duties and imposts, laid by any State on imports or exports, shall be for the use of the Treasury of the United States; and all such laws shall be subject to the revision and control of the Congress.

No state shall, without the consent of Congress, lay any duty of tonnage, keep troops, or ships of war in time of peace, enter into any agreement or compact with another State, or with a foreign power, or engage in war, unless actually invaded or in such imminent danger as will not admit of delay.

ARTICLE II

SECTION 1. The executive power shall be vested in a President of the United States of America. He shall hold his office during the term of four years, and, together with the Vice-President, chosen for the same term, be elected, as follows:

Each state shall appoint, in such manner as the legislature thereof may direct, a number of electors, equal to the whole number of senators and representatives to which the State may be entitled in the Congress: but no senator or representative, or person holding an office of trust or profit under the United States, shall be appointed an elector.

The electors shall meet in their respective States, and vote by ballot for two persons, of whom one at least shall not be an inhabitant of the same State with themselves. And they shall make a list of all the persons voted for, and of the number of votes for each; which list they shall sign and certify, and transmit sealed to the seat of the Government of the United States, directed to the President of the Senate. The President of the Senate shall, in the presence of the Senate and House of Representatives, open all the certificates, and the votes shall then be counted. The person having the greatest number of votes shall be the President, if such number be a majority of the whole number of electors appointed; and if there be more than one who have such majority, and have an equal number of votes, then the House of Representatives shall immediately choose by ballot one of them for President; and if no person have a majority, then from the five highest on the list the said House shall in like manner choose the President. But in choosing the President, the votes shall be taken by States, the representation from each State having one vote; a quorum for this purpose shall consist of a member or members from two-thirds of the States, and a majority of all the States shall be necessary to a choice. In every case, after the choice of the President, the person having the greatest number of votes of the electors shall be the Vice-President. But if there should remain two or more who have equal votes, the Senate shall choose from them by ballot the Vice-President.

The Congress may determine the time of choosing the electors, and the day on which they shall give their votes; which day shall be the same throughout the United States.

No person except a natural born citizen, or a citizen of the United States, at the time of the adoption of this Constitution, shall be eligible to the office of President; neither shall any person be eligible to that office who shall not have attained to the age of thirty-five years, and been fourteen years a resident within the United States.

In case of the removal of the President from office, or of his death, resignation, or inability to discharge the powers and duties of the said office, the same shall devolve on the Vice-President, and the Congress may by law provide for the case of removal, death, resignation, or inability, both of the President and Vice-President, declaring what officer shall then act as President, and such officer shall act accordingly, until the disability be removed, or a President shall be elected.

The President shall, at stated times, receive for his services, a compensation, which shall neither be increased nor diminished during the period for which he shall have been elected, and he shall not receive within that period any other emolument from the United States, or any of them.

Before he enter on the execution of his office, he shall take the following oath of affirmation:- 'I do solemnly swear (or affirm) that I will faithfully execute the office of President of the United States, and will to the best of my ability, preserve, protect and defend the Constitution of the United States.'

SECTION 2. The President shall be Commander in Chief of the Army and Navy of the United States, and of the militia of the several States, when called into the actual service of the United States; he may require the opinion, in writing, of the principal officer in each of the Executive Departments, upon any subject relating to the duties of their respective offices, and he shall have power to grant reprieves and pardons for offenses against the United States, except in cases of impeachment.

He shall have power, by and with the advice and consent of the Senate, to make treaties, provided two-thirds of the senators present concur; and he shall nominate, and by and with the advice and consent of the Senate, shall appoint ambassadors, other public ministers and consuls, judges of the Supreme Court, and all other officers of the United States, whose appointments are not herein otherwise provided for, and which shall be established by law: but the Congress may by law vest the appointment of such inferior officers, as they think proper, in the President alone, in the courts of law, or in the heads of departments.

The President shall have power to fill up all vacancies that may happen during the recess of the Senate, by granting commissions which shall expire at the end of their next session.

SECTION 3. He shall from time to time give to the Congress information of the state of the Union, and recommend to their consideration such measures as he shall judge necessary and expedient; he may, on extraordinary occasions, convene both houses, or either of them, and in case of disagreement between them, with respect to the time of adjournment, he may adjourn them to such time as he shall think proper; he shall receive ambassadors and other public ministers; he shall take care that the laws be faithfully executed, and shall commission all the officers of the United States.

SECTION 4. The President, Vice-President and all civil officers of the United States, shall be removed from office on impeachment for and conviction of, treason, bribery, or other high crimes and misdemeanors.

ARTICLE III

SECTION 1. The judicial power of the United States shall be vested in one Supreme Court, and in such inferior courts as the Congress may from time to time ordain and establish. The judges, both of the supreme and inferior courts, shall hold their offices during good behavior, and shall, at stated times, receive for their services, a compensation, which shall not be diminished during their continuance in office.

SECTION 2. The judicial power shall extend to all cases, in law and equity, arising under this Constitution, the laws of the United States, and treaties made, or which shall be made, under their authority; to all cases affecting ambassadors, other public ministers and consuls; to all cases of admiralty and maritime jurisdiction; to controversies to which the United States shall be a party; to controversies between two or more States; between a State and citizens of another State; between citizens of different States; between citizens of the same State claiming lands under grants of different States, and between a State, or the citizens thereof, and foreign States, citizens, or subjects.

In all cases affecting ambassadors, other public ministers and consuls, and those in which a State shall be party, the Supreme Court shall have original jurisdiction. In all the other cases before mentioned, the Supreme Court shall have appellate jurisdiction, both as to law and to fact, with such exceptions, and under such regulations as the Congress shall make.

The trial of all crimes, except in cases of impeachment, shall be by jury; and such trial shall be held in the State where the said crimes shall have been committed; but when not committed within any State, the trial shall be at such place or places as the Congress may by law have directed.

SECTION 3. Treason against the United States, shall consist only in levying war against them, or in adhering to their enemies, giving them aid and comfort. No person shall be convicted of treason unless on the testimony of two witnesses to the same overt act, or on confession in open court.

The Congress shall have power to declare the punishment of treason, but no attainder of treason shall work corruption of blood, or forfeiture except during the life of the person attainted.

ARTICLE IV

SECTION 1. Full faith and credit shall be given in each State to the public acts, records, and judicial proceedings of every other State. And the Congress may by general laws prescribe the manner in which such acts, records and proceedings shall be proved, and the effect thereof.

SECTION 2. The citizens of each state shall be entitled to all privileges and immunities of citizens in the several States.

A person charged in any State with treason, felony, or other crime, who shall flee from justice, and be found in another State, shall on demand of the executive authority of the State from which he fled, be delivered up, to be removed to the State having jurisdiction of the crime.

No person held to service or labor in one State, under the laws thereof, escaping into another, shall, in consequence of any law or regulation therein, be discharged from such service or labor, but shall be delivered up on claim of the party to whom such service or labor may be due.

SECTION 3. New States may be admitted by the Congress into this Union; but no new State shall be formed or erected within the jurisdiction of any other State; nor any State be formed by the junction of two or more States, or parts of States, without the consent of the legislatures of the States concerned as well as of the Congress.

The Congress shall have the power to dispose of and make all needful rules and regulations respecting the Territory or other property belonging to the United States; and nothing in this Constitution shall be so construed as to prejudice any claims of the United States, or of any particular State.

SECTION 4. The United States shall guarantee to every State in this Union a republican form of Government, and shall protect each of them against invasion; and on application of the legislature, or of the executive (when the legislature cannot be convened) against domestic violence.

ARTICLE V

The Congress, whenever two-thirds of both Houses shall deem it necessary, shall propose amendments to this Constitution, or, on the application of the legislatures of two-thirds of the several States, shall call a convention for proposing amendments, which, in either case, shall be valid to all intents and purposes, as part of this Constitution, when ratified by the legislatures of three-fourths of the several States, or by convention in three-fourths thereof, as the one or the other mode of ratification may be proposed by the Congress; provided that no amendment which may be made prior to the year one thousand eight hundred and eight shall in any manner affect the first and fourth clauses in the Ninth Section of the First Article; and that no State, without its consent, shall be deprived of its equal suffrage in the Senate.

ARTICLE VI

All debts contracted and engagements entered into, before the adoption of this Constitution, shall be as valid against the United States under this Constitution, as under the Confederation.

This Constitution, and the laws of the United States which shall be made in pursuance thereof; and all treaties made, or which shall be made, under the authority of the United States, shall be the supreme law of the land; and the judges in every State shall be bound thereby, anything in the Constitution or laws of any State to the contrary notwithstanding.

The Senators and Representatives before mentioned, and the members of the several State legislatures, and all executive and judicial officers, both of the United States and of the several States, shall be bound by oath or affirmation, to support this Constitution; but no religious test shall ever be required as a qualification to any office or public trust under the United States.

ARTICLE VII

The ratification of the conventions of nine States shall be sufficient for the establishment of this Constitution between the States so ratifying the same.

Done in convention by the unanimous consent of the States present the seventeenth day of September in the year of our Lord one thousand seven hundred and eighty seven and of the Independence of the United States of America the twelfth. In witness whereof we have hereunto subscribed our names.

GEO. WASHINGTON,
Presid't and deputy from Virginia.

Amendments

AMENDMENT I

[Ratification of the first ten amendments was completed 15 December 1791.]

Congress shall make no law respecting an establishment of religion, or prohibiting the free exercise thereof; or abridging the freedom of speech, or of the press; or the right of the people peaceably to assemble and to petition the Government for a redress of grievances.

AMENDMENT II

A well regulated militia, being necessary to the security of a free State, the right of the people to keep and bear arms, shall not be infringed.

AMENDMENT III

No soldier shall, in time of peace be quartered in any house, without the consent of the owner, nor in time of war, but in a manner to be prescribed by law.

AMENDMENT IV

The right of the people to be secure in their persons, houses, papers, and effects, against unreasonable searches and seizures, shall not be violated, and no warrants shall issue, but upon probable cause, supported by oath or affirmation, and particularly describing the place to be searched, and the persons or things to be seized.

AMENDMENT V

No person shall be held to answer for a capital, or other infamous crime, unless on a presentment or indictment of a grand jury, except in cases arising in the land or naval forces, or in the militia, when in actual service in time of war or public danger; nor shall any person be subject for the same offence to be twice put in jeopardy of life or limb; nor shall be compelled in any criminal case to be a witness against himself, nor be deprived of life, liberty, or property, without due process of law; nor shall private property be taken for public use, without just compensation.

AMENDMENT VI

In all criminal prosecutions, the accused shall enjoy the right to a speedy and public trial, by an impartial jury of the State and district wherein the crime shall have been committed, which district shall have been previously ascertained by law, and to be informed of the nature and cause of the accusation; to be confronted with the witnesses against him; to have compulsory process for obtaining witnesses in his favor, and to have the assistance of counsel for his defence.

AMENDMENT VII
In suits at common law, where the value in controversy shall exceed twenty dollars, the right of trial by jury shall be preserved, and no fact tried by a jury, shall be otherwise re-examined in any court of the United States, than according to the rules of the common law.

AMENDMENT VIII
Excessive bail shall not be required, nor excessive fines imposed, nor cruel and unusual punishments inflicted.

AMENDMENT IX
The enumeration in the Constitution, of certain rights, shall not be construed to deny or disparage others retained by the people.

AMENDMENT X
The powers not delegated to the United States by the Constitution, nor prohibited by it to the States, are reserved to the States respectively, or to the people.

AMENDMENT XI   [Ratified 8 January 1798]
The judicial power of the United States shall not be construed to extend to any suit in law or equity, commenced or prosecuted against one of the United States by citizens of another State, or by citizens or subjects of any foreign State.

AMENDMENT XII   [Ratified 25 September 1804]
The electors shall meet in their respective States and vote by ballot for President and Vice-President, one of whom, at least, shall not be an inhabitant of the same State with themselves; they shall name in their ballots the person voted for as President, and in distinct ballots the person voted for as Vice-President, and they shall make distinct lists of all persons voted for as President and of all persons voted for as Vice-President, and of the number of votes for each, which lists they shall sign and certify, and transmit sealed to the seat of the government of

the United States, directed to the President of the Senate;—The President of the Senate shall, in the presence of Senate and House of Representatives, open all the certificates and the votes shall then be counted;—The person having the greatest number of votes for President, shall be the President, if such a number be a majority of the whole number of Electors appointed; and if no person have such majority, then from the persons having the highest numbers not exceeding three on the list of those voted for as President, the House of Representatives shall choose immediately, by ballot, the President. But in choosing the President, the votes shall be taken by States, the representation from each State having one vote, a quorum for this purpose shall consist of a member or members from two-thirds of the States, and a majority of all the States shall be necessary to a choice. And if the House of Representatives shall not choose a President whenever the right of choice shall devolve upon them, before the fourth day of March next following, then the Vice-President shall act as President, as in the case of the death or other constitutional disability of the President.—The person having the greatest number of votes as Vice-President, shall be the Vice-President, if such number be a majority of the whole number of Electors appointed, and if no person have a majority, then from the two highest numbers on the list, the Senate shall choose the Vice-President; a quorum for the purpose shall consist of two-thirds of the whole number of senators, and a majority of the whole number shall be necessary to a choice. But no person constitutionally ineligible to the office of President shall be eligible to that of Vice-President of the United States.

AMENDMENT XIII   [Ratified 18 December 1865]
SECTION 1. Neither slavery nor involuntary servitude, except as a punishment for crime whereof the party shall have been duly convicted, shall exist within the United States, or any place subject to their jurisdiction.
SECTION 2. Congress shall have power to enforce this article by appropriate legislation.

AMENDMENT XIV   [Ratified 28 July 1868]
SECTION 1. All persons born or naturalized in the United States, and subject to the jurisdiction thereof, are citizens of the United States and of the State wherein they reside. No State shall make or enforce any law which shall abridge the privileges or immunities of citizens of the

United States; nor shall any State deprive any person of life, liberty, or property, without due process of law; nor deny to any person within its jurisdiction the equal protection of the laws.

SECTION 2. Representatives shall be apportioned among the several States according to their respective numbers, counting the whole number of persons in each State, excluding Indians not taxed. But when the right to vote at any election for the choice of electors for President and Vice-President of the United States, representatives in Congress, the executive and judicial officers of a State, or the members of the legislature thereof, is denied to any of the male inhabitants of such State, being twenty-one years of age, and citizens of the United States, or in any way abridged, except for participation in rebellion, or other crime, the basis of representation therein shall be reduced in the proportion which the number of such male citizens shall bear to the whole number of male citizens twenty-one years of age in such State.

SECTION 3. No person shall be a senator or representative in Congress, or elector of President and Vice-President, or hold any office, civil or military, under the United States, or under any State, who, having previously taken an oath, as a member of Congress, or as an officer of the United States, or as a member of any State legislature, or as an executive or judicial officer of any State, to support the Constitution of the United States, shall have engaged in insurrection or rebellion against the same, or given aid or comfort to the enemies thereof. But Congress may by a vote of two-thirds of each House, remove such disability.

SECTION 4. The validity of the public debt of the United States, authorized by law, including debts incurred for payment of pensions and bounties for services in suppressing insurrection or rebellion, shall not be questioned. But neither the United States nor any State shall assume or pay any debt or obligation incurred in aid of insurrection or rebellion against the United States, or any claim for the loss or emancipation of any slave; but all such debts, obligations, and claims shall be held illegal and void.

SECTION 5. The Congress shall have power to enforce, by appropriate legislation, the provisions of this article.

AMENDMENT XV   [Ratified 30 March 1870]

SECTION 1. The right of citizens of the United States to vote shall not be denied or abridged by the United States or by any State on account of race, color, or previous condition of servitude.

SECTION 2. The Congress shall have power to enforce this article by appropriate legislation.

AMENDMENT XVI   [Ratified 25 February 1913]
The Congress shall have power to lay and collect taxes on incomes, from whatever source derived, without apportionment among the several States, and without regard to any census or enumeration.

AMENDMENT XVII   [Ratified 31 May 1913]
SECTION 1. The Senate of the United States shall be composed of two senators from each State, elected by the people thereof, for six years; and each senator shall have one vote. The electors in each State shall have the qualifications requisite for electors of the most numerous branch of the State legislature.

SECTION 2. When vacancies happen in the representation of any State in the Senate, the executive authority of such State shall issue writs of election to fill such vacancies: *Provided*, That the legislature of any State may empower the executive thereof to make temporary appointments until the people fill the vacancies by election as the legislature may direct.

SECTION 3. This amendment shall not be so construed as to affect the election or term of any senator chosen before it becomes valid as part of the Constitution.

AMENDMENT XVIII   [Ratified 29 January 1919. Repealed by the
                                                         21st Amendment]
SECTION 1. After one year from the ratification of this article the manufacture, sale, or transportation of intoxicating liquors within, the importation thereof into, or the exportation thereof from the United States and all territory subject to the jurisdiction thereof for beverage purposes is hereby prohibited.

SECTION 2. The Congress and the several States shall have concurrent power to enforce this article by appropriate legislation.

SECTION 3. This article shall be inoperative unless it shall have been ratified as an amendment of the Constitution by the legislatures of the several States, as provided in the Constitution, within seven years from the date of the submission hereof to the States by the Congress.

AMENDMENT XIX   [Ratified 26 August 1920]
SECTION 1. The right of citizens of the United States to vote shall not be denied or abridged by the United States or by any State on account of sex.
SECTION 2. Congress shall have power to enforce this article by appropriate legislation.

AMENDMENT XX   [Ratified 6 February 1933]
SECTION 1. The terms of the President and Vice-President shall end at noon on the 20th day of January, and the terms of Senators and Representatives at noon on the 3rd day of January, of the years in which such terms would have ended if this article had not been ratified; and the terms of their successors shall then begin.
SECTION 2. The Congress shall assemble at least once in every year, and such meeting shall begin at noon on the 3rd day of January, unless they shall by law appoint a different day.
SECTION 3. If, at the time fixed for the beginning of the term of the President, the President elect shall have died, the Vice-President elect shall become President. If a President shall not have been chosen before the time fixed for the beginning of his term, or if the President elect shall have failed to qualify, then the Vice-President elect shall act as President until a President shall have qualified; and the Congress may by law provide for the case wherein neither a President elect nor a Vice-President elect shall have qualified, declaring who shall then act as President, or the manner in which one who is to act shall be selected and such person shall act accordingly until a President or Vice-President shall have qualified.
SECTION 4. The Congress may by law provide for the case of the death of any of the persons from whom the House of Representatives may choose a President whenever the right of choice shall have devolved upon them, and for the case of the death of any of the persons from whom the Senate may choose a Vice-President whenever the right of choice shall have devolved upon them.
SECTION 5. Sections 1 and 2 shall take effect on the 15th day of October following the ratification of this article.
SECTION 6. This article shall be inoperative unless it shall have been ratified as an amendment to the Constitution by the legislatures of three-fourths of the several States within seven years from the date of its submission.

AMENDMENT XXI   [Ratified 5 December 1933]
SECTION 1. The eighteenth article of amendment to the Constitution of the United States is hereby repealed.
SECTION 2. The transportation or importation into any State, Territory, or possession of the United States for delivery or use therein of intoxicating liquors, in violation of the laws thereof, is hereby prohibited.
SECTION 3. This article shall be inoperative unless it shall have been ratified as an amendment to the Constitution by conventions in the several States, as provided in the Constitution, within seven years from the date of the submission hereof to the States by the Congress.

AMENDMENT XXII   [Ratified 1 March 1951]
SECTION 1. No person shall be elected to the office of the President more than twice, and no person who has held the office of President, or acted as President, for more than two years of a term to which some other person was elected President shall be elected to the office of President more than once. But the Article shall not apply to any person holding the office of President when this Article was proposed by the Congress, and shall not prevent any person who may be holding the office of President, or acting as President, during the term within which this Article becomes operative from holding the office of President or acting as President during the remainder of such term.
SECTION 2. This article shall be inoperative unless it shall have been ratified as an amendment to the Constitution by the legislatures of three-fourths of the several States within seven years from the date of its submission to the States by the Congress.

AMENDMENT XXIII   [Ratified 29 March 1961]
SECTION 1. The District constituting the seat of Government of the United States shall appoint in such manner as the Congress may direct:
A number of electors of President and Vice-President equal to the whole number of Senators and Representatives in Congress to which the District would be entitled if it were a State, but in no event more than the least populous State; they shall be in addition to those appointed by the States, but they shall be considered, for the purpose of the election of President and Vice-President, to be electors appointed by a State; and they shall meet in the District and perform such duties as provided by the twelfth article of amendment.

SECTION 2. The Congress shall have power to enforce this article by appropriate legislation.

AMENDMENT XXIV   [Ratified 23 January 1964]
SECTION 1. The right of citizens of the United States to vote in any primary or other election for President or Vice-President, for electors for President or Vice-President, or for Senator or Representative in Congress, shall not be denied or abridged by the United States or any state by reason of failure to pay any poll tax or other tax.
SECTION 2. The Congress shall have power to enforce this article by appropriate legislation.

AMENDMENT XXV   [Ratified 10 February 1967]
SECTION 1. In case of the removal of the President from office or of his death or resignation, the Vice-President shall become President.
SECTION 2. Whenever there is a vacancy in the office of the Vice-President the President shall nominate a Vice-President who shall take office upon confirmation by a majority vote of both Houses of Congress.
SECTION 3. Whenever the President transmits to the President pro tempore of the Senate and the Speaker of the House of Representatives his written declaration that he is unable to discharge the powers and duties of his office, and until he transmits to them a written declaration to the contrary, such powers and duties shall be discharged by the Vice-President as Acting President.
SECTION 4. Whenever the Vice-President and the majority of either the principal officers of the executive departments or of such other body as Congress may by law provide, transmit to the President pro tempore of the Senate and the Speaker of the House of Representatives their written declaration that the President is unable to discharge the powers and duties of his office, the Vice-President shall immediately assume the powers and duties of the office as Acting President.
Thereafter, when the President transmits to the President pro tempore of the Senate and the Speaker of the House of Representatives his written declaration that no inability exists, he shall resume the powers and duties of his office unless the Vice-President and a majority of either the principal officers of the executive departments or of such other body as Congress may by law provide, transmit within four days to the President pro tempore of the Senate and the Speaker of the House of Representatives their written declaration that the President

is unable to discharge the powers and duties of his office. Thereupon Congress shall decide the issue, assembling within forty-eight hours for that purpose if not in session. If the Congress, within twenty-one days after receipt of the latter written declaration, or, if Congress is not in session, within twenty-one days after Congress is required to assemble, determines by two-thirds vote of both Houses that the President is unable to discharge the powers and duties of his office, the Vice-President shall continue to discharge the same as Acting President; otherwise, the President shall resume the powers and duties of his office.

AMENDMENT XXVI   [Ratified 30 June 1971]
   The right of citizens of the United States, who are 18 years of age or older, to vote shall not be abridged by the United States or by any State on account of age.

AMENDMENT XXVII   [Ratified 7 May 1992]
   No law varying the compensation for the services of the Senators and Representatives shall take effect, until an election of Representatives shall have intervened.

Appendix II

Presidents and Vice-Presidents of the United States

Appendix II

Presidents and Vice-Presidents of the United States

	Name	Term of Office	Party	State of Res.	Vice-President
1	George Washington	1789–97	Fed.	Virginia	John Adams
2	John Adams	1797–1801	Fed.	Mass.	Thomas Jefferson
3	Thomas Jefferson	1801–9	Dem. Rep.	Virginia	Aaron Burr George Clinton (from 1805)
4	James Madison	1809–17	Dem. Rep.	Virginia	George Clinton E. Gerry (from 1813)
5	James Monroe	1817–25	Dem. Rep.	Virginia	D. D. Tompkins
6	John Quincey Adams	1825–9	Dem. Rep.	Mass.	John C. Calhoun
7	Andrew Jackson	1829–37	Dem.	Tennessee	John C. Calhoun Martin Van Buren (from 1833)
8	Martin Van Buren	1837–41	Dem.	New York	R. M. Johnson
9	William Harrison*	1841	Whig	Indiana	John Tyler
10	John Tyler	1841–5	Whig	Virginia	—
11	James Polk	1845–9	Dem.	Tennessee	George M. Dallas
12	Zachary Taylor*	1849–50	Whig	Louisiana	Millard Fillmore
13	Millard Fillmore	1850–53	Whig	New York	—
14	Franklin Pierce	1853–7	Dem.	New Hampshire	William R. King
15	James Buchanan	1857–61	Dem.	Pennsylvania	J. C. Breckinridge
16	Abraham Lincoln†	1861–5	Rep.	Illinois	H. Hamlin Andrew Johnson (from 1865)
17	Andrew Johnson	1865–9	Dem.	Tennessee	—
18	Ulysses S. Grant	1869–77	Rep.	Ohio	S. Colfax H. Wilson (from 1873)
19	Rutherford B. Hayes	1877–81	Rep.	Ohio	W. A. Wheeler

	Name	Term of Office	Party	State of Res.	Vice-President
20	James A. Garfield†	1881	Rep.	Ohio	Chester A. Arthur
21	Chester A. Arthur	1881–5	Rep.	New York	—
22	Grover Cleveland	1885–9	Dem.	New York	A. Hendricks
23	Benjamin Harrison	1889–93	Rep.	Indiana	Levi P. Morton
24	Grover Cleveland	1893–7	Dem.	New York	Adlai E. Stevenson
25	William McKinley†	1897–1901	Rep.	Ohio	G. A. Hobart / Theodore Roosevelt (from 1901)
26	Theodore Roosevelt	1901–9	Rep.	New York	C. M. Fairbanks (from 1905)
27	William H. Taft	1909–13	Rep.	Ohio	J. S. Sherman
28	Woodrow Wilson	1913–21	Dem.	New Jersey	T. R. Marshall
29	Warren G. Harding*	1921–3	Rep.	Ohio	Calvin Coolidge
30	Calvin Coolidge	1923–9	Rep.	Mass.	Charles Davies (from 1925)
31	Herbert Hoover	1929–33	Rep.	California	Charles Curtis
32	Franklin D. Roosevelt*	1933–45	Dem.	New York	John N. Garner / Henry A. Wallace (from 1941) / Harry S. Truman (from 1945)
33	Harry S. Truman	1945–53	Dem.	Missouri	Alben Barkley (from 1949)
34	Dwight D. Eisenhower	1953–61	Rep.	New York	Richard M. Nixon
35	John F. Kennedy†	1961–3	Dem.	Mass.	Lyndon B. Johnson
36	Lyndon B. Johnson	1963–9	Dem.	Texas	Hubert Humphrey (from 1965)
37	Richard M. Nixon	1969–74	Rep.	New York	Spiro Agnew / Gerald R. Ford (from 1973)
38	Gerald R. Ford	1974–7	Rep.	Michigan	Nelson Rockefeller
39	Jimmy Carter	1977–81	Dem.	Georgia	Walter Mondale
40	Ronald Reagan	1981–9	Rep.	California	George Bush
41	George Bush	1989–93	Rep.	Texas	Dan Quayle
42	Bill Clinton	1993–	Dem.	Arkansas	Al Gore

*Died in office †Assassinated

Appendix III

Glossary

Affirmative action programs. Policies that are designed to favour minorities (for example, in job recruitment) and remedy past discrimination.

Amicus curiae. A person or organization that is not a party in a case but has an interest in it and is allowed by the court to file a brief and present arguments as a 'friend of the court'.

Appellate jurisdiction. The powers of a court to re-examine or review a case on appeal from a lower court.

Appropriation. The process by which Congress determines the actual amounts of money each government department and agency can spend.

Balanced budget. A budget in which revenues are equal to or exceed expenditures. A Constitutional Amendment to force an end to deficit spending by the federal government has been proposed which would mandate a balanced budget except in particular circumstances such as wartime.

'Balancing the ticket'. The practice of attempting to make a party's candidates attractive to broad sections of the nation by nominating people from different ethnic, religious or regional backgrounds.

Band-wagon effect. The process by which reports of voters' or delegates' intentions can influence the outcome of an election or nominating convention.

Beltway issue. An issue that is of concern to those involved in Washington politics but not to the people outside the beltway—the interstate highway that surrounds the capital.

Bicameralism. Having a two-chamber legislative body.

Bill of Rights. The first ten Amendments to the US Constitution, ratified in 1791, guaranteeing individual and state rights.

Bipartisanship. Cooperation between the two parties and their leaders on a political issue.

Blue ribbon commission. A panel of eminent and distinguished citizens, possibly with particular expertise, formed to investigate a problem and make recommendations for action.

Calendar. A list of pending business awaiting legislative action.

Caucus. A meeting of party members to plan strategy or select candidates.

Certiorari, Writ of. An order from a court to a lower court directing that the record of its proceedings be put forward for review—'to be made certain'.

Checks and balances. The principle of having government institutions exercising certain checks and constraints over one another's activities.

Cloture (closure). The process of setting a time limit and terminating debate on a bill.

Coat-tails effect. The result of voters casting their votes for one popular candidate and also voting for the rest of the party's candidates for other offices.

Concurrent powers. The authority possessed by both the federal and the state governments simultaneously (*e.g.* taxation).

Conference committee. A committee made up of members of both houses of Congress whose job is to iron out differences between House and Senate versions of a bill and recommend one version to the two houses for final approval.

Continuing resolution. Legislation that provides funding for executive branch activities to continue at a particular level, when the regular appropriation has not been passed by the start of the fiscal year.

'Dark horse' candidate. A candidate for political office who has little support at a convention but who may be a compromise choice if there is a deadlock between the major contenders.

Direct mail fund-raising. A technique to raise money directly from the public using computerized mailing lists.

Divided government. A government where the legislative and executive branches are controlled by different parties.

Due process of law. The right of citizens against arbitrary action by government, protected by following established judicial procedures.

Executive agreement. An agreement made by the President with a foreign power that has the same force as a treaty but does not require Senate approval.

Executive privilege. The argument that the communications between a

President and his advisers are confidential and should not be revealed without the permission of the President.

Exit polls. Election-day polls taken as people leave the polling stations, used by media to predict results and for analysis of the way sections of the electorate voted.

Fat cats. Wealthy contributors to political campaigns.

'Favourite son' candidate. A state politician who is nominated for President at a convention by delegates from his own state but is not usually a serious contender. Often used for bargaining purposes or personal publicity.

Filibuster. The obstruction of Senate action on a bill by taking advantage of the rule of unlimited debate and 'talking the bill to death'.

Founding Fathers. Those individuals who played a major role in the establishment of the new nation, in winning independence and writing the Constitution.

Freshmen. Congressmen serving their first term in office.

Frontrunner. A candidate whom politicians and the media have identified as the likely winner.

Gender gap. A pattern of clear and consistent difference in the voting behaviour or in the opinions on policy issues between men and women.

Gerrymandering. Dividing voters into electoral districts in such a way as to give one party or faction an unfair advantage.

GOP. Grand Old Party or Republican party, which was formed in 1856.

Grand jury. A jury whose rule is to investigate whether there is sufficient evidence to justify holding for trial an individual who has been arrested.

Grants-in-aid. A financial subsidy provided by the federal government to state and local governments (or by states to local government) to be used for specific purposes.

Hispanic. A term used to include persons of Mexican–American, Puerto Rican, Cuban, Central or South American, or other Spanish origin.

Home Rule. The practice of states allowing their local governments to draft their own charters and manage their own affairs with less direction from the state than is normal.

Honeymoon period. The period, often relatively short, after a President takes office when he experiences harmonious relations with Congress, the media and the public.

Hundred days. The first hundred days of a new administration when it attempts to pass major legislation while support is still strong following election success, such as Roosevelt's policies to counter the Great Depression in 1933.

Impeachment. The formal accusation of misconduct on the part of an executive or judicial official by the House of Representatives, starting the process by which the individual can be removed from office after a trial by the Senate.

Implied powers. The powers Congress has been given to carry out its specified tasks, implied by the 'necessary and proper' clause of the Constitution.

Impoundment. The refusal by the President to spend funds appropriated by Congress for particular purposes.

Incumbent. The person currently holding a particular office.

Initiative. The process by which state laws or constitutional amendments can be enacted by direct popular vote, having been placed on the ballot paper as a result of a petition signed by a specific number of electors.

Interstate commerce. Business or activity between or among several states and subject to federal government regulation.

Intra-state commerce. Business or activity within the boundaries of one state and subject only to regulation by that state authority.

Item veto. The ability of some state Governors to prevent particular sections of a bill from becoming law while allowing the rest to go on to the statute books.

Jim Crow laws. Laws passed by Southern states requiring segregation and racial discrimination between blacks and whites.

Judicial review. The power of the judiciary to declare the actions of the legislative or executive branches unconstitutional.

Keynote address. The major speech at a party national convention, other than the nominee's acceptance speech, that sets out the party's themes and vision for the forthcoming election.

'Lame duck'. An office-holder who has lost an election but holds power until the inauguration of a successor.

Legislative veto. A provision of a law in which Congress asserts the power to nullify the actions of the executive branch.

Lobbyist. An individual who works on behalf of a pressure group and tries to influence the decisions of the legislature or administration on impending legislation or policy.

Log-rolling. The practice whereby legislators will trade votes in order to achieve their own individual legislative objectives.

Merit system. The system used in public employment whereby personnel are recruited and promoted on the basis of qualifications and
ability rather than by political patronage.

Metropolitan area. A large area or conurbation made up of several large
cities and the areas between them; also known as a 'megalopolis'.

Negative advertising. Paid commercials which attack an opponent and
his policies in an election campaign.

Open seat. A constituency in which the incumbent member is not seeking re-election.

PAC. A political action committee set up by a pressure group to raise and
distribute campaign finance to particular candidates in elections.

Patronage. The appointment of positions by executive officials on the
basis of party, usually as a reward to friends or supporters.

Pigeon-hole. To set aside indefinitely; the practice of Congressional committees in not considering bills sent to them.

Platform. A statement of party policies, made up of clauses on different
subjects.

Plurality. The largest number of votes cast in an election for one candidate who wins whether or not he has an absolute majority over all
the other candidates.

Pocketbook issue. A political issue which directly affects the disposable
income of electors, such as taxation and inflation.

Pocket veto. Refusal by the President to give assent to legislation after
the adjournment of Congress. As there is no opportunity for the
legislature to override the veto, the bill dies.

Pork-barrelling. The appropriation of public money secured by legislators for projects which will favour their local constituencies, and
help their re-election.

Precinct. An electoral subdivision of a city, probably small enough for all
the residents to be able to vote at one polling station.

Primary. An election held before the general election to nominate a
party's candidate for office. If it is 'closed', only registered or
declared party supporters may vote; if it is 'open', a voter may vote
for the nomination of any of the candidates regardless of his party
affiliation.

Ranking member. The member of a political party on a committee who
has the longest continuous service on that committee.

Reapportionment. The redrawing of electoral districts and redistribution
of legislative seats to take into account the changes in population
settlement.

Recall. The procedure by which voters can remove an elected official from office before the end of his term if there is evidence of corruption, negligence or incompetence. About one-quarter of the states provide such a procedure in their constitutions, although such attempts are rarely successful.

Referendum. A popular vote on a new state constitution or amendment, or on a statute already approved by the legislature. A petition signed by a specific number of voters is necessary to refer such legislation to the electorate.

Reserved powers. The powers possessed by the states under the Tenth Amendment to the Constitution, that is all those not delegated to the federal government or denied to the states. Also known as the 'residual powers'.

Revenue sharing. The allocation of a portion of tax moneys by the federal government to states and local governments to spend with few or no conditions as to how it should be used.

Rider. A provision included in legislation that is not related to the main subject of the bill it is riding on.

Senatorial courtesy. The process by which the President consults with Senators of his own party when he makes an appointment to one of the states, thus helping to secure confirmation of the appointment by the Senate.

Seniority system. The system by which priority or status is given to an individual on the basis of his length of service in an organisation.

Separation of powers. The principle that power should be distributed between three independent branches of government—the legislature, executive and judiciary.

Smoke-filled room. A phrase that grew out of the 1920 Republican Convention, symbolizing the secret meeting of political bosses to select a candidate.

Soft money. Money contributed to a political party ostensibly to support its organizational activities but also used to help the party's candidates financially outside of the scope of federal election regulations.

Sound-bite. The use in news programmes of a brief excerpt of a candidate's or politician's speech.

Special districts. A local government unit that is created to administer one particular service.

Special election. A by-election that has been specially arranged to fill a vacancy when a member has resigned or died in office before the expiry of his term.

Splitting tickets. The process whereby a voter selects candidates of different parties for different offices on the same ballot paper.

States' rights. The opposition to increasing federal government power at the expense of the states.

Sunbelt. The southern states, characterized by mild and warm weather, that experienced considerable population growth in the 1980s.

Term limit. A legal or constitutional restriction on an office-holder serving more than a defined number of terms in the same position.

Treaty. A formal agreement between sovereign states establishing certain relationships between them. US treaties must be approved by a two-thirds vote in the Senate.

Veto. The power of the President to prevent legislation passed by the legislature. The President's veto can be overridden if both houses of Congress support the bill by a two-thirds majority.

Whips. Legislators who can act as communication links between leaders and ordinary Congressmen and who make sure party members are present for crucial votes.

Write-in candidate. A candidate whose name does not appear on the printed ballot and whose supporters must therefore write his name themselves.

Index